THE LIBRARY

W9-CLV-920

BOTSWANA'S SEARCH
FOR AUTONOMY
IN SOUTHERN AFRICA

"You'll be all right — you'll be among friends"

Source: *Punch* 251, no. 6569 (3 August 1966): 169. Reprinted with permission of *Punch*, London, England.

BOTSWANA'S SEARCH FOR AUTONOMY IN SOUTHERN AFRICA

Richard Dale

Contributions in Political Science, Number 358

GREENWOOD PRESS
Westport, Connecticut • London

Library of Congress Cataloging-in-Publication Data

Dale, Richard.
    Botswana's search for autonomy in southern Africa / Richard Dale.
       p.   cm.—(Contributions in political science, ISSN 0147–1066
 ; no. 358)
    Includes bibliographical references and index.
    ISBN 0–313–29571–9 (alk. paper)
    1. Botswana—Politics and government—1966- . 2. Botswana—Foreign
relations—1966- . 3. Botswana—Economic conditions—1966-
4. Africa, Southern—Politics and government. 5. Africa, Southern—
Economic conditions. I. Title. II. Series.
DT2496.D35   1995
  968.83—dc20   95–2087

British Library Cataloguing in Publication Data is available.

Copyright © 1995 by Richard Dale

All rights reserved. No portion of this book may be
reproduced, by any process or technique, without the
express written consent of the publisher.

Library of Congress Catalog Card Number: 95–2087
ISBN: 0–313–29571–9
ISSN: 0147–1066

First published in 1995

Greenwood Press, 88 Post Road West, Westport, CT 06881
An imprint of Greenwood Publishing Group, Inc.

Printed in the United States of America

The paper used in this book complies with the
Permanent Paper Standard issued by the National
Information Standards Organization (Z39.48–1984).

10 9 8 7 6 5 4 3 2 1

To Athern P. Daggett, Edgar Dale, and Joseph C. Pillion

In Memoriam

Contents

Preface

When President F.W. De Klerk announced in Parliament on 2 February 1990 that the cluster of anti-apartheid organizations, some of which had been banned as far back as 1960 (see the Chronology), were now at liberty to resume their operations, South African politics were dramatically changed. What Samuel P. Huntington had called the third wave of democratization was well under way in South Africa.[1] Later that month African National Congress (ANC) leader Nelson Mandela was released, and the transition to a nonracial South Africa, marked by the first democratic general elections of 27 April 1994, had begun.[2] Following the installation of Nelson Mandela as president of South Africa, South Africa once again became a full member of the international community of nations, rejoining the Commonwealth of Nations and becoming a member of the Organization of African Unity (OAU) and of the Southern African Development Community (SADC). South Africa once again was able to participate in the work of the United Nations (UN) General Assembly.

Such a shift away from apartheid and toward a nonracial democratic order in South Africa raises both hopes and questions about South Africa's relations with the rest of the world and its neighbors in southern Africa.[3] One of its neighbors, Botswana,[4] has earned a remarkable reputation, particularly in the West, for economic growth and prudence,[5] for a democratic political system,[6] and for a relaxed, tolerant racial climate. On a per capita basis, in 1989 it received the highest level of foreign aid of all nations belonging to the World Bank.[7] However, this reputation needs to be juxtaposed with the condition of Botswana at the close of the Second World War. By that time, it was not clear whether there was a nation-to-be, for the future of Botswana (then known by its colonial name of the Bechuanaland Protectorate) was widely thought to be absorbed into the Union of South Africa. The range and depth of the links between this British protectorate and the Union and Southern Rhodesia reflected the prevailing norms of white power and imperial power.

This book deals with Botswana in the post–1945 era, spanning both colonial and post-colonial Botswana. The inquiry terminates with the admission of South Africa into the SADC at the end of August 1994. The principal focus of the inquiry is Botswana's four neighbors: South Africa, Namibia, Zambia, and Zimbabwe.[8] Not all four neighbors receive equal coverage because Botswana's patterns of interaction are heavily oriented toward South Africa and Zimbabwe, the two most economically powerful states in southern Africa.

The data were restricted to those patterns of conflict and cooperation that traversed national borders, to activity that had a readily recognizable international dimension. To delimit the conflictual and cooperative patterns and to make them manageable and significant, I have followed the precedent of the literature of international relations, supplemented by several research trips to Botswana. I divided the patterns into high politics and low politics.[9] In this study high politics includes these three sectors: national territorial integrity; international refugee traffic; and police, security, and armed forces. Low politics covers the following five sectors: education and science; administration; transportation, tourism, and communications; commerce, finance, and investment; and international labor migration.

These sectors are frequently mentioned in the dependency-related literature on Botswana and southern Africa.[10] They also permit analysis over both the colonial and the post-colonial periods. Such a long-term analysis will show how, and to what extent, Botswana has attempted to reduce, if not remove, obstacles to its freedom to maneuver in the political, security, and economic realms.[11]

Such constraints are usually associated with Botswana's southern and eastern neighbors, namely, South Africa and Zimbabwe. The restraints, especially in the South African case, can be thought of as links, so that one finds reference in the literature to the task of "de-linking" majority-ruled southern Africa from South Africa.[12] This analysis, then, explores the origins, development, and status of the various links, which enables one to follow the de-linking activity in sectoral, temporal, and regional terms. Occasionally, the regional significance of a particular sector is underscored by the addition of the term *diplomacy* following the designation of the sector, as in business diplomacy or transport diplomacy.[13]

Unlinking one sector from the companion sector in a contiguous state, usually South Africa and sometimes Zimbabwe, may be necessary, but it is hardly sufficient to enhance Botswana's autonomy (a term I shall define shortly). Botswana usually will need to replace the neighborly link with a regional, continental, or global one, which necessitates the consideration of the costs and benefits of such replacement policies. Does this unlinking signify, as sometimes suggested in the literature, that Botswana is a captive state of South Africa?[14] Does it also mean that Botswana lacks autonomy? These are significant questions not only for Botswana but also for most of the states which belonged to the Southern African Development Coordination Conference (SADCC), which became the SADC in 1992.

Those scholars who endorse dependency theory appear to answer both questions affirmatively.[15] They suggest that as SADCC (which included Botswana) tried to extricate itself from the economic grip of South Africa, it had to rely upon Western resources. Such reliance, they argue, increased SADCC's indebtedness to, and dependence upon, the West, thus exchanging one dependency for another.[16] Such analysis tended to be time-bound and nation-bound. It was linked to the present and the near future, and it concentrated unduly on apartheid South Africa. Although one could transcend dependency theory provided one thought far enough ahead to visualize southern Africa without South African apartheid,[17] to have done so was to have expanded the time span and the geographical span of inquiry.

Such analysis, often emotive and polemical on the subject of South Africa, appeared to be grounded on the assumption that the advent of majority rule in South Africa would tend to reduce South Africa's hegemonic power. It was one thing to excoriate the system of entrenched racism in South Africa, but it was quite another to assume that a regime change would alter the calculus of regional power. African majority rule in South Africa would not necessarily mean a major realignment of economic power differentials within southern Africa; South Africa would probably remain what John Sullivan calls the "regional hegemon."[18]

In addition to being suffused with rhetoric and sometimes unbridled emotion with respect to South Africa, the literature seemed to have a blind spot with regard to Zimbabwe, Botswana's eastern neighbor and probably the second-ranked economic powerhouse of southern Africa. Despite Zimbabwe's hard-won independence, at the cost of many lives, the destruction or absence of white minority rule in Zimbabwe did not end its disagreements with Botswana. Later chapters will indicate the nature of the economic, military, and political conflicts between Botswana and Zimbabwe.

Although this study closes with the admission of South Africa into

SADC at the end of August 1994, there is no a priori reason to think that Botswana's relations with Namibia will be entirely free of any conflict and controversy. It is more likely, however, that significant conflicts will occur with those neighbors with which Botswana interacts most frequently and most intensely. To paraphrase the title of a popular journalistic account of Mexico, Botswana and Namibia, as well as Botswana and Zambia, are "distant neighbors."[19] Geographical propinquity and intensity of interaction are key elements in the regional pattern of conflict and cooperation.

Relations with neighbors vary over time and with the sector involved. These patterns of interaction bring up the question of the balance or imbalance in the relationship between the states, which leads to the topic of autonomy. The term *autonomy* seldom appears in the southern African international relations literature, even though it is helpful in explorations of weak states' behavior.[20] Hans Mouritzen suggests that autonomy carries the connotation of "defensive power" and that it also entails an element of unpredictable state behavior.[21] That unpredictable behavior implies the notion of choice of which policies to implement as well as the choice of when to put them into force.

This study uses the straightforward definition of autonomy offered by M. Crawford Young in his *Ideology and Development in Africa*, that is, the focus is upon the ways in which Botswana has been able "to enlarge—within the relatively narrow range of possibility—the range of choices available."[22] The concern here is with the idea of both creating and making choices or options in the face of economic, political, and strategic constraints. The core concept of autonomy does not rule out the possibility that dependence may well be the fate of numerous African states, particularly if one concentrates on external dependence between nation-states, which entails the notion of domination and an unequal pattern of exchange. Asymmetry is thus a crucial element in the notion of dependency.[23] In this study I concentrate upon Botswana's regional dependency patterns (that is, Botswana has been, is now, or in the future will be dependent upon state X for goods or services Y) on a sector-by-sector and neighbor-by-neighbor basis.[24]

After describing and explaining the nature of the various dependencies, I then observe whether there has been any shift in the sectors or neighbors involved and ask how those shifts have taken place, primarily, but not entirely, since Botswana's independence in 1966. Shifts will signal attempts to reduce the level of dependence in a specific sector or to replace dependence upon a single neighbor with dependence upon one or more regional, continental, or even non-African states and organizations. This is often the case with respect to seeking out any array of aid donors to avoid being completely beholden to one donor. Foreign aid and investment represent two means to attenuate the burden and risks of dependence, the former involving the public sector and the latter the private sector. This study focuses on the creation and subsequent utilization of options for altering, reducing, and perhaps eliminating dependence in several interrelated sectors.[25] Thus I carefully examine the host of activities subsumed under low politics, that is, those that entail such international economic interactions as migrant labor, customs receipts, railway, road, and air passenger and freight traffic, and tourism flows.

Usually the low politics areas will be characterized by cooperation, but occasionally they become conflictual. As one moves toward the classic high politics sectors, economic dependence becomes less helpful as an organizing concept. Territorial sovereignty and integrity, along with liberal and democratic value systems, are more relevant in exploring the nature of Botswana's international boundaries, its security forces, and its treatment of political exiles from neighboring states in southern Africa.

Autonomy, rather than dependence, becomes a more creative and parsimonious concept. It challenges one to think in terms of "political maneuver"[26] and of "political space."[27] The concern, then, is with how Botswana responded to threats to its territorial integrity from any of its neighbors and how it turned to external donors for assistance to keep political, military, and economic space between itself and hostile neighbors.

Acknowledgments

During the course of the research for this book, I visited or wrote to a wide array of archives, special collections, and libraries in the United States, the United Kingdom, and southern Africa. Their directors and staffs were remarkably generous with their time and resources. In particular, I am most indebted to the Africa Institute of South Africa (Pretoria); American University; National Archives (Gaborone); Botswana National Library Service (Gaborone); British Museum Newspaper Library (London); Catholic University of America; Center for Research Libraries; *The Chronicle* (Bulawayo); Duke University; *Financial Mail* (Johannesburg); George Washington University; Georgetown University; The Hoover Institution on War, Revolution, and Peace; Howard University; Imperial War Museum (London); Institute for Contemporary History (University of the Orange Free State); Institute of Commonwealth Studies (University of London); Institute of Strategic Studies (University of Pretoria); International Institute for Strategic Studies (London); Johannesburg Public Library; Land Tenure Center (University of Wisconsin, Madison); Lincoln University (Lincoln University, Penn.); Military Information Bureau (Pretoria); National Archives of Namibia (Windhoek); National Archives of Zambia (Lusaka); National Archives of Zimbabwe (Harare); National Institute of Development Research and Documentation (University of Botswana); Northwestern University; Public Record Office (London); Rhodes House (University of Oxford); Royal Commonwealth Society (London); Royal Institute of International Affairs (London); Royal Military Academy, Sandhurst; Royal United Services Institute for Defense Studies (London); The Scandinavian Institute of African Studies (Uppsala); School of International Studies

(Fort Bragg, N.C.); School of Oriental and African Studies (University of London); South African Institute of International Affairs (Johannesburg); South African Institute of Race Relations (Johannesburg); Southern Illinois University at Carbondale; Stanford University; *The Star* (Johannesburg); The State Library (Pretoria); Transvaal and Central Archives Depot (Pretoria); United States Naval War College; University of Botswana (Gaborone); University of California, Berkeley; University of Illinois, Urbana; University of Iowa; University of Massachusetts, Amherst; University of Minnesota; University of North Carolina, Chapel Hill; University of Stellenbosch; University of Wisconsin, Madison; and Yale University.

For travel and other financial support for research in, and on, southern Africa I am particularly grateful to the American Philosophical Society, the Earhart Foundation, the program underwritten by the US Intergovernmental Personnel Act (administered for the School of International Studies at Fort Bragg, N.C., by Southern Illinois University at Carbondale), the Inter-University Seminar on Armed Forces and Society, as well as the Department of Political Science, the College of Liberal Arts, and the Office of Research Development and Administration of Southern Illinois University at Carbondale.

I have benefited enormously by those who very kindly read and commented on some or all of this book: Chawa Bogosi; Wilhelmus J. Breytenbach; Robert L. Clinton; Jacobus J. N. Cloete; C. John R. Dugard; Peter J. Duignan; E. Brian Egner; Sir R. Peter Fawcus; Lewis H. Gann; Kenneth W. Grundy; Thomas H. Henriksen; H. C. L. Hermans; Richard Holway; J. Derek Jones; G. M. Erich Leistner; Victor T. Le Vine; the late Connie Minchin; Clay Morgan; E. Philip Morgan; Edwin S. Munger; Thomas P. Ofcansky; Q. Neil Parsons; James H. Polhemus; Leslie I. Rubin; Dan L. Seiters; Timothy M. Shaw; James D. Simmons; Paul S. Van der Merwe; Mildred Vasan; J. Richard T. Wood; James J. Zaffiro; Werner M. Zepp; and anonymous readers.

For their help in providing interviews, counsel, data, cartography, encouragement, and hospitality during the course of the research and writing, my thanks go to Douglas G. Anglin; David A. Bennett; F. P. Blignaut; John L. K. Brett; the late Gwendolen M. Carter; Olaf Claus; William H. Clennell; David S. Cownie; the late Michael Crowder; Allie A. Dubb; Leslie C. Duly; T. J. Denis Fair; Edward E. Feit; Churchill Gape; Stephanie Grant; John J. Grotpeter; Daniel W. Henk; Christopher R. Hill; Richard Hodder-Williams; John D. Holm; David W. Joy; Thomas G. Karis; Peter H. Katjavivi; Margaret R. Legum; Ambrose B. Masalila; Terry D. Mathias; Spencer P. and the late

Connie Minchin; Kenneth J. Mommsen; Riecks Morake; R. Frederic Morton; Samuel A. Mpuchane; Tom Obondo-Okoye; Jack D. Parson; Moeng Pheto; Louis A. Picard; Joe Podbrey; Christian P. Potholm; John A. Scanlon; Barry M. Schutz; John J. Seiler; the late Anthony Sillery; Walter A. E. Skurnik; Joseph P. Smaldone; J. E. Spence; Eric B. Stander; Richard P. Stevens; Newell M. Stultz; Scott A. Sylvester; Thomas Tlou; Philip V. Tobias; the staff of the US Embassy, Gaborone; Joan K. Wadlow; Bernhard Weimer; Richard F. Weisfelder; Denis J. Worrall; and James Young.

My wife Doris merits a special place in the acknowledgments, considering how many roles she played while this book was in progress. She gave freely of her time and talents while still pursuing her own academic career here or as a visiting professor at other universities. She kept the faith throughout the entire project.

Carbondale, Illinois
5 November 1994

Abbreviations

This list of abbreviations and acronyms includes those used in the text and notes with the place of publication for material published outside the United States and the location of institutions and libraries outside the United States.

AA	*African Affairs* (London)
AB	*African Business* (London)
AC	*Africa Confidential* (London)
ACRASD	*Africa Contemporary Record: Annual Survey and Documents*
AD	*African Development* (London)
AECI	African Explosives and Chemical Industries
AI	*Africa Insight* (Pretoria)
AIB	*Africa Institute Bulletin* (Pretoria)
AISA	Africa Institute of South Africa (Pretoria)
AJES	*American Journal of Economics and Sociology*
AMAX	American Metal Climax
ANC	African National Congress (of South Africa)
ANSAC	American Natural Soda Ash Corporation
APSR	*The American Political Science Review*
APTU	African Postal and Telecommunications Union
AR	*Africa Report*
ARBEFTS	*Africa Research Bulletin: Economic, Financial and Technical Series* (Exeter)
ARBPS	*Africa Research Bulletin: Political Series* (Exeter)
ARBPSCS	*Africa Research Bulletin: Political, Social, and Cultural Series* (Oxford)

AS	*African Studies* (Johannesburg)
AT	*Africa Today*
AW	*African World* (London)
AWL	*African Wild Life* (Johannesburg)
BBC	British Broadcasting Corporation
BC	*The Bulawayo Chronicle* (Bulawayo)
BCC	Botswana Christian Council
BCL	Bamangwato Concessions Limited
BCR	Botswana Council for Refugees
BCSO	Botswana. Central Statistics Office
BDC	Botswana Development Corporation
BDF	Botswana Defense Force
BDIPER	Botswana. Directorate of Personnel
BDN	*Botswana Daily News* (Gaborone)
BDP	Bechuanaland/Botswana Democratic Party
BDWNP	Botswana. Department of Wildlife and National Parks
BED	Botswana. Education Department
BG	*Botswana Guardian* (Gaborone)
BGG	Botswana. *Government Gazette*
BLAJ	*Botswana Library Association Journal* (Gaborone)
BLS	Botswana, Lesotho, and Swaziland
BNA	Botswana National Archives (Gaborone)
BNAORH	Botswana. National Assembly. Official Report (Hansard)
BNDP	Botswana, *National Development Plan*
BNR	*Boswana Notes and Records* (Gaborone)
BP	Bechuanaland Protectorate
BPAACM	Bechuanaland Protectorate. African Advisory Council, *Minutes*
BPARC	Botswana. Police. *Annual Report of the Commissioner*
BPEACM	Bechuanaland Protectorate. European Advisory Council, *Minutes*
BPEDAR	Bechuanaland Protectorate. Education Department. *Annual Report*
BPF	Botswana Police Force
BPIBBR	Bechuanaland Protectorate. Information Branch, *Bechuanaland Report for the Year*
BPJACM	Bechuanaland Protectorate. Joint Advisory Council, *Minutes*
BPLAORH	Bechuanaland Protectorate. Legislative Assembly. *Official Report* (Hansard)

BPLCORH	Bechuanaland Protectorate. Legislative Council. *Official Report* (Hansard)
BPNACM	Bechuanaland Protectorate. Native Advisory Council, *Minutes*
BPP	Bechuanaland/Botswana People's Party
BPPARC	Bechuanaland Protectorate. Police, *Annual Report of the Commissioner*
BPSL	Bechuanaland Protectorate, *Statute Law*
BRST	Botswana Roan Selection Trust
BS	The Botswana Society (Gaborone)
BSAC	British South Africa Company (of Southern Rhodesia)
BSAP	British South Africa Police (of Southern Rhodesia)
CAS	Colonial Administrative Service
CBAA	*A Current Bibliography on African Affairs*
CCTA	Commission for Technical Cooperation South of the Sahara
c.e.	city edition
CH	*Current History*
chap(s).	chapter(s)
CILJSA	*Comparative and International Law Journal of Southern Africa* (Pretoria)
c.l.e	city late edition
c.l.h.e.	city late home edition
c.l.s.e.	city late sport edition
Cm(n)d.	command paper
CO	Colonial Office
col(s).	column(s)
comp.	compiler
CONSAS	Constellation of Southern African States
CPBLS	*Country Profile: Botswana, Lesotho, Swaziland* (London)
CRBNLS	*Country Report: Botswana, Namibia. Lesotho, Swaziland* (London)
CRNBLS	*Country Report: Namibia, Botswana, Lesotho, Swaziland* (London)
CRO	Commonwealth Relations Office
CS	*Comparative Strategy*
CSA	Scientific Council for Africa South of the Sahara
CSM	*The Christian Science Monitor*
CSO	Central Selling Organization
CT	*The Cape Times* (Cape Town)
CUP	Cambridge University Press
diss.	dissertation

DO	Dominions Office
doc.	document
DRC	Dutch Reformed Church
EAER	*Eastern Africa Economic Review* (Nairobi)
ed.	edition or editor(s)
EDCC	*Economic Development and Cultural Change*
EEC	European Economic Community
EG	*Economic Geography*
EIU	Economist Intelligence Unit (London)
EPH	*Eastern Province Herald* (Port Elizabeth)
FAO	Food and Agricultural Organization (of the United Nations)
FBISDRMEA	Foreign Broadcast Information Service Daily Report: Middle East and Africa
FBISSSA	*Foreign Broadcast Information Service Daily Report: Sub-Saharan Africa*
f.e.	final edition
FM	*Financial Mail* (Johannesburg)
FPRSA	*Focus on Political Repression in Southern Africa* (London)
FT	*The Financial Times* (London)
GP	The Government Printer
HCT	High Commission Territory/Territories (of Basutoland, Bechuanaland Protectorate, and Swaziland)
HMSO	His/Her Majesty's Stationery Office (London)
IA	*International Affairs* (London)
IAB	*International Affairs Bulletin* (Johannesburg)
i.a.w.e.	international airmail weekly edition
ICSUL	Institute of Commonwealth Studies, University of London
IDAFSA	International Aid and Defense Fund for Southern Africa (London)
IDSB	*Institute of Development Studies Bulletin* (Sussex)
IISS	The International Institute of Strategic Studies (London)
IJAHS	*The International Journal of African Historical Studies*
ILO	International Labor Organization
IM	*Immigrants and Minorities* (London)
IMR	*International Migration Review*
IntOrg	*International Organization*
ISQ	*International Studies Quarterly*

i.w.e.	international weekly edition
JAS	*Journal of African Studies*
JCAS	*Journal of Contemporary African Studies* (Pretoria/Grahamstown)
JCCP	*The Journal of Commonwealth and Comparative Politics* (London)
JCH	*Journal for Contemporary History* (Bloemfontein)
JDA	*Journal of Developing Areas*
JDS	*Journal of Development Studies* (London)
JMAS	*The Journal of Modern African Studies*
JSAS	*Journal of Southern African Studies* (Oxford)
l.e.	late edition
l.f.e.	late final edition
l.l.a.e.	late London air edition
l.l.e.	late London edition
LNOJ	League of Nations, *Official Journal*
LNPMCM	League of Nations. Permanent Mandates Commission, *Minutes*
LPSSSO	List of Post Secondary Students Studying Outside Botswana and at the U.B.L.S.
l.s.e.	late sport edition
LWF	Lutheran World Federation
MB	*The Military Balance* (London)
m.f.e.	morning final edition
MMBG	*Mafeking Mail and Botswana Guardian* (Mafikeng)
MMPG	*Mafeking Mail and Protectorate Guardian* (Mafikeng)
MOD	Ministry of Overseas Development (London)
MP(s)	Member(s) of Parliament
mtg.	meeting
MWD	*Mmegi wa Dikgang/The Reporter* (Serowe and Gaborone)
NA	*New African* (London)
NAZA	National Archives of Zambia (Lusaka)
n.d.	no date of publication given
NMAG	National Museum and Art Gallery (Gaborone)
NMB	National Museum of Botswana (Gaborone)
n(n).	note(s)
no.	number
n.p.	no publisher given
NR	*The New Rhodesia* (Harare)
NRC	Native Recruiting Corporation
n.s.	new series
NYT	*The New York Times*

OAU	Organization of African Unity
OUP	Oxford University Press
P	Pula (currency of Botswana)
PA	*Public Administration* (London)
PAC	Pan-Africanist Congress (of South Africa)
para(s).	paragraph(s)
PBJAS	*Pula: Botswana Journal of African Studies* (Gaborone)
PLAN	People's Liberation Army of Namibia
PMU	Police Mobile Unit(s) (of the Bechuanaland Protectorate/Botswana Police)
PRO	Public Record Office (London)
PSAJPS	*Politikon: The South African Journal of Political Science* (Johannesburg)
pseud.	pseudonym
PSQ	*Political Science Quarterly*
pt.	part
PTA	Preferential Trade Area
QERNBLS	*Quarterly Economic Review of Namibia, Botswana, Lesotho, Swaziland* (London)
R	Rand (South African currency)
RDM	*Rand Daily Mail* (Johannesburg)
res.	resolution
rev. ed.	revised edition
RH	*Rhodesia Herald* (Harare)
RHL	Rhodes House Library (University of Oxford)
RRJ	*Race Relations Journal* (Johannesburg)
RST	Rhodesian/Roan Selection Trust
RT	*The Round Table* (London)
SA	South Africa(n) or *South Africa* (London)
SABC	South African Broadcasting Corporation
SACU	Southern African Customs Union
SAD	*South African Digest* (Pretoria)
SADC	Southern African Development Community
SADCC	Southern African Development Coordination Conference
SADEX	Southern African Development Information/ Documentation Exchange
SADF	South African Defense Force
SAFR	*South Africa Foundation Review* (Johannesburg)
SAHJ	*South African Historical Journal* (Johannesburg)
SAIIA	South African Institute of International Affairs (Braamfontein)

SAIPAJPA	*SAIPA: Journal for Public Administration* (Pretoria)
SAIRR	South African Institute of Race Relations (Johannesburg)
SAJAA	*The South African Journal of African Affairs* (Pretoria)
SAJE	*South African Journal of Economics* (Johannesburg)
SALC	Southern African Labor Commission
SAPEM	*Southern Africa: Political & Economic Monthly* (Harare)
SAPHAD	South Africa. Parliament. House of Assembly, *Debates*
SAPSD	South Africa. Parliament. Senate, *Debates*
SATS	South African Transport Services
SAYIL	*South African Yearbook of International Law* (Pretoria)
SBR	*Standard Bank Review* (London)
SCR	*Standard Chartered Review* (London)
sess.	session
SIAS	The Scandinavian Institute of African Studies (Uppsala)
s.l.	no place of publication given (*sine loco*)
SP	*Sunday Post* (Johannesburg)
s.p.e.	stop press edition
SRLAD	Southern Rhodesia. Legislative Assembly, *Debates*
SRPD	Southern Rhodesia. Parliament, *Debates*
SRPHAD	Southern Rhodesia. Parliament. House of Assembly. *Debates*
SRRSA	*A Survey of Race Relations in South Africa* (Johannesburg)
SRSA	*Strategic Review for Southern Africa* (Pretoria)
ST	*Sunday Times* (Johannesburg)
suppl.	supplement
SWAPO	South West Africa People's Organization (of Namibia)
TCAD	Transvaal and Central Archives Depot (Pretoria)
TEBA	(The) Employment Bureau of Africa
TF	*Transafrica Forum*
UB	University of Botswana (Gaborone)
UBLS	University of Botswana, Lesotho, and Swaziland (Roma)
UCP	University of California Press
UDF	Union (of South Africa) Defense Force
UK	United Kingdom

UKCOBPR	United Kingdom. Colonial Office, *Bechuanaland Protectorate Report*
UKCRO	United Kingdom Commonwealth Relations Office
UKCROBPR	United Kingdom. Commonwealth Relations Office. Bechuanaland Protectorate Report
UKMOD	United Kingdom. Ministry of Overseas Development
UKPHCD	United Kingdom. Parliament. House of Commons, Debates, 5th series
UKPHLD	United Kingdom. Parliament. House of Lords, *Debates*, 5th series
UN	United Nations
UNESCO	United Nations. Educational, Scientific, and Cultural Organization
UNGA	United Nations. General Assembly
UNGAOR	United Nations. General Assembly, *Official Records*
UNHCR	United Nations High Commission(er) for Refugees
UNISA	University of South Africa (Pretoria)
UNSC	United Nations. Security Council
UNSCOR	United Nations. Security Council, *Official Records*
USDS	United States. Department of State
USGPO	United States Government Printing Office (Washington, D.C.)
UTA	Union de Transports Aériens (Air Transport Union) (private French airline)
vol(s).	volume(s)
WA	*Windhoek Advertiser* (Windhoek)
w.a.e.	weekly air edition
WCC	World Council of Churches
WD	*World Development* (Oxford)
w.e.	weekly edition
WFP	World Food Program
w.n.c.l.e.	world and national city late edition
WNLA	Witwatersrand Native Labor Association
w.n.s.p.e.	world and national stop press edition
WP	*World Politics*
WT	*The World Today* (London)
YJIL	*Yale Journal of International Law*
yr.	year
YUP	Yale University Press
ZANU	Zimbabwe African National Union
ZAPU	Zimbabwe African People's Union
ZIPRA	Zimbabwe People's Revolutionary Army
ZV	*The Zebra's Voice* (Gaborone)

Chronology of Significant Events in Botswana and Southern Africa

Year	Event
1866	Discovery of gold in the Tati area
1867	Discovery of diamonds in Griqualand West
1884	South West Africa became a German protectorate
1885	Bechuanaland became a British protectorate
1886	Discovery of gold in the Witwatersrand
1888	Creation of the British South Africa Company
1889	Creation of Northern Rhodesia
1890	Pioneer Column transited the Bechuanaland Protectorate and reached Southern Rhodesia
1891	Creation of Nyasaland
1894	Completion of the railway to Mafikeng
1895	Visit of three Batswana chiefs to London
1895	The Cape Colony incorporated British Bechuanaland
1895	Transfer of Bechuanaland Protectorate headquarters from Vryburg to Mafikeng
1895	Jameson raid on the Transvaal launched from Pitsani in the Bechuanaland Protectorate
1897	Completion of the railway through the Bechuanaland Protectorate to Bulawayo
1899	Beginning of the Anglo-Boer War
1899	Beginning of the siege of Mafikeng
1900	End of the siege of Mafikeng
1902	End of the Anglo-Boer War
1904	Beginning of the German-Herero war in South West Africa
1907	End of the German-Herero war

1907   The Dominions Department of the United Kingdom Colonial
       Office became responsible for the administration of the
       Bechuanaland Protectorate
1909   Passage of the South Africa Act creating the Union of South
       Africa
1910   Inauguration of the Union of South Africa, with the British
       high commissioner doubling as the governor-general and
       Louis Botha serving as the prime minister
1910   Customs union among South Africa, Basutoland, the
       Bechuanaland Protectorate, and Swaziland
1912   Formation of the African National Congress and of the
       National Party in South Africa
1914   South African and Southern Rhodesian forces invaded
       German South West Africa
1915   South Africa completed the conquest of German South West
       Africa
1915   Customs union agreement among the three High Commission
       Territories, Northern Rhodesia, and Southern Rhodesia
1919   Establishment of the Native Advisory Council in the
       Bechuanaland Protectorate
1919   Jan C. Smuts became South African prime minister following
       the death of Louis Botha
1920   Establishment of the European Advisory Council in the
       Bechuanaland Protectorate
1920   League of Nations awarded a class C mandate to South
       Africa for South West Africa
1921   South West Africa included in the 1910 customs union
       linking South Africa and the three High Commission
       Territories
1922   White voters in Southern Rhodesia rejected incorporation by
       the Union of South Africa in a referendum, preferring
       responsible government
1922   Customs agreement between Northern Rhodesia and Southern
       Rhodesia
1922   Bechuanaland Protectorate officials began to administer the
       eastern Caprivi Strip of South West Africa for South
       Africa
1924   South African general election giving victory to the National
       and Labor Parties, with James B. M. Hertzog becoming
       the prime minister
1925   United Kingdom Dominions Office assumed responsibility for
       the administration of the three High Commission
       Territories

1929   South Africa resumed its administration of the eastern
        Caprivi Strip of South West Africa
1930   Customs agreement between South Africa and Southern
        Rhodesia
1930   Customs agreement between the Bechuanaland Protectorate
        and Southern Rhodesia
1931   The British high commissioner in South Africa no longer
        served as governor-general of the Union of South Africa
1933   Pim Commission report on the financial and economic
        position of the Bechuanaland Protectorate
1939   Report of the Anglo-South African Joint Advisory
        Conference on Cooperation
1939   Jan C. Smuts became South African prime minister
1946   United Nations General Assembly rejected South Africa's
        proposal to incorporate South West Africa
1947   The Dominions Office of the United Kingdom became the
        Commonwealth Relations Office
1948   National Party won the general election in South Africa and
        began to design and apply its policy of apartheid, with
        Daniel F. Malan as prime minister
1948   Marriage of Seretse and Ruth Khama in London
1949   Harrigan report on the succession to the chieftainship of the
        Bamangwato in the Bechuanaland Protectorate (not
        published until 1985)
1950   Seretse Khama began his exile in London
1951   Establishment of the Joint Advisory Council in the
        Bechuanaland Protectorate
1953   Creation of the Central African Federation of Southern and
        Northern Rhodesia and Nyasaland
1954   Johannes G. Strijdom became South African prime minister
1956   Customs agreement between the three High Commission
        Territories and the Central African Federation
1956   Seretse Khama returned to the Bechuanaland Protectorate
1957   Bechuanaland Protectorate assumed control over its
        telecommunications system
1958   Hendrik F. Verwoerd became South African prime minister
1959   Formation of the first political party in the Bechuanaland
        Protectorate
1959   South African Railways became responsible for running the
        southern portion of the railway traversing the
        Bechuanaland Protectorate
1960   Constitution for the Bechuanaland Protectorate
1960   South African Police killed sixty-nine demonstrators in

Sharpeville, the African township outside Vereeniging in
the Transvaal
1960   South African Government banned the African National
Congress and the Pan-Africanist Congress
1961   The United Kingdom Colonial Office became responsible for
the administration of the Bechuanaland Protectorate
1961   Establishment of the Legislative Council in the Bechuanaland
Protectorate
1961   Formation of the Bechuanaland People's Party
1961   South Africa left the Commonwealth of Nations
1962   Formation of the Bechuanaland Democratic Party
1963   End of the Central African Federation
1963   Independence of Malawi
1963   The position of the resident commissioner in the
Bechuanaland Protectorate was elevated in status to Her
Majesty's commissioner (equivalent to a governor)
1963   Bechuanaland Protectorate's Prohibition of Violence Abroad
Act
1963   Bechuanaland Protectorate assumed control over its postal
system
1964   Independence of Zambia
1964   Conclusion of Rivonia trial, with the sentencing of Nelson
Mandela and seven others to life imprisonment
1965   Transfer of Bechuanaland Protectorate headquarters from
Mafikeng to Gaborone
1965   Bechuanaland Protectorate granted self-government by the
United Kingdom
1965   Southern Rhodesian Unilateral Declaration of Independence
1965   British troops guarded the Francistown radio relay station
1966   International Court of Justice's advisory opinion on Namibia
and the beginning of the war for Namibian independence
at Omgulumbashe
1966   Balthazar J. Vorster became South African prime minister
1966   South Africa relinquished the administration of the southern
portion of the railway line through the Bechuanaland
Protectorate to the Rhodesia Railways
1966   Luke Report on the localization of the Bechuanaland
Protectorate civil service
1966   Independence of Botswana and Lesotho
1967   Diamonds discovered at Orapa
1968   Independence of Swaziland
1969   Amendment of the South Africa Act to reflect the
independence of Botswana, Lesotho, and Swaziland

1969   Renegotiation of the Southern African Customs Union
1969   Lusaka Manifesto on Southern Africa
1969   South African-Botswana extradition treaty
1970   Botswana imposed minor economic sanctions against
         Southern Rhodesia
1971   Orapa diamond mine began production
1972   Botswana balanced its recurrent budget without British grants
1973   Construction began on the road linking Botswana with
         Zambia
1973   South African-Botswana labor treaty
1974   *Coup d'état* in Portugal
1974   Completion of the Beitbridge-Rutenga railway connection
         between Southern Rhodesia and South Africa
1975   Independence of Angola and of Mozambique
1975   Botswana signed the Lomé Convention linking the European
         Economic Community with African, Caribbean, and Pacific
         states
1976   Diamonds discovered at Jwaneng
1976   Formation of the Front Line States, which included Angola,
         Botswana, Mozambique, Tanzania, and Zambia
1976   African student protest in Soweto (acronym for South West
         Townships around Johannesburg) which spread to other
         townships
1976   Botswana issued its own currency
1976   Botswana's road link to Zambia finished
1977   United Nations Security Council authorized a mandatory
         arms embargo against South Africa
1977   Inauguration of the Republic of Bophuthatswana
1977   Botswana applied further minor economic sanctions against
         Southern Rhodesia
1977   Formation of the Botswana Defense Force
1977   United Nations mission to Botswana
1978   Pieter W. Botha became South African prime minister
1979   Southern Rhodesian forces sank the Botswana-Zambian ferry
         at Kazungula
1979   South Africa proposed the creation of a Constellation of
         Southern African States
1980   Creation of the Southern African Development Coordination
         Conference
1980   Creation of the Southern African Labor Commission
1980   Death of President Khama and election of Q.K.J. Masire as
         the president of Botswana
1980   Botswana's Foreign Enlistment Act

1980   Botswana-Zambian ferry at Kazungula back in operation
1980   End of economic sanctions against Southern Rhodesia
1980   Independence of Zimbabwe
1982   Conclusion of a nonaggression pact between South Africa
        and Swaziland
1982   Jwaneng diamond mine became operational
1984   Nkomati nonaggression pact between South Africa and
        Mozambique
1984   Pieter W. Botha became president of South Africa
1984   Seretse Khama Airport opened
1985   South African Defense Force attack on Botswana
1986   Simultaneous South African Defense Force attacks on
        Botswana, Zambia, and Zimbabwe
1986   Botswana's National Security Act
1988   Botswana-Zimbabwean trade agreement
1989   Completion of the Botswana Railway's takeover of its
        railway system from the National Railways of Zimbabwe
1989   Internationally supervised elections for the Namibian
        Constituent Assembly
1989   Frederik W. De Klerk became president of South Africa
1990   February 2: Lifting of the ban on African National Congress
        and Pan Africanist Congress in South Africa
1990   February 11: Nelson Mandela left prison
1990   March 21: Independence of Namibia
1994   April 27: First multiracial elections in South Africa
1994   May 9: Mandela became president of South Africa
1994   May 24: South Africa joined the Organization of African
        Unity
1994   June 1: South Africa rejoined the Commonwealth of Nations
1994   July 30: Ending of the Front Line States grouping
1994   August 29: South Africa joined the Southern African
        Development Community

Sources: Compiled, in part, from material in the text and notes as well as
from Heribert Adam and Kogila Moodley, *South Africa without Apartheid:
Dismantling Racial Domination*, Perspectives on Southern Africa no. 39
(Berkeley: UCP, 1986), 265–267; Christopher L. Colclough and Stephen J.
McCarthy, *The Political Economy of Botswana: A Study of Growth and
Distribution* (New York: OUP, 1980), 249–252; Derek J. Hudson, "[A] Brief
Chronology of Customs Agreements in Southern Africa, 1855–1979," BNR 11
(1979) 89–95; Robert S. Jaster, Moeletsi Mbeki, Morley Nkosi, and Michael
Clough, *Changing Fortunes: War, Diplomacy, and Economics in Southern
Africa*, South Africa Update Series ([New York]: Ford Foundation and the

Foreign Policy Association, 1992), 203–216; Q. Neil Parsons, "Seretse Khama and the Ba[ma]ngwato Succession Crisis, 1948–1953," in *Succession to High Office in Botswana*, ed. Jack D. Parson, Monographs in International Studies, Africa Series, no. 54 (Athens: Ohio University Center for International Studies, 1990), 75–77; *Encyclopedia of Southern Africa*, comp. and ed. Eric Rosenthal (London: Frederick Warne & Co., Ltd., 1961), 429–433, 486–488, 494–496, and passim; *South Africa, 1989–90: Official Yearbook of the Republic of South Africa*, fifteenth ed., ed. Elise Keyter (Pretoria: Bureau for Information on behalf of the Department of Foreign Affairs, circa 1989), 23–50; Donald L. Sparks and December Green, *Namibia: The Nation after Independence* (Boulder, CO: Westview Press, 1992), 165-66; "The Past Months," SAFR 20, no. 3 (May–June 1994):1–2; no. 4 (July–August 1994):1–2; no. 5 (September–October 1994):1–2; and "SADC: South Africa Joins," ARBEFTS 31, no. 8 (16 August–15 September 1994):11812–11813.

Map of Botswana

Map of Southern Africa

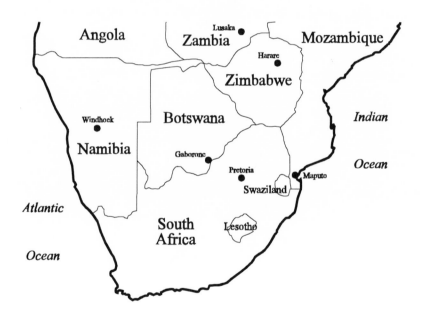

CHAPTER ONE

Introduction

THE FOCUS ON AUTONOMY

African nationalists and their coalition allies indicated in 1969 that they preferred to promote nonracialism by pacific means, but that they would take up arms if the white minority regimes in southern Africa did not abandon oligarchical rule.[1] The position of the white-led states was reinforced by their regional economic strength, with South Africa being the premier economic power in southern Africa. South Africa developed a formidable military capacity despite UN arms embargoes, thus transforming much of its wealth into an impressive arsenal.

Because of the disparity in economic capabilities between Botswana and its eastern and southern neighbors, analysts dwelt upon the gap between the weak Botswana and the strong white oligarchies of South Africa and Zimbabwe (at least until the independence of Zimbabwe in 1980). They often explained the poverty of Botswana relative to its white-ruled neighbors in terms of dependency theory, which had roots in Latin American experience. Although one need not accept all the tenets of dependency theory, one still must specify those sectors in which Botswana is dependent upon South Africa (or Zimbabwe)[2] and realize, in turn, that South Africa is dependent upon Botswana, albeit to a much smaller extent.[3]

Furthermore, the link between dependency and vulnerability is crucial in a hostage or client-type relationship. The most significant goal of Botswana was to reduce its vulnerability to its powerful neighbors.[4] In the last analysis, Botswana engaged in what M. Crawford Young termed "the diplomacy of dependency."[5] This pattern of diplomacy concentrated on building up what Willie Henderson described in "Seretse Khama and the Institutionalisation of the Botswana State" (p. 172) as "areas of freedom" for the decision-makers in Gaborone. These areas of autonomy shifted in significance over time, involved different sectors of the Botswana polity and economy, and concerned different neighbors.

This study also examines the matter of destabilization, a pejorative term that sometimes lacked conceptual rigor and clarity.[6] The term was often employed to describe South African policy, which had plausible deniability and which was seen by the people of the target state and their allies as malevolent. It suggested that conflict with South Africa was both ceaseless and ubiquitous and that South African policymakers intended to reinforce or expose the dependency or helplessness of Botswana or of other African majority-ruled states in the region.[7]

The core of this study is autonomy, dependency, vulnerability, and low and high politics in Botswana. Although this analysis could be replicated for all of South Africa's majority-ruled neighbors in a series of dyadic studies, there are five compelling reasons to select Botswana. The first reason in the absence of violence in the independence process and the peaceful transition to majority rule, which was not the case with neighboring Zimbabwe and Namibia but does apply to Zambia. The graceful transition to independence was a source of price to both the Batswana and their British mentors. Relations between the two states have usually been harmonious. The British royal family was well received in 1947, 1966, and 1979, and Sir R. Peter Fawcus, the Queen's commissioner, was invited to return for the twentieth anniversary celebrations of independence.[8]

Second, Botswana had earned high marks for the practice of democracy in Africa. Although the democratic tradition has not fared well in Africa, there are indications that improvements may be expected. Yet until more of the continent moves over into the democratic fold, Botswana stands as an exception and exemplar.[9]

Third, Botswana follows a policy of nonracialism, one which Swaziland has also endorsed.[10] The policy, which established the norm of nondiscrimination between African and non-African, had much stronger roots in Botswana and had attracted international interest.[11] The policy was dramatized by the political consequences of an interracial marriage involving the first and only prime minister (1965–1966) and subsequent president of Botswana (1966–1980). In 1948 Seretse Khama, heir to the chieftainship of the largest ethnic group in Botswana (the Bamangwato), married Ruth Williams, a Briton, without securing the consent of his uncle, Tshekedi, who was Seretse's regent. Seretse's mixed marriage jeopardized the future of the Bamangwato chieftainship, and the British government banished him from Botswana until 1956.

This marriage and the subsequent turmoil over the succession to the Bamangwato chieftaincy focused international attention on racial attitudes in southern Africa. Whites in neighboring South Africa and Zimbabwe were alarmed by miscegenation, fearing that it would undercut the status and power of the minority whites in the region. Many Britons were ashamed to see their government capitulating to the southern African white minority regimes by chastising Seretse and depriving him of his political inheritance. For the more liberal Britons, Seretse's marriage personified a policy of nonracialism at a time when and place where racism was the dominant way of thought and life.[12]

President Khama wanted Botswana's nonracial policy to serve as an example for other states in the region. Presumable the leaders of neighboring countries needed to be reassured that African majority rule would not be threatening to whites. Botswana and apartheid South Africa represented antipodes of racial etiquette, with Botswana's relaxed society offering a welcome alternative, particularly to those South Africans who sought an antidote to apartheid.[13]

A fourth attractive feature of Botswana is its stunning economic performance. The Johannesburg *Financial Mail* claimed that Botswana had "the best-managed economy in Africa,"[14] while Swedish economist Jan A. Isaksen asserted that "Botswana stands out as the wonderboy of growth during the seventies."[15] In 1989, for example, Gerhard De Kock, the later governor of the South African Reserve Bank, told the members of the Council on Foreign Relations in New York that Botswana had "one of Africa's most stable and prosperous economies."[16]

Such economic growth was all the more spectacular given the economy's sorry state at independence, when the nation was in the midst of a long drought and many Batswana participated in a food-for-work program underwritten by international agencies. A careful stewardship of resources aided by a largely expatriate group of economic planners, substantial public foreign aid, and infusions of private foreign capital in the mining sector led to some of the record levels of economic performance. A restructuring of the customs union linking Botswana with South Africa, Lesotho, and Swaziland also enabled Botswana to dispense with British grants-in-aid.[17] Botswana's economy was so well managed that it was held up as a "showpiece of economic stability" for Namibia to follow after independence.[18]

Fifth, Botswana merits careful attention because of its location at the geographical center of a politically turbulent area. What the Danish scholar Erling Bjøl has called "the *security geography* of the small state" comes into play.[19] Botswana, a landlocked state, is centrally located at the crossroads of southern Africa, where is served as a haven to political refugees from both white- and black-ruled southern African states. Its borders have been violated by its neighbors bent on either hot pursuit or on reprisal raids. American political scientist Thomas M. Callaghy alliteratively labeled the area "the intensifying vortex of violence."[20] Even though the South Africans claimed that destabilization was a double-edged sword that Africans have used as well, Pretoria's destabilization policy has extracted a heavy toll in treasure, lives, and lost opportunities for its neighbors.[21]

BOTSWANA AND HIGH POLITICS

Under the paradigm prevailing in American political science after the Second World War, students of international politics concentrated heavily on the conflict between states. After a global war that left the League of Nations in shambles, it is little wonder that members of the discipline reappraised their understanding of the dynamics of world politics. Woodrow Wilson and other idealists of the interwar period lost their appeal, and the school of realists became the academic elite within international relations. Their scholarship was predicated upon the primacy of power, and Hans J. Morgenthau of the University of Chicago became the leading realist.

From the perspective of the realists, high politics dealt with the cultivation and judicious application of military power and with the preparations for, or deterrence of, war. The realists accepted the concept of national sovereignty as well as a considerable amount of international anarchy as part of the backdrop for the national pursuit of national ends in a global arena. They assumed that high politics would take precedence over the more pedestrian socioeconomic matters involved in low politics. Supporters of the realist approach accepted the distinction between the two types of international politics. Their successors, however, have questioned whether this distinction provides a useful analytical tool.[22]

Expanding the conventional definition of high politics to include the topic of regime legitimacy, as Ronald Ingelhart did,[23] is an effective way to organize and analyze southern Africa data. Not only does the phrase *high politics* include the customary military and security component but it also, following Inglehart's change, covers the idea of territorial integrity. The rationale for this less restrictive interpretation is that territorial claims, irredentist goals, and boundary disputes are at the core of African international politics despite the Organization of African Unity's nearly inflexible position that colonial borders are sacrosanct.[24]

High politics covers two distinct sets of territorial and legitimacy issues: the international recognition of colonial Botswana as a separate, nondivisible entity with its own institutions, values, and status; and the related topic of the illegitimacy of the system of apartheid in neighboring South Africa (until 1994) and the persistence of white domination in neighboring Zimbabwe (until 1980) and Namibia (until 1990).

In terms of the first territorial and legitimacy issue, the independence of Botswana was not a foregone conclusion once the Union of South Africa was formed in the wake of the 1899–1902 Anglo-Boer War (see Chapter Two). White South African political leaders indicated to the British authorities their determination to include the High Commission Territories (HCT) in an enlarged South African state, while their Zimbabwean counterparts expressed an interest to the British government in expanding their realm by including some or all of Botswana's territory. Neither South Africa nor Zimbabwe could expand its borders to include all or some of Botswana. Some of the white residents of Botswana wanted to transfer the white enclaves in eastern Botswana to South Africa or Zimbabwe.[25]

Regarding the second territorial and legitimacy issue, the Batswana were deeply troubled by the system of white rule in southern Africa. Although their nation was almost enveloped by white-ruled states when it became independent in 1966, Botswana's officials cautiously supported African aspirations for majority rule. They contributed to the cause of national liberation at a time, place, and manner of their choice.[26] This involved some risk because of the superior military strength of neighboring Zimbabwe and South Africa, which had also dispatched its armed forces to Namibia to combat African nationalist guerrilla activity there.

The nub of this aspect of Botswana's high politics was to avoid any semblance of legitimating or condoning white rule in a neighboring state. In the South African case, Botswana steadfastly refused to exchange ambassadors with apartheid South Africa. President Khama established this policy to signal Botswana's distaste for minority rule. Nevertheless, the two states conducted business over the telephone and dispatched officials to confer with their opposite numbers on matters of mutual concern.[27]

Supplementing this high politics position on diplomatic exchanges is the low politics concern with welfare of Batswana migrant workers in South Africa. The Botswana Labor Office in Roodeport, South Africa, established in 1971, not only served as a guardian for the interests of these miners in various Transvaal mines but also handled a range of consular tasks for Batswana visiting and working in South Africa. This low politics institution performed tasks that could not be undertaken at a higher diplomatic level because of the dictates of high politics. The South Africans, in turn, used a similar tactic with their trade mission to Lesotho, Mozambique, Swaziland, and Zimbabwe, four other majority-ruled nations that did not exchange ambassadors with Pretoria.[28]

A special target of President Khama's nonrecognition policy concerned the creation of separate homelands for separate African ethnic groups in South Africa. When South Africa granted the Tswana-speaking homeland, known as Bophuthatswana, independence in 1977, neither Botswana nor any other member of the Organization of African Unity (OAU) granted it diplomatic recognition. Botswana, however, conducted some business with Bophuthatswana, and Bophuthatswana sought diplomatic recognition from Botswana.[29]

BOTSWANA AND LOW POLITICS

The realm of low politics is much less dramatic than that of high politics, yet it is grist for the mill of those political scientists concerned with transaction analysis and with technical arrangements and transfers between political entities. If high politics is the stuff of wars and national security affairs, then surely low politics is the stuff of business as usual.[30] The former is usually regarded as competitive, threatening, and conflictual, while the latter is viewed as uncompetitive, friendly, and cooperative.

Low politics is an important component of the international integration studies that explore whether, and to what extent, political space between nation-states is decreasing or increasing. Although the creation of the European Community has intellectually inspired much of international integration research, Africans, including South Africans, have questioned the relevance of the Western European experience to their own situation.[31]

In southern Africa, low politics can serve to diminish economic and social, if not political, space along regional states. But so much depends upon which state defines the significance of that space. In Botswana's case, the assumption was that apartheid South Africa was too close for comfort and that the African majority-ruled states are too distant to be of much comfort. From South Africa's perspective, though, Botswana was not close enough for comfort, and that was the nub of the asymmetry. As shown in Chapter Two, once South Africa abandoned its goal of expanding its northern border by incorporating Botswana, it found other means of keeping Botswana in near-thralldom. The Pretoria regime was anxious to build a bulwark of weak, dependent majority-ruled states, including the former homelands of Bophuthatswana, Ciskei, Transkei, and Venda. In its search for clients, rather than for equals, South Africa began to utilize the tools of low politics to create and maintain a safe outer perimeter in such fields as transportation, finance, customs, banking, technology, tourism, and managerial skills.[32]

The majority-ruled southern African states attempted to acquire greater leverage relative to South Africa in the low politics zones. In 1980 they formed a multilateral institution called SADCC, which became SADC in 1992, to attempt to offset the resources that South Africa could muster in its Constellation of Southern African States (CONSAS).[33] High politics is the home of the realist school of international politics, while low politics is better suited to those who consider themselves pluralists. In the pluralist world, international politics extends beyond the state and involves transnational forces and entities. Low politics questions the state-centered view of international politics and includes an array of nonstate actors, such as multinational corporations and revolutionary and philanthropic organizations. The pluralist school, though, doubts the sharpness of the distinction between high and low politics, arguing that they are coupled together.[34] A variant of that argument is that it is best to array high and low politics along a continuum.[35]

Previously I indicated a shuffling between high and low politics in the area of diplomatic recognition by which Botswana employed its Office of the Labor Representative in Roodeport as a de facto consulate for Batswana resident in South Africa. Low politics supplanted high politics in that instance. Conversely, what South Africans have called "transport diplomacy"[36] assumed an aspect of high politics when South African railway freight cars, especially refrigerated ones for Botswana's frozen beef, were not delivered on time or were somehow lost or misplaced.[37] This sends a very strong signal. The same was true in terms of the Bophuthatswana railway imbroglio, a topic covered in Chapter Seven. In southern Africa, air and rail transportation services tend to be state rather than private enterprises. But a number of nonstate or private actors are involved in low politics.

As explained in Chapter Five, missionaries have helped to develop primary and secondary education in colonial Botswana. This is an example of low politics when, during the pre-independence period, Batswana left Botswana to continue their education at such missionary-sponsored institutions as the famous Tiger Kloof Institution in the Cape Province, a school sponsored by the London Missionary Society. Many of the political elite of Botswana are alumni of Tiger Kloof. Yet when one considers the role of missionary and church groups with such international connections and patrons as the Lutheran World Federation (LWF) and its local representative in the management of the refugee camp at Dukwe, one moves into the realm of high politics. Refugee policy, as shown in Chapter Three, is high politics and has strained Botswana's relations with both South Africa and Zimbabwe.

In the low politics zone of private foreign investment, discussed in Chapter Eight, I examine the dominant role of such South African-based multinational corporations as the Anglo-American Corporation and its various subsidiaries, in the diamond, copper-nickel, and soda ash mining sectors. The arrangements between Botswana and South Africa regarding the exploitation of soda ash at Sua Pan, located in the northern part of the nation, took on added significance when placed in the context of international trade sanctions against South Africa. Equally important has been the increase in private South African investment in manufacturing establishments in Botswana that export their products to Zimbabwe. Authorities in Zimbabwe, concerned about the level of the local content of these exports, feared that they were little more than thinly disguised South African exports. Low politics thus offered an escape hatch for South African firms determined to avoid international economic sanctions. South Africa's economic well-being, in turn, could be regarded as closer to the high politics end of the continuum than to the low politics end because of the nation's economic isolation. Conversely, Botswana's ability to withstand any South African counter-sanctions moved away from the low politics zone and into the high politics zone.[38] Clearly in southern Africa, low politics can be harnessed to the service of high politics.

REFASHIONING THE WEB OF HIGH AND LOW POLITICS

Why the web of high and low politics that enfolds Botswana and its neighbors in southern Africa? Does it merely confirm the conventional wisdom about South Africa as the dominant state or hegemon in southern Africa?[39] What did the transaction flows involved in low politics have to do with southern African international relations?[40] To describe and analyze these flows over time is to map the dependency position of Botswana. As Larry W. Bowman and his colleagues testified before the Subcommittee on Africa of the Committee on Foreign Affairs of the US House of Representatives, "a complete analysis of relations between particular states . . . requires that the various dimensions of dependency be analyzed separately and that room be left for autonomous riposte."[41]

If one accepted the allegation that, at the time it became independent in 1966, Botswana was primarily a client state beholden primarily to South Africa and secondarily to Zimbabwe, did that mean that these asymmetrical relations persisted, frozen in time? Did it also imply that Botswana's political leadership could not fashion what Professor Bowman called an "autonomous riposte"? Not necessarily so. Using the concept of high and low politics, this political mapping exercise shows to what extent, and why, Botswana was dependent upon its neighbors, especially those two powerful states, and to what extent that dependency has been modified. This entails tracking the sector and the neighbor involved in the dependency relationship to indicate Botswana's needs, and prospects for, autonomy. Autonomy, in short, will be treated in a disaggregated fashion.

Considering the profound distaste that Africans had for white minority rule in southern Africa and their equally profound relief in its replacement by majority-rule systems in southern Africa, one should not be surprised if this emotional euphoria is coupled with political myopia about the region. There is nothing a priori to prevent a large and powerful majority-ruled state in southern Africa, such as Zimbabwe now or post-apartheid South Africa, from becoming the new or remaining the old regional hegemon. Although the racial designation of the rulers changes, the rank order remains the same. Even the members of SADCC and other perceptive observers recognized that the imbalance between that organization and South Africa could not be transformed with the advent of majority rule in South Africa.[42]

This book describes, analyzes, and explains the pattern of links between Botswana and its four neighbors in terms of high and low politics. Even though these lines were usually uneven, favoring South Africa and Zimbabwe, Botswana has taken several deliberate steps since 1966 to reduce its dependence upon South Africa.[43] By exploring how these networks have been refashioned in the independence era, one can locate strengths and weaknesses in different sectors within the webs of high and low politics. Moreover, one can ascertain which neighbors are dominant in which sectors. Employing a high politics–low politics continuum, which considers the separate sectors and the separate neighbors, illuminates some of the dynamics of transnational relations within southern Africa and demonstrated how much of an "autonomous riposte" Botswana's leaders have been able to fashion to respond to those who capitalize upon their nation's weakness. There is an inverse relationship, as F. John Ravenhill has observed, between weakness and choice, which is the quintessential element of autonomy. "Weakness constrains choice" was the way he expressed it.[44]

M. Crawford Young has indicated that autonomy entails "enlarging the scope of choice and reducing the impact of external constraints on policy options."[45] Botswana has expanded its options by drawing upon regional and extraregional material and human resources. This prompted British scholar Willie Henderson to remark that the regime in Gaborone "was turned into an efficient aid gathering machine . . . [for garnering] foreign aid and foreign investment."[46] Botswana, moreover, negotiated with its strongest neighbor, South Africa, on the basis of enhanced collective bargaining strength as well as on the basis of reciprocal advantage. By doing so, it has been chipping away at the various layers of dependency binding it to South Africa. It created room for maneuver in its neighborhood by cultivating other neighbors and a host of public and private aid donors, particularly in the West.

Following President Khama's interpretation of his nation's role, one recognizes that dependency does not necessarily hobble national leaders. There is scope for the "autonomous riposte" in this approach. Such cautious optimism, though, it less likely to spring from the dependency theory school of thought which assumes more of a global approach than either the realist or pluralist schools. As such, it tends to undervalue the areas of choice and maneuver open to innovative diplomats and planners. Botswana, for example, was quite skillful in its relations with South Africa, thereby avoiding some, but not all, of the heavy costs associated with the application of South African destabilization policies.[47] The dependency theory approach nevertheless correctly underscores the trade-off between SADCC's efforts to diminish its members' reliance upon South Africa and a corresponding increase in their need for Western assistance.[48]

PART ONE

ISSUES IN HIGH POLITICS

CHAPTER TWO

Territorial Integrity and Identity

THE PROPOSED TRANSFER OF BOTSWANA TO SOUTH AFRICA

Joseph Hanlon's description of South Africa as "king of Southern Africa" characterizes the relations between Botswana and the Union (later the Republic) of South Africa.[1] Until after the Second World War, Botswana's territorial integrity and identity were precarious, its autonomy at risk because of the hegemonic aspirations of the "king of Southern Africa." This chapter explores the political implications of the South African threat to incorporate Botswana. Such incorporation would have ended Botswana's hopes for autonomy. Now, at least Botswana enjoys juridical sovereignty, which, argued Stephen D. Krasner, is the vital underpinning for those international activities of the Third World states intended to redistribute more equitably some of the world's resources.[2]

Prior to the formation of the Union of South Africa in 1908–1909, Bechuanaland had been divided into two unequal portions, with the portion south of the Molopo River becoming part of the Cape Province in 1895. The Cape segment was termed British Bechuanaland after 1885, while the portion north of the Molopo River was called the Bechuanaland Protectorate (BP) after its proclamation in 1885.[3] The Cape Province was the linchpin between the two Rhodesias (now Zimbabwe and Zambia) and German South West Africa (now Namibia).

British Bechuanaland served as the administrative headquarters and railway corridor for the BP, which became Botswana at independence in 1966. Bechuanaland's first capital was located in Vryburg, Cape Province, until 1895, when it was moved north along the railroad to

Mafikeng (then called Mafeking), another small town in the Cape. The BP's administrative headquarters remained in South Africa in an area of Mafikeng known as the Imperial Reserve.[4] In 1965 the BP's capital was finally moved from outside South Africa to inside the BP at a place further north along the railway line known as Gaborone (called Gaberones at that time). From 1897, when the rail line was opened from Vryburg to Bulawayo, until September 1974, when the line was completed from Rutenga to Beitbridge, one could not travel by rail from South Africa to Zimbabwe without transiting Botswana.[5]

From the inauguration of the Union of South Africa in 1910 until a year after South Africa became a republic in 1961, BP's existence as a separate entity was largely contingent on the state of Anglo-South African relations. At the 1962 meeting of the Transvaal National Party, South African Prime Minister Hendrik F. Verwoerd asserted that the transfer of the three High Commission Territories (HCT) to South Africa was no longer feasible.[6] He repeated this policy statement in the House of Assembly (the lower chamber of the South African parliament) early the next year.[7] This, to all intents and purposes, ended roughly a half century of diplomatic maneuvering between the United Kingdom (UK) and the "king of Southern Africa."

Such a conflict stemmed from the permissive wording of the 1909 South Africa Act, which allowed, but did not require, the transfer of the HCT to South Africa with the British government's permission. In terms of Section 151 of that act, the initiative rested with the South African Parliament, which was to request such a transfer from the British monarch who would be guided by the Privy Council's decision in the matter. If and when such a transfer took place, the governance of the HCT would follow the guidelines set forth in the Schedule to the act. According to Section 150 of the 1909 Act, a similar request from the South African Parliament would be necessary were the incorporation of Southern Rhodesia to be sought.[8] South Africa proposed, the UK disposed was the logic of these two sections. Not until the 1968 meeting of the Orange Free State National Party did the South African Prime Minister indicate that these anomalous sections of the constitution would be dropped. This was done in the 1969 South Africa Act Amendment Act.[9]

Six aspects of the triangular relationship among the UK, the BP, and South Africa bear on the question of Botswana's autonomy. First, with respect to ethnographic considerations, a proposed transfer of the lip to South Africa would have rejoined groups that had been rent asunder by colonial boundaries. Presently, more than twice as many Setswana-speakers reside in South Africa than in Botswana itself—1.7 million versus roughly 0.75 million, respectively.[10]

Despite the appeal of kith and kin arguments, white South Africans seemed more impressed than the Batswana of the BP with the ethnic arithmetic and geographic configurations in the 1954 Tomlinson Commission Report, an eighteen-volume report that called for the development of the Union's homeland areas, usually called Bantustans, for Africans.[11] The Tomlinson Commission Report represented the apotheosis of separate-development philosophy, nurtured by Verwoerd, who was the intellectual force behind the concept of territorial apartheid as exemplified by the Bantustans. Although never fully adopted by the government, the Tomlinson Report hinted at, but was not predicated upon, the inclusion of the three HCT within the Union. When the House of Assembly debated the Tomlinson Report, Verwoerd, then Minister of Native Affairs, emphasized that any mention of the HCT in the report was inadvertent because the terms of reference for the commission on the homeland areas did not mention the Territories.[12] Yet thirty years earlier, the leadership of the Transvaal National Party clearly saw the link between implementing a system of strict geographical segregation in the Union and the need for additional land reserved for African occupation in the HCT.[13]

In 1977 South Africa granted independence to the Setswana-speaking homeland termed Bophuthatswana, part of which abuts on Botswana's southeastern border. Botswana refused to legitimize South Africa's separate development policy by extending diplomatic recognition to Bophuthatswana. Only South Africa recognized this, or any other, erstwhile homeland. The South African–Botswana rail line, which traversed Bophuthatswana, afforded Bophuthatswana an opportunity to pressure Botswana for recognition.[14] To allay anxiety about this vulnerable segment of the railway, Botswana's Minister of External Affairs indicated that informal arrangements not requiring Botswana to recognize Bophuthatswana's travel documents would be made for travel to and from Bophuthatswana.[15]

A second consideration underlying the question of the BP transfer to South Africa was white access to BP's land, a matter of concern at the time of British acquisition.[16] Land hunger, particularly among the impoverished Afrikaners, concerned the British in Southern Rhodesia, which was contiguous to the Union's Transvaal Province.[17] One reason the white Rhodesians rejected the 1922 South African proposal to join the Union (provided for by Section 150 of the South Africa Act) was hostility to Afrikanerdom and the fear of Afrikaner immigration.[18] The BP, however, did offer possibilities in the way of Crown lands. The ownership of these lands was vested in the state, that is, the Crown in the BP. Local white ranchers were anxious to secure personal title to these lands.[19] Indeed, two South African cabinet members, P.M.K.

Le Roux and J.J. Serfontein, became nonresident landowners in the Tati area of the BP.[20] Some of the residents in the eastern white enclaves of the Protectorate sought territorial incorporation by the Union.[21] In their view, the Union provided better protection and a more congenial economic environment than the BP for the pursuit of their livelihoods.[22]

International prestige and status for South Africa was a third consideration in the diplomacy of transfer.[23] Having been defeated by the British in the 1899–1902 South African War, the Afrikaners transferred the contest for primacy in South Africa from the battlefield to the political, economic, and diplomatic fields. These Afrikaner nationalists wanted a republic rather than a monarchy, which was symbolized in South Africa by the governor-general, a Briton (and later a South African) representing the British crown.

In addition to symbolic changes, the nationalists were eager to reduce British influence over and intrusion into South African legislation and foreign policy, especially in the highly sensitive area of South African neutrality were the UK to get involved in war.[24] The Afrikaners wanted to shape their own domestic and foreign policies, including racial, trade, and defense links with neighboring colonies. Although the question of the transfer of the HCT to South Africa goes back to 1908,[25] the more active, aggressive phase was pursued under General James B.M. Hertzog's and Daniel F. Malan's premierships from 1924 to 1939 and 1948 to 1954, respectively.[26] Thereafter, the issue abated slowly, even though as late as December 1962 the United Nations General Assembly cautioned South Africa (without naming it) not to incorporate the HCT, lest it be charged with an act of aggression.[27] Prime Minister Malan expressed South Africans' resentment at second-class treatment by the British over the HCT in Cape Town on 9 February 1951 when he charged that South Africa "is compelled to harbour territories . . . belonging to and governed by another country." This affront would not be endured by other Commonwealth states, including the UK. Consequently, the Union, in his view, did not have "real equality . . . [or] even full independence" and was thus "relegated to a position of inferiority and . . . to the position of a semi-independent and third-class country."[28]

The fourth aspect of the BP transfer to South Africa involves the definition of consultation with the inhabitants, which is fundamentally a question of self-determination for the people of the BP.[29] No public evidence exists that the UK ever considered holding a referendum on the question of transfer, even though it tenaciously held to the position that the affected parties would be consulted about transfer.[30] Evasive and ambiguous when queried about the mechanics of consultation,

British policymakers said the time was not opportune when the South Africans pressed the issue of transfer, which led Hyam to epitomize the British response as the "doctrine of The Unripe Time."[31] Unsystematic as it was, the evidence indicates that the leaders of the eight principal Tswana groups represented on the Native (later, African) Advisory Council expected unflagging British protection against South African incorporation. These elites agreed to British protection,[32] which piqued Malan, who, in his address to the 1953 congress of the Orange Free State National Party, reminded the UK that its policy was inconsistent because it made no parallel attempt to secure African consent in Nyasaland and Southern and Northern Rhodesias when building the Central African Federation.[33]

A fifth consideration of the transfer question, which arose in the mid-1930s, has had an impact upon South African policy toward the independent HCT. This can be called the functionalist approach to South African regional policy.[34] The roots of this approach can be found in the 1938 Anglo-South African agreement to broaden and deepen the technical, scientific, and economic links between the Union and the HCT, with a view to creating a more favorable climate of local opinion with respect to the prospective transfer.[35] To facilitate this enterprise, the Hertzog government allocated the sum of £35,000, much to the dismay of Malan's opposition Purified National Party, which forced, and lost, a parliamentary vote or division on the matter.[36] The Batswana had their doubts about what they perceived as Pretoria's Trojan horse, which would ultimately lead to incorporation.[37]

Still, the two governments established a Joint Advisory Conference on Cooperation, which included the resident commissioners of all three HCT and the South African secretaries of agriculture, finance, and native affairs. It filed its first report in May 1939, which, because of the Second World War, was not published until 1952, when the transfer issue arose again.[38] The Southern Rhodesians also stressed their functional cooperation when discussing territorial expansion into the BP, so the South Africans did not have the low politics field all to themselves.[39] A number of the links—the financial, commercial, banking, and transport ties—between the BP and South Africa were unaffected by either South Africa's departure from the Commonwealth in 1961 or by Botswana's independence in 1966. From such links came various South African proposals for regional cooperation, as well as the concerns of the SADCC for "delinking" its members from South Africa.[40]

Finally, there are considerations of defense. Here we need to be more speculative because the available evidence is skimpy. Armed black South Africans have been allied with or utilized by white South

African military forces before the twentieth century,[41] but in this century white South Africans were reluctant to arm African members of the Union Defense Force (UDF) to fight in overseas or regional wars.[42] This cultural and political constraint suggested that South African military considerations regarding the BP would be more likely to focus on geography and strategic location than on African manpower resources.

After the First World War, the British government considered the idea of loaning UDF units—along with South African Air Force overflights and intelligence-gathering activities by UDF officers in mufti—to the HCT to quell disorder. Sensitive to the ill will these activities would generate among the African residents of the HCT, the British apparently never acted upon these ideas.[43] Yet in 1933 British sailors and marines from *H.M.S. Carlisle* were dispatched by train from Simonstown to Serowe to provide a show of force to help discipline Tshekedi Khama of the Bamangwato,[44] and during the Second World War the UDF staged maneuvers on the Union-BP border.[45] After that war the Pretoria authorities undertook discussions with the British government about the prospect of building a radar screen, using the HCT, conducting military overflights, and securing an emergency access route to Namibia for UDF vehicles via the BP, all of which suggests that the South Africans viewed the BP as a northern defense perimeter.[46] The well-publicized South African Defense Force (SADF) strikes into Botswana in 1985 and 1986 reflect some of that perception.

ZIMBABWEAN TERRITORIAL DESIGNS ON BOTSWANA

The threat that South Africa posed to the territorial identity and integrity of the BP was compounded by a secondary threat from Southern Rhodesia, which also had claims on the BP. Recently Q. Neil Parsons averred that Southern Rhodesia's role with regard to westward and southerly expansion into the BP has been neglected because of the fascination with the South African attempt to include the three HCT within its domain.[47] His historical revisionism focused attention on the Southern Rhodesian position, particularly when the official records of the European Advisory Council in the BP indicated that "dismemberment of the territory" was a topic of Southern Rhodesian concern not long after it became self-governing in 1923.[48]

Cecil J. Rhodes' British South Africa Company (BSAC), which received its charter in 1889, posed the principal threat to the BP.[49] From 1889 to 1894, negotiations with the British government had proceeded to the point where, with the approval of the imperial authorities who saw the proposed acquisition as a means of reducing the cost of colonial rule, the Company was ready to incorporate the territory. The BSAC would handle the administrative expenses incurred in managing its new domain. The BP was particularly attractive because it would become a rail corridor between Southern Rhodesia and the Cape, because gold had been discovered in 1866 in the northeastern Tati area, and because its land could be sold to white ranchers. Finally, the acquisition of the BP would provide strategic benefits for the British Empire, which could block eastward expansion of the Germans in South West Africa and northern expansion of Afrikaners in the Transvaal. The location of the territory prompted Cecil Rhodes to regard it as a landward Suez Canal. Yet the visit of three Batswana chiefs to Britain in 1895 and the ill-fated cross-border raid on Johannesburg led by Rhodes' compatriot Leander S. Jameson in the last week of 1895 furnished the occasion for the imperial government to curb the expansion of the BSAC into the BP.

These chiefs had ceded some eastern land to the BSAC, and, by 1897, the rail line traversed what had once been their land to reach Bulawayo.[50] The railway was subsequently linked to the Mozambican port of Beira, thus providing the BP and Southern Rhodesia with access to the Atlantic (at Cape Town) and the Indian Ocean (at Beira). The railway did not become Botswana's property until 1987, when the Zimbabwean Railway relinquished control of the line to the National Railways of Botswana.[51] By 1909 the BSAC once again pushed the incorporation question with the authorities in London now that it had secured ownership of three parcels of land for white occupancy in the eastern perimeter known as the Gaborone, Lobatse, and Tuli blocks.[52] Rhodes had been a patron to a number of Afrikaners who trekked into Ngamiland to establish themselves at Ghanzi, but the BSAC did not acquire the land there; instead the BP government granted the land titles.[53] The final enclave catering to white settlement was the Tati district, including the town of Francistown, which served as the gateway to Southern Rhodesia. The Tati district had close ties with the Matabeleland portion of Southern Rhodesia and became part of the BP in 1892.[54]

Rebuffed by the British government in its attempt to secure the Tuli block in 1909, the BSAC would not drop the matter.[55] Jameson told the Chartered Company shareholders in 1913 that the imperial government had thwarted its economic development plans for the BP, which, he told his audience, was "our inheritance." He declared that the British government was following a "dog-in-the-manger policy" in the Protectorate by checking BSAC activities, on the one hand, and being remiss in developing the territory, on the other.[56] These comments riled South African Prime Minister Botha, who cautioned the authorities in London that such remarks "caused suspicion in the Union as to the destination of that Protectorate." General Botha also indicated "that the Union Government would offer strenuous opposition to any such transfer of Bechuanaland . . . [to] the Chartered Company."[57] South African opposition to Southern Rhodesian territorial ambitions in the BP rarely changed for the next half century.

From Jameson's 1913 address to the BSAC shareholders until Botswana's independence, the Southern Rhodesian challenge to South African expansion tended to assume three forms:[58] the total challenge, requesting the whole of the BP; the northern challenge, requesting the northern portion of the BP; and the block challenge, requesting one or more of the blocks allocated to white settlement. The Tati area (which includes the commercial and railway hub of Francistown) was the block most frequently mentioned.[59] Except for the northern challenge, the initiative often came from white residents of the Protectorate and involved petitions, visits, and speeches in the BP European Advisory Council. The matter often surfaced in parliamentary debates in Salisbury and sometimes in London. Indeed, on two separate occasions high-level British officials considered the fragmentation of the BP.[60]

Turning to the block challenge, white residents of the Tati district contacted the Colonial Office in early 1918 to explore the possibility of merging that district with Southern Rhodesia.[61] Although London ignored their case, the Tati whites persisted, directing their lobbying efforts at members of the Southern Rhodesian Legislative Council. In 1921 that council passed a motion calling upon the "Administration [to] approach the Colonial Office and the inhabitants of the Tati district with a view to arranging for the immediate incorporation of the . . . Tati Territory with Southern Rhodesia."[62] This motion said nothing about the views of the Africans residing there, and the Colonial Office thought that Prime Minister Jan Smuts should be consulted about this matter. Although Smuts remonstrated, the Africans of Tati objected to the incorporation. In addition, BP officials doubted that the whites of Tati were unified regarding the proposed transfer.[63]

Members of Parliament (MPs) raised questions about the incorporation of the Tati area in the British House of Commons,[64] as did members of the Southern Rhodesian Legislative Assembly.[65] By 1933 the topic surfaced as a formal motion in the Legislative Assembly. This motion called upon "the Government to lay down as a definite objective the incorporation of Tati with Southern Rhodesia.[66] Prime Minister Moffat of Southern Rhodesia pressed his country's claims to the Tati area at a Bulawayo banquet of the British Empire

Service League on Armistice Day 1929, where the senior guest was the BP Resident Commissioner Rowland M. Daniel. Moffat asserted that Tati "rounds off our Southern Rhodesia[n] boundary. Geographically, historically and politically it should belong to Southern Rhodesia.[67]

In the years just before the BP received self-government, the white residents of the Tati area considered secession and merger with Southern Rhodesia or the subsequent Central African Federation[68] or even independence.[69] They even entertained the idea of raising the issue of secession from the BP with the International Court of Justice, which was then considering the South West African cases.[70] Their legal adviser was Lourens Beyers, a Pretoria lawyer and prominent Tati landowner.[71] This separatist policy alarmed African political leaders in the Bechuanaland People's Party (BPP)[72] and in the Bechuanaland Democratic Party (BDP), who quickly denounced any notion of territorial fragmentation.[73]

At the northern challenge level, the idea of a bifurcated BP seemed to have a wider, more irredentist appeal to white Rhodesians. Bifurcation was more useful than the block approach as a check against South African encroachment because it affected a larger audience in southern Africa. References exist to incorporating the northern portion[74] of the BP in parliamentary debates in Salisbury in the late 1920s,[75] as well as in the 1930s,[76] and the idea was even bruited about by a well-known clergyman, the Rev. Alfred E. Jennings (a London Missionary Society missionary in the BP) in his 1938 address to the Bulawayo Rotary Club.[77]

After the 1948 South African general election, which marked the end of the Smuts era and the second accession to power of Afrikaner nationalism since 1924, the total approach came into vogue. Early in 1949, members of the BP European Advisory Council considered joining with Southern Rhodesia in the larger context of Central Africa.[78] The matter was handled in a cursory fashion in the counterpart African Advisory Council.[79] Journalists' impressionistic samplings of opinion in 1949 and 1950 among whites and Africans in the BP indicated only a grudging acceptance of such an incorporation as an alternative to absorption by South Africa.[80] The Protectorate showed little sustained interest in the prospect of merger with Southern Rhodesia. Yet in Southern Rhodesia, the press noted the European Advisory Council's position,[81] and an official Southern Rhodesian visit to London in late 1949[82] revived claims to at least the northern portion of the BP, if not the entire protectorate.[83] There are grounds for believing that Southern Rhodesian businessmen liked the idea of including the BP.[84]

Malan objected to the Southern Rhodesian claims to BP territory, particularly because Salisbury had not cleared the matter with Pretoria. South African objections apparently did not distinguish between the Southern Rhodesian half or total approaches, which were not mutually exclusive bargaining positions. A South African[85] English-language press report suggested that Prime Minister Malan overreacted to the Southern Rhodesian bargaining position (which asked that the imperial government take into account the Southern Rhodesian position "if any change in the status of Bechuanaland were contemplated") primarily to placate its National Party constituents. Bashing the British on the HCT was hardly a novel stratagem in South Africa. The Southern Rhodesians quickly noted that their government had not been consulted when Prime Minister Malan had broached the matter of the proposed South African incorporation of the BP.[86]

In addition to the irredentist claim based upon BSAC and other historical records, which seemed to appeal more to the whites of the BP than to the Batswana,[87] there were ethnic linkages between the Africans of the BP and Southern Rhodesia. The Bira and especially Bakalanga have kinsmen on both sides of the Botswana-Zimbabwe border.[88] Those Bakalanga living in Botswana appealed to Radio Botswana to broadcast in their own language.[89] With kinship ties to the Ndebele in Zimbabwe, the Bakalanga in the Francistown area tend to side with the BPP rather than with the BDP, which they perceived as a Bamangwato instrument.[90] Historically they have disliked the Bamangwato.[91] There have been no boundary disputes between the two neighboring states[92] following the demarcation of the border by a joint team in 1959[93] and the negotiation of a post-independence boundary agreement.[94]

BOTSWANA AND THE STATUS OF NAMIBIA

As a landlocked territory, Botswana has access to the sea by way of South Africa on its southern border and Namibia on its western border. Its other two neighbors, Zimbabwe and Zambia, are also geographically separated from the Indian and Atlantic Oceans. This chapter explores Botswana's relations with Namibia in terms of Walvis Bay as an outlet to the Atlantic Ocean, Namibia's quest for internationally recognized independence from South Africa, temporary colonial administrative arrangements between the BP and Namibia, and territorial claims.

Placed under imperial German rule in 1884, South West Africa (as Namibia was then called) possessed only two mediocre ports, Swakopmund and Lüderitzbucht. Previously the Cape Colony had annexed Walvis Bay, the best harbor, but British imperial policy ruled out northward expansion from the Cape Colony. Taking advantage of this, the Germans encircled Walvis Bay with their own territory. Except for a brief period during the First World War when it was overrun by the Germans, Walvis Bay remained under Cape authority all through the German era. Until 1977 it was treated administratively as if it were part of Namibia, but thereafter until the end of February 1994 South African legislation has made it a part of the Cape Province.[95]

With regard to Namibia's international status, Regent Tshekedi Khama of the Bamangwato organized four BP chiefs (of the Bakwena, Bangwaketse, Batlokwa, and Bamalete) to oppose South Africa's annexation of South West Africa after World War II.[96] He lobbied the British, rather than the South African government, about South West Africa because at that time the Dominions (later, the Commonwealth Relations) Office bore the responsibility for Anglo-South African relations and the governance of the HCT. Tshekedi and his fellow chiefs presented their written case to the British government,[97] and he discussed the topic with the British high commissioner in South Africa. Yet the British would not help him present the case in London, possibly to avoid embarrassing the Smuts government.[98] The Undersecretary of State for Dominion Affairs of the Attlee government assured the House of Commons that Tshekedi did not need to visit the United Kingdom to discuss the matter in person. He pointed out that "the interests of the Bechuanaland Protectorate cannot be regarded as involved in the future status of South-West Africa."[99]

Subsequently the undersecretary reiterated this position on the "interests" of the Protectorate—without referring to the Protectorate's inhabitants[100]—and the prime minister informed the House that the British delegation to the United Nations was familiar with the views of these BP chiefs on the proposed incorporation of South West Africa.[101] The gist of the chiefs' position, which Tshekedi relayed to the British high commissioner in Cape Town, was that incorporation would jeopardize future access to Walvis Bay if a connecting railway link were constructed. Incorporation also would be politically unwelcome in terms of BP's future because of South Africa's racial policies. In their view, the incorporation of the mandated territory would permit South Africa to acquire greater economic leverage against the BP and increase the possibility of the transfer of the BP to the Union.[102] The chiefs' memorandum could thus be seen as a preemptive move against the United Kingdom and, indirectly, an attempt to cultivate a constituency within the British public, if not the governing Labor Party. Tshekedi and his nephew Seretse later put such public relations skills to greater use in the Bamangwato dynastic disputes of the 1950s.[103]

As the pace of decolonization accelerated in southern Africa, the British government again became involved with the international status of South West Africa. Charged with the responsibility for monitoring South Africa's stewardship of the mandate, a UN General Assembly group wanted to visit the territory and had to transit the BP to do so. In 1961 the British government, acting through the high commissioner in Salisbury, withdrew visas for entry into the BP for members of the UN Committee on South West Africa because the committee would not agree to confine its activities to the BP. The South African government had warned that committee not to cross over the BP border into South West Africa on pain of arrest and subsequent deportation. To make that threat credible, the South Africans stepped up security patrols along the border.[104]

In terms of high politics, Botswana's relations with Namibia have been less strained than those with South Africa and Zimbabwe because there was no threat of complete or partial annexation. Until 1990 Namibia was not an independent political entity and could not make irredentist claims. Namibia was much more closely tied to South Africa than to Southern Rhodesia after World War I and, unlike Southern Rhodesia, was subject to international scrutiny as a League of Nations mandated territory. For Botswana, the Namibian connection had the high politics element of avoiding the precedent of South African incorporation of a neighboring territory as a prelude to the transfer of the three HCT to South Africa. High politics were also involved in the exodus of political refugees from Namibia into pre- and post-independent Botswana.

About 1962, distinguished American political scientist Quincy Wright suggested a joint UN trusteeship for the BP and South West Africa. The UN, the British, or the South Africans seemed never to have entertained this idea.[105] In 1962 African nationalists from South West Africa, influenced by the pan-African concepts popularized by President Nkrumah of Ghana, briefly considered the possibility of a merger of Botswana, Namibia, and Angola.[106] Despite these administrative and pan-African dreams, Botswana and Namibia are relatively distant neighbors.

Another of Botswana's concerns with Namibia involved the administration of the eastern Caprivi Strip of South West Africa in the interwar period. Because BP officials had easier geographical access to that portion of the Caprivi Strip, Pretoria delegated administrative responsibility for its governance from 1922 until 1929 to the BP Administration.[107] South Africa remunerated the BP Administration for the expenses it incurred in this task.[108] The League of Nations' Permanent Mandates Commission in Geneva, which monitored the administration of South West Africa, was concerned at the South African delegation of authority to the BP administrators. At several of its annual meetings, the commission deemed this delegation of authority to be unconventional and undesirable.[109]

In 1934 Prime Minister Huggins of Southern Rhodesia discussed the Strip's future with Prime Minister Hertzog of South Africa, perhaps hoping to register a Southern Rhodesian claim to the Strip.[110] Another ineffectual Southern Rhodesian claim to this Strip was made in 1953.[111] The claimants would probably have considered the role the Southern Rhodesian forces played in conquering the Caprivi Strip in the opening stages of the German South West African campaign.[112]

G. Heaton Nichols, who had served as the South African high commissioner in London, suggested in 1951 that South Africa transfer the Strip to Northern Rhodesia because of ethnic considerations with the Barotseland area of Northern Rhodesia,[113] which had administered the Strip for a brief period after the Southern Rhodesian military had seized it in the opening days of the First World War.[114] Cool to the suggestion, Prime Minister Malan argued that the Union needed to hold the Strip for a future railway link with states to the north.[115]

The last of Botswana's concerns with Namibia were claims to the Caprivi Strip[116] by the Lozi of Barotseland as well as the Batawana of the BP.[117] Mr. T.T. Tsheko cited the ethnic considerations of the Bayei, Hambukush, Tonga, and Subyia who had lived in the Strip,[118] the 1922–1929 BP administrative interlude, and a desire to secure better economic access to Angola and Northern Rhodesia as reasons to introduce an irredentist motion on the Caprivi Strip in the BP Legislative Council in 1963.

Tsheko asserted that the Caprivi Strip "belongs to Bechuanaland and should be administered by Bechuanaland." Although strongly supported by future Botswana president Masire, the motion was defeated without a formal vote. Anticipating this lack of support, Tsheko declined to withdraw his motion because "in future when the British are no . . . [longer] here we might continue the claim."[119] That claim surfaced once again during a press interview in London with Masire after the BP had advanced to the self-governing stage.[120]

By independence, the demarcation of the boundary on the ground had covered the western border and had begun at the western Caprivi Strip, moving eastward toward the Chobe River.[121] As the Caprivi's southern border was demarcated, some Batswana found themselves displaced south of the boundary line,[122] thus raising the issue of compensation for land transferred to the Caprivi Strip.[123]

The status of the Caprivi Strip attracted the attention of some Batswana legislators, who expressed an interest in that part of the Strip which presumably was part of the BP before the British ceded it to the Germans pursuant to the 1890 Anglo-German treaty. The Botswana government position, explained by the attorney-general and the minister of external affairs, was that the northern boundaries of Botswana could be decided by the two nations only after Namibia became an independent state.[124]

Once Namibia achieved its independence, President Sir Ketumile Masire was the first head of state to visit, during which time he and President Sam Nujoma signed an agreement to create a Joint Commission on Defense and Security. Given the task of handling matters along the joint border, this commission held its first plenary session in Windhoek on 15 November 1990, following a meeting of the Joint Technical Committee at Kasane two weeks earlier. The commission held its second plenary session in Maun a year later. Both states have laid claim to an island in the Chobe River called Kasikili Island in Namibia[125] and Sidudu in Botswana. The dispute involved the 1985 findings of a joint Botswana-South African survey team[126] and led to small-scale clashes between the armed forces of Namibia and Botswana.[127] Both nations are anxious to resolve the difficulty and have sought to employ a technocratic process by appointing a commission of six experts,[128] by involving the good offices of President Mugabe of Zimbabwe, and by agreeing to arbitration.[129]

BOTSWANA AND ITS ZAMBIAN NEIGHBOR

Until the independence of Zimbabwe in 1980, Zambia's significance to Botswana was primarily political because Zambia represented the southernmost point of majority-ruled Africa. Ian R.D. Elgie argued that this boundary between majority- and minority-ruled Africa has slowly shifted southward as "an ideological frontier."[130] When Botswana received its independence in 1966, Zambia was the only one of its neighbors that belonged to the OAU. Shortly after the 1965 general elections, which ushered in a new era of self-government with Seretse Khama as prime minister, President Kenneth Kaunda of Zambia (independent only since 1964) invited Prime Minister Khama for a state visit.[131] As president, Sir Seretse reciprocated the Zambian hospitality, inviting President Kaunda for a state visit in 1968,[132] and, in 1971, the Zambian High Commission opened its chancery in Gaborone.[133]

An ethnic overlay involving the Subyia and Tonga exists between

Botswana and Zambia (known as Northern Rhodesia prior to 1964).[134] The area of Zambia contiguous to Botswana is the Barotse Province, whose political leaders had cherished independence from Lusaka. Gerald L. Caplan indicated that the Pretoria regime was interested in cultivating separatist feelings in Barotseland, thereby undercutting Lusaka's control over Barotseland, some of which bordered on the Caprivi Strip.[135]

South African dominion over the Caprivi Strip did not adversely affect the Botswana-Zambian relationship until Gaborone authorities claimed a common frontier with Zambia as a preliminary legal step involved in the construction of the Botswana-Zambia road. This common frontier also involved the Caprivi Strip. The road linking Botswana with Zambia traversed the confluence of the Chobe and the Zambezi Rivers opposite Kazungula, with the Chobe River separating the Caprivi Strip from Botswana, while the Zambezi River bordered Zambia and the eastern end of the Caprivi Strip. Such a road could be used to decrease dependence upon the rail line that traversed Botswana and Southern Rhodesia, meaning that goods could enter Zambia directly from Botswana and not have to travel by rail through Southern Rhodesia.[136]

A ferry had operated between the two countries since 1874, serving as the corridor to Northern Rhodesia's western portion until 1904. Thereafter, the bridge at Victoria Falls spanned the Zambezi River.[137] Tourists from Livingstone were ferried across the Zambezi by the Chobe River Hotel in BP, which handled ferry traffic in the 1960s.[138] The ferry provided access to the village of Kasane, which is the eastern gateway to the Chobe Game Reserve.[139] Because it also became the workhorse for transporting political refugees from white-ruled southern Africa into African-ruled Zambia, the ferry earned the cognomen of "freedom ferry."[140] This new traffic flow may have prompted the BP administration in 1964 to establish a police post by the ferry.[141] By 1973 the Zambian government assumed the responsibility for the ownership and operation of the ferry,[142] with the Lusaka authorities levying no charge on the Gaborone regime for this service.[143]

The border imbroglio with South Africa began in 1970 when South Africa challenged Botswana's contention that it shared a border with Zambia in the middle of the Zambezi River, where it joined the Chobe River, which marks the southern boundary of the eastern Caprivi Strip.[144] Even though South Africa was illegally occupying Namibia, in the view of the United Nations, it still controlled the Caprivi Strip, where SADF units were based. South Africa complained that the highway bridge that was to span the confluence of the Zambezi and

Chobe Rivers actually violated the Caprivi Strip's territorial limits,[145] contending that the four-nation boundary (of Botswana, Zambia, the Caprivi Strip, and Southern Rhodesia) constituted a "pinpoint" or imaginary intersection in the center of the rivers, with the bridge infringing upon the Caprivi Strip portion of the "pinpoint." South Africa asserted that the riverine corridor was too narrow to construct a bridge, making the bridge trespass on the Caprivi Strip territory.[146]

Both the United States, which was underwriting the R 4.5 million Botswana-Zambia (Botzam) highway,[147] and Botswana indicated that there were no plans to build a bridge and that an improved ferry service would handle the traffic.[148] That remained the official position until the early 1980s, when Botswana and Zambia agreed to construct a R 180 million bridge over the rivers, with the cost borne by the SADCC.[149] The Norwegian Agency for Development furnished the technical personnel for appraisal of the bridge project.[150]

South African and Southern Rhodesian concern with the construction of the bridge and the operation of the ferry stemmed from the conduct of counterinsurgency warfare. In 1979 elite Southern Rhodesian forces had put the ferry out of action.[151] The South Africans feared that the link, which involved the construction of a 200-mile road joining the ferry with Nata in northeastern Botswana, would invite the influx of armed insurgents,[152] while the Southern Rhodesians were worried about the transport of war supplies for units of the Zimbabwe People's Revolutionary Army (ZIPRA), the military component of the Zimbabwe African People's Union (ZAPU).[153] In 1979 Southern Rhodesian special forces raided sites in Francistown, which they claimed housed the military headquarters of ZIPRA.[154] Botswana later indicated that no foreign power (Zambia or South Africa) would be granted access to any Botswanan roads for its military vehicles.[155] The South African journalist J.H.P. Serfontein speculated that Pretoria's objections on the common border with Zambia perhaps were meant to impress local National Party stalwarts with its toughness, although such a position may have undercut its outward policy, which was the name given to its foreign policy of creating friends in the continent and thereby breaking out of its externally imposed diplomatic isolation.[156]

Shortly before independence, the official position in the BP was that the boundary at Kazungula had not been surveyed or demarcated.[157] Nevertheless, Zambia and Botswana believed that a common border, not a pinpoint, separated the two states.[158] During the 1970 contretemps with South Africa, President Khama indicated that the common border was fifty yards wide.[159] Yet it appeared that the matter would not be resolved until Namibia became independent and could sign a multilateral boundary agreement. That, at least, was

Botswana's view.[160] How, and to what extent, an independent Namibia would respond to any Barotse-based Zambian claims on the Caprivi Strip is conjectural.[161]

In terms of high politics, two of Botswana's neighbors lodged major territorial claims against the BP. South Africa based its quest for incorporation of the HCT on the Schedule to the 1909 South Africa Act, while Southern Rhodesia varied its claims from all the protectorate to just the white farming and ranching enclaves on the border. Had either South African or Southern Rhodesia claims been successful, they would have resulted in either the termination or fragmentation of the BP. Territorial autonomy and integrity would have been sacrificed. The BP, in turn, attempted to adjust its border with South West Africa and Northern Rhodesia with respect to the Caprivi Strip.

Between the First and Second World Wars, the political map of Anglophone Southern Africa became even more confusing with an array of schemes for territorial amalgamation. In 1921 the BSAC entertained the possibility of turning Barotseland into an administrative fiefdom of the BP.[162] The next year, the BP served as an administrative sub-metropole for the eastern Caprivi Strip, an arrangement that lasted until 1929. In 1932 one member of the Northern Rhodesian Legislative Council, who represented the Livingstone area, took a hard look at the Caprivi Strip, which Southern Rhodesian forces seized from the Germans. He proposed that the Strip link the Atlantic with the two Rhodesias, Nyasaland (now Malawi), and the BP, all of which would be amalgamated into a British Central African dominion.[163] Some of his plan was realized by the creation of the Central African Federation in 1953. The Federation, which included Southern and Northern Rhodesia and Nyasaland, collapsed in 1963 without ever including the BP.

In the case of South Africa, the matter of territorial integrity was finally settled in 1969, when South Africa amended its constitution, indicating that the Schedule to the South Africa Act (which was retained during the transition from the Union to the Republic of South Africa in 1961) was null and void.[164] In the case of the three other borders, there seems to be no clear and present danger to Botswana's territorial integrity. The independence of Namibia in 1990 brought to the fore territorial claims and counterclaims which have not fundamentally jeopardized the peaceful cooperative relations between these two Commonwealth member states.

CHAPTER THREE

The Burdens and Management of Political Refugees

BOTSWANA AS A REFUGEE CORRIDOR

When it became independent in late 1966, Botswana was surrounded by minority-rule regimes in South Africa, Southern Rhodesia, and South West Africa. Only in the north did it share a riverine border with African majority-ruled Zambia. Landlocked, Botswana could serve as a corridor for those who crossed over its borders and then headed north. The decision to grant political asylum to those fleeing from what Leon Gordenker has termed "insurrectionary social structures,"[1] such as the South African, Southern Rhodesian, or South West African ones, has significant consequences in terms of high politics. Botswana's governmental officials cooperated with representatives of local and transnational nongovernmental organizations to fashion policies intended to protect and guard political refugees while incurring minimal economic, political, and security costs.

Refugee policy can be traced back at least to 1896, when the BP provided political asylum to members of the Herero community fleeing from the German Schutztruppe in German South West Africa.[2] A second group of Hereros fled eastward through the Kalahari Desert in 1904 and sought refuge primarily among the Batawana in the Ngamiland region of the BP, although some traveled further east to urban areas along the railway. The BP authorities made no attempt to repatriate the Hereros after the South Africans defeated the Germans in South West Africa in the First World War. These refugees remained in Botswana, although many of them identified with the Herero in South West Africa.[3]

The Herero exodus of 1904 was prompted by military defeat.

Making neither overt nor covert attempts to stage cross-border raids against the German colonial troops, the Hereros posed no military threat; nor did they seem to create friction between the neighboring colonial powers. This was not the case with the Namas of South West Africa, who started their campaign against the German forces only after the Hereros rebelled. German military authorities and Cape police cooperated to curb the Namas, who excelled at guerrilla warfare.[4] The experience with the Namas and the German authorities underscored BP's need for a refugee policy that both protected the refugees from military retaliation and maintained the neutrality of the host country.

For the next half century, there was no influx of refugees into the BP nor any cross-border security problems. In 1945, however, the British administration considered drawing upon the military might of South Africa and Southern Rhodesia to bring to heel a group of Bakalanga (the Mswazis) who defied the authority of Tshekedi Khama (the Bamangwato regent). The matter was resolved without violence, and the Mswazis returned from Southern Rhodesia.[5]

At the end of the 1950s, a group of Transvaal Africans known as the Bafurutse, from nearby Zeerust, fled to the BP to escape apartheid.[6] BP authorities thought these particular refugees came to the BP to avoid the authority of their own leader, who remained in South Africa, and perhaps to evade taxation. The Bafurutse did attract some attention from overseas, but only briefly,[7] so the BP was not yet faced with the need to develop an elaborate refugee policy. That came in the 1960s.

The varied nature of Botswana's refugee population[8] forced the Gaborone regime to consider the requirements of the transient refugee who would move on to Zambia and even to Tanzania as well as those of the permanent refugee who desired a less adventurous, more traditional, rural way of life. Similarly, a refugee policy needed to coordinate efforts to find housing, employment, medical services, and schools for the newcomers as well as to insure their physical safety.[9]

Refugee control, which is an integral part of Botswana's regional policy, affects Botswana's domestic tranquility. The development and application of refugee control and management policies provide an example of what James N. Rosenau has termed linkage politics.[10] Such politics represent the intersection of domestic and international politics. Thomas Omestad's neologism—"intermestic issues," meaning "international issues with strong domestic consequences"—captures the intertwining of the two types of politics.[11]

Because of political and economic conditions in the early 1960s, BP refugee policy encouraged transit through the country unless the refugees could find employment there. Politically, BP administrators feared economic sanctions if they offended South Africa. Moreover, British authorities had no wish to host "political hot-heads" while they were engaged in moving the BP on the path to self-government. Economically destitute, unemployed refugees would present an unwelcome liability.[12] The white residents of the BP also made the refugees feel unwelcome.[13]

During the 1960s, modern political parties were founded in the BP,[14] where ethnic solidarities and rivalries were also significant in building a popular base for nationalist doctrine and organization.[15] In addition, the omnipresent threat of incorporation, especially by South Africa, galvanized the Batswana.[16] Nevertheless, the development of political institutions, such as the Legislative Council that facilitated the development of political parties in the BP,[17] tended to lag behind that in other parts of British-ruled Africa.[18] Interlopers from South Africa or South West Africa with access to the political process might put the territory at risk by compromising the BP's cultivated neutrality.[19]

By 1964 Zambia had achieved independence, making it possible to think of an overland route north from the BP out to black-ruled Africa, where refugees would not be liable to arrest and return to the country of origin. The significance of the Southern Rhodesian–South African link for refugees was underscored in 1962, when British High Commissioner Sir John Maud arranged the release of three South West African prisoners from a train enroute through BP territory. The prisoners were being sent back to South Africa for illegal departure from South West Africa and for illegal entry into the Central African Federation. Sir John instructed the BP authorities to free them because they had committed no offense in the BP. The three had intended to go to Dar es Salaam and then to the United States, where they were to continue their education.[20] One of them, Peter H. Katjavivi, later became a high-ranking South West Africa People's Organization official and earned his doctorate at the University of Oxford. Subsequently, he was elected to the Namibian Constituent Assembly and became vice chancellor of the University of Namibia.

The principal exit route was through Lobatse, north to Francistown, and thence to Kazungula, where the refugees could take the ferry across the Zambezi to Zambia.[21] Because it was used to transport so many refugees, the ferry soon earned the sobriquet of "freedom ferry."[22] It was also possible to leave the country by air, with Francistown being the main departure point for Tanganyika[23] or even Zaire.[24] Francistown became the focal point of refugee activity as well as a site of anti-refugee violence.[25]

DEVELOPING AND IMPLEMENTING REFUGEE POLICIES

As African nationalist activity in neighboring South Africa increased during the 1960s, the level of rhetoric and violence rose. When passive resistance failed to secure majority rights, nonviolence lost some of its appeal. Correspondingly, government surveillance and control over African movement and activity escalated. As early as 1955, South African authorities, who possessed an impressive intelligence service, began to look much more carefully at the foreign travels of its nationals. They attempted, by means of the Departure from the Union Act, to close a loophole permitting some South Africans to visit the Soviet bloc in a roundabout way. British subjects were entitled to travel to the United Kingdom (UK) without South African passports. From there, they would secure travel documents enabling them to visit Eastern Europe, where they allegedly engaged in anti-regime activities. They could return to the United Kingdom and thence to South Africa, which could not prosecute them for subversive activities abroad if they had been a resident of one of the HCT for a year before taking their European trip. Entry into and exit from the HCT required no South African passports. Those whom Pretoria deemed to be Communists or fellow travelers could evade South African security measures designed to curtail travel behind the Iron Curtain.[26]

Once South Africa left the Commonwealth of Nations in 1961, additional legislation was required to establish the legal relationship between South Africa and the neighboring British HCT. In his policy statement before the House of Assembly on 29 April 1963, the South African Foreign Minister Eric Louw explained that the British and South African governments had considered the matter of access to South Africa and the HCT by the nationals of each territory. Travel documents would be required for persons wishing to enter South Africa or the HCT after 1 July 1963. These rules applied to South West Africa and the HCT as well. Louw noted that the government would establish fourteen passport control posts to monitor the flow of persons to and from BP.[27] By January 1964, fifteen such control posts were in operation along the border with BP.[28]

In September 1963 the South African Minister of Transport B.J. Schoeman announced new regulations on the use of South African airspace in the wake of a dramatic escape from a Johannesburg jail by Arthur Goldreich and Harold Wolpe.[29] Awaiting trial for internal security offenses, these two white South Africans escaped to Swaziland. From there they overflew South Africa in a chartered aircraft to get to the BP, continuing on to the UK by way of Tanganyika.[30] During their escape, an East African Airways plane that was to fly the two of them and other refugees out of Francistown was destroyed on the ground. Who destroyed the airplane is not known. The BP authorities sheltered the two refugees in the Francistown jail to protect them from being kidnapped[31] and provided an escort for them to drive to Palapye, where they boarded a flight in an aircraft owned by Arusha Air Charters (Tanganyika) to Kasane and thence to Elisabethville in Zaire and on to Dar es Salaam, Tanganyika.[32] This dramatic escape in 1963 embarrassed the Pretoria regime, but it was handled in a tactful way by the BP, especially by the Francistown District Commissioner, Phillipus L. Steenkamp, an Afrikaner born in Kenya and educated there and in South Africa. He saw to it that the two refugees were given police protection. Later, Steenkamp became a Botswana citizen and a high-ranking civil servant in the Office of the President.[33]

Demonstrating South Africa's sovereignty over its airspace, Schoeman stipulated that, except for regularly scheduled flights to and from the HCT and those used by the diplomatic corps in South Africa, civilian aircraft would need to make an in-country stop enroute to or from the HCT. The minister asserted that carrying refugees or criminals out of South Africa would be cause for revoking an air carrier's South African license. Thus he terminated East African Airways' permit to conduct scheduled flights between Johannesburg and Nairobi and between Durban and Nairobi. Evidence does not indicate whether East African Airways responded in kind to South African Airways.[34] Subsequently, the minister specified the airports within South Africa at which aircraft traveling to and from the HCT must land.[35] The next step was to consolidate South African control over its skies by bringing the 1949 Air Services Act[36] up to date in 1964.[37]

In London, MPs raised questions in the House of Commons about these South African actions, but the Douglas-Home government found no international fault with the protection of South African airspace. Indeed, Minister of State for Foreign Affairs P.J.M. Thomas observed that such restrictions were permitted under international law.[38] These border control measures were soon followed by two other South African statutes. The first was the 1965 Police Amendment Act, which permitted searches and seizures without search warrants in a one-mile corridor parallel to the South African border. This legislation expanded the search rights previously granted in the Customs Act, and the minister of justice indicated that his concern was with those trying to cross into South Africa with the intent of performing hostile acts.[39]

The second South African statute, the 1965 Criminal Procedure Act, empowered the government to detain witnesses in internal security cases. Introducing the bill for its second reading, the minister of justice reminded the MPs that the government had apprehended 133 persons attempting to leave South Africa for sabotage training at five unnamed centers in African states, which included Tanzania and Ethiopia.[40] In addition, the authorities arrested eighty-five persons who had received such training when they returned to South Africa. To prosecute these cases, the government needed state witnesses, and the minister observed that six such witnesses had been murdered and twelve others had managed to escape from South Africa. This legislation would thus insure that state witnesses could be placed under custody and restrained from fleeing the country.[41]

On the eve of BP's independence, Prime Minister Verwoerd, in discussing future relations between South Africa and the HCT, indicated that South Africa had no extradition treaty with any HCT. He made it clear that "No modern state makes provision for the extradition of political fugitives," adding that an extradition treaty was something that South Africa and the BP would have to negotiate once the BP became independent. He was anxious that neither neighbor be used as a site for launching attacks or undertaking conspiracies against the other. Here he anticipated the subsequent South African policy of offering neighboring states nonaggression treaties.[42]

During the final days of British rule, the BP began to pay attention to its immigration statutes. In late 1965 its legislature revised the basic immigration law granting the government power to remove prohibited immigrants from the BP. The government also could deport aliens even though they had secured legal domicile in the BP.[43] As a part of the legal package accompanying South Africa's departure from the Commonwealth, BP ended its extradition agreement with South Africa that applied to neighboring South West Africa; South Africa had terminated such rights with its 1962 Extradition Act, and the BP reciprocated.[44]

Shortly after Botswana became independent, the South African government indicated that it was negotiating an extradition agreement with Botswana.[45] Even when South Africa was still a Commonwealth member, the British government made it clear in the House of Commons that it would not return those who had fled to the HCT from South Africa for political reasons.[46] Even the South African minister of justice conceded that political offenses were generally not included in extradition treaties. The minister pointed out, however, that what is meant by a political offense differs from nation to nation.[47]

President Khama had made it a cardinal principle of his nation's foreign policy that Botswana would welcome genuine political refugees, provided they did not abuse the hospitality of their host.[48]

Botswana's refugees could not participate in political activity that could endanger the country's safety and public order.[49] Yet the BDP government was quick to notice that the Opposition seemed to have cultivated a clientele among the refugees and that consequently the BDP had to act circumspectly regarding the refugees.[50] The Opposition included persons with well-established anti-apartheid credentials and experience in African political groups in South Africa.[51]

From the political and legal perspective, Botswana continued to modify its refugee legislation to permit greater governmental control over refugee activity[52] and to fashion its policy to secure international recognition and assistance in reducing the costs of providing political asylum. Regional problems thus could be managed, if not solved, by access to extraregional resources. By 1967 the government was ready to establish rules regarding the management of refugees; the title of the act (Refugees [Recognition and Control] Act) indicated the government's priorities. In brief, the act created an advisory board to recommend who should be granted political refugee status, and it also indicated that a refugee's status would be reexamined every six months. Despite the considerable element of control that such a policy entailed, the government affirmed that it would not deport a refugee to a nation where the refugee would be placed at risk.[53]

Shortly thereafter, two United Nations High Commission for Refugees (UNHCR) representatives visited Botswana to confer with the president, government leaders, World Council of Churches officials, and leaders of refugee organizations in Botswana.[54] According to the minister of state,[55] the UNHCR informed the Khama government that the 1967 Refugees (Recognition and Control) Act was not in harmony with international standards expressed in the 1951 Convention Relating to the Status of Refugees.[56] Although the government subsequently amended the 1967 act to bring it into conformity with the 1951 Convention, it nevertheless indicated its objections to that convention. The act's amended version, which employed a less constrained definition of the term refugee[57] and allowed refugees to be considered as potential citizens,[58] was well received by the Opposition. The government, in turn, expected UN assistance as a benefit of the liberalized legislation.[59]

Early in 1968, the South African press indicated that the former HCT and South Africa were negotiating bilateral extradition treaties.[60] When the Botswana government presented the National Assembly with a draft of the Botswana-South African extradition treaty later that year, the minister of state declared that the treaty would not become operative until the National Assembly approved it. Then the government introduced the 1968 Extradition Act, which stipulated the general principles applicable in any extradition treaties that Botswana might subsequently accept.[61] By 1969 the two governments signed an extradition treaty, which provided that "Extradition may be refused if the offence in respect of which it is requested is regarded by the requested Party as a political offence or as an offence connected with a political offence."[62] Such a phrasing enabled Botswana to protect genuine South African political refugees from extradition.

In addition, the text of the 1969 treaty did not mention South West Africa, which could have been a reflection of the 1964 BP legislation repealing the Extradition and Fugitive Offenders (South West Africa) Act, noted earlier. But it also could have represented a conscious choice in Gaborone to avoid recognition of South African jurisdiction over the territory. Botswana sought international legitimacy for its refugee policy in January 1969 by accepting the 1951 Convention Relating to the Status of Refugees and the 1967 United Nations Protocol Relating to the Status of Refugees. With few reservations, it adhered to both international conventions.[63] By accepting the 1951 Geneva Convention, Botswana effectively endorsed the position the British government had taken in 1960 when it applied the Geneva Convention to the BP. Finally, in 1969 Botswana signed the OAU Convention Governing the Specific Aspects of Refugee Problems in Africa, but did not ratify the OAU Convention even though it accepted the less stringent definition of a refugee in the 1969 OAU document.[64]

THE ECONOMIC BURDENS OF POLITICAL ASYLUM

There has been no complete accounting of the total costs that Botswana has incurred by caring for refugees. To defray these expenses, Botswana has turned to local and international humanitarian organizations for financial, as well as technical, assistance.[65]

During the pre-independence period, the London-based Joint Committee for Relief Work in the High Commission Territories provided weekly rations to the refugees lodged at what was called "the white house" in Francistown.[66] This Joint Committee had arranged to have a refugee center built to replace the unsatisfactory quarters. A local representative for Amnesty International oversaw the construction, while the British Labor Party underwrote the building.[67] Just before the refugee center was to be opened in 1964, however, it was destroyed by a bomb.[68] Under the aegis of the Zambian Ministry of Home Affairs from 1964 to 1967,[69] the International Refugee Council of Zambia supplied refugees at Kazungula with food.[70]

Shortly after Botswana became independent, the British United

Nations Association recruited and paid the expenses for a full-time refugee officer who could draw upon funds from three other organizations: the International Rescue Committee, the Emergency Program for Ecumenical Action in Africa, and the Church World Service.[71] Also the locally based Botswana Christian Council (BCC) took over the tasks of the Joint Committee[72] (an umbrella-type nongovernmental organization), which had brought together such groups as the Society of Friends (Quakers), Amnesty International, the British Labor Party, the Oxford Committee for Famine Relief (Oxfam), Inter-Church Aid of the World Council of Churches (WCC), the War on Want, and several others.[73] By this time, the Joint Committee was hard pressed for money.[74] The BCC, which was inaugurated in 1965,[75] served as the conduit for funds granted by the UNHCR.[76]

The WCC was involved in the Angolan resettlement project at Etsha, along with the UNHCR, the World Food Program (WFP), Oxfam, the Red Cross, and different Botswana government units.[77] Together the UNHCR and the WFP underwrote about two-thirds of the cost of R 230,000. The Botswana government and the WCC combined took care of roughly 30 percent of these expenses, while the remainder was borne by Oxfam and the Red Cross.[78]

Near the end of 1973, the BCC and the government of Botswana created the Botswana Council for Refugees (BCR) to coordinate humanitarian assistance to refugees and thus relieve the BCC of that responsibility. The BCC, the LWF, and the UNHCR provide the funding for the BCR, while the Botswana government, the Quakers, the Red Cross, the BCC, the UNHCR, and the LWF serve on the executive committee of the BCR.[79] The government, the UNHCR, and the LWF cooperated in the management of refugee camps in the north at Selebi-Phikwe and Francistown, which bore the brunt of handling the influx of refugees from Southern Rhodesia.[80]

In February 1977 a United Nations mission headed by Abdulrahim A. Farah, the Assistant Secretary-General for Special Political Questions, assessed Botswana's needs in light of the Southern Rhodesian war. The Farah mission noted the expenses the influx of Southern Rhodesian refugees created for Botswana, recommending that funds be allocated to Botswana for projects to assist these refugees.[81] By 1978 Botswana developed an additional refugee camp at Dukwe, located eighty miles northwest of Francistown.[82] Following the 1985 SADF attack on Gaborone, Botswana again sought help from the UN to meet the needs of its refugee community. Farah headed a second UN mission to the country in July–August 1985.[83]

Botswana has secured funds for different aspects of its refugee maintenance program from different nations and nongovernmental organizations, such as the LWF, which has shared the responsibility of running the Dukwe refugee camp with the Botswana government since 1980.[84] As the refugee population—which fluctuated from a low of 207 in 1967 to a peak of about 30,000 in 1980 when Zimbabwe became independent[85]—diminishes, so can the burden of expense. The population at the Dukwe camp changed dramatically in the 1980s, shifting from 466 refugees in 1980 to 4,461 in 1985, because of refugees from Zimbabwe, who constituted 90 percent of the 1985 figure.[86] The Dukwe refugee population fell to 691, in addition to 250 refugees located in urban areas.[87]

The Farah mission report indicated that the economy was not growing fast enough to provide employment for the increasing population.[88] Obviously, then, refugees have been allowed minimal access to the job market.

A consistent theme in the questions posed by the MPs in the National Assembly is the breadth, depth, and speed of localization in the public[89] and private[90] sectors. The theme also appears in parliamentary motions. This nationalization of employment to the detriment of most refugees was institutionalized in the 1981 Employment of Non-Citizens Act, which required refugees to have Botswana work permits.[91] Such legislation thus permits a considerable measure of control over the economic well-being of refugees,[92] which seems congruent with the slow erosion of some civil liberties that observers have noted and decried.[93]

THE REFUGEE COMMUNITY AND POLITICAL VIOLENCE

One of the byproducts of Botswana's granting asylum to political refugees has been the United Nations Security Council accolade in 1977[94] and the awarding of the Nansen Medal to Sir Seretse Khama in 1978 for his service to refugees.[95] Still another has been acts of violence that dissident individuals or members of foreign security and defense forces directed at specific refugees or at groups of refugees and their possessions. Such acts presumably were committed to force the government to take a much harder line against political refugees by declaring them to be prohibited immigrants and then deporting them, or by moving them much more swiftly through the refugee pipeline on to the second country of asylum. In some cases the identity of the purveyors of violence was known, while in others it was only suspected. The threat of external force, and its demonstrable use, have been linked with the South African destabilization strategy,[96] but South Africa was not alone in employing violence against refugees.

Violence has taken several different forms. Vehicles used or owned by refugees have been damaged, as have aircraft chartered to fly refugees out of the country. Refugee housing has been destroyed. Automobile bombs have been detonated by the driver. Then there is the parcel bomb which explodes when the package is unwrapped. Finally, there is abduction across the border. In all these cases, there is the nagging question of protection afforded by the host country as well as the anxiety about the extent to which the refugee community has been infiltrated by hostile agents. Consequently, many refugees are frightened and perhaps even disoriented, and they sometimes can be difficult for host country authorities to monitor.[97]

The first known case of violence took place in Lobatse in the latter half of November 1963, when an explosion damaged a Land Rover purchased with ANC funds, and titled to a South African refugee who was an official of the Mpho wing of the BPP. The BPP officer in turn allowed another South African refugee in the Protectorate to drive Harold Wolpe and Arthur Goldreich from Lobatse to Francistown after their escape from South Africa by way of Swaziland. The explosion caused no personal injuries, and damage was minimal.[98] According to a former South African intelligence agent, South African operatives, working for the Bureau of State Security, damaged the vehicle.[99]

Of much greater interest to the BP police was the sabotaging in August 1963 of the East African Airways DC-3 aircraft parked at the Francistown airport, an airplane chartered to fly Goldreich and Wolpe out of the BP. Aided in their investigations by the Assistant Air Attaché of the British Embassy in Pretoria,[100] BP police found no suspects in this case.[101]

During this year, the Protectorate Legislative Council passed the Prohibition of Violence Abroad Act, which is still on the statute books. It was given its first reading on 19 November 1963, only two months after the Lobatse Land Rover incident. The second reading debate on the bill was perfunctory and dominated by the chief secretary, the administration secretary, and the attorney-general. The Lobatse and Francistown events were not mentioned.[102]

The act forbade anybody within the BP to participate in any conspiracy to undertake any act of violence that is an offense under BP law or an offense in the foreign state. Conviction brought a maximum fine of R 1,000 or three years imprisonment or both.[103] The other two HCT also enacted such laws,[104] which could be construed as signaling the Pretoria regime that the British had the upper hand in dealing with refractory or dangerous refugees, even though there was no extradition treaty between any HCT and South Africa.[105]

Less than a year after the destruction of the East African Airways

DC-3, violence erupted once more in Francistown. During the early morning hours of 26 July 1964 a blast destroyed a center for housing refugees two miles away from this town, with no reported injuries or loss of life. At the time of the explosion, it was estimated that there were one hundred South African refugees in Francistown.[106] Again the BP police investigated the incident but made no arrests.[107]

Much more dramatic and much more deadly were the 1985 and 1986 SADF raids in the Gaborone area that destroyed homes or apartments used by members of the refugee community. Unlike the 1963 and 1964 events in Francistown, those responsible were definitely agents of a foreign power.[108] South Africa was taken to task in the United Nations Security Council. Botswana unsuccessfully hectored the South African government for damages inflicted in the 1985 Gaborone raid. The South African justification for the raids boiled down to the projection of power in self-defense to neutralize what they regarded as significant ANC operatives in Gaborone. Violating the territorial integrity of Botswana irked the remainder of the world far more than it did the South Africans, who rationalized the use of state power beyond their borders. Strangely enough, the South Africans, in their public statements, did not refer to the 1963 Prevention of Violence Act, which the British put, and the Batswana retained, on the statute books to protect South Africa.

Even though the SADF spokesmen refer to Botswana's cordiality to the ANC,[109] they are not especially careful to distinguish among the levels of activity that Botswana appears to have permitted, nor do they seem to acknowledge the application of the cluster of Botswana's statutes that apply to the importation of articles of war.[110] Although Botswana has granted asylum to individual ANC members, the ANC itself has received only marginal recognition or status in Botswana,[111] and Botswana ended this status in 1986.[112]

Earlier evidence suggested that claiming affiliation with some exiled Southern African political party would facilitate, rather than hinder, a refugee's entry into Zambia.[113] To control the activities and movements of refugees, Botswana has placed large numbers of them in camps, particularly at remote Dukwe, which was not appealing to urban South African refugees. The Botswana government has had to round up refugees to relocate them at Dukwe.[114] Botswana Defense Force (BDF) soldiers guarded the refugee camps,[115] while the government kept close tabs on the movement of refugees assigned to these camps.[116] On a more covert level, the South Africans also have taken an interest in the refugees for reasons of their own. In one case a South African agent posed as a journalist,[117] while in another case a South African policeman was convicted of attempted bribery to obtain information about refugees.[118]

Following the 1985 SADF raid, the Botswana National Assembly passed the 1986 National Security Act aimed at curbing the activities of South African intelligence operatives or their Batswana informants.[119] The 1986 Act specified a number of criminal offenses, such as receiving secret information or divulging this type of information to unauthorized personnel, using official vehicles, uniforms, or passes without permission, or entering security areas or buildings. Such intelligence data were useful to the SADF in its 1985 raid. The attorney-general was empowered to decide whether to prosecute, and the maximum penalty for contravention of the act was thirty years' imprisonment. The act, which applies to citizens and noncitizens,[120] has not been well received, especially by the intelligentsia[121] and the parliamentary opposition[122] because it made inroads on traditional civil liberties for which Botswana had been internationally acclaimed.[123]

In addition to the destruction of housing, automobile and parcel explosives are killing and injuring people. A South African active in the South African Students' Organization, Abraham Tiro, had left South Africa for Botswana and was still awaiting a Botswana government decision on his refugee status when he was killed in early 1974 by a parcel bomb delivered to his residence at a Roman Catholic mission school outside Gaborone.[124] Another South African exile and ANC member was killed in Gaborone by a car bomb a month before the SADF raid in 1985.[125]

Both the South Africans and the Southern Rhodesians have resorted to abduction. Perhaps the best publicized kidnapping concerned the physician Dr. Kenneth Abrahams, who was abducted in 1963 from near Ghanzi and taken across the border into South West Africa. Following a court appearance in Cape Town, Abrahams was permitted to return to the BP.[126] During Southern Rhodesia's war, Southern Rhodesian Selous Scouts, a long-range commando and reconnaissance unit, captured documents and personnel from the ZIPRA headquarters in Francistown in Operation Petal on 13 April 1979.[127]

Botswana earned high marks for its willingness to accept refugees. As the 1985 SADF commando raid illustrated, this put the country at risk. Botswana served as both a hospitality house and what South African journalist Allen Pizzey called a "halfway house," depending upon the time and the circumstances.[128] The British began the hospitality approach with the Herero, who fled the German regime in Windhoek following their defeat. Some of them considered returning to their ancestral land once Namibia became independent.[129]

When the flow of refugees increases, and particularly when the influx includes highly politicized refugees bent on liberating their own countries by violent means, the matter becomes one of high politics. After the 1976 riots in the cluster of Johannesburg African townships known as Soweto, African secondary school students fled to Botswana. By mid-1977 there were roughly five hundred such refugees in Botswana, with about fifty arriving each month.[130] The arrival rate dropped to about thirty a month later in 1977.[131]

Such an ingress can be considered to be a case of high politics because, in the southern African situation, South Africa and Southern Rhodesia had both the capacity and the will to inflict violence on neighboring Botswana.[132] This cycle of internal repression, a refugee exodus from the neighboring state, and armed intrusion or the perpetration of violent acts by the security forces or irregulars of the neighboring state was one that drained Botswana's local resources and tempted its citizens to increase their economic protectionism or reduce the threat of violent retribution. Refugee protection is a basic concern for Botswana[133] irrespective of which policy—hospitality house or halfway house—was pursued. The halfway house approach to refugee management, which was adopted by the British colonial authorities in the 1960s, clearly was an attempt to anticipate violence and to take precautionary measures by passing the refugees further northward.

Some refugees have been assimilated into the Botswana polity and consider the country to be their home, particularly if they became citizens. Many have brought skills to Botswana and have contributed to the development of the nation in economic and intellectual ways. They represent a net gain in infrastructural resources.[134] Where the state was burdened with refugee-related expenses, it turned to international governmental and nongovernmental organizations such as the UNHCR and the LWF for funding and management skills. UNHCR data suggest that from 1963 until 1981, Botswana had an annual average of 5,920 refugees and that it had received UNHCR funds for fourteen years. The annual average amount of UNHCR funding was $754,200, which meant that each refugee received an average amount of $121.46. That per capita UNHCR refugee aid figure was higher for Lesotho ($241.78) and for Swaziland ($192.19), which dealt with a smaller average annual refugees, namely, 470 for Lesotho and 2,700 for Swaziland during the 1963–1981 period.[135]

The Dukwe camp was closed once the bulk of the Zimbabwean refugees were repatriated. It would be tempting to think that Botswana (aided by international patrons) would no longer have to bear the political and economic burdens of serving as a host nation, particularly because Zimbabwe and Namibia have made the transition to majority rule. But there is no a priori reason to predict the end of refugee flows and possible political entanglements. Botswana has served as host for refugees from Lesotho, Chad, Burundi, Ghana, Kenya, Uganda, Angola, Mozambique, Zaire, Somalia, and Malawi, as well as from South Africa and Namibia.[136]

Ethnic fragmentation, coupled with political violence, might push more refugees into Botswana. Botswana, for example, provided asylum to a number of Zimbabweans from Matabeleland in western Zimbabwe during the period of considerable tension between the Shona and Ndebele groups. In 1988 it took the good offices and persuasive skills of ZAPU leader Joshua Nkomo to convince the 3,678 Zimbabweans at Dukwe camp to return to their homes.[137] Comparable refugee flows might come from Namibia, as well as from South Africa itself. These shifts in the balance of racial or ethnic power may generate political violence that could spill over into Botswana or that could intrude into its domestic political process. The search here is not so much for autonomy but rather for the reduction of refugee-linked internal and cross-border violence. Refugee management is a vexing task, with few rewards except symbolic ones, such as international recognition for a difficult job well done.[138]

CHAPTER FOUR

Responding to Cross-Border Violence

BUILDING UPON THE POLICE AND MILITARY TRADITIONS

From the inception of British rule in the nineteenth century, the police force served as the administrative mainstay of the BP, as suggested by the high proportion of the BP's budgets allocated to the police.[1] The colonial era lacked a strong martial (as distinct from police) tradition, partly because of the deeply ingrained and widespread white racial attitudes regarding the impropriety of arming and deploying black soldiers.[2] The British colonial administration in the BP maintained no standing army, although the whites and Batswana served with either British or South African units in the First and Second World Wars. In accordance with the prevailing racial norms in southern Africa, the Batswana served primarily in noncombatant military labor contingents.

Neighboring Southern Rhodesia, whose cross-border strikes in the 1970s precipitated the creation of an army in Botswana, had both a strong police force (called the British South Africa Police or BSAP) and a more highly developed martial tradition, particularly among the whites who also fought with the British in the South African and two world wars.[3]

The BSAP were used in the Protectorate to quell violence in Serowe in early 1952, which sprang from the dispute within the Bamangwato people between the adherents of Seretse Khama and his uncle Tshekedi Khama.[4] Additional reinforcements were secured from the police in the other two HCT.[5] The BP police, in turn, were deployed as reinforcements in Swaziland in 1963 during a general strike.[6]

During the self-government interlude (from March 1965 until

September 1966), there were no sweeping organizational changes in the BP police force except those necessitated by the transfer of the administrative headquarters of the Protectorate from Mafikeng to Gaborone in 1965.[7] By 1964 the police force included a mobile contingent[8] that the colonial authorities revamped and termed a General Service Unit, a name later changed to Police Mobile Unit (PMU).[9] This component was further subdivided into three platoons of forty-one policemen each. Two of the three platoons were based in Gaborone, while the third was stationed at Francistown.[10] The PMU was headed by a British police officer who had previously served in Uganda. Less than enthusiastic about the quality of some of the long-serving officers in the force, he was committed to accelerating the localization of the BP police.[11]

On 11 November 1965, eight months after the BP achieved self-governing status, neighboring Southern Rhodesia unilaterally declared itself independent of the British Crown. In an attempt to counter this rebellion, the British broadcast their policy over the airwaves, building a radio relay station on the outskirts of Francistown. Although well situated for sending transmissions into Southern Rhodesia,[12] the Central African Relay Station was located in a rather pro-Southern Rhodesian and pro-South African enclave of the BP. Based on their experience with violence toward refugees, the British authorities had reason to anticipate that the relay station would be damaged by local sympathizers of the Smith or Verwoerd regimes. They dispatched British army units from Swaziland to safeguard it.[13]

Ironically, Prime Minister Khama declared in the BP Legislative Assembly on 13 December 1965 that "There are persistent rumours that the [Francistown radio] station is in some way connected with the possibility of troops being sent to Bechuanaland," but he claimed that "there is no foundation for any suggestion that it is intended to station troops or commandos in Francistown."[14] The British Parliamentary Under-Secretary of State for the Colonies, Eirene White, visited the BP ten days after Prime Minister Khama made this statement.[15] A day later, the first batch of British troops arrived from Swaziland. One South African newspaper account suggested that White and the queen's commissioner in the BP pressured the prime minister and his cabinet colleagues to accept the presence of British armed forces at the Francistown relay station,[16] which would account for the discrepancy between Sir Seretse's parliamentary assurances and the stationing of British troops at the radio relay station.

Sir Seretse reportedly was concerned that the construction and operation of the radio relay station would jeopardize the operation of the Rhodesia Railways line through the BP.[17] The opposition

Bechuanaland Independence Party (which failed to win any parliamentary seats in the 1965 general election) protested the militarization of the Francistown station,[18] which was sited only fifteen miles from the Southern Rhodesian border.[19]

Three months after the arrival of the British Army contingents at Francistown, the parliamentary opposition BPP introduced a motion in the Legislative Assembly favoring the development of an indigenous military force. The debate over the motion was relatively short, not particularly lively, and the motion was defeated without a formal vote or division.[20] This matter had been broached earlier during the parliamentary consideration of the independence constitution, when BPP spokesmen drew attention to the perils of a premature independence without having an army to defend the national territory: "I cannot think of any country in the world which was ever pushed into independence without a single soldier," said one opposition MP.[21]

Such an institutional deficiency bothered only the Opposition and attracted little notice among the BDP MPs. Still not satisfied, the Opposition returned to the topic once more in the Legislative Assembly before independence was conferred. Prime Minister Khama's response was to rely upon the local police force.[22] The United Kingdom seemed unwilling to offer any security guarantees in the form of a defense treaty but declined to make the point publicly.[23] On independence day in 1966, a United Kingdom–Botswana agreement on the status of the British armed forces (guarding the Francistown relay station) went into effect.[24] Nevertheless, the British did not follow the practice of the French government, which undertook formal defense commitments with their former African dependencies.[25]

Shortly after independence, the Botswana government announced its socioeconomic priorities, which included strengthening the PMU.[26] The British government provided two army personnel to train PMU members in 1967,[27] and the two governments concluded an agreement in 1968 about furnishing British army instructors for the Botswana police force.[28] From August 1967 until May 1968, the PMU handled the guard duties at the Central African Relay Station in Francistown, thereby replacing the British army contingents.[29] From 1965 to 1968, the British government spent £0.739 million to build, equip, and guard the Francistown station.[30] The BPP, which relied upon the Francistown area for its electoral support, was able to make some political capital out of the British military presence, which, in their view, had a baleful effect upon the local residents.[31]

Along with its work at Francistown, the PMU also undertook patrols to locate and apprehend African nationalist insurgents— officially called "armed infiltrators"[32]—from neighboring countries, who most likely would have belonged to the ANC in South Africa or to ZAPU in Zimbabwe.[33] The Khama government had authority to do so by virtue of the 1963 Prevention of Violence Abroad Act,[34] and a week after independence, Sir Seretse Khama announced before the National Assembly his government's policy to insure that Botswana would not become a base of operations for attacking any neighbor.[35] The 1963 legislation had to be supplemented by border surveillance, a reliable intelligence network, a highly trained and impartial police force, and a judiciary willing to enforce the germane statutes. The Khama government arrested, tried,[36] imprisoned,[37] and deported to Zambia[38] insurgents who drifted into, or were forced to flee into, Botswana.

Occasionally, Zimbabwean guerrillas used Botswana's territory, although Botswana was not a major theater of operations for the insurgents.[39] Especially annoyed at the presence of South African police units in Southern Rhodesia,[40] the Botswana government supported opponents of the Smith government by granting asylum to political refugees.[41] In general, however, it followed a modest policy with respect to the Liberation Committee of the OAU, which bore the responsibility for orchestrating resistance to white minority-ruled states.[42]

As it became more experienced in seeking and securing aid donors, the Botswana government devoted more attention to its police force. From 1965 until 1967, the force grew by 300 personnel, most of whom were in the PMU. In the five years from 1968/69 to 1972/73, recurrent expenditure of the police force was projected to be R 5.237 million out of the total of R 69.123 million, that is, roughly 7.5 percent of the total recurrent expenditures for the period. Capital expenditures were estimated to be much lower, namely, R 0.318 million out of a total of R 69.273 million, which is only 0.45 percent of the total.[43]

In yet another, revised development plan, the government complained that, in comparison with Malawi and Zambia, Botswana had too few policemen: there was one policeman for every 211 square miles in Botswana, whereas there was one for every thirty-five square miles in Zambia and one for every fourteen square miles in Malawi.[44] The plan emphasized that "The Republic of Botswana is one of the few independent states in Africa which has no standing army or military establishment,"[45] meaning that its police force had to assume conventional and paramilitary roles. To assist the police force in meeting these challenges, the government wanted to increase the manpower levels by 16 percent, which would raise the police force from 1,090 to 1,265 personnel.[46] President Khama nevertheless expressed his displeasure at expanding the security forces, continuing to take pride in the absence of an army.[47]

As violence in Southern Rhodesia escalated, Botswana MPs[48] charged that officials of the Smith regime violated Botswana's territorial sovereignty by arresting individuals inside Botswana's borders.[49] The Southern Rhodesian authorities, for example, turned Michael Dingake over to the South African government, which tried and imprisoned him in Robben Island off Cape Town from 1965 until 1981.[50] The British House of Lords also expressed concern.[51]

The political situation deteriorated to such an extent that, in late 1976, Botswana notified the UN Security Council of a number of border violations.[52] The Security Council debated the matter[53] without permitting the Southern Rhodesian government to present its position,[54] and adopted a resolution in early 1977 that condemned the Smith regime for such transgressions.[55] Shortly thereafter, a visiting UN mission examined the impact of the deteriorating security situation upon Botswana and recommended several projects that needed foreign donor support. The essential idea was that Botswana was diverting scarce resources from development projects to deal with the effects of the war in Southern Rhodesia. The total cost of the aid package was estimated to be $53.5 million over the course of three years.[56]

Regional instability and a somewhat improved budgetary position because of mining revenue, a renegotiated customs union with South Africa, Lesotho, and Swaziland, and higher multilateral aid levels enabled Botswana to explore the creation of the defense force it had repeatedly rejected on economic grounds since 1966. With the PMU serving as the basis for the development of a national army, police and military traditions could be now be nurtured.

ACQUIRING MILITARY RESOURCES AND SKILLS

Once the necessary framework legislation was passed in 1977, the BDF began recruiting and training its personnel.[57] The logical place to begin was with the PMU, which had functioned as a quasi-army. Ian Khama, the commander of one of two PMU, transferred to the newly formed BDF and became second in command as a brigadier.[58] Mompati Merafhe, the deputy commissioner of the Botswana Police Force (BPF), became the BDF commander with the rank of major general.[59]

The nation's economic situation made recruitment easy. The emoluments and conditions of service in the BDF were better than those offered by the police force.[60] Batswana could now join their own national army, not a foreign one, as they had in the past. Henceforth, under the terms of the 1980 Foreign Enlistment Act, Batswana were forbidden to join any other army unless they had the written permission of the president.[61] The government wanted to prevent the SADF from recruiting Botswana nationals, particularly the Basarwa (sometimes called Bushmen), for counterinsurgency operations in Namibia.[62] After the war ended in Namibia, some of them returned to Botswana.[63]

Even though several foreign observers[64] have been quite critical of disciplinary lapses among the troops, that view is not universally shared.[65] In 1978 a noncommissioned officer was acquitted in a well-publicized trial for allegedly killing three civilians (including one Briton) in the Tuli block area of Botswana.[66] Five years later, two BDF soldiers were found guilty of killing two civilians (one of whom was a South African citizen) in the Chobe region.[67] One soldier was sentenced to twenty-four years in prison, the other to nine years.[68] President Masire pardoned both of them a month later because of their age and extenuating circumstances.[69]

In 1987 a British national was killed in an altercation with BDF soldiers manning a roadblock near Francistown.[70] His widow successfully sued the government for monetary damages.[71] Additional shooting occurred; by 1990 the BDF was responsible for the deaths of thirteen civilians.[72] The BDF has also been criticized for its low educational standards for recruitment.[73] This did not escape the attention of the BDF commander who, in a public address before the Botswana Society, indicated that the BDF was "under tremendous pressure from civilians to admit into the Army people who have no sound educational background."[74] Nevertheless, the BDF enjoys prestige, some of which can be traced to the ascriptive reason that President Khama's eldest son, Ian, became the commanding officer of the force in 1989.[75] In May 1979 he was installed as the chief of the Bamangwato,[76] a status that the British denied to his late father. Major General Ian Khama was the first Motswana to attend the Royal Military Academy at Sandhurst.[77]

Sixteen other BDF officers have been trained there.[78] In addition, nine BDF officers studied at the US Army Command and General Staff College at Fort Leavenworth, Kansas, and two others attended the Air Command and Staff College at Maxwell Air Force Base, Alabama.[79] At a lower echelon, one Motswana cadet has attended the US Military Academy at West Point as an exchange student.[80] Recently, ninety members of the elite British Special Air Services Regiment undertook a six-week military exercise in Botswana, where they trained BDF instructors and officers.[81] Subsequently, the BDF and US forces conducted a joint training exercise.[82]

Only the British, who concentrate on "combat related skills," and the Indians, who specialize in "technical skills," provide in-country training for the BDF. The United States and Zambia have resident military attachés or security assistance officers in Botswana, while the British, French, and Canadian military attachés are located in Harare.[83]

Published sources indicate that the BDF has a total strength of 3,800 men, of whom 150 are designated an air arm and the remaining 3,650 an army.[84] The 2,850 army personnel are organized into one infantry battalion group, which includes five infantry companies and five specialized companies concerned with support, logistics, engineering, communications, and reconnaissance work. Data regarding the number, ranks, and ethnic affiliation of commissioned and noncommissioned officers are not presently published. There seems to be little anxiety about the ethnic mix in the BDF, with all ethnic groups except the Basarwa represented. Both neighboring Zambia and Zimbabwe accept women in their armies, and Botswana is likely to do the same. Such women soldiers would receive equal pay for equal military rank, yet they would be involved only in the administrative side of the BDF.

Regarding armaments, the BDF made it clear from the outset that it preferred standardized military equipment.[85] The BDF acquired its first aircraft, three Britten Norman Islander Defenders, in 1977 for border surveillance and sent its pilots to the UK for training on this aircraft.[86] By 1988 the BDF had begun to purchase used jet fighter aircraft, starting with nine British-built Strikemaster fighters from Saudi Arabia.[87] These aircraft were supplemented by six transport airplanes, and five helicopters, two of which were provided by France.[88] Except for thirty BTR-60 armored personnel carriers, a T-34 main battle tank, AK-47 rifles, recoilless rifles, and one hundred SAM-7 missiles from the USSR,[89] the weaponry and vehicles are British or American,[90] although American military aid to Botswana started only in fiscal year 1981.[91] The Germans provided trucks, while the Chinese furnished air artillery.[92] Some small arms may be of Soviet and Chinese origin.[93]

The Soviet arms connection created anxiety in South African circles.[94] Four Soviet personnel accompanied the arms shipment, but they left, and 710 Soviet military personnel remain in Botswana.[95] The Indian army has sent fifteen instructors to assist the BDF in the use of Soviet equipment as well as in aviation, medicine, and engineering.[96] The American military education and training aid package level rose from $70,000 in fiscal year 1980 to $356,000 in fiscal year 1987 and involved 168 Batswana during that period. Correspondingly, from fiscal year 1981 to fiscal year 1985 the US foreign military sales financing program for Botswana grew from $500,000 to $5 million, with the total expenditure amounting to $18 million by fiscal year 1987.[97] Although the Americans supplied the BDF with TOW anti-tank missiles and Vulcan anti-aircraft weaponry,[98] there has been less willingness to provide military credits to Botswana and apprehension about the ramifications of increasing defense expenditures.[99]

UTILIZING THE BOTSWANA DEFENSE FORCE

It would be neither prudent nor economically feasible for the BDF to prepare itself for large-scale combat against the massive, battle-hardened SADF. As Charles P. Snyder has advised, the idea of "force development" draws attention to the relationship between threat and force structure; the former shapes the latter to the extent that personnel and budget permit.[100] It made political, economic, and military sense for the BDF to be able to repulse or deter small-scale incursions, whether from SADF units stationed in South Africa or previously posted to the Caprivi Strip in Namibia or from the South African-sponsored Bophuthatswana Defense Force. To a lesser extent, the notion of force development was applied to deal with cross-border operations undertaken by the Southern Rhodesian Army from 1970 to 1980.[101]

In May 1977 a Southern Rhodesian unit, crossing into Botswana by helicopter and armored personnel carriers, overran a small BDF camp at Mapoka. Forced to withdraw, the Botswana soldiers suffered no casualties, and the Southern Rhodesians pulled back when BDF reinforcements were dispatched.[102] The next February, during a hot pursuit raid near Kazungula, the Rhodesians killed fifteen and wounded eight BDF soldiers one kilometer inside Botswana's territory.[103] A year later the Southern Rhodesians, using bogus BDF license plates and uniforms, sank the Zambia-Botswana ferry at Kazungula and kidnapped fourteen ZAPU activists from Francistown.[104] Southern Rhodesian cross-border activity continued that year in the area around Francistown and even involved aerial combat between Southern Rhodesian helicopters and a BDF military aircraft.[105] Following the policy laid down in 1963 regarding the prevention of violence abroad, the BDF, in cooperation with the BPF, ferreted out and arrested Zimbabwean guerrillas using Botswana's territory.[106]

Even after the termination of the war in Southern Rhodesia and its subsequent internationally recognized independence in 1980, fragmentation and rivalry persisted within the Zimbabwean nationalist ranks. This factionalism spilled over into Botswana from Matabeleland, the stronghold of Joshua Nkomo's ZAPU, which fared poorly against Robert Mugabe's Zimbabwe African National Union (ZANU) in the 1980 elections. Part of the problem was a perception in Harare that Botswana was offering a safe haven to ZAPU militants.[107] The absence of a bilateral extradition treaty between Botswana and Zimbabwe[108] and Nkomo's sudden departure for London via Botswana increased the strain between the neighboring Commonwealth states.[109]

The BDF bore much of the brunt of the border tension, which included sporadic engagements with the formidable Zimbabwean army.[110] British observers Paul L. Moorcroft[111] and Joseph Hanlon,[112] as well as American political scientist Richard F. Weisfelder[113] charged that the South Africans were attempting to destabilize the Mugabe government through the manipulation of ZAPU dissidents, which might explain some of the border turmoil the BDF faced. Botswana had experienced an influx of Zimbabwean refugees at this time, straining the relations between Gaborone and Harare. The refugees identified with ZAPU, and the authorities in Harare looked askance at an opposition group called super-ZAPU, which they regarded as a destabilizing force. The Dukwe refugee camp functioned as a recruiting depot for this group of dissidents, they claimed.[114] Once again the matter of Botswana's neutrality was at stake, just as it was with regard to the ANC of South Africa.

Less than a year after the Smith government unilaterally declared its independence of the British Crown, African nationalists in what was then South West Africa took up arms against the Pretoria regime. The guerrillas of the People's Liberation Army of Namibia (PLAN), the military wing of SWAPO, began their war in northern South West Africa in 1966. Rising levels of violence and cross-border strikes into Zambia and Angola came to characterize SADF operations in Namibia.[115]

Considering Namibia's location, it was only logical that members of PLAN should have attempted to enter the country from the north or east. Botswana provided one of the three corridors for infiltration, with Angola and Zambia serving as the principal paths. PLAN made only limited use of the Botswana route,[116] probably without the knowledge of the Gaborone authorities.[117] The clashes the BDF has experienced along this part of the border more often have been with SADF ground[118] and river patrols operating from bases in Namibia.[119] In 1981 President Masire expressed his displeasure with the South African Air Force for trespassing on Botswana's airspace on its flights from the Transvaal Province to Namibia.[120] The next year, the BDF shot down a South African civilian aircraft that violated Botswana's airspace,[121] and it has charged SADF members with game poaching in the Chobe area.[122] Some of the friction, especially in the Caprivi area, has resulted from differing perspectives on border demarcation, and both parties have cooperated to resolve the issue.[123]

In 1985 and 1986 the SADF launched cross-border raids from South Africa and perhaps even from Bophuthatswana, challenging the BDF in a different way.[124] In the early morning hours of 14 June 1985, approximately fifty armed South African soldiers crossed into Botswana near the Tlokweng border post not far from Bophuthatswana. Transported in eighteen vans with falsified Botswana government license plates, their mission in Gaborone, nine miles from that border post, was to neutralize eight houses and two offices located within a radius of twelve kilometers. The South African authorities claimed that these ten sites served as focal points of hostile ANC planning and activity.[125]

To minimize retaliation from BDF units, the attacking force cut the telephone wires to the BDF barracks and sprinkled metal spikes on the road from those barracks to puncture the tires of any pursuing vehicle. The raid, which began at about 1:40 A.M., lasted roughly forty minutes, during which time the SADF teams demolished four houses and severely damaged the other four. On the way back, the SADF regrouped, put up their own roadblocks, and crossed back over the border to their military base, avoiding the roadblocks that the BDF and the BPF had erected. Neither the location of their base of operations nor the exact units to which they belonged has been disclosed.[126] Security legislation and regulations affecting border areas in South Africa make such obscurity likely.[127]

No South African soldiers were killed, but one was slightly wounded, apparently by his own forces because there was no exchange of fire between the SADF and Botswana's security forces. The SADF raiding party encountered only BPF personnel whom they apparently convinced not to interfere with the attack. In addition to destroying property they claimed was used by ANC operatives, the SADF commandos seized arms, documents, and a computer. With twelve dead and six wounded on the Botswana side, obviously the BDF was inadequately equipped or trained to challenge a commando raid.

Major General Mompati Merafhe, the senior BDF officer, held a press conference shortly after the SADF raid because of rumors that the BDF received advance warning of the raid, which might explain why there was no exchange of fire between the BDF and the SADF.[128] Major General Merafhe asserted that the BDF had not been warned about the raid, stressing that the BDF responded to the attack by closing the roads leading to and from Gaborone to intercept the South

African soldiers. Moreover, the BDF felt that to engage in a firefight with the SADF in an urban area could create even greater loss of civilian life and destruction of buildings.[129]

Major General Merafhe also noted that the lengthy border between Botswana and South Africa gave South Africa the strategic advantage because the BDF lacked the personnel to deploy over great distances.[130] Merafhe further asserted that the BDF could not be placed on constant alert status.

The BDF, he said, would review its techniques for handling such attacks, perhaps hoping that such a review would forestall investigation by either the National Assembly or by other appropriate civilian authorities. Given what appears to be a credible South African intelligence network in Botswana, his guarded and ambiguous remarks about a review process were prudent.[131] The South African National Intelligence Service was one of the four government departments (along with the police and the Departments of Foreign Affairs and of Defense) that favored the Gaborone raid.[132] The public evidence suggests that the BDF's performance during the 1985 raid did not invite recriminations, trigger demands for a different set of military leaders, or even give rise to threats of a military coup. Civilian control over the BDF remained intact, with hostility focused upon South Africa and its SADF, not upon the BDF.

Botswana's diplomats turned to the UN Security Council, as they had done in 1977 following a series of border transgressions by the Southern Rhodesians, and presented Botswana's case[133] against the South African government, whose representative argued that South Africa was simply countering the aggression of the Botswana-based ANC.[134] The council unanimously passed[135] a resolution condemning South Africa for the incursion, insisting that it pay reparations to Botswana.[136] Although a UN mission to Botswana assessed the raid's cost,[137] South Africa did not pay any reparations to Botswana for the damage the SADF caused.[138] Botswana rebuilt one of the houses in Gaborone as a memorial to those killed in the 1985 attack.[139]

Relations between Botswana and South Africa deteriorated as a result of a second SADF raid on a cluster of five private houses about a half mile from the BDF barracks at Mogoditshane.[140] The South Africans asserted that these houses were ANC transit sites. The attack on Mogoditshane, which is about three miles outside Gaborone, occurred at approximately 6:15 A.M. on 19 May 1986. The ten-minute Mogoditshane raid was not a replica of the 1985 attack. It differed from the previous raid in five distinct ways.

First, it entailed the use of a SADF spotter aircraft and eight helicopters, so it was less camouflaged than the first raid, which used no standard, marked SADF vehicles. The airplanes also scattered anti-ANC literature. Second, it took place at dawn, when there would be greater visibility and, presumably, greater opportunity to identify targets with care, and to avoid mistakes (which Botswana had pointed out in its outrage at the 1985 attack on an urban area). The SADF fired on the BDF barracks, but this time the BDF returned the fire, without destroying any aircraft. Third, the loss of life was much less than earlier: one killed and three wounded (including one BDF member) on the Botswana side, with no reported SADF casualties. Fourth, the raid was coordinated with similar cross-border attacks that same day on alleged ANC targets in Zambia and Zimbabwe. No such strategy was used in 1985. Finally, the 1986 air assault took place during the visit of the Eminent Persons Group from the Commonwealth of Nations, a group that had visited Gaborone in late February 1986, which demonstrated even less South Africa concern than before for world and regional opinion.

Although the United States did not recall its ambassador to Pretoria this time, it dismissed Brigadier Alexander Potgetier, the senior South African Defense Attaché in Washington. As in 1985, the UN Security Council considered the SADF raids,[141] but the use of a double veto by the American and British delegations—both of which opposed the strong sanctions of the draft resolution—prevented the council from adopting a resolution.

From the South African perspective, the SADF attacks were extraterritorial responses to internal threats. As a guarantor of the system of white hegemony, the SADF was obligated to fend off attacks by armed African nationalists aimed at the South African heartland. The SADF perceived that there was a "total onslaught" against South Africa and responded with a "total strategy,"[142] which involved rooting out ANC operatives based outside the country—in Botswana and elsewhere. The preferred and most efficient solution to this problem was for the SADF to subcontract the job and to let the host state do the work. That, after all, was the essence of the system of nonaggression treaties that South Africa has proposed. The text of a proposed bilateral South African–Botswana nonaggression treaty obligated Botswana to supply South Africa with data about South African refugees.[143]

Had it accepted such a treaty,[144] Botswana would have become a branch office of the South African National Intelligence Service. The South Africans have persisted in their charges that Botswana was a staging area for ANC guerrillas who infiltrated into the Transvaal Province.[145] Botswana, in turn, has closed down the ANC's office and required the two ANC representatives to depart.[146] But it still offered asylum to bona fide refugees and demanded that no one abuse its hospitality by using it as a base for attacks.[147] Such laws are difficult to enforce, but the record shows that Botswana has imprisoned several ANC activists.[148]

An unpleasant byproduct of the SADF raids has been the adoption of the National Security Act of 1986. During the parliamentary debates on this bill, the 1985 commando attack was mentioned, with the memorandum introducing the bill drawing attention to that raid and three bomb explosions in 1985.[149] The act constricted civil liberties and contained a provision that contravenes the basic Western tenet that one is presumed innocent until proven guilty.[150] To that extent it resembled South African security legislation which was odious to the Batswana. Because of the act's protean nature, members of opposition parties in Botswana regarded it as a BDP-inspired device to silence opposition voices and the private press.[151] There was concern that the activities of the BDF are off-limits to the press.[152] Nevertheless, the Masire government has prosecuted captured South African soldiers and their local accomplices under the act.[153]

Not unexpectedly, the BDF has increased spending,[154] causing concern.[155] If the BDF budget is a lagged reflection of the South African security threat, then a reduction in the South African threat and in the ability to carry out the threat would induce lower BDF spending levels. Even though the SADF, whose budget has been reduced,[156] is by far the most capable defense force in southern Africa, it would be a mistake to regard South Africa as the only adversary for Botswana. As noted earlier, in 1983 there were clashes between the BDF and Zimbabwean units, and Namibia created an army for itself, with British assistance.[157]

In terms of its missions, however, the BDF has developed a wider geographical focus, for it sent a contingent to participate in the UN operation in Somalia[158] and in Mozambique.[159] Probably the only realistic way to reduce defense spending in Botswana is for a balanced, regional arms and force reduction.[160] If the military expense of high politics were diminished or even curtailed, then more resources and energy could be devoted to the pursuit of low politics.

PART TWO

ISSUES IN LOW POLITICS

CHAPTER FIVE

Developing an Educational and Scientific Infrastructure

REGIONAL STATES, MISSIONARIES, AND EDUCATION

Changing the focus from high to low politics entails shifting from a concern for reducing dependence upon white-ruled neighbors to one for increasing areas of autonomy. The next five chapters covering selected areas of low politics establish the baseline for dependence primarily upon South Africa and secondarily upon Southern Rhodesia. From that point, I will examine the efforts of Botswana's decision-makers to expand their zones of autonomy, including long-range plans as well as a willingness to tap foreign donors for resources and personnel. In some cases, Botswana has overcome severe infrastructural weaknesses, while in others enlarging the zone of autonomy takes considerable time, effort, and funds. I begin with the field of education and science because creating skilled bureaucratic, professional, and business leaders in Botswana is both an end in itself and a prerequisite for a more productive economy, a higher quality of life for its citizenry, and a more effective role in regional, continental, and global affairs.

The term "missionaries' road" appears in the historical accounts of the BP's founding in 1885, while historians have emphasized what they regard as the imperial sentiments and activities of missionary figures in Botswana's history.[1] My concern here is with the missionary establishment as a link to education outside the BP. I consider how the government and people of the protectorate utilized South African, Southern Rhodesian, and South West African facilities and practices. This focus illustrates how Botswana has reduced its educational clientage upon its neighboring, white-ruled states.[2] This approach fits within the political science literature that explores educational dependencies in the post-colonial world.[3]

Until 1964, classroom instruction followed the Southern African separatist system, with one school system for Africans, a second for Eurafricans, and another for whites,[4] with the African system funded at the lowest per capita basis.[5] For African children, education was limited to the primary level; a curriculum preparing them for the South African university matriculation examination was not introduced until 1954.[6] The first state secondary school (in Gaborone) was built in 1965 at the time of the transfer of the administrative headquarters from Mafikeng to Gaborone. Prior to independence in 1966, Africans could take post-Junior Certificate level work at only two protectorate schools (Moeng and Kgale), one of which was a missionary institution.[7]

The South African and missionary nexus was essentially a Cape Provincial link characterized by the Tiger Kloof Institution. Operated by the London Missionary Society outside Vryburg, this particular Cape boarding school received a subsidy from the BP administration for the education of Protectorate Africans.[8] Although Batswana attended other missionary-run secondary schools in South Africa, such as Lovedale Institution (sponsored by the Church of Scotland) in the Cape[9] and Adams College (a Congregational school) in Natal,[10] the Tiger Kloof Institution is probably best known and most closely linked with the BP. In 1951, for example, over half (31 out of 56) the African secondary school students from the BP studying outside the country were enrolled in Tiger Kloof.[11] Most of the Batswana members of President Khama's first post-independence cabinet were Tiger Kloof alumni.[12]

Few Batswana could afford to attend boarding school in the United Kingdom[13] or Eire,[14] although relatively senior British colonial officials in the BP would be more likely to be able to afford to send their children to a British boarding school because they received an educational allowance.[15] Nevertheless, South Africa, and to a lesser extent Southern Rhodesia and South West Africa, became the academic metropole throughout most of the colonial period. This was the case for African[16] as well as for white students.[17]

Students whose parents resided along the northern part of the railway line were likely to have attended Southern Rhodesian institutions.[18] After 1951, however, these schools did not welcome students from territories not scheduled to become a part of the Central African Federation.[19] A small number of white children from Ghanzi, however, attended boarding school in South West Africa, which was closer to their homes than either South Africa or Southern Rhodesia.[20] Education emphasized the transitory nature of the white children's residence in the BP.

According to Ernst G. Malherbe's report on education for white pupils in the BP, the major purpose of their education was "*to educate them for escape*" from the BP.[21] He thought the protectorate offered few economic prospects for white inhabitants because of the depressed livestock industry.[22] That South African, Southern Rhodesian, and South West African institutions were regarded as means to facilitate white exodus from the BP was more of an economic statement than a political one. It complements the effort of the white residents to have their enclaves incorporated into either South Africa or Southern Rhodesia.

The BP schools utilized South African syllabi, examinations, textbooks, and teachers.[23] The South African syllabi and examinations replaced the Southern Rhodesian ones before the Second World War.[24] Instruction in Afrikaans at BP schools illustrated the extent of South African influence. Although not a compulsory school subject,[25] Afrikaans instruction remained in the school system until after independence, when this language was replaced by Setswana, one of the two official languages of Botswana.[26] Its use has concerned MPs, who raised questions in the different legislative bodies about the status of the language.[27] Afrikaans is taught as an elective subject in some private schools that meet the needs of South African expatriates who want their children to follow the curriculum of South African schools and universities.[28]

During the colonial era, a high percentage of white students were Afrikaners,[29] who needed mother tongue instruction, while those non-Afrikaners who sought employment or further study in South Africa found the study of Afrikaans necessary or useful. After the Second World War, access to South African schools became more difficult for African students from the BP.[30] Under the regime of segregated education designed for Africans in South Africa, known as Bantu education, Tiger Kloof Institution ceased to operate as a missionary school.[31] It was reconstituted as Moeding College by the sponsoring London Missionary Society at Otse, between Gaborone and Lobatse, and began classes in 1962.[32]

In the educational and cultural sector, the BP used South African consultants for primary education for the white community[33] and for Batswana at remote cattle posts,[34] while the South African Dutch Reformed Church (DRC) operated a homecraft center for the Bakgatla in Mochudi.[35] The BP provided access for the South African anthropologist Isaac Schapera, whose work was discussed in several meetings of the African Advisory Council[36] and who was recognized in 1985 with an honorary doctorate from the University of Botswana.[37]

This heavily skewed relationship favoring South Africa as educational donor was only partially offset by the contribution that renowned BP missionary Rev. Alfred E. Jennings made in the field of Setswana orthography and as an examiner in that language for the University of Cape Town.[38]

At the post-secondary level, residential university education in South Africa was generally segregated, except for such nominally open English-medium institutions as the Universities of Cape Town and the Witwatersrand.[39] BP Africans usually were restricted to the Pretoria-based nonresidential University of South Africa (UNISA), which taught by correspondence, or to the residential Fort Hare University College near the secondary school at Lovedale in the Cape.[40] This was southern Africa's premier African university at the time and the alma mater of the late President Khama.[41] Zachariah K. Matthews, who built his academic reputation at Fort Hare, later became Botswana's first permanent representative to the United Nations, where he served with four of his former Fort Hare students who became ambassadors.[42]

When Fort Hare was closed to extra-Union Africans in 1959,[43] Batswana could still enroll in UNISA. UNISA helped the Roman Catholic Pius XII College (founded in Roma, Basutoland in 1945) make the transition to regular university status, complete with a royal charter from the British government.[44] Previously, the colonial regime had considered linking up with the university for the Central African Federation in Salisbury but chose not to do so because BP schools did not offer the lengthy secondary school curriculum (sixth form) required by the university in Salisbury. The interterritorial university at Roma, which had the less arduous and expensive fifth form entrance requirement prevailing at South African institutions, enabled the BP to reduce its reliance upon South African institutions of higher learning in the post-independence years.[45]

Until the University of Botswana (UB), in a joint arrangement with the University of Edinburgh, established a legal curriculum in 1981,[46] the BP often depended upon individual South African lawyers for legal services.[47] There was only one Motswana lawyer in the country at the time of independence in 1966, and the second one did not qualify until 1975.[48] These extraterritorial lawyers could practice in the BP, as well as in Botswana,[49] and even serve on its Court of Appeal.[50] Not only were there practical reasons of speed and expense to engage South African lawyers, but also the legal system in pre- and post-independent Botswana draws upon the Cape system of law.[51]

When he became chief justice of Botswana in 1968, John R. Dendy-Young, a former member of the Southern Rhodesian High Court who had broken with the Smith government, introduced an element of regional balance.[52] The Southern Rhodesian government provided cultural and educational assistance to the BP and Botswana by serving as the repository for a large number of BP archival materials from 1961 until 1967, and their staff inventoried a considerable amount of this material.[53] South African corporations provided funds to purchase books for the National Archives.[54]

EXTRAREGIONAL FACULTY AND INSTITUTIONS

By the time the University of Basutoland, Bechuanaland, and Swaziland was inaugurated in 1964,[55] South Africa had left the Commonwealth of Nations and reassessed its relations with the HCT. In the next two decades BP began to reverse the direction and strength of its educational ties with its white-ruled neighbors.

Botswana's parliamentarians began to urge the government to expand the opportunities for secondary education,[56] and a larger number of urban Batswana secured places in secondary schools. The school system, moreover, replaced the South African examination standards with British ones (the Cambridge School Certificate), which permitted access to Commonwealth African and British universities for sufficiently gifted students.[57] In the year of independence eleven students from Botswana had gone to British institutions, twelve had gone to the United States, four were at the University of Zambia, one had gone to Kenya, three were in Southern Rhodesia, two were studying in Uganda, thirty were enrolled at the University of Botswana, Lesotho, and Swaziland, one had gone to India, another to Canada, and still another to Australia.[58] Four years later, there were no students from Botswana enrolled in either Southern Rhodesian or South African residential universities.[59]

Given the projected national personnel needs, however, the pool of secondary students was too small,[60] partly because of the need for adequately trained teachers at the secondary level.[61] Indeed, the civil service often attracted the better qualified teachers, which only compounded the difficulty.[62] The employment of expatriate teachers, some of whom were South Africans,[63] and the utilization of foreign volunteers,[64] such as those from the US Peace Corps,[65] the UN International Voluntary Service, and the UK Voluntary Service Organization,[66] were palliative measures.

South Africans contributed to the teaching profession in the form of such innovative schools as Swaneng Hill School in Serowe and the Maru-a-Pula School in Gaborone. Patrick van Rensburg, a former

South African diplomat who subsequently became active in the Liberal Party, founded the progressive Swaneng Hill School, which provided a novel blend of academic work and vocational instruction.[67]

In 1968 Deane Yates, former headmaster of St. John's College in Johannesburg, became the first headmaster of the Maru-a-Pula School,[68] a private, fee-paying, multiracial school with a scholarship program to support students from less affluent homes.[69] This school won the respect of President Khama. Not only did President Khama's two sons but also Vice President Masire's daughter attended Maru-a-Pula School.[70] Maru-a-Pula faculty included several white American teachers,[71] one of whom had been the first US chargé d'affaires in Botswana,[72] as well as a South African Rhodes Scholar.[73] Maru-a-Pula is the only secondary school in Botswana offering the A-level, advanced British university preparatory curriculum[74] as well as the one school in Botswana whose alumna, Liyanda Lekalake, became the first Motswana Rhodes Scholar.[75]

Other South Africans helped to build a school for the Basarwa run under the auspices of the DRC,[76] while American volunteers with the Crossroads Africa program have assisted with the construction of schools or libraries at Serowe, Kanye, and Ootsi.[77] Some African teachers from South Africa were not well received in Botswana, and those who earned their teaching credentials in South Africa after 1962 (when the system of Bantu education went into effect) were denied professional status because Botswana did not recognize the legitimacy of the Bantu education curriculum in South Africa.[78]

The South African academic link weakened as the multinational University of Botswana, Lesotho, and Swaziland (UBLS), in Roma, received funding from the American, Australian, British, Canadian, Dutch, French, and Swedish governments, the UN, South African mining houses,[79] and an American private foundation.[80] Botswana did not regularly send a proportionate number of students to Pius XII College and its successors.[81] When Lesotho withdrew from the UBLS in 1975, the other two parts of the combined university became the University of Botswana and Swaziland in 1976. The Gaborone campus of the University of Botswana and Swaziland, which began operating in 1971, was termed the University College of Botswana.[82]

Out of this dual university came the UB, located in Gaborone, in 1982. Even though the university in Gaborone does not include the wide range of academic disciplines and professional schools that universities in the developed nations do,[83] it still plays a vital role in Botswana. The acquisition of a university represents a hallmark of independence for the citizens of Botswana, and it also serves as the repository for, and patron of, Botswana's national culture and identity.[84] For example, the faculty of the department of history has been heavily involved in teaching students to integrate oral history into their historical research on Botswana. The tape recordings and transcriptions of the interviews that the students conducted in the course of these research projects at the UB are deposited in the Botswana National Archives. The arrangement between the department of history and the National Archives appears to be informal, but one that contributes to the quality of the student theses and to the wealth of local historical materials.[85] The university library, which the Algerian government helped to finance, also has a special Botswana collection room.[86]

In the final years of the Protectorate, several American institutions provided scholarships for Batswana students.[87] Since that time, Botswana has created a wider network of patrons and friends to help improve its educational institutions. For obvious reasons of language, this educational network is composed primarily of Commonwealth states, but it includes the UN family of organizations, which started to provide educational planning assistance in 1964.[88] Within southern Africa, the provision of places for Batswana students in Zambian educational institutions was particularly welcome, especially in the immediate post-independence period when both states had a strained relationship with Southern Rhodesia.[89] Other Batswana have attended universities in non-Commonwealth African states (Liberia) and in the Commonwealth of Nations (Canada, Kenya, Malaysia, Nigeria, Sierra Leone, Tanzania, Uganda, the UK, and Zambia).[90]

The Soviet Union has provided Botswana several scholarships in such technical fields as architecture, engineering, metallurgy, telecommunications, veterinary science, computer science, and analytical chemistry.[91] The BPP or other nationalist groups also secured unofficial scholarships for Batswana to study in the Soviet Union or Eastern Europe.[92] Those with Soviet qualifications will not occupy the upper echelons of the administrative elite in Botswana under a BDP Government,[93] however, even though one political party leader, Kenneth Koma of the Botswana National Front, holds an advanced Soviet degree.[94]

Institution-building in the cultural area is an adjunct of creating an infrastructure for secondary and post-secondary education. Along with the creation of the National Archives, there is the National Art Gallery and Museum in Gaborone. Their displays and folk art exhibits, along with their quarterly bilingual (English and Setswana) publication, *The Zebra's Voice* (the zebra is the logo of the museum), are contributions to the nation's cultural life. Aid for the museum came from Southern Rhodesian and South African business firms,[95] as well as from the

Batswana, with the Southern Rhodesian museums providing technical training.[96] The museum developed ties with American, Belgian, British, and Zambian institutions[97] and has received funding from Denmark and the UN.[98] It has a small training program to prepare those interested in the museum and archaeological field for university work.[99]

Operating out of the museum is the Botswana Society, a private, nonprofit organization founded in 1969 to promote the study of Botswana's history and culture. The society, which sponsors symposia and lectures, publishes the annual *Botswana Notes and Records*, which covers the natural, physical, and social sciences as well as special topical symposia.[100] Complementing these publications is *Pula: Botswana Journal of African Studies*, begun in 1978, which concentrates on social sciences and language. Finally, the National Institute of Development Research and Documentation, a unit of the UB, publishes working papers, bibliographies, research notes, seminar proceedings, and directories.

REGIONAL SCIENTIFIC AND TECHNICAL COOPERATION

In the latter half of the 1930s, the British government negotiated with the South African one over the transfer of the HCT to the Union. At that time, both governments developed an institutional arrangement (the Joint Advisory Conference) to facilitate technical cooperation between the HCT and South Africa.[101] This low politics approach demonstrated South Africa's interest in functionalism at both the regional and international level.[102] The 1933 report of Sir Alan Pim to the Secretary of State for Dominion Affairs on the BP's financial and economic position noted the linkages forged between the BP and South West Africa as well as between the Protectorate and the Union and Southern Rhodesia.

Both the Union and the Southern Rhodesian governments provided many services to the administration and people of the BP.[103] This chapter probes the low politics areas of wildlife and natural sciences research and management, water resources, agricultural and livestock research and marketing, medical services, and anthropological research. Chapters Six through Nine investigate low politics of administrative skills and arrangements, communications, transportation and tourism, the Southern African Customs Union and the financial nexus, and transnational employment. Although these fields overlap, they demonstrate the range of possibilities for the application of South African low politics as well as the extent to which Botswana has been able to provide these services itself, thereby enhancing its own autonomy.[104]

Wildlife research and management typify the technical, supposedly nonpolitical approach to closer cooperation in the Southern African region. A significant example is the Kalahari Gemsbok Park in the Gordonia District of the Cape Province, which became a South African national park in 1931.[105] The South African government later added more land to this park,[106] while in 1940 the BP created a contiguous game preserve administered by the South African National Parks Board.[107] This board and the South African staff shared its data with the BP and served as game wardens for both parks.[108] The BP paid an annual fee to the South African government for the management of the BP portion of the park and reimbursed the National Parks Board for water drilling operations in the BP park.[109] By 1990, because of the need to even out tourist flows to various parks in southern Africa, South Africa was prepared to merge its Kalahari Gemsbok Park with Botswana's Gemsbok National Park. Presumably, South Africa would be the steward for Botswana's interests in the portion of the combined park that lies east of the Nossob River, which is the international border between South Africa and Botswana.[110]

At the unofficial level, the Okavango Wildlife Society in Johannesburg has been interested in the Moremi Wildlife Reserve in Botswana's Ngamiland area, acting as a patron of research activities[111] and providing support for, and information about, the reserve among interested South Africans.[112] The South African Wildlife Foundation, associated with Afrikaner business magnate Anton Rupert, has paid for equipment for Botswana's national parks.[113] Other assistance has come through the activities of faculty members of South African universities[114] or, for example, from scientists at the Entomological Department of the South African Institute for Medical Research, who undertake fieldwork in Botswana. The research findings are often published in the Johannesburg journal, *African Wild Life*.[115] Finally, the South Africans sponsor scholarly meetings devoted to wildlife topics.[116]

With regard to water resources, interest in the Okavango as a source of water for drought-prone Botswana[117] dates back to at least 1920 with the publication of Ernest H. L. Schwarz's work, *The Kalahari or Thirstland Redemption*.[118] Since then, the South African government sponsored two trips, one in 1925, led by Dr. A. L. Du Toit[119] and the other in 1945 by Senator E. A. Conroy (the Minister of Lands),[120] to ascertain the possibilities of irrigating much of the BP, thus opening arid land to settlement and improving the BP's economy, perhaps making the Protectorate a more attractive territory to transfer to the Union.

In addition to promoting the domestic utilization of water for irrigated farming, other considerations include the possibility of using water resources from Botswana in South Africa, which has difficulty meeting its water needs in the Witwatersrand industrial complex.[121] Such proposals supplement other South African international water plans involving Lesotho. South Africa also assisted BP authorities on well boring operations and on matters related to water supplies for the capital at Gaborone.[122] In 1985 officials of both governments showed an interest in a West German geographer's proposal for a water pipeline from Kazungula to the Witwatersrand, with outlets for southern Botswana. The estimated cost for the 744-mile line was R 4 billion, and the project has not been undertaken so far.[123] Such a project would have environmental costs and would probably need the support of Botswana farming and cattle ranching interests, which have a proprietary interest in the availability of water in Botswana. Increasingly, environmental concerns affect water use policies, particularly in the Okavango area.[124]

Agricultural and livestock research work and marketing received ample coverage in the Pim Report.[125] Botswana and South Africa have belonged to the Pretoria-based Southern African Regional Commission for the Conservation and Utilization of the Soil (SARCCUS), along with Lesotho and Swaziland, Angola and Mozambique, Malawi, Namibia, Southern Rhodesia, and São Tomé and Principe.[126] Another mutual concern has been in arresting the depredation of insects and birds upon crops, in particular the brown or red locust[127] and the quelea (weaver bird).[128] Botswana and South Africa were both members of the International Red Locust Control Service, which included Lesotho, Angola and Mozambique, Zaire, Ruanda and Burundi, Zambia, along with Kenya, Uganda, and Tanzania. Begun in 1934, this body received considerable financial support from South Africa[129] but was disbanded in 1970 when six African states withdrew for political reasons.[130]

South African cattle ranchers, who for quite some time have been economically favored by import restrictions upon BP cattle,[131] gave an independence gift of breeding stock to Botswana, presented by the South African minister of agricultural technical services J. J. Fouché (who later became the state president).[132] Livestock producers from South Africa and Botswana share an interest in containing the spread of foot-and-mouth disease,[133] in control of the tsetse fly (particularly in Ngamiland),[134] and in improving the health of their animals. South African authorities, particularly at Onderstepoort Veterinary Research Institute,[135] provided advice, personnel, and different types of animal vaccines to Botswana.[136] As in other scientific fields, personnel consult with their counterparts on veterinary matters,[137] and the two states, in addition to Lesotho, Swaziland, Zimbabwe, Malawi, and Mozambique, are members of the Inter-Territorial Foot-and-Mouth Advisory Committee.[138]

Marketing arrangements between Botswana and South Africa cover a rather small range of products. These arrangements include the South African Livestock and Meat Industries Control Board,[139] along with the Dairy Industry Control Board, the Mealie Industry Control Board, the Oilseeds Control Board,[140] and the marketing cooperative for karakul sheep in Upington.[141] Such marketing arrangements are difficult to document adequately and exist on an ad hoc basis for Botswana, Lesotho, and Swaziland. No treaties cover these matters, although the three HCT were granted advisory status on the South African Maize Board.[142]

In terms of medical assistance, the South African Institute of Medical Research has undertaken studies on plague carriers in the BP,[143] while the Union Public Health Department has aided in plague control.[144] South African radiographic facilities were used before the Second World War in connection with the diagnosis of pulmonary disease,[145] while the Union took care of the BP's more seriously mentally ill patients.[146] The DRC appointed a physician to serve at its mission in Mochudi, and Batswana received rudimentary dental assistant training in South Africa and Southern Rhodesia.[147] Those whites of BP who needed medical assistance traveled to South West Africa, Northern Rhodesia, Southern Rhodesia, or South Africa.[148]

Not until 1945 did a Motswana begin to study medicine in South Africa at the University of the Witwatersrand.[149] The BP administration did not employ either of the Scottish-educated Molema brothers as physicians in Mafikeng—presumably because of British racial attitudes.[150] On occasion, patients from the BP were sent to South African hospitals for special or emergency treatments,[151] and even the late President Khama was hospitalized in South Africa in 1968.[152] South African medical students from the University of the Witwatersrand performed professional duties in Botswana.[153]

In the nursing profession, the Transvaal Chamber of Mining financed the local training of nurses at a level which would meet some of the medical needs of the BP but yet not enable the nurses to be professionally employed in South Africa.[154] Batswana women were attracted to nursing, and the BP began to employ them as nurses in the early 1930s.[155] In addition, African registered nurses from South Africa were able to find employment in the BP.[156] It was not until 1948 that a Motswana, who had trained in South Africa, became a registered nurse.[157] The HCT utilized the professional standards of, and examiners from, the South African Nursing Council both before and after independence.[158]

In the anthropological field, the focus was upon the San (or Basarwa or Bushmen) of the Kalahari, who assume a prominent place in the ethnological literature on Botswana. During the late 1930s, when functional cooperation began in a systematic fashion, the BP administration, the Universities of Cape Town and the Witwatersrand, the native affairs department of the South African government, and the South West African government created a committee to consider investigation on the Basarwa. Isaac Schapera wrote a report for the committee on its research agenda.[159]

Later, the BP government commissioned research on the Basarwa, with George B. Silberbauer's report being published in 1965. In the introductory chapter of his report, *Bushman Survey*, Silberbauer took note of his graduate work in social anthropology and linguistics at the University of the Witwatersrand in 1957–1958, drawing attention to the scholarly activities of the Kalahari Research Committee of that university.[160] The interdisciplinary committee included researchers from the Dental and Medical School and undertook frequent scientific expeditions to the BP. According to committee chairman Phillip V. Tobias, no other South African university carried on such an extensive research program on the Basarwa of Botswana. The members of the University of Witwatersrand Kalahari Research Committee compiled a remarkable scholarly publication record, and Tobias has developed an international scientific reputation.[161]

After independence, the Botswanan government systematized the process by which research work would be permitted by the passage of the 1967 Anthropological Research Act, which has been extended to cover other academic disciplines, including, for example, political science. Although it was published in the *Government Gazette* as the Anthropological Research Act,[162] it was designated as the Anthropological Research and Bushman Protection Bill in the parliamentary record of the debates.[163] The Office of the President issues these permits, which obligates the research worker to send copies of his or her research papers and publications to the National Archives and Records Service.

DIVERSIFYING SCIENTIFIC IMPORTS AND CHOICES

Bequeathed a meager educational and scientific infrastructure at independence, Botswana has to enlarge its pool of trained personnel while simultaneously engaging in the long-term task of raising the qualifications of its own citizens, including its attempts to achieve greater autonomy in the field of scientific personnel. Sending students outside the region primarily to English-speaking nations for specialized undergraduate and graduate training would not only meet projected manpower needs in the coming decades but would also furnish candidates for localization of posts. This would strengthen Botswana's autonomy.

Botswana's enlarged circle of patrons grew logically from the intracolonial and intercolonial patterns for the promotion and application of scientific research modified in the age of decolonization. The inter-colonial organizations, namely, the Scientific Council for Africa South of the Sahara (CSA) and the companion Commission for Technical Cooperation South of the Sahara (CCTA), were established in the wake of the Second World War and included the UK as well as South Africa.[164] Neighboring Southern Rhodesia and then the Central African Federation were members of both organizations until 1962.[165] The three governments of the UK, the Federation, and South Africa paid just over 40 percent of the budget of the CCTA in 1958.[166] Archival sources suggested that the BP scientific officers were kept abreast of the work of the commission through various communications and memoranda.[167]

Turning to the wildlife sector, there was no major break in the South African linkage in terms of the Kalahari Gemsbok National Park management.[168] Probably the Botswana authorities found the arrangement to be cost effective, particularly in terms of transportation and communication expenses. Because of its location at the extreme southwestern edge of the country off the major trunk roads and rail line,[169] it is more likely to attract South African, rather than overseas, tourist clientele.[170]

Another useful link is the Okavango Wildlife Society which, though South African, has underwritten the research of two American zoologists working in the Central Kalahari Game Reserve.[171] Prior to independence, a biologist from the National Museums of Southern Rhodesia undertook zoological and ornithological investigations in the BP, financed by the British government. South African wildlife ecologists conducted other wildlife research, which was supported by the International Union for Conservation of Nature and the Food and Agricultural Organization (FAO) of the UN.[172] American Fulbright scholar W. H. Elder of the University of Missouri also conducted wildlife research during this period.[173]

Since independence, US Peace Corps volunteers attached to the Department of Wildlife and National Parks have published the results of their research.[174] This represented a marked change from the early group of volunteers who often had no undergraduate scientific training[175] and who usually worked in secondary schools or with the cooperative movements.[176] To meet its personnel needs, the Botswana government sent students to Tanzania[177] and Australia to pursue work in wildlife management.[178]

Regional cooperation was channeled through Malawi, which accepted responsibility for wildlife matters in the Southern African Development Coordination Conference (SADCC).[179] Yet some of the funding will come from private bodies in the West, such as the National Geographic Society and the Frankfurt Zoological Society, which already have sponsored research projects in Botswana.[180] The National Science Foundation of the United States[181] and the FAO also funded wildlife investigations in Botswana.[182] The most likely pattern is localization coupled with selected funding by a medley of public and private donors for particular wildlife projects.

The area of water resources is particularly well suited to international assistance[183] and has high visibility because of the recurrent droughts in Botswana.[184] This has ramifications for both agriculture and for the generation of hydroelectric power. In terms of the former, Botswana, Lesotho, and Zimbabwe share the tasks within SADCC that bear upon water as a factor of agricultural production,[185] while there seems to be an interest in, but no specific country assigned to deal with, hydroelectric power.[186]

Botswana uses its own coal to generate electrical power, and for economic reasons probably will not use the waters of the Zambezi for this purpose. At the outset of independence, Nationalist China dispatched an agricultural mission to Botswana to provide technical assistance in the matter of irrigated farming.[187] Assistance for research in this sector is likely to come from UN agencies, probably supplemented by talent in the universities and scientific institutes in Johannesburg and Pretoria, if not in Harare. Presently, however, irrigated agriculture does not seem to be a high priority.[188]

Turning to agricultural and livestock research and marketing, Botswana was designated the nation to oversee crop research and animal disease under the SADCC.[189] As the beef export market becomes increasingly oriented toward the European Economic Community,[190] probably a wider range of patrons can be found for what has been the mainstay of the Botswana economy, a way of life, and a business investment for urban political elites in Botswana.[191] Indeed, the donation of cattle under the slogan of "one man, one beast" was a highly visible means of supporting public causes, particularly the UB in 1976 as it disengaged from the UBLS and established itself in Gaborone.[192] Consequently, considerable emphasis will be placed upon the quality, availability, and affordability of veterinary services and supplies.

Analyzing the territorial manpower situation in the BP just before independence, a British-sponsored investigation pointed to the dominance of expatriates in the field of veterinary medicine and observed that local persons would be unable to fill the positions requiring advanced education for six years.[193] In the final years of the Protectorate, a British economic survey team observed that not even one Motswana was being groomed for professional veterinary studies. The BP had established a school for technicians or paraprofessionals in the veterinary field, but that would not enable it to replace expatriate veterinarians at the highest departmental levels.[194]

This is not an area where the University of Botswana can be expected to carry the total burden, except at the pre-professional level. Thus a regional approach to professional education would be a cost-effective means to meet this need. The most likely short-term strategy will be to place Batswana in pre-veterinary and veterinary curricula in Commonwealth universities. The training and nurturing of scientific staff is one of the most challenging tasks facing African states and will take years.[195]

Botswana loosened its links to the South African veterinary research establishment at Onderstepoort when it found support for the production of a vaccination to protect the national herd against the dreaded foot-and-mouth disease, which has been a continuous problem to Batswana livestockmen and their neighbors. This vaccination manufacturing facility, funded by the European Economic Community[196] and provided for through a French firm, Institut Merieux, was anticipated to have export potential.[197] The problem of localizing the veterinary staff in the livestock field is beginning to be resolved, for a total of eleven Batswana have qualified as veterinarians since 1973, and seven more are now in veterinary schools.[198]

In the realm of medical services, missionary societies and hospitals have filled in the gaps to supplement government services. Members of the government came to the parliamentary defense of the DRC, which supported a medical complex in Mochudi, when it (and the South African variant of its ideology) was subject to attack by the BPP Opposition in the National Assembly.[199] In addition, one medical missionary, Dr. Alfred M. Merriweather of the Scottish Livingstone Hospital in Molepolole, served as the first Speaker of the National Assembly as well as President Khama's physician.[200]

It is unlikely that missionary medical personnel can be obtained in sufficient numbers on a long-term basis; hence health care must depend upon the willingness and ability of foreign donors to furnish physicians, rapidly increasing the number of Batswana practitioners, and the willingness of physicians in the region to emigrate to Botswana.[201] Along with those in the veterinary medicine field, Botswana has been sending prospective medical students for study abroad.[202] Botswana's medical and dental professions have now been organized as a single group known as the Medical Association of Botswana, which publishes a scientific journal for its members.[203] This may, in time, loosen the formal, organizational ties to South African counterpart organizations. It is an area in which UN activity would complement the work undertaken by the SADCC, which appointed Swaziland as the coordinating member state for health matters.[204]

One significant aspect of the temporary importation of scientific talent is the long-term effect it is likely to have upon the local scientists. One public administration specialist who has spent time in Botswana training public servants has drawn attention to the professional relationship between the imported and the Batswana scientists.[205] This relationship improves the scientific climate in Botswana, and it is also likely to bring unanticipated future scientific benefits for Botswana.

CHAPTER SIX

Developing an Administrative Infrastructure

THE COMMONWEALTH RELATIONS OFFICE AND SOUTH AFRICA

The last chapter indicated that Botswana had only a meager educational infrastructure at the time of its independence. In terms of low politics, it utilized the resources of South Africa and, to a much smaller extent, the educational and scientific communities of Southern Rhodesia. Educational and scientific traffic tended to move between Botswana and these two technologically advanced neighbors rather than between Botswana and the British metropole. The administrative as well as the educational policy were in the realm of low politics. In this chapter I explore the dimensions of low politics with respect to South African personnel and administrative sites during the colonial era before showing how the South African connection was replaced by short-term reliance on other states and on international organizations for administrative expertise.

British governance of the BP was unlike that elsewhere in Anglophone Africa, where the chain of command extended from the district officer in the field to the governor in the capital and thence to the Colonial Office (CO) in London. The BP pattern,[1] which applied to the other two HCT, had two added elements that reflect the significance of the South African factor in imperial management. First, an extra level in the colonial hierarchy linked the resident magistrate (called district commissioner after 1936[2]) at the local level to the metropole. This was the Dominions (later called the Commonwealth Relations) Office, which was responsible for relations with South Africa. A second peculiarity was the siting of BP's administrative capital on South African territory in Mafikeng, the headquarters of the resident commissioner of the BP, a colonial position equivalent to lieutenant-governor.[3]

Turning to the administrative chain of command, BP, as well as Southern and Northern Rhodesia, fell under the jurisdiction of the Dominions Department of the British CO from 1907 to 1925.[4] In 1925 the newly created Dominions Office (DO) assumed responsibility for the three HCT and Southern Rhodesia,[5] while the CO remained in charge of Northern Rhodesia.[6] In 1947 the name of the DO was changed to the Commonwealth Relations Office (CRO),[7] which continued to administer the BP. The CO, however, took over responsibility for the BP in 1961, when South Africa left the Commonwealth of Nations.[8]

Southern Rhodesia continued its link with the CRO, although the resident commissioners handled the actual administration in each HCT. The British high commissioner in South Africa—the link between the three resident commissioners and the DO—also functioned as governor-general of South Africa from 1910 to 1931.[9] Thereafter, the high commissioner also served as the UK's resident ambassador to Pretoria, combining governance and diplomatic functions in this single office.[10]

This fusion of colonial and diplomatic functions ended when a direct line of responsibility was established between the CO and the resident commissioner, whose title was changed to Her Majesty's commissioner in 1963. The new designation meant that the post was upgraded to the status of governor within the British colonial hierarchy; the next year the British government eliminated the position of high commissioner, which was no longer necessary now that Her Majesty's commissioner reported directly to London.[11] The Foreign Office assumed responsibility for South African diplomatic ties.[12]

Critics, citing the BP administrative chain of command from Mafikeng to London,[13] were concerned that the governance of the BP took place within the administrative framework of Anglo–South African relations, within the confines of the DO or the CRO. The line of responsibility, they argued, should have stretched directly from the BP to the CO, as this was one measure of the status of a dependency and its rulers.[14] Retired Resident Commissioner Sir Charles F. Rey suggested that the link with the DO be replaced by one with the CO. He recommended that the position of resident commissioner be elevated within the imperial hierarchy,[15] arguing that the CO would befriend the BP administration in its conflicts with South Africa much more than would the DO.[16]

Retired BP Resident Commissioner Anthony Sillery indicated three reasons why the BP should fall under the CO's jurisdiction rather than the CRO's: Sillery felt that the CRO lacked expertise in the area of colonial rule; he contended that the high commissioner in South Africa, who combined the tasks of senior administrator and diplomat, need not necessarily be conversant with the tasks of colonial governance to secure appointment, although he found little substance in this argument if only because the high commissioner had three able resident commissioners to handle that task; and he argued that conflict between the two representative roles of the high commissioner would be resolved in favor of South Africa. He suggested that the high commissioner's administrative tasks be jettisoned and that the three resident commissioners be elevated in rank to facilitate direct communication with the CRO. In brief, the Pretoria intermediary bothered him more than the affiliation of the HCT with the CRO.[17]

Former BP District Commissioner Hugh Ashton warned that the high commission in Pretoria favored South African over British colonial economic legislation and policies. This bias apparently included some South African racially discriminatory practices. Ashton emphasized that "the more weighty interests of Dominion affairs and harmony" often displaced the needs and concerns of the HCT,[18] suggesting the presence of bureaucratic politics at work along the lines of the famous aphorism attributed to Don K. Price: "where you stand depends on where you sit."[19] Thus the BP was boxed in with the Union in the organization of the British High Commission, and observers commented on the bureaucratic hegemony of South Africa in this setting.[20]

Additionally, London Missionary Society members[21] and the chiefs of the Barolong, the Bamangwato, and the Bangwaketse[22] preferred CO over DO rule. Tshekeo Tsheko, a future Botswana cabinet minister, then an African Advisory Council member, also favored breaking the link with the CRO in favor of the CO.[23] They perceived the CO to be more responsive than the DO or the CRO to African political needs and aspirations, feeling that they and their allies could more effectively lobby the CO than the DO or CRO.

Several members of the House of Commons throughout the 1950s[24] and early 1960s[25] wanted to separate the British high commissioner's governing and ambassadorial roles. The admixture of the two functions, said John Dugdale, "is about as foolish as it would be to combine the post of Ambassador to Italy with the Governorship of Malta."[26] Another suggestion, also rebuffed, was to establish direct links between the HCT and the CRO without the intervening High Commission.[27] A veiled criticism of the dual post of the high commissioner was that a senior officer could spend only a short time in each of the three HCT,[28] inferring the high commissioner was not devoting adequate time to the governing role. In the House of Lords, Lord Harlech, who had been high commissioner from 1941 to 1944, observed that the two hats should be worn by two different persons.[29] Sir William Clark, high commissioner from 1935 to 1940, did not share this view.[30] Parliamentary pressure appeared to have no effect upon this peculiar administrative arrangement, which was routinely defended by government spokesmen,[31] including the prime minister.[32]

The debate about the preferred method of governing the HCT seems interminable, with not even the British proconsuls in agreement on the subject. Louis A. Picard, after studying the records available in the PRO, posited a distinction without much of a difference in competence between the DO/CRO and the CO because the former had access to the expertise of the latter.[33] Q. Neil Parsons, a British historian who has written extensively on BP matters, indicated that CO–CRO cooperation took place at the highest levels and that there was some rotation of staff between London and the HCT, but more often the rotation took place within southern Àfrica itself.[34] Yet the BP was closeted with South Africa and with Southern Rhodesia (and the Central African Federation) within the confines of the CRO and its predecessor; this bureaucratic propinquity was not the best position from which to wage battles for vital interests.[35]

Perhaps the one area in which the CRO paid more attention to the sensibilities of white South Africans and Southern Rhodesians than to the Batswana was in the political retribution it extracted for Seretse Khama's interracial marriage (see Chapter One). Recently released archival evidence indicates that the British government was more sensitive to the views of the white community in the Union than it cared or dared to admit. Of all the instances of South African bureaucratic hegemony in the High Commission, this marriage is doubtless the most dramatic one, if not the one with the longest legacy.[36]

ADMINISTRATIVE HEADQUARTERS IN MAFIKENG

Within Mafikeng, the BP's administrative headquarters occupied a 640-acre enclave known as the Imperial Reserve. The BP also owned a number of houses in the town for official use. The resident commissioner lived in Mafikeng, and the Protectorate lay sixteen miles beyond Mafikeng. In addition, Mafikeng was the capital of the chief of the Barolong peoples who lived in both British Bechuanaland (later the Cape Province) and in the BP. A representative of the chief resided at Good Hope, a farm in the Barolong area in the extreme southeast of the BP.[37] The authority of the South African-based chief over his kinsmen in Botswana continued until 1970, when it was ended by the government of Botswana itself.[38]

After the First World War, when the inhabitants of the BP were given a limited forum for voicing their views through racially segregated councils meeting annually in Mafikeng, the Protectorate's whites took a lively interest in moving the administrative headquarters into the BP, raising the matter at the second session of the European Advisory Council in 1921,[39] discussing it intermittently every decade until the early 1950s.[40]

The counterpart African body did not deal with the relocation of the Imperial Reserve,[41] although they considered the closely related matter of incorporation. One explanation of this discrepancy might be that, other than incorporation, which involved British pledges to consult the inhabitants of the HCT, "high politics" were off-limits to the Africans.[42] This certainly was the case when it came to the consideration of BP joining the Central African Federation.[43]

The Pim Report urged that the capital be transferred into the BP,[44] and the matter was under review in Mafikeng.[45] In 1936 in London, a high-level committee composed of representatives of the DO, the CO, and the Treasury echoed the Pim Report's exhortation to relocate the administrative headquarters.[46] At this time the idea of functional cooperation between South Africa and the HCT as a way of resolving the incorporation issue began to interest the British and South African political elites and technocrats. Yet in 1946, when the British high commissioner urged Whitehall to move the capital, the DO rejected his proposal on the grounds that it might antagonize Prime Minister Jan Smuts and adversely affect the delicate Anglo–South African balance over the transfer of the HCT issue.[47]

As the incorporation issue faded and the territory looked as though it would enjoy an existence outside South Africa's territorial domain, the Imperial Reserve's position became a political embarrassment, the more so because BP Africans grew more vocal about racial discrimination. After all, Mafikeng was part of South Africa and thus represented a way of life that African nationalists and their overseas supporters had rejected.[48] The British government's opposition to moving the capital into the BP became more embarrassing once South Africa had left the Commonwealth of Nations in 1961.

Relocating the capital inside the borders of the BP would provide a highly visible symbol of official British as well as of Batswana resistance to the transfer of the Protectorate to South Africa, as originally envisioned in the South Africa Act. In addition, transferring the capital would provide African politicians and officials with easier access to central administrators and facilitate their training for higher positions.[49] By 1956 the authorities in Mafikeng decided to move the meetings of the two (African and European) Advisory Councils from the Imperial Reserve to Lobatse.[50]

Anthony Sillery indicated that, despite the expense in doing so, the British government should move the Imperial Reserve over into the BP. In his view, the move would have "obvious economic and administrative advantages," but the practical problem would be to choose a spot in the Protectorate that offered "convenient position, good communications, [and] plentiful water."[51] The site, then, would be near the country's railway axis, along which ran the principal road and the main telecommunications line. If the site were close to the railway, it would be within reach of four-fifths of the people of the BP.[52] At one time Lobatse and Mahalapye, both of which are located along the railway line, were considered as possible relocation sites.[53]

In 1961 the resident commissioner asked his staff to recommend sites for the new capital. They considered nine different locations in the BP and used Sillery's criterion of available water supplies. They also looked for a consensus between whites and Africans in the territory, proximity to centers of population in the BP, balance between the northern and southern portions of the country, and ample room for growth.[54] This committee of experts selected Gaborone (spelled Gaberones until 1968[55]) and reported their findings in a White Paper to the Legislative Council, which superseded the segregated councils and the Joint Advisory Council linking the two.[56]

With the Bamangwato the key voting group in the choice of Gaborone over Francistown,[57] the Legislative Council concurred without dissent.[58] The selected site had ample room for expansion because it included Crown land, thus meeting the expansion criterion. It also enveloped the white farming block (the Gaborone block) and the African reserve of the Batlokwa, one of the eight principal ethnic units in the BP. Being the smallest of the eight units, the Batlokwa were in no position to threaten any of the larger groups. Thus the selection of Gaborone meant there was an acceptable balance in terms of the criteria of ethnic arithmetic, north-south interests, and white-African race relations.[59]

Citing expense, the imperial government had long opposed relocating the capital from Mafikeng to Gaborone. Yet the members of the European Advisory Council persisted because moving from Mafikeng into the BP would have visible economic benefits for those engaged in wholesale and retail trade and other private sector economic activity,[60] which presumably would shift away from Mafikeng into the BP.[61] British authorities sold the Imperial Reserve to the South African government for R 0.42 million, using these funds to defray the cost of building the new capital at Gaborone.[62]

THE SOUTH AFRICAN EXPATRIATES

One recurring theme in the early administrative history of many British dependencies, including the BP, has been the tendency to curtail colonial expenses and to minimize the burden on the metropolitan taxpayer. The imperial government expected colonies to be economically self-sufficient and provide for their own maintenance.[63] As long as the British believed that the BP would be transferred to the Union as provided for in the 1909 South Africa Act, they could make a case that the UK was underwriting personnel and infrastructural expenses that subsequently would be assumed by the Union.[64] From the British perspective, it might be more economical to hire personnel from South Africa, especially if the white South Africans could be recruited without the additional perquisites (such as home leave to the UK) needed to attract personnel from the metropole.[65]

Although the same arguments about lower overhead costs applied to Southern Rhodesia, the UK expressed little concern about the employment of white Southern Rhodesians in the BP civil service, perhaps because Southern Rhodesian territorial ambitions regarding the BP were smaller than the South African ones. Southern Rhodesian ambitions, moreover, were much less damaging to British economic and strategic interests than were those of the more militant Afrikaner nationalists.

The Southern Rhodesian component of the BP civil service also points to a related and practical research question: how does one define a South African in this administrative context? The BP staff lists, which are public documents, indicate the employee's date of birth, salary, and the dates of his or her first appointment to the BP, to his or her present office, and to the BP pensionable establishment. Only personnel records include the place of birth of any given employee. The Botswana National Archives staff had privileged access to individual personnel records, which necessarily constrained the depth and breadth of my research.[66]

At the outset, I defined a South African employee as one born in South Africa, even though the employee might have exchanged his or her South African citizenship for a British one or enjoyed the status of dual citizenship (UK and SA). The obverse could be true as well; a South African could be born in the UK and carry SA and UK passports. The place of birth criterion thus is not a perfect indicator of nationality, but it was the only one available to me.[67]

Next, I assumed that salary levels were commensurate with levels of authority and responsibility, so that those with higher salaries enjoyed greater responsibility and status within the establishment. This assumption allowed me to examine the hierarchy of civil service employment. Presumably, the interest in, and anxiety about, South Africans in the civil service would be greater if they had monopolized the higher echelons of the civil service.

I scrutinized the staff levels at approximately ten-year intervals, beginning in 1945 and ending in 1964, which indicated trends within the BP civil service during the two decades leading up to independence, the years when Afrikaner nationalism flourished in South Africa and when apartheid was institutionalized. This period also marked the end of the Commonwealth connection for South Africa. Although I made personnel and institutional comparisons over this period, I encountered two difficulties. First, some personnel files were destroyed or not available, which meant that all the relevant South African civil servants could not be identified. Specifically, as suggested in Table 6.1 below, I found the gaps much more serious in the early period.

Table 6.1 - Availability of Data

Year	Total Selected	Data Available	Percentage Available
1945	62	36	58%
1955	95	80	84%
1964	152	131	86%

Published sources for tables 6.1 to 6.6:

For 1945:   BP, Staff List, 1 April 1945 (s.l.: n.p., n.d.), 2–23 (tables I–XIII).

For 1955:   BP, Senior Service Staff List, 1 April 1955 (s.l.: n.p., n.d.), 1–68 (tables I–XVIII).

For 1964:   BP, Staff List, Scale A/P and T/E Officers, 1 April 1964 (s.l.: n.p., n.d.), 1–122.

Second, as indicated in Table 6.2 below, the functional organization of the civil service shifted from 1945 to 1964, with more divisions in the latter years. This meant that I could follow trends in employment by sector only when the same organization was found in subsequent staff lists.

My initial purpose was to discover whether the South Africans were at the commanding heights of the BP administration. To do so, I limited myself to the top quartile of the civil service as determined by salary. I arranged the top quartile in descending order by salary, in ranges of £100 (for 1945 and 1955) or R 500 (in 1964). The totals in Tables 6.3, 6.4, and 6.5 indicate that the number of civil servants in each of the salary ranges was not uniform. Furthermore, the number

Table 6.2 - Departmental Distribution of South African Nationals

Department	1945	1955	1964
Agriculture	2	2	2
District Administration	7	4	3
Education	0	2	7
Finance	NA	NA	3
Game	NA	NA	1
Geological Survey	0	1	3
Medical	1	3	4
Police	2	5	8
Posts and Telegraphs	0	2	4
Public Works	0	4	8
Secretariat	1	3	NA
Township Works and Communications	NA	NA	1
Treasury	2	1	3
Tribal Affairs and Social Services	NA	NA	1
Tsetse Fly Control	NA	NA	1
Veterinary	4	7	7
Total	19	34	56

NA not applicable

Table 6.3 - 1945 Staff List Nationalities

Level	Salary Range (in Pounds Sterling)	Born in United Kingdom	Born in British Empire Common-wealth	Born in South Africa	File Destroyed	No File	Total
1	1,000 or more	3	0	2	0	3	8
2	900–999	1	0	1	1	1	4
3	800–899	2	1	3	0	0	6
4	700–799	3	0	1	1	1	6
5	600–699	0	1	3	2	4	10
6	500–599	4	2	9	2	11	28
Total		13	4	19	6	20	62

Table 6.4 - 1955 Staff List Nationalities

Level	Salary Range (in Pounds Sterling)	Born in United Kingdom	Born in British Empire Common-wealth	Born in South Africa	File Destroyed	No File	Total
1	1,500 or more	4	1	1	0	2	8
2	1,400–1,499	3	0	5	0	0	8
3	1,300–1,399	6	1	2	1	0	10
4	1,200–1,299	2	1	3	1	0	7
5	1,100–1,199	7	1	6	0	2	16
6	1,000–1,099	9	0	3	1	2	15
7	900–999	4	1	7	0	1	13
8	800–899	6	0	7	3	2	18
Total		41	5	34	6	9	95

Table 6.5 - 1964 Staff List Nationalities

Level	Salary Range (in Pounds Sterling)	Born in United Kingdom	Born in British Empire Commonwealth	Born in South Africa	Born Elsewhere	File Destroyed	No File	Total
1	6,000 or more	3	0	0	0	0	1	4
2	5,500–5,999	6	0	5	0	0	3	14
3	5,000–5,499	0	0	4	0	0	0	4
4	4,500–4,999	10	2	6	0	0	0	18
5	4,000–4,499	18	1	9	5	I	9	43
6	3,500–3,999	9	1	12	0	2	3	27
7	3,000–3,499	18	2	20	0	1	1	42
Total		64	6	56	5	4	17	152

Table 6.6 - The Top Quartile

Year	Total in Staff List	Total Selected	Percentage Selected
1945	251	62	25%
1955	352	95	27%
1964	621	152	24%
Total	1224	309	25%

of civil servants in the sequence of salary ranges did not always increase, range by range, as one descended the salary scale. There was, nevertheless, an approximate pyramid based on salary levels.

Bearing in mind the incompleteness of the data (see Table 6.1), the absolute number of South Africans in the top quartile of the BP civil service rose from nineteen in 1945 to fifty-six in 1964. The numbers increased from nineteen to fifty-six during this period. During that same time, however, the establishment's size, and therefore of the top quartile, more than doubled (Table 6.6). As a percentage of the top quartile, the South Africans dropped from 53 percent (nineteen out of thirty-six persons for whom I have nationality data) in 1945 (Tables 6.1 and 6.3) to 43 percent (fifty-six out of 131 persons for whom I have nationality data) in 1964 (Tables 6.1 and 6.5).

This raised the question of whether there was a corresponding decrease of South Africans in the upper reaches of the BP civil service. Although an unequal number of salary ranges in the nationality table made the comparisons approximate, there was a decline in absolute numbers of South Africans in the highest salary level from two in 1945 (Table 6.3) to none in 1964 (Table 6.5). At the next salary level there was an increase from one in 1945 (Table 6.3) to five in 1964 (Table 6.5). This same pattern of increase from 1945 to 1964 held for the third level as well. When percentages were used for the first three levels, the South African proportion declined in the highest level from 40 percent to zero percent in the first level and from 50 percent to 45 percent in the second level; but it jumped from 50 percent to 100 percent at the third level.

In the lowest three salary levels of the top quartile from 1945 to 1964, there was some evidence of a decline in the percentage of South African nationals. At the very lowest level (the sixth in 1945 and the seventh in 1964), the South African proportion fell from 60 percent (nine out of fifteen) in 1945 (Table 6.3) to 50 percent (twenty out of forty) in 1964 (Table 6.5). A much more marked drop occurred at the next lowest level (the fifth in 1945 and sixth in 1964) from 75 percent (three out of four) in 1945 to 54 percent (twelve out of twenty-two) in 1964. Moving up one more level on the salary scale (the fourth in 1945 and the fifth in 1964) showed a very slight increase from 25 percent (one out of four) in 1945 to 27 percent (nine out of thirty-three) in 1964.

Thus the percentage of South Africans in the top quartile of the BP civil service declined from 1945 to 1964, with the sharpest decline coming at the highest salary level and rather marked at the two lowest salary levels. A very small drop at the second salary level coincided with a very large increase at the third salary level. At the fourth (1945) and fifth (1964) levels there was a tiny jump. Although the absolute numbers of South Africans in the top quartile of the BP civil service grew during this period as did the size of the quartile, the South African percentage fell at the top and bottom, but increased at the middle, of this quartile. The South Africans' grip on the commanding heights of the civil service, in other words, was diminished.

Regarding the functional distribution of the South Africans, their specialties would have obvious implications for localization planning and costs. The most obvious change from 1945 to 1964 (Table 6.2) was a decline in the number of South Africans in the district administration, the core of the British system of colonial governance where the elite were generalist administrators. The next largest group of South Africans in 1945, those in the veterinary service, increased their numbers in 1955 and remained constant thereafter. Similarly, the South Africans also clustered in the BP's medical service, increasing in numbers over this period. They were also well represented in other technical areas such as posts and telegraphs, public works, and the geological survey, along with business-oriented divisions such as the treasury and finance divisions. South Africans also contributed sizable numbers to the police force and to the area of education.

Overall, the South African presence was most visible in those sectors where university scientific and professional credentials were needed for entry-level positions: geologists, engineers, veterinarians, and physicians. In addition, the South Africans increased their numbers in the education department and police department. A careful analysis of these two critical departments for 1964 shows that (judging from names alone) two of the seven South Africans in the education department were black South Africans. In addition, there were two Britons and two BP-born Batswana in that department, both of whom later became foreign ministers of Botswana. In the educational field, the director of education was South African-born and his deputy was British-born. The South African connection could have been explained in large measure in terms of the use of South African, rather than British, educational models for much of the colonial period.[68]

As for the police, the department included five Britons in addition to the eight South Africans. Even though the commissioner of police was British, his second-in-command was South African. British authorities attempted to isolate the South African policemen in terms of access to sensitive information, especially about refugees, fearing that the South African and Southern Rhodesian police had unwarranted access to those members of the BP police force who were sympathetic to the concerns of these two white-ruled regimes.[69]

Little published data exist regarding the Batswana reaction to white South African civil servants. During a discussion in the African Advisory Council—which represented the Africans in the BP—on the matter of the color bar in the territory, Councillor Sefhako Pilane of the Bakgatla hinted that "the Dutch people" from South Africa—the Afrikaners—in the BP civil service might leave something to be desired.[70] Insofar as the white South Africans, as a group or as individuals, acted in a racist fashion (as defined by the Batswana) then they were unwelcome. South Africans did not hold a monopoly on such behavior, however.

A former colonial officer who became a high-ranking administrator in Botswana, H.C.L. Hermans, noted that the South Africans in the BP civil service were among the best and among the worst, with a number of them concerned about harmonious race relations.[71] According to one retired resident commissioner of the BP, South Africans in the upper reaches of the BP administration during the 1934–1960 period held attitudes which were as liberal as those of their British counterparts.[72] The BP civil service utilized a system of emoluments that Batswana regarded as racist,[73] and their African civil service association voiced their concerns about the racially related system of remuneration.[74] In the period immediately before independence, a number of white South African expatriates thought that they were being economically discriminated against by the British government[75] and decided to leave the civil service.[76]

EXPATRIATES IN BOTSWANA

Q. Neil Parsons has argued[77] that the term *expatriate* should be restricted to those persons who left their country of nationality for employment in Botswana for a period of two to three years and who received additional financial rewards from their home government as an inducement to take up this overseas employment. He suggested that the first Colonial Administrative Service (CAS) officer to be posted to Botswana, Sir Edwin Arrowsmith in 1933, could be so described.[78] In Parsons's view, those recruited locally who were not CAS types would not be regarded as expatriates. In this study, however, I have used a less restricted interpretation than Parsons and treated those who were not born in the BP and who were not nationals of the BP as expatriates.[79] Thus I have regarded the British, the South Africans, and nationals of southern African states or territories other than the BP as expatriates. At some point (retirement or earlier) they would be expected to return to their legal domicile outside the BP. Some expatriates became citizens of Botswana. The position of the expatriate employee in post-colonial Botswana was subject to negotiation between the donor government and the government in Gaborone.[80]

During the Anglo–South African negotiations over the possible transfer of the HCT to South Africa in the last half of the 1930s, British authorities indicated their interest in using South African technical experts—on loan from the Union to the BP—on a short-term basis.[81] South African expatriates at this time were an integral and widely accepted part of the BP civil service. The notion of short-term technical personnel aid was a vital part of functional cooperation between South Africa and the UK. Such cooperation would create a climate of goodwill between the two states and, in due course, facilitate the transfer. Good works would lead to favorable attitudes.[82] This was essentially an exercise in what students of international organization have termed functionalism.

During the Protectorate era, the British extended the search for experts beyond southern Africa and the UK. They called upon faculty members in the United States to serve on two separate commissions, one to investigate the prospects for ranching in the western part of the BP[83] and the other to assess the economic performance and needs of all three HCT.[84]

Prior to independence, the American consul at Mbabane, Swaziland, initially was responsible for forging links with the BP, but by April 1966 the American government appointed its first consul and opened its consulate in Gaborone.[85] The previous October, the UK had granted the US and the Norwegian governments permission to establish consular links with the BP.[86] About fifty years earlier, the British had granted Belgium similar rights, on a nonresident basis, with respect to the three HCT.[87] This put the United States in a strong position not only to receive but also to evaluate requests for, and offers of, American public and private sector aid. In addition, twenty-seven UN technical advisers had been at work in the BP as early as 1963.[88]

Even before granting self-government to the BP in 1965, the imperial government implemented a government localization policy that, intended or not, eventually reduced the size of the South African contingent in the BP civil service.[89] In 1962 BP authorities enumerated a wide range of positions that would be closed to those who were not locals. Those born outside the BP would still be considered locals if their parents were BP residents.[90] In a more positive manner, the UK provided the BP administration with a subsidy to acquire or retain certain expatriates with needed skills.[91]

Expatriates whose salaries were subsidized were termed designated officers, usually recruited in London, while the nondesignated ones tended to be South Africans. It was cheaper for the BP authorities to hire designated expatriates when and where required rather than nondesignated ones because of the British subsidy provided to the BP exchequer for designated expatriates. South African civil servants often resigned under these circumstances.[92]

By the time of independence in 1966, other expatriates were replacing the South African civil servants. This was possible in part because of the willingness of private and public organizations to provide volunteers, some of whom had fairly high level skills. Probably the best known group of volunteers is the American Peace

Corps, but there are others from Canada, Denmark, Germany, the Netherlands, Norway, Sweden, and the United Kingdom, as well as United Nations volunteers.[93]

In particular, the Peace Corps has provided a number of lawyers. As early as 1961, Syracuse University arranged for lawyers and economists to be sent to Botswana as district officers under the Africa Public Service Fellowship Program.[94] The resident commissioner of the BP was extremely impressed with the quality of the Americans who served in the BP under the auspices of that program and thought they compared very favorably to the best British Colonial Service District Officers.[95] Syracuse University also trained the initial group of Peace Corps Volunteers scheduled to serve in Botswana.[96]

Although not all of these volunteers served in the highest echelons, they provided a youthful pool of talent in the teaching and development fields for Botswana[97] while its secondary schools turned out some of those who, as university graduates, localized the civil service. While the utilization of volunteers was only a temporary arrangement. it contributed to the reduction of the South African presence in the civil service and probably cost far less than the employment of expatriates on contract.

The regular contract expatriates recruited by the government of Botswana provided additional personnel. In a few cases, particularly involving African teachers from South Africa, expatriates became citizens and thus were counted among the citizens in the civil service.[98] The need for expatriates in the higher reaches of the civil service, particularly in the professional and technical branches, has continued,[99] and the localization issue has tended to be subordinated to economic development.[100] This expansion has generated a need for an even larger civil service establishment, resulting in a shortfall not only in posts filled by expatriates but also in vacant posts.[101] The national rather than the district level of government tended to get the well-qualified citizens.[102]

Eventually, Botswana citizens will displace any remaining South Africans who have not become naturalized Botswana citizens. The rate of localization was much slower at levels requiring advanced academic or professional credentials, and the government of Botswana did not expect to have a thoroughly indigenous civil service in the immediate future. Mentz and Picard recently estimated that complete localization will not be possible in this century, making Botswana dependent upon outside, extraregional assistance in the short run.[103] Lately it has been turning to Asian and African states for skilled personnel, who are less expensive than their North Atlantic counterparts.[104] Botswana has been able to attract talented African professionals from other parts of the region and continent.[105]

Supplementing the administrative talents furnished by volunteers and contract expatriates, private and public sector training has been available from overseas for Batswana civil servants or prospective civil servants on either an institutionalized or ad hoc basis. One obvious source of external assistance is the UN family of organizations, which had operated in the territory since before independence. The UN, often working in conjunction with national donors, provided assistance in such fields as instructor training in vocational fields with the National Center for Vocational Training.[106] In addition, the three former HCT, the Canadian and Norwegian aid agencies, and the Ford Foundation cooperated to establish the Institute of Development Management in Gaborone.[107] The Ford Foundation, an example of a transnational organization,[108] provided two advisers to assist in civil service management matters.[109]

Such activities, which need not be exhaustively documented, are intended to develop Botswana's potential for self-sustained growth in administrative personnel and management skill. These must be linked to the educational and scientific efforts. But for the time being, global expatriates are needed to fill gaps in the civil service caused by the departure of the South Africans. Botswana has moved beyond southern Africa and relies upon the developed world and its national, international, and transnational organizations. Botswana fortunately lost very few of its highly educated administrators to international organizations, which have very attractive terms of remuneration compared with that available in Botswana.[110] In some instances educated nationals did not return to Botswana following their training and instead sought employment in South Africa or in the former South African homelands, such as Bophuthatswana, where salaries were higher than in Botswana. Unfortunately, there are few hard, systematic data about such an exodus of skilled Batswana.[111]

The management of BP, particularly prior to the Pim Report of 1933, was in the hands of South African nationals. This situation developed in part because the recruitment of locals was less expensive than importing CAS talent from London or from the remainder of the British colonial empire. At a time when the transfer of the HCT to the Union was a distinct possibility, administration was a significant domain of low politics. Since that time, the South Africans have continued to stress, as part of their public relations campaign aimed at both southern African states and the West, that they are knowledgeable about conditions in southern Africa. This theme of South African foreign policy occurs most frequently in the technical fields, which includes public administration. To the extent that the incorporation of the BP into South Africa was part of the agenda of high politics, then the low politics of administrative and technical personnel was a logical consequence of a proposed territorial merger. The retention of Mafikeng as an extraterritorial administrative headquarters epitomized the interplay between high and low politics. It also reflected an element of economizing on expenses, for the move to Gaborone was costly. Administrative arrangements in London, linking the supervision of BP colonial policy in the CRO rather than in the CO, was yet another reflection of the administrative low politics nexus between South Africa and the BP. In the independence era, there was a distinct move away from the South African low politics link and a search for a wider range of suppliers, particularly in the Third World, to spread the net of dependence and to economize on personnel costs. Patrick P. Molutsi of the University of Botswana has estimated that roughly 10 percent of all public service employees are expatriates.[112] Any antagonism to these foreign managers and experts was muted by Botswana's exceptional economic growth, argued public administration scholars Johannes C.N. Mentz and Louis A. Picard. They believe that the subject of localization has become depoliticized.[113]

CHAPTER SEVEN

Transportation, Tourism, and Communications

REGIONAL ROADS

This chapter deals with road, railway, and air transportation and the closely related tourism and communications sectors that rely upon and supplement Botswana's transportation network, concentrating on the manner in which Batswana and foreigners travel across the nation's borders and communicate with one another and investigating how foreigners might be attracted to visit Botswana. Transportation and communication policies are an integral part of the network of low politics involved in the relationship between Botswana and South Africa and with its other three neighbors. Transportation is vital to South Africa in terms of what J.G.H. Loubser, former manager of the South African Railways, called "transport diplomacy."[1] Others, less bland, have used the phrase "transport weapon.[2]

By the end of the British protectorate, the nation had a mere twelve miles of tarred roads,[3] all located in Francistown, Gaborone, and Lobatse.[4] Beginning in 1964, thanks to a loan from the International Development Association, the BP authorized the building of a road linking the commercial center of Francistown to Maun in the northwest.[5] The major road, however, ran from Francistown in the north to Lobatse in the south parallel to the railroad. This north–south trunk road made economic and geographic sense, considering that only one-fifth of the population resides more than fifty miles from that line of rail.[6] At independence, Botswana acquired a meager roadway network primarily oriented as a distribution center linking the villages to the railway trunk line.[7] The national government maintained 2,657 of the 4,996 miles of roads that Botswana had at independence. The district authorities assumed responsibility for the other 2,339 miles.[8] By 1985 the road network had grown to 8,880 miles, 4,968 miles of which are paved.[9]

After independence, Botswana began to develop an international road network linking it to its northern neighbor, Zambia. The Botswana portion of the road between Botswana and Zambia, sometimes termed the Botzam road, opened for traffic in January 1977.[10] Providing a direct passage to Zambia, this road avoided Southern Rhodesian territory. Running between the railheads of Francistown in Botswana, and Livingstone in Zambia, by way of Nata and the Kazungula ferry, the road enabled freight to be hauled directly to Zambia rather than by rail via Bulawayo and the Victoria Falls. It was a strategic route[11] in case either Botswana's or Zambia's borders with Southern Rhodesia were closed, as happened to the Zambian–Southern Rhodesia border from 1973 until 1978.[12] The $19 million, 155-mile tarred road from Nata to Kazungula was financed by the United States, Norway, and the European Economic Community.[13]

A little-publicized aspect of this international road project was a spur linking Ngoma in the Namibian Caprivi Strip with Kazungula. This forty-mile east-west couple enabled the SADF, which had a base at Katima Mulilo, to secure access to Southern Rhodesia via the bridge across the Chobe River at Ngoma. The Ngoma–Kazungula road was constructed at the request of the United States to secure South African acquiescence in building the Nata–Kazungula trunk road linking Botswana with Zambia. The Botswana government found the road to Ngoma to be politically disconcerting.[14]

Intended to diminish Botswana's vulnerability to economic pressure from its white-ruled neighbors, the Botzam road also stimulated the economic growth of the northeastern part of the country.[15] In 1989 construction began on another international road system linking Jwaneng, site of Botswana's newest diamond mine, with Mamuno, a town bordering on Namibia.[16] The Namibian component of this trans-Kalahari highway involved the building of about 62 miles of road from east of Gobabis to the border,[17] while the Botswana section extended 447 miles from Mamuno to Jwaneng.[18]

Botswana depends upon South African trucking firms for its road haulage needs,[19] but it now requires work permits of expatriate truck drivers operating vehicles with a Botswanan registry.[20] South African authorities gave preference to their own nationals, allowing Botswana's drivers to operate only in those areas of South Africa not covered by the South African Transport Services (SATS, now called Transnet).[21] Furthermore, South African firms have a corner on the freight-forwarding business.[22] So far, there has been no bilateral agreement to regulate trucking between Botswana and South Africa.[23] The authorities in Gaborone want to create further opportunities for the employment of their own nationals in this sector of the economy,[24] and they are concerned about road repair costs involved because of heavy South African truck traffic between Zeerust in the south and Kazungula in the north.[25]

REGIONAL RAILWAY SYSTEMS

Botswana's principal road artery is the north-south one running parallel to the 398 miles of rail line joining Botswana to South Africa and to Zimbabwe.[26] The railway, rather than the highways, is vital for the transportation of goods. About three-fourths of the freight that leaves or arrives in Botswana travels by railroad, with most of the remainder traveling by road rather than by aircraft.[27] Air freight, however, is used for the export of diamonds.[28]

Built under the aegis of the BSAC from 1896 to 1897[29] and vital to foreign trade, the railway system was part of the National Railways of Zimbabwe, formerly Rhodesia Railways.[30] To ship its goods to the Indian Ocean ports of Durban, Beira, or Maputo, landlocked Botswana must transit South Africa or Zimbabwe or Mozambique; thus it cannot completely control the entire route to the sea, no matter what the political or racial nature of the neighboring regimes might be.

From 1949 to 1963, BP representatives served on the board of the Rhodesia Railways, which became a Southern Rhodesian government entity in 1949.[31] The land on which the railroad was erected belonged to the BP,[32] and the Rhodesia Railways paid royalties and wayleave for its use.[33] Yet the BP was not involved in the daily operations of the line connecting Bulawayo with Mafikeng. From 1959 until the day before Botswana became independent in 1966, the South African Railways acted as a subcontractor for the Rhodesia Railways and assumed responsibility for the southern portion of the line, with Mahalapye being the point of division between the two railways.[34]

No permanent repair workshops existed in BP; neither were there any marshaling yards for making up freight trains.[35] With no locomotives, freight cars, passenger cars, or other rolling stock, the BP had little equity in the system.[36] The Batswana, in turn, held no significant technical or managerial posts in the railway.[37] Localization would open up opportunities for skilled Batswana to assume such positions. Some progress has already been made in the training of locomotive drivers,[38] but localization at the managerial level will take longer.[39]

When Southern Rhodesia unilaterally declared its independence in 1965, the Botswana government assured Southern Rhodesia that it would not interfere with the railway line.[40] As the authorities in Gaborone implied in their *note verbale* of 27 February 1967 to the UN, Southern Rhodesian ownership and management of this economic lifeline meant that Botswana was Southern Rhodesia's hostage. Had Botswana applied any but the most nominal economic sanctions against the Smith regime, Southern Rhodesia undoubtedly would have retaliated by closing the Botswana line after linking the Southern Rhodesian and South African railway systems at Beitbridge, just inside Southern Rhodesia.[41]

"Any substantial curtailment in the operation of the railway through Botswana," observed the Gaborone authorities, "would contribute an economic blow which would be so serious that Botswana could never recover without the injection of substantial additional aid in the form of providing capital and technical assistance."[42] On 3 February 1967, Prime Minister Ian Smith announced that Parliament had tabled the Beitbridge Commission Report. He noted that there were no immediate plans to build the connecting rail link.[43]

By early September 1974, the Rhodesia Railways completed the Beitbridge–Rutenga link with the Transvaal, allowing the Smith regime to bypass Botswana.[44] Later that month, President Khama announced that Botswana would consider assuming control of the Botswana portion of the Rhodesia Railways.[45] Canadian railway experts explored the ramifications and calculated the costs of Botswana's proposed nationalization.[46] By 1977 Botswana began to localize railway personnel, with Malawi and Kenya handling some of the staff training.[47] The price tag for the nationalization was set at approximately £27 million for the rolling stock, plus the salaries of expatriates whose services might be required as well as any compensation for fixed assets that might have to be paid for as part of the nationalization.[48] By 1978 the Khama government began to acquire its own rolling stock from South Africa,[49] although it took much longer to add diesel-electric locomotives to the inventory.[50] Botswana received assistance from Sweden,[51] Denmark,[52] the People's Republic of China,[53] and Canada[54] to facilitate the takeover of the Botswana portion of the National Railways of Zimbabwe, which was planned for 1 January 1987.[55]

Shortly before the 1987 transfer date, neighboring Bophuthatswana, which controlled the rail line between South Africa and Botswana, challenged Botswana. The government insisted that the locomotive crews from Botswana or Zimbabwe needed visas to traverse fourteen miles before exchanging places with the SATS (now termed Spoornet) crews at Mafikeng. Neither the Gaborone nor Harare authorities acceded to the visa requirement which, in their view, was a gambit to win the diplomatic recognition denied to Bophuthatswana since South Africa granted it independence in 1977.[56] The Mangope regime in Boputhatswana sought to be included in the arrangements between the South African Railways and the Botswana Railways once the latter assumed the rights and responsibilities of the National Railways of Zimbabwe.[57] The matter was resolved by bilateral arrangements between South Africa and Botswana, which permitted the South African locomotive crews to assume control of the trains headed south at Rakhuna Halt,[58] six miles inside Botswanan territory.[59]

This encounter with Pretoria regarding the international status of the Mmbatho regime illustrates graphically how low politics can shade into high politics. Transport diplomacy subsumed the high politics of international recognition of one of the South African homelands. The Botswana government proceeded with the takeover arrangements, and Botswana Railways completed the task in March 1989. Botswana paid P 83 million for the assets of the National Railways of Zimbabwe, including the land, the track, telecommunications and signaling equipment, bridges, and stations. Botswana did not, however, purchase the rolling stock of the National Railways of Zimbabwe,[60] instead renting locomotives[61] and freight cars from Spoornet.[62]

Ever since the Southern Rhodesian unilateral declaration of independence, Botswana officials understood the vulnerability of the rail line connecting Botswana to the sea via South Africa and Southern Rhodesia. Despite Southern Rhodesian armed intrusions into Botswana, neither Southern Rhodesian military nor clandestine commando units sabotaged the Rhodesia Railways line inside Botswana. The only economic target the elite Southern Rhodesian Special Air Service attacked was the ferry at Kazungula, which it destroyed in April 1979.[63] Thus South Africa made only sparing use of its transport weapon against Botswana. On one occasion, though, South Africa reportedly withheld refrigerated freight cars from Botswana to express its displeasure with Botswana's anti–South African stance at the UN.[64]

Botswana's experience with limited economic sanctions against Southern Rhodesia and with dependence upon South Africa for its petroleum supplies pointed to the importance of developing petroleum reserves for its vehicles and diesel-electric locomotives.[65] With West German[66] and Arab[67] help in the late 1970s, Botswana developed its strategic petroleum reserve at Gaborone and Francistown, a reserve that could serve as a hedge against economic counter-sanctions imposed by South Africa.[68] Botswana feared that South Africa might attempt to pass on at least some of the adverse effects of international oil sanctions, such as the one imposed by several Arab states in 1973, to its African-ruled, landlocked neighbors.[69] In 1980–81 South Africa held up the delivery of the oil for the strategic reserve, an indication of its use of economic leverage against Botswana.[70] Botswana, in turn, has received EEC[71] and Canadian financial backing in its oil prospecting endeavors, but so far the search has not been rewarding.[72]

THE INTERNATIONAL AIRLINE SYSTEM

The principal flying operation in the Protectorate was undertaken by the Witwatersrand Native Labor Association (WNLA), the South African mine labor recruiting organization,[73] which had its own airport at Francistown.[74] The Botswana government purchased that airport in 1977, and improved its facilities.[75] Shortly after the Second World War, the Southern Rhodesian carrier, Central African Airways, initiated air service linking Bulawayo to Francistown and Maun.[76] A commercial loss, it was quickly terminated.[77] In the early 1960s, BP authorities were responsible for the upkeep of twenty-eight airfields and landing strips used to handle freight and passengers arriving from South Africa, the Central African Federation, South West Africa, Basutoland, Swaziland, and Tanganyika. Charter flights and air mail were available.[78]

By 1965 Bechuanaland National Airways—aided by a government grant—replaced privately owned Bechuanaland Airways, considerably improving commercial aviation. This subsidized airline operated as a domestic and foreign carrier, with flights to Zambia, Southern Rhodesia, and South Africa.[79] Financial setbacks to the Botswana National Airways and to its successor, Botswana Airways Corporation Ltd., caused organizational changes reflecting the economics of the industry and the inexperience of the management. In 1972 Air Botswana (Pty.) Limited was established,[80] with Air Botswana Holdings handling the ownership and leasing arrangements for the aircraft and serving as the holding company for Air Botswana.[81] The national airline functioned as a subsidiary of the larger Botswana Development Corporation,[82] but that link was severed in 1988 when Air Botswana achieved the status of a parastatal body[83] under the jurisdiction of the Ministry of Works and Communications.[84] The government purchased both Air Botswana and Air Botswana Holdings in 1988.[85]

Air Botswana (Pty.) Ltd. functioned as a contractor for various flight services, which were subcontracted to South African Protea Airways, while Air Botswana was responsible for ticketing flights on

Zambia Airways, South African Airways, and British Overseas Airways Corporation (now British Airways).[86] British Airways got the contract to manage Air Botswana.[87] Having no fleet of its own, Air Botswana undertook no major aircraft maintenance within the country.[88] Recently, Air Botswana has tried to develop not only its local maintenance capabilities[89] but also to increase the number of Batswana pilots.[90]

The Khama government appreciated the significance of airline links between Botswana and the outside world, anticipating the need for an international airport at Gaborone. The initial economic plan called for the necessary pre-investment survey for such an airport.[91] By 1969 the private firm of Sir Alexander Gibb and Partners completed a feasibility study, followed by an airport plan in 1974. Additional preliminary studies and engineering drafts followed in 1977, with the planning work underwritten by a loan from the African Development Bank, which quickened the pace. Several funding organizations sent officials to Botswana to evaluate the proposed international airport, while the National Assembly passed the necessary loan legislation in 1978 and 1980.[92]

When the National Assembly considered the project in 1978, future minister of external affairs Gaositwe K.T. Chiepe proclaimed the time was opportune to construct an international airport and pointed to what she thought was the circular reasoning that delayed the project: insufficient international traffic to justify building such an airport and, conversely, the fact that such traffic was not possible without this kind of airport.[93] Even though constructing such an airport would require a leap of faith, backbench and opposition MPs as well as cabinet ministers accepted the need, emphasizing Botswana's landlocked position. They viewed the new airport as a strategic project, along with the Botzam road, and placed the construction within the framework of economic disengagement from minority-ruled southern Africa.[94] Future vice-president L. M. Seretse termed it a means "to disengage from the dependence on countries around us who do not hold out any promising future for us."[95]

Further, the MPs—particularly those who had become seasoned travelers—emphasized the delays and backtracking necessary when transiting Jan Smuts Airport in Johannesburg, implying that somehow those flying out of and into Botswana could bypass Jan Smuts Airport, saving time and money.[96] Then there was the political aspect of being able to travel outside the region if one were a persona non grata with the South African and Southern Rhodesian regimes. Here the presumption was that both regimes acted as passenger turnstiles and would not issue transit visas to passengers holding valid round-trip airplane tickets to points outside the immediate region. Clearly there was the implied hope that all passengers could enter and exit from Botswana without using the South African or Southern Rhodesian corridor.[97]

Construction of the P 57 million airport seven miles outside Gaborone began in April 1982. On 10 December 1984, the Seretse Khama Airport was open for traffic,[98] handling flights from Lusaka, Harare, Matsapha (Swaziland), and Johannesburg.[99] The airport and the expanding air traffic pattern have grown to the extent that Air Botswana flew to all ten SADCC states and twenty different locations by 1991.[100] Lesotho Airways, Zambia Airways, Kenya Airways, Air Tanzania, Air Zimbabwe, and Air Malawi use this airport, along with South African Airways, British Airways (which took over British Caledonian, which was awarded the route from Gatwick to Gaborone),[101] and UTA, the French airline which began its weekly flights to Paris via Luanda in November 1989.[102] Just prior to its independence in 1990, Air Botswana, in conjunction with Namib Air, began a service to Windhoek via Maun.[103]

At the official opening ceremonies for the Sir Seretse Khama Airport in early 1988, President Masire signified that the government planned to relieve the South Africans of the responsibility for air traffic control operations in Botswana. The president noted the commission of a feasibility study for the transfer of this function of control over Botswana's airspace.[104] The British firm Plessey Radar secured the contract for the development of Botswana's flight information region.[105] This had both military and civilian significance, particularly as the president had protested to the South Africans about the intrusion of South African Air Force into Botswana airspace.[106] South African military aircraft were overflying Botswana en route from the Transvaal to Namibia.[107]

Had international economic sanctions against South Africa been expanded to cover cross-border flights, then the Sir Seretse Khama Airport would have been well positioned to take advantage of such an interruption. Flights originating in Western Europe could have landed at this airport, which is close to the South African border, and the passengers could have traveled by bus to their final South African destinations or to nearby South African airports serviced by commuter aircraft.[108] Conversely, South African passengers could have reversed the route and exited South Africa en route to Western Europe via Botswana.[109] Botswana is thus strategically located and could help to circumvent air passenger sanctions against South Africa, which the Organization of African Unity called for as early as 1963.[110]

The most important and visible role of the aviation sector in

Botswana is the transportation of government officials on official business and providing rapid and efficient access to Botswana for foreign businessmen, foreign tourists, expatriates, and international agency officials[111] who are very sensitive to the timing and convenience of flights.[112] Although the government will construct aircraft maintenance facilities at the Seretse Khama Airport,[113] thus reducing the amount of servicing undertaken at foreign airports, it is not likely that the industry will be labor intensive. Probably the most significant international aspect of this sector of transportation, which caters only to the affluent in Botswana and hence has a small constituency,[114] is in its links with the tourist industry.[115] The link is clearly demonstrated by the construction of a new airport at Kasane, which borders on the Chobe National Park.[116] This project was funded by the European Community.[117]

THE INTERNATIONAL TOURIST INDUSTRY

When a team, cosponsored by the United Nations' Food and Agricultural Organization and the International Union for the Conservation of Nature and Natural Resources, visited the territory in 1962 and applauded the quantity and quality of its wildlife resources, the BP received international recognition.[118] In that same year, the first East African safari organization, Andrew Holmberg Company, began to function in BP.[119] Subsequently the 1965 Porter Mission of the UK Ministry of Overseas Development recommended that the game department of BP, established in 1956,[120] be enlarged to monitor the safari industry, provided funding for this could reasonably be derived from increasing fees for hunting licenses.[121] It also suggested that the Chobe Game Reserve become a tourist site, especially because of its propinquity to the Victoria Falls, which presumably would be the point of entry for the anticipated tourist traffic.[122]

By 1968 the Chobe Game Reserve had become the Chobe National Park,[123] with accommodations at the family-owned Chobe River Hotel (later the Chobe River Lodge) for those interested in viewing game and in sport fishing. The hotel, which opened in 1963, catered to guests who generally were more interested in game viewing than in angling. The Victoria Falls were located sixty miles east of the hotel, but the overland road was crude[124] The private Kazungula ferry, originally built from large drums and utilizing twin outboard motors, was nearby and used to transport the hotel guests until replaced by a much more modern craft.[125]

American big game hunter Harold M. Prowse conducted the first scientific survey of the safari clientele in 1969,[126] and in 1972 the Bureau of Market Research of UNISA sponsored research on tourism and air travel prospects.[127] Prowse noted that the safari industry was sensitive to political stability and turmoil, which had been one of the reasons that the Andrew Holmberg Company (later termed Andrew Holmberg Safaris [Botswana] Ltd.) had wanted to move from East Africa to the then BP.[128]

Prowse saw a great variety among safari clients and tourists, with some interested in hunting expeditions while others preferred game viewing. The safari and tourist industries required appropriate marketing strategies.[129] The Bureau of Market Research study revealed that telecommunications and lodging facilities were not as efficient and attractive as the more affluent traveler needed or wanted, especially in Maun.[130]

Five years after independence, the government established a Department of Tourism,[131] and in 1972 the Central Statistics Office established a Tourist Statistics Unit to collect and monitor tourist data.[132] For political reasons, the government avoided official ties with the South African Tourist Corporation (SATOUR) and the Southern African Tourism Conference (SARTOC),[133] composed of South Africa, Malawi, Mauritius, and Swaziland.[134] The Department of Tourism, however, has bilateral and multilateral links (through SADCC) with the Zambian National Tourist Bureau to facilitate tourist promotions and marketing, particularly for tours covering both nations.[135]

The South African connection is the most significant one in terms of tourist flows, as suggested by the official data for 1989, when roughly 45 percent (309,747 out of 691,041) of the foreign nationals entering Botswana were South African or Namibian citizens. The next largest group came from Zimbabwe and Zambia; they constituted 36 percent (249,283 out of 691,041) and nearly 4 percent (25,241 out of 691,041), respectively. Then came the United Kingdom, Ireland, and the remainder of Europe accounting for nearly 4 percent (25,735 out of 691,041) and 5 per cent (34,340 out of 691,041), respectively, of the foreign visitors to Botswana. Looked at differently, citizens of Botswana's four neighbors accounted for slightly over 84 percent (584,271 out of 691,041) of the foreign arrivals to Botswana in 1989.[136] Some of the tourist flows between South Africa and Botswana involve family visits, especially for the Batswana[137] and for those who live in border areas,[138] and do not represent much economic benefit for Botswana.

As Hanlon observed in his study of southern African regional politics, the South African tourist market is significant and the South African government hopes to keep neighboring states open to their citizens. He has also suggested that Pretoria could gain economic leverage if it throttled the flow of its tourists into neighboring states. In 1983 South African tourists spent P 18 million in the country, an amount that jumped to P 33 million in 1984.[139] In 1984, Botswana's total income from tourism was reported to be P 45 million.[140]

South Africans were attracted in part by what were called the "forbidden fruits"[141] of gambling and prostitution, if the experience of Swaziland and Lesotho with their casinos is any guide.[142] Prostitution concerned members of parliament, who dealt with the matter in more than one debate on the topic introduced by the Opposition BPP.[143]

The multinational Holiday Inn firm petitioned the government to begin casino operations there in 1969. Anticipating that Gaborone would be a growing urban area, but lacking land to expand the President Hotel in the mall, government officials were receptive to the idea of having another elaborate hotel catering to international visitors in Gaborone. Were this second hotel to appeal only to those on vacation or to those on business trips, the cost could not be rapidly amortized. Hence, the idea of a casino was introduced.[144]

The casino is hardly a labor-intensive employer and initially the croupier positions there were held by South African nationals,[145] although they have since been localized.[146] Equally significant, luxury hotels diminish their net earning capacity by consuming a considerable amount of imports from South Africa.[147] In his study of the tourist industry of Botswana commissioned by the Kalahari Conservation Society of Botswana, John D. Fowkes estimated that tourism created slightly more that 1,000 permanent jobs in Botswana, primarily in the Ngamiland and Chobe areas, and ranked fourth (with textiles) as a foreign exchange generator, following diamonds, livestock, and copper-nickel matte.[148] In addition, tourist spending adds an attractive multiplier in Botswana. In 1989, 582,871 visitors spent roughly P 107 million in the country;[149] using the factor of four as the multiplier (which the tourist industry does),[150] then P 428 million coursed through Botswana's economy. Services and sales—automobile rentals, lodging, construction of tourist facilities, gasoline sales, and boating trips—generated these funds, and they helped the rural economy in the northwestern region of Botswana.[151]

Although large numbers of South African tourists visit Botswana, the government of Botswana has opted for a policy of low tourist numbers with high income generation, which will reduce environmental damage to the national parks.[152] Many South African tourists who drive to Botswana do not generate much income there because they bring in most of their own food and supplies in their own all-terrain vehicles.[153] Consequently, on 1 July 1989, the Botswana government raised its daily park entry fee to P 60 and camping fee to P 24 and vehicle fees to P 12 for nonresidents.[154] This was in line with this policy of "high cost, low volume,"[155] keeping the number of nonresident tourists low, expecting that this small clientele would be generous spenders. Such fees would deter all but affluent tourists.[156]

Botswana's representatives have participated in an American travel exposition designed to appeal to North American customers.[157] The European Economic Community, moreover, is furnishing technical assistance in the tourist sector[158] and is underwriting the salary of one adviser to the Department of Tourism.[159] Botswana has sent government representatives and tour operators to the International Tourism Bourse in West Berlin, the World Travel Market in London, and the Travel Trade Workshop in Montreaux.[160] The principal market for Botswana travel advertisement is British; the government undertakes no advertising within the SADCC nations, leaving the initiative to the private sector.[161]

Possibly American, British, Canadian, West European, and Irish tourists who plan vacations in South Africa can be induced to add Botswana to their itinerary[162] or even bypass South Africa for Botswana. Just as political violence adversely affected tourism in the Chobe area during the final days of the war in Zimbabwe,[163] so too could violence, along with economic sanctions, deter overseas tourist travel to South Africa. With the independence of Namibia and the establishment of air service between these two neighbors, there is private sector cooperation in developing tourist packages covering both nations. The new airport at Kasane will facilitate the promotion of tourist packages involving Zimbabwe.[164]

Tourism, one of the components of low politics where quantification is possible and appropriate,[165] can enable Botswana to improve its position of autonomy and reduce its vulnerability, particularly to South Africa. This industry has been closely linked with the private service and investment sectors of the economy[166] and with the public transportation sector, particularly the national scheduled airline, Air Botswana. Tourism, though, depends upon political tranquility[167] and individual security, as demonstrated by the debilitating experience with the Zimbabwean civil war in the Chobe area[168] and with the South African foreign minister's warning in 1990 about the safety of South African visitors to Botswana.[169] Nevertheless, Botswana's central geographical location and political quietude have enabled it to serve as a political innkeeper hosting significant conferences among southern African states and interest groups.[170] Air Botswana now publicizes itself as the premier SADCC airline because it flies to the capital of every SADCC member state.[171]

Botswana's tourist potential, though, is more closely related to the status of wildlife in the nation, as Prowse clearly saw in the 1960s. Because of this link,[172] threats to wildlife can adversely affect tourism. These threats materialize from the ecological conflict between vested cattle interests, which have significant domestic political leverage, and environmental groups such as the Kalahari Conservation Society,[173] Botswana-based and one of the most effective public interest lobbies in the nation.[174] As cattle rangelands are expanding and are being fenced to prevent the spread of animal-borne disease, these fences have changed the migration patterns of wildlife,[175] and the death of such wildlife has resulted in adverse publicity for Botswana.[176] This controversy will detract from Botswana's very favorable tourist image, such as the one created in 1975 by Richard Burton when he remarried Elizabeth Taylor in the Chobe Game Lodge.[177]

REGIONAL TELECOMMUNICATIONS, RADIO, AND PRESS

As noted in Chapter Six, the BP's administrative cadre had more of a South African than a British composition, especially in the communications field during the colonial era. The southern African link extended to the postal service, the telecommunications network, radio broadcasting, and the publishing field. The telecommunications web, in fact, has bound the BP primarily to the communications and publications systems of South Africa and Southern Rhodesia. This inquiry in low politics explores how, and the extent to which, such ties were developed, persist, and in some cases have been severed as Botswana searches for greater autonomy.

Responsibility for the postal and telegraphic services in the BP was divided between the Postmasters-General of South Africa and Southern Rhodesia.[178] Telegraphic services—essentially an adjunct of the Rhodesia Railways—were operated by BP personnel as well as by Southern Rhodesians and South Africans.[179] A limited telephone service also operated near the South African and Southern Rhodesian ends of the rail line, with the South Africans maintaining the southern portion and the Southern Rhodesians the northern portion.[180] The Southern Rhodesian government paid part of the salaries of the personnel in the BP's posts and telegraphs division.[181] By 1957 the BP took charge of its own telecommunications system,[182] and six years later it assumed responsibility for its postal system.[183] The South African authorities also ended their agricultural parcel post system in the HCT in 1963.[184]

The BP (and later Botswana) and South Africa were linked together in the African Postal and Telecommunications Union (APTU) since 1935, along with the other two former HCT, Namibia, Southern Rhodesia, Zaire, Angola, Mozambique, and Malawi. The APTU members belonged to the larger Universal Postal Union and the International Telecommunications Union. South Africa provided the site[185] for and finances of the Bureau of the APTU, and, in the colonial era, made arrangements concerning the enhancement and operation of the telecommunications circuits directly between the BP and South Africa as well as through the British High Commission. Technical cooperation continued through the independence period.[186]

Dating back to 1936, radio broadcasting in the BP was primarily a police and government activity, with the principal operating base at the administrative headquarters in Mafikeng.[187] By 1949 ten radio stations operated within the Protectorate, four of which were owned by WNLA, which permitted the government to use them when necessary.[188] Radio programming was handled in Mafikeng in cooperation with the South African Broadcasting Corporation (SABC), which also supported the small station there (station ZNB).[189] In 1963 a local station in Lobatse began broadcasting in Setswana, and it carried British Broadcasting Corporation (BBC) material.[190] The Lobatse station ZND provided the training needed for the relocation of broadcasting services in the new capital at Gaborone.[191] Its successor, Radio Botswana, broadcasts in both official languages (English and Setswana), for a total of 119 hours a week, and permits no commercial advertisements. The government does not require licenses for radio owners,[192] but earlier, those who owned radios in the BP paid license fees to the SABC.[193] By 1963 South Africa no longer controlled radio matters in the HCT and was not empowered to assign radio frequencies to stations in the HCT. However, the three HCT continued to cooperate with the South African authorities in this matter.[194]

In May 1962 the Johannesburg Afrikaans Sunday newspaper, *Dagbreek en Sondagnuus*, suggested that the inauguration of a broadcasting system in the HCT would be politically significant. The newspaper maintained that the HCT would begin beaming broadcasts to South Africa designed to undermine the country's political beliefs. Should that happen, warned the newspaper, South Africa might consider jamming the offensive broadcasts.[195] About two months later, the BP information department made it clear that "We are not interested in beaming programmes to South Africa."[196] That was the end of the matter, particularly after the HCT authorities assured the Pretoria regime that their radio stations would not handle "hostile political matter."[197]

A more serious problem arose in 1965 after BP received self-government and after the Smith government made its unilateral declaration of independence. British Prime Minister Wilson's government decided to conduct psychological warfare against Southern Rhodesia by beaming BBC programs from BP into Southern Rhodesia. For this purpose, the British built a radio relay station in Francistown. The Wilson government utilized British troops to defend the relay station against possible attack, presumably by those BP whites in the Francistown area who might be sympathetic to the Smith government or perhaps by Southern Rhodesian commando units (which later operated on Botswana territory). Although it never attacked or damaged the Francistown radio transmitter, Southern Rhodesia jammed its broadcasts.[198]

In another area of communications, the number of telephones in the country almost trebled from 1,907 in 1965 to 5,500 in 1973.[199] By early 1980, the Botswana government had acquired a P 1 million earth satellite facility to transmit overseas calls directly rather than through the international telephone exchange in Cape Town. Located at Kgale near Gaborone, this facility handled a maximum of sixty channels, permitting the simultaneous transmission of calls.[200] The British firm Cable and Wireless Company secured the contract from the Department of Telecommunications for the improvement of the nation's domestic and foreign communications capabilities.[201] Assisted by the Swedish and Norwegian governments, Zimbabwe developed direct microwave communications links with Botswana via Francistown,[202] thereby bypassing South Africa as the turnstile of overseas telecommunications for southern Africa.[203] By 1986 Botswana had improved its telecommunications system so that it could handle direct-dialed international calls without relying on the South African facilities. The African Development Bank helped finance part of this modernization program, insuring greater autonomy for Botswana in telecommunications.[204]

In the publications field, one of the oldest links between the BP and South Africa has been the Tswana press, which dates as far back as 1858 as an outgrowth of the evangelizing work of the missionaries.[205] During the Second World War, the BP administration published a small weekly news sheet in English and Setswana. It also subsidized the Tswana newspaper, *Naledi ya Batswana*, published in Johannesburg in one form or another from 1944 to 1954 and from 1958 through 1964. In 1965 the *Bechuanaland Daily News* started publication, changing its name to the *Botswana Daily News* in 1966.[206] Beginning in January 1962, the BP Information Branch in Mafikeng launched the Setswana–English monthly magazine, *Kutlwano* (meaning mutual understanding),[207] edited by Kgosi Lebotse, the previous editor of *Naledi ya Batswana*.[208]

A number of extraterritorial newspapers circulated in Botswana,[209] which had no significant private sector newspapers until 1982.[210] The most popular newspapers have been two Johannesburg dailies, *The Star* and the *Rand Daily Mail* (until its demise in 1985); the Bulawayo daily, *The Chronicle*; and the Mafikeng weekly, *The Mafeking Mail and Protectorate Guardian*, which subsequently became *The Mafeking Mail and Botswana Guardian* after independence. The Mafikeng newspaper, which used English and Afrikaans in its columns, served as a transnational weekly connecting the Protectorate with the administrative headquarters. Now known as *The Mail*, it is trilingual (Afrikaans, English, and Setswana) and covers Bophuthatswana, while including material from Botswana. During the heyday of the Liberal Party of South Africa in the late 1950s and early 1960s, its biweekly *Contact* circulated in the BP,[211] carrying a number of items on African and refugee politics in the BP. One can safely assume that the South African weekly, *New Age*, which was further to the left, had readers in the BP.[212]

The newspaper-reading public in Botswana depends upon the South African and Zimbabwean press. The editor of the weekly *Mafeking Mail* estimated that about 240 to 480 copies per week went into the BP from 1945 to 1960, with the number rising thereafter to 480 to 720 per week.[213] The distribution manager of *The Mail*, the leading weekly newspaper of Bophuthatswana, indicated that it sent 250 copies to Botswana.[214] As for the two English—language dailies from the Witwatersrand area, in 1972 the *Rand Daily Mail* had a circulation of 475 to 513, while *The Star* was roughly the same, that is, 384 to sos.[215] The Botswana Book Center, the premier bookstore in Gaborone, in 1987 received 810 copies of *The Star*, 2,600 copies of the *Sunday Times* (Johannesburg), 1,150 of the *Sunday Star*, 500 of *The Citizen* (Johannesburg), and 450 of the *Sowetan* (Johannesburg).[216]

From the north, *The Chronicle* in Bulawayo sent out 98 copies daily in 1965, which climbed to 140 by 1975,[217] and the Botswana Book Center received 160 copies of this newspaper in 1987, along with 70 copies of the *Sunday News* from Zimbabwe.[218] Almost no newspapers cross the Namibian border, with one recorded subscription to *Die Suidwester*,[219] none to the *Allgemeine Zeitung*, and two to the *Windhoek Advertiser*,[220] all of which are published in Windhoek. In 1987 ten copies of the *Namibian* were sent to the Botswana Book Center, which carried no Zambian newspapers for its customers.[221] Estimates on newspaper circulation in Botswana indicated sales of 7,500 copies of South African, Zimbabwean, and other foreign newspapers, as well as of 10,000 Sunday newspapers (presumably from the same group of nations).[222] By way of contrast, the English–Setswana *Daily News*, referred to earlier, published a run of 25,000 copies,[223] which expanded to 50,000 copies by 1987.[224]

Along with the growth of the *Daily News* has been the development of a private sector media with the publication of two weekly newspapers (*The Examiner* and *The Botswana Guardian*) in Gaborone in 1982,[225] and one (*Mmegi Wa Dikgang/The Reporter*) in Serowe in 1984.[226] A fourth, *The Gazette*, is primarily a business-oriented publication.[227] These private newspapers, which the government often perceived as refractory, have experienced considerable economic hardship, particularly in terms of advertising revenue.[228] In 1981 Botswana created its own wire service, known as BOPA (Botswana Press Association),[229] and in 1986 it joined the larger Pan-African News Agency,[230] enabling it to reduce its reliance on the Western wire services for coverage of African events.[231]

Batswana journalists have been trained overseas at the diploma, undergraduate, and graduate levels in Australia, Canada, Ghana, Kenya, the United States, and Zimbabwe. These journalists banded together to form the Botswana Press Club in the 1970s, which was subsequently replaced by the Botswana Journalists Association (known as BOJA). Although foreign reporters do travel to Botswana, only one full-time foreign journalist (from *Xinhua*, the Chinese news agency) is based in Gaborone. In addition, *Agence France Presse*, the French news agency, has an officer in South Africa to cover the news in Botswana.[232] There is a nascent commercial publishing industry in the nation, including local branches of the well-known British firms, Longman and Macmillan,[233] and this growth has been accompanied by improvements in the national library system. Sweden, the United Kingdom, and Zambia, as well as South African mining houses, have provided funds and personnel for the expansion of library services.[234]

What conclusions can be drawn from this survey of the low politics of transportation, tourism, and communications? How have these policy areas evolved from colonial to post-colonial times? The least mutable factor for Botswana is its landlocked geographical position, which makes it vulnerable, to varying degrees, no matter what regimes are installed in Lusaka, Harare, Windhoek, or Pretoria. As a member of SADCC, Botswana appreciated the primacy of transportation[235] as the means to edge away from the hegemony of South Africa, the strongest littoral state in southern Africa. Even though it finally assumed full control over its entire railway system in 1987 from the Zimbabweans and rejected the claims of Bophuthatswana for transit rights, Botswana still must depend upon Spoornet for access to the Atlantic and Indian

Oceans for its bulky exports. In a more circuitous way, it can send its goods on to Mozambican ports, thereby increasing the distance its freight must travel, but equally increasing its leverage against Spoornet.

Since independence Botswana has made a determined effort to strengthen its transportation system and to extend it north and west, improving its links with Zambia and Namibia. The Zambian connection can be traced to the Zimbabwean war of independence which highlighted the need to have direct riverine access to Zambia. The new trans-Kalahari highway may have considerable utility in promoting economic development, trade, and perhaps tourism in western Botswana. Botswana's northern perimeter along the Caprivi Strip is important as a tourist attraction, and the completion of the airport in Kasane enhances the country's ability to handle tourist traffic flows, particularly those associated with package tours involving Zimbabwe and Namibia.

The Sir Seretse Khama Airport in Gaborone allowed Botswana to handle flights to other SADCC states and to cater to the affluent North American and Western European tourist clientele. Such airport diplomacy had the potential for leverage against South Africa were air traffic sanctions tightened against Pretoria. It could, as critics have charged, also have been a convenient location for South African-inspired countermeasures to evade or attenuate external economic sanctions.

Botswana now has acquired considerable autonomy in the communications policy area because of its extensive modernization program, no longer dependent on South Africa in terms of its posts, telegraphs, and telephone services. Although it has its own radio network, Radio Botswana, it has no television station, and viewers in the south sometimes get their news from television in neighboring Bophuthatswana.[236] No published data indicate which neighboring radio stations Batswana listen to and conversely who listens to Radio Botswana outside the frontiers of Botswana.[237]

In terms of their reading habits, the attentive public in Botswana relies on neighboring English language South African newspapers from the Transvaal Province. Some do read the Zimbabwe press, and the number probably increases the closer one travels to Francistown. These readership patterns are doubtless related to the economics of rail transportation. Although the authorities in Gaborone are attempting to improve the quality of their own journalists, and to take a more assertive position in terms of news gathering and dissemination through its own press agency, more needs to be done in the private sector of the press[238] and of the publishing industry to enhance its intellectual and educational autonomy. The economies of scale make the task formidable; the market for such endeavors is small.[239]

CHAPTER EIGHT

Trade, Currency, Investment, and Aid

INTERNATIONAL TRADE AND THE CUSTOMS UNION

Although foreign and South African political observers[1] have stressed the devastating effects of South African military power on the erstwhile HCT and other SADCC states, the more persistent pattern of domination has not been destabilization. Rand diplomacy has provided the most persistent pattern of regional hegemony and the most difficult form of power projection to parry or diminish. Yet diminishing that power was central to the mission of SADCC. In the low politics areas of trade, currency, and investment, what Richard J. Payne labeled "the web of regional interdependence" is most visible and durable.[2]

Botswana and the other two former HCT are joined in a customs union with South Africa, with the four members restructuring this union in 1969 to provide a slightly better balanced arrangement. Botswana secured greater economic autonomy when it left the South African-sponsored monetary system it had inherited from its British rulers. It developed its own monetary system based on the Pula and the Thebe (the fundamental units of Botswana's currency). Securing private investment and public funds to improve its economic infrastructure and performance is a central component of Botswana's low politics.

Under the terms of the Southern African Customs Union Agreement concluded at Potchefstroom on 29 June 1910,[3] the Union and the HCT constituted a single area within which there was to be free exchange of goods, along with an external tariff.[4] Eleven years later, the membership of the Customs Union was expanded through the 1921 Customs and Excise Act of South Africa to include the mandated territory of South West Africa, which was treated as though it were a component part of South Africa.[5]

While article two of the 1910 customs agreement called for "a free interchange of the products and manufactures of the Union and the [High Commission] Territories" within this large region, South African authorities construed such language to mean that quantitative restraints on intraregional trade could be imposed.[6] In the case of the BP, South African officials placed weight limitations on the importation of live cattle from the Protectorate destined for Johannesburg abattoirs, thereby protecting South African beef producers in the Transvaal during difficult economic times. Not only were South African cattle ranchers protected; the white ranchers in the Protectorate were best placed to meet the weight restrictions because their cattle were heavier than those of the Batswana.[7] White cattle ranchers in the BP also purchased cattle from the Africans expressly for further feeding in preparation for marketing in South Africa.[8]

No provision in the 1910 agreement provided for joint policymaking,[9] so that the South African interpretation of the phrase "freedom of trade" in article two of the agreement could not be challenged in any meaningful way. Further, the British imperial authorities did not stop this South African agricultural trading practice. South Africans used this economic lever to secure the political aim of incorporation of the Protectorate by the Union.[10]

In terms of common customs, the three HCT received a fixed percentage of the customs duties South Africa levied upon all imports, and the South African proportion (98.69 percent) remained constant throughout the life of the agreement. The remaining 1.31 percent was divided unevenly among the three HCT, with the BP receiving 0.28 percent, Basutoland 0.88 percent, and Swaziland 0.15 percent.[11] This asymmetrical allocation was based upon the consumption pattern of dutiable goods from April 1907 to March 1910.[12] According to Stephen J. Ettinger, however, the proportion of the customs duties allocated to the BP apparently did not take into account the goods destined for use in the BP administrative headquarters because Mafikeng was located within South African territory.[13] In 1965, following the 1963 report of Exeter University statistician F.M.M. Lewes,[14] the British government altered the distribution within the three HCT, increasing the Swaziland proportion to 0.53 percent and the BP portion to 0.31 percent, but trimming back Basutoland's share to 0.47 percent.[15] Because South Africa did not participate in this rearrangement, it continued to pay out the same amount to each of the three HCT, while the British government made the necessary inter-HCT financial adjustments.[16]

Low levels of British funding after 1910 made these customs receipts important sources of revenue for BP.[17] When the South African economy, particularly after 1925, began to move away from an agricultural base, it used a system of protective tariffs to encourage industrial growth,[18] which meant that customers within the HCT effectively underwrote this expansion of South African manufacturing by purchasing commodities that they might have been able to buy from less expensive suppliers from outside the customs area.[19] Such was the polarization cost of a less-advanced economy (BP) being linked in tandem with a fast-growing, powerful industrializing neighbor.[20]

When it received self-government, the Khama government made it clear that it intended to press for a revised customs union agreement,[21] officially announcing its intentions of doing so in 1966 in the National Assembly[22] and in its 1966 economic planning document.[23] From 1967 to 1969, authorities in Botswana, along with those in Lesotho and Swaziland, became involved in restructuring the institutions and processes of the 1910 agreement. This time the negotiations were quadrilateral (the three former HCT and South Africa)[24] rather than bilateral (United Kingdom and South Africa) as they had been in 1910.[25] The South African government negotiated within the context of Prime Minister B. J. Vorster's outward policy of creating new regional and continental friends for South Africa. Because of the forthcoming 1970 general election, the South African National Party did not want to appear to be unduly generous to the three former HCT in a renegotiated customs agreement lest it alienate its more conservative Afrikaner followers.[26]

From a policy point of view, the 1910 agreement permitted the parties to change the tariff gradients, yet these levels were set by South Africa, the dominant partner, giving the HCT no control over the rates of the common external tariff.[27] The junior partners, moreover, had no right of consultation, much less the right of veto, regarding future South African economic policies. Hence they lacked institutions through which to express their preferences.[28] Whatever views were exchanged on this topic were between London and Pretoria. South Africa approached the United Kingdom about revamping the customs union once the Pretoria government had left the Commonwealth of Nations in 1961.[29]

In the 1969 revision of the customs union,[30] the four parties agreed to the creation of a common organization—the Customs Union Commission—which was required to meet at least once a year and as often as needed. Although an improvement over the 1910 arrangement, the 1969 agreement granted the Commission neither executive nor legislative functions; nor did it provide any recourse to international arbitration.[31] The Commission established subcommittees to handle technical matters, and the meetings of the Commission were devoted to matters of policy. Matters were resolved in a consensual manner, rather than by voting.[32]

Another significant change in the 1969 treaty was the recognition of the polarization effect of combining two different economies into one customs union that favored the stronger South African economy.[33] To compensate Botswana, Lesotho, and Swaziland (BLS) for this asymmetrical combination, a multiplier of 1.42 was used in the formula to compute the amount of revenue from the common pool due each of the BLS partners.[34] Unlike the 1910 treaty, which froze the percentages due each HCT, the 1969 one provided for a variable percentage based upon the relationship of its dutiable imports, consumption, and manufactures to that of the entire customs union,[35] including Namibia.[36] The percentage was calculated on the basis of data for the financial year two years prior to the current one.[37]

Because such a lagged calculation required that BLS gather more detailed trade data than ever before, Botswana created its own Department of Customs and Excise to undertake this task.[38] Payments, which fluctuated, are made to Botswana in several installments based upon predicted and then upon actual common pool customs receipts.[39] In 1976 members of the customs union revised the benefits formula to reduce the fluctuations from 17 to 23 percent of the value of the dutiable imports, consumption, and manufactures, making the average 20 percent, which corresponds to the revenue other Commonwealth African states receive from their customs systems.[40] Receiving no accrued interest, BLS informed South Africa of their displeasure with the lagged system of payments from the customs pool, but they obtained no redress of this grievance.[41]

Regarding regional trade, the 1965 Porter Mission from the British Ministry of Overseas Development asserted: "All economic planning in Bechuanaland must take account of economic relations with the Republic of South Africa,"[42] a statement that remains apposite. The direction of trade clearly manifests such dependence, especially in terms of Botswana's imports from South Africa. At independence, 67.3 percent of Botswana's estimated imports came from South Africa and 24.9 percent from Southern Rhodesia, leaving a residue of 7.8 percent for the rest of the world.[43] Ten years later Botswana's imports from South Africa had jumped to 81.4 percent, with 12.2 percent coming mainly from Southern Rhodesia, and 6.4 percent from the rest of the world. International sanctions imposed upon Southern Rhodesia and a corresponding trade diversion to South Africa accounts in some measure for this shift.[44]

Earl L. McFarland, Jr., an economic consultant to the Botswana Ministry of Finance and Development Planning, estimated that Botswana's propensity to import from South Africa generated 25,500 manufacturing and 38,200 nonmanufacturing jobs in South Africa.[45] On the export side of the ledger, the asymmetry in trade links is less marked. Export data indicate that South Africa's share of Botswana's exports dropped from 38 percent to 15 percent from 1974 to 1976.[46] By 1979 Botswana sent only 6.9 percent of its exports to South Africa.[47] Such a reduction in exports to South Africa reflects the growth of the copper-nickel and diamond mining industries as well as Botswana's access to the lucrative European Economic Community (EEC) beef market through the several Lomé Conventions. By 1977 this triad of diamonds, copper-nickel, and beef constituted 87.1 percent of Botswana's export trade.[48] Diamond export earnings were so significant that by 1985 Botswana had realized its first foreign trade surplus since 1961.[49]

Botswana's trading links with Southern Rhodesia date back to 1903, when the BP was included in a larger customs union with Southern Rhodesia, Basutoland, and the four future provinces of the Union of South Africa. This was followed by multilateral customs agreements with Southern and Northern Rhodesia signed in 1910 and in 1915.[50] In 1930 Southern Rhodesia and the BP developed a free trade area, and in 1937 the governor of Southern Rhodesia and the British high commissioner (representing BP) signed an agreement for handling the transfer of South African goods between Southern Rhodesia and the BP. When the two Rhodesias and Nyasaland federated in 1953, a customs agreement was concluded three years later to cover all three HCT and the three members of the Central African Federation. Following the Federation's demise in 1963, only Northern Rhodesia discontinued the customs arrangement with BP in which locally produced goods could be exchanged without duties.[51] Why Northern Rhodesia did so in 1964 is not clear, but it meant that it relinquished its special access to the BP.[52]

When British authorities in Gaborone imposed economic sanctions upon the Salisbury government for its unilateral declaration of independence in 1965, Southern Rhodesia supplied roughly 15 percent of the BP's imports.[53] The level of exports (cattle and dairy products[54]) from the BP to Southern Rhodesia was quite low, with the balance of trade favoring Southern Rhodesia.[55] Following independence, the Botswana government continued the very limited sanctions policy initiated by the British administration.[56] Economically vulnerable to Southern Rhodesian counter-sanctions, Botswana arranged with the UN to apply only a limited range of constraints upon

Southern Rhodesia.[57] Gaborone authorities exempted the Chobe area from the national sanctions policy in terms of imports of cigars, cigarettes, tobacco, and beer.[58] The sanctions caused South African goods gradually to replace Southern Rhodesian ones in the Botswana marketplace.[59]

Botswana's most important trade links in southern Africa outside the Southern African Customs Union are with Zimbabwe, the leading economic power within SADCC.[60] Trade between the two operated under the provisions of a 1956 agreement between the BP and the Central African Federation,[61] which permitted free trade in locally produced or manufactured goods.[62] In 1988 Botswana and Zimbabwe concluded an agreement, amending the 1956 free trade accord.[63] These two states were SADCC members, but Botswana is a Southern African Customs Union (SACU) member and has not adhered to the Preferential Trade Area (PTA) agreement, which includes Zimbabwe and fourteen other southern and eastern African states.[64]

According to the PTA agreement, Zimbabwe could offer only those trade preferences to nonsignatories that were extended to signatories.[65] Under the terms of the SACU, Botswana required South Africa's consent to enter into trade pacts with nonmembers of the union, and such consent was given in 1982. Yet Botswana did not join the PTA because its decision-makers feared that South Africa would respond adversely, estimating that PTA membership was not economically or politically appealing.[66] Botswana's trade with Zimbabwe proved profitable, while the level of Botswana's exports seemed unusually high to the Zimbabwean authorities, who thought Botswana was merely reexporting goods it had imported from South Africa. Officials in Gaborone worried about the competition its textile industry faced in Zimbabwe. Botswana, in turn, paid premium prices for its sugar imports from Zimbabwe[67] and handled all Zimbabwe's beef exports to the EEC.[68] Consequently, each partner had something to lose had there been no revised trade agreement.

Botswana's other neighbors loom large in the foreign trade matrix. In Namibia, a coopted fellow member of the SACU, the trade data were not disaggregated from those of South Africa, in part because Namibia had no customs department; available data suggest that Namibia exported to South Africa and to Western Europe and derived its imports from Western Europe and South Africa. Botswana did not appear in the Namibian direction of trade data.[69] The two economies tend to resemble, rather than complement, each other in terms of mineral and agricultural exports and both are dependent upon South African imports. Once it became independent, Namibia joined Botswana in the Commonwealth, SACU, SADCC, and accepted the

Lomé Convention. It is an observer of, but not a member of, PTA.[70]

Plans for the trans-Kalahari rail link from Botswana to Walvis Bay depend upon the largesse of foreign donors. The idea of the east-west couple appealed to the Harare authorities,[71] who saw it as a way to expedite their exports to Western Europe. The trans-Kalahari railway would reduce the shipping time from Zimbabwe, and its proponents saw it as an instrument for regional economic growth, providing a convenient outlet for Botswana's coal. Some question exists, however, regarding the type of imports that would travel over the route to Botswana.[72] Although feasibility studies of the railway line were undertaken as late as 1985,[73] the proposal has shifted into the background with the announcement of a proposed trans-Kalahari road link.[74]

In terms of Zambia, the bilateral trade links are comparatively small. This trade was at the level of $.3 million in 1973–1974[75] but grew fivefold to $1.54 million by 1981.[76] It may possibly increase if the highway bridge over the Zambezi River at Kazungula is built. The Norwegian Agency for Development undertook the feasibility study for the Kazungula bridge, which will replace the ferry operation.[77] This link between Botswana and Zambia became a SADCC project, estimated to cost between $20 million and $25 million. Because it has proven difficult to find foreign donors to finance the project,[78] especially after Zimbabwe became independent, it, along with the trans-Kalahari railroad, may have to be shelved for want of funding.

THE BANKING AND MONETARY SYSTEMS

Another element in the low politics between Botswana and its neighbors entails using banking institutions and currency closely linked to South Africa and, to a lesser extent, Zimbabwe. Only after the Second World War was there a resident commercial bank in Botswana. Consequently, financial business had to be handled in commercial banks in Namibia, South Africa, or Zimbabwe.[79] Five years after the Second World War, the Mafikeng branch of the Standard Bank of South Africa Limited and Barclays D.C.O. (Dominion, Colonial, and Overseas) began regular weekly trips to Lobatse.[80] By 1953, both these commercial banks had established branches in Francistown,[81] which had enjoyed resident banking services from the South African-based African Banking Corporation Limited from 1897 to roughly 1907.[82]

The Standard Bank conducted operations in Botswana from South Africa until 1962, when the responsibility shifted to the London office. Barclays Bank shifted its Botswana activities from South Africa to the

United Kingdom only in 1971.[83] The South African Reserve Bank controlled the credit policies of both these commercial banks.[84] The two British-based banks, which utilized South African banking styles,[85] then became incorporated as Botswana firms in 1975, and the government of Botswana kept its current account in the Standard Bank until 1977, when it shifted over to the Bank of Botswana.[86]

Within the Protectorate, individuals could handle small accounts through the South African Post Office Savings Bank, which invested its earnings in South Africa rather than in the BP.[87] Although BP took charge of its own postal and telegraphic services in 1957, the Union government still operated this bank.[88] The director of posts and telegraphs for the BP assumed the responsibilities of the South African postmaster-general for the operation of this bank in early 1963.[89] At the time of the transfer, twenty-one branches of this bank functioned within the Protectorate, nearly treble the number that existed in 1953 (eight) when the commercial banks came to Francistown.[90]

A private savings institution in Botswana, known as the United Building Society, was superseded in 1977 by the Botswana Building Society, which acquired the assets of this South African organization. The United Building Society provided some managerial advice to the Botswana Building Society, while the government of Botswana provided P 1.6 million to purchasea number of shares to put the local firm on a secure footing.[91] The banking sector became further enlarged when the (now liquidated) Bank of Credit and Commerce International (BCCI) began operations in Botswana in 1982,[92] followed by the Zimbank Botswana Limited in 1990 and by the First National Bank of South Africa (which bought the local BCCI) in 1991.[93]

This transfer of responsibility for the Post Office Savings Bank, as well as the extraterritorial nature of banking until 1977, demonstrates the close banking links between the Protectorate and the Union that complemented those in the Customs Union.

A similar network existed in the currency field. In 1895 Cape bank notes and British coins were legal tender in the BP,[94] and by 1920 Transvaal coins were also legally acceptable. By 1932 the Protectorate recognized as legal tender the bank notes of the South African Reserve Bank,[95] which began to operate in 1921.[96] The BP never received any revenue from the circulation of these South African Reserve Bank notes, even though it earned a modest amount from the circulation of the Cape bank notes before the creation of the Union of South Africa. In the case of the coins the South African Mint produced, payments from the profits of the operation (seigniorage) were made to Zimbabwe from 1926 to 1931, where they were legal tender, but no such payment was made to the BP, which also used South African coins. Botswana, according to Basil C. Muzorewa, probably can press a claim against South Africa for such past profits.[97]

When Pretoria issued the Rand to replace the South African pound in 1960, the three HCT followed suit and used the decimalized Rand as legal tender,[98] although until the end of November 1965 it permitted the free exchange at par value of old and new South African currency, Zambian currency, Zimbabwean currency, and Malawian currency.[99] Many of the financial transactions in the Tati area had been conducted in terms of Southern Rhodesian currency.[100] The BP continued to use the South African Rand as its currency until 1976, when Botswana first introduced the Pula, its own decimalized currency.[101]

Botswana relied upon the South African Rand for a decade after independence, still another manifestation of the asymmetrical economic links between the two neighbors. Charles Harvey described the country as "a monetary province of South Africa" until it issued its own currency.[102] Sovereign Botswana may have chosen to remain and then to have left the Rand Monetary Area (RMA) because it could tap South Africa's tourist business. South Africans could spend an unlimited number of Rand within the BLS states but could carry only R 250 per person to other contiguous states. Or perhaps Botswana remained in the RMA to save the added expense of developing and administering a separate currency. By using the Rand, BLS did not frighten away potential investors familiar with that currency.[103] Still another inducement to stay within the RMA was that affluent individuals within Botswana could invest their savings in South African financial institutions.[104]

Despite these attractions, authorities in Gaborone understood the disadvantages of belonging to the RMA, calling attention to them in the development plan drawn up on the eve of independence.[105] By not drawing interest from the South African Reserve Bank for the reserves it kept to support the South African currency circulating in Botswana, Gaborone officials lost R 100,000 annually. Further, with no representation on the Board of the South African Reserve Bank, Botswana could not defend its own economic interests.[106] Nor could Botswana be master of its own economic house in terms of foreign exchange rates and controls, prevailing interest rates, general macroeconomic policy formulation and execution, and the investment of foreign currency reserves.[107] Finally, it did not benefit financially from the creation of South African fiduciary issues.[108] By leaving the RMA, the Botswana government assumed that it could divert the flow of savings from Botswana away from South Africa and back into Botswana where it could generate national wealth. The 1989 development of the Botswana Share Market, a stock exchange,[109] indicates that domestic savings can be successfully tapped and need not be lost to the country.[110]

In 1969 Botswana, Lesotho, and Swaziland began to consider changes in the RMA,[111] an international association built upon customary practices.[112] Three years later, BLS notified South Africa that reforms were needed in the RMA. Negotiations with South Africa took place during 1973 and 1974, but by September 1974 the Botswana government left the quadripartite RMA talks and declared that it would found its own national bank and issue its own currency.[113] In 1975 the Bank of Botswana was established, assuming the previous responsibilities of the Monetary Preparatory Commission.[114]

The transition from the South African Rand to the Botswanan Pula (the Setswana term for rain) and Thebe (meaning shield), which is one-one hundredth of a Pula, went rather smoothly in 1976. On Pula Day, 23 August 1976, the new bills began to circulate, while the coins were issued two weeks later. The Bank of Botswana purchased the foreign exchange holdings of Botswana residents, who received Pulas in return. At the time, there was an even (one-for-one) exchange rate between the US dollar and the Rand, with the Botswana authorities pegging the Pula to the dollar,[115] which is customary among African states.[116] The government of Botswana continued the equality between the Pula and the Rand until the end of November that year.[117]

By June 1980 Botswana ceased to peg the Pula to the declining US dollar, moving instead to the basket of foreign currencies.[118] One currency in that basket was the South African Rand, a currency in which the bulk of Botswana's imports are denominated.[119] Consequently, changes in the Pula-Rand exchange rate have a significant bearing upon the pattern of Botswana's imports from South Africa.[120] The Rand comprised about 50 percent of the basket of foreign currencies to which the Pula was pegged; the remainder was composed of Special Drawing Rights of the International Monetary Fund.[121] The Rand's weight in that basket increased to 75 percent in 1985, but that proportion dropped in 1986 to the 60 to 65 percent range to offset the depreciation of the Rand.[122]

Botswana's diamond sales are denominated in US dollars.[123] So far, the country has had a remarkably low debt-service ratio. The ratio, which indicates the proportion of national export earnings needed to amortize foreign debts, was as low as 2 percent in 1980 and increased to 3.5 percent in 1989.[124] Botswana also has accumulated large foreign reserves[125] that enable its inhabitants to enjoy a rather liberal foreign exchange policy.[126]

PRIVATE FOREIGN INVESTMENT AND THE MINING SECTOR

Turning to private foreign investment, principally in the mining sector, it is worth recalling that during the colonial era, there was little, if any, interest in the country as a source of minerals. Although gold was mined in the BP from 1869 until 1964,[127] the gold strikes in the Witwatersrand area of the adjacent South African Republic (subsequently the Transvaal) in 1886 were of far greater economic significance and attracted overseas investment as well as African migrant workers from Southern African territories.

The Bechuanaland Copper Company mined copper on a small scale from 1908 to 1918 at the Bushman Mine, near Dukwe.[128] Surface mine dumps left from the decades of the 1950s and 1960s in the Tati area will be reworked, and one underground gold mine has been opened.[129] This new gold mine, Map Nora, which began operating in 1989,[130] is expected to generate about two hundred jobs during the course of its operations which are anticipated to last only a decade.[131]

In 1887, twenty-one years after German geologist Karl Mauch's discovery of gold in Tati,[132] Bamangwato ruler Khama III agreed to let the Northern Gold Fields Exploration Syndicate prospect. This syndicate, in turn, created the Bechuanaland Exploration Company, whose prospecting rights later were taken over by the BSAC. Chief Khama III accepted a subsequent agreement with the BSAC in 1893. Thirty years later he wanted to terminate the concession, perhaps fearing that the influx of miners would eventually lead to the loss of his tribe's territory and autonomy. His visit to London in 1895, after all, concerned protection for the Bamangwato against the BSAC. He did not live long enough to end the mining concession. His heir, Sekgoma II, brought the matter to the attention of the BP resident commissioner, but nothing was settled during his brief reign from 1923 until his death in 1925.[133]

In 1929 the British authorities suggested that Tshekedi Khama, who became the regent of the Bamangwato following the death of his brother Sekgoma II, accept a revised concession. In 1932 the regent signed an agreement with the BSAC to permit prospecting in the Bamangwato domain. By 1959 the Bamangwato had concluded a ten-year prospecting agreement[134] with Rhodesian (subsequently Roan) Selection Trust (RST), a large firm involved in copper mining in Zambia. The 1959 agreement allowed Bamangwato Concessions Limited (BCL) to prospect. In 1963 and 1965 BCL located copper-nickel deposits at Selebi and Phikwe, respectively. BCL indicated in early 1967 that there were substantial amounts of ore at these sites in Bamangwato country.[135]

Not long after the BCL announcement, the newly independent government consolidated and improved its mineral ownership and mining policy. Since 1964 the idea had gained currency that mineral rights vested in the various tribal authorities—public subnational entities—should be transferred to the central government. After discussion with the tribes, the chiefs, as members of the upper house of parliament known as the House of Chiefs, agreed to the change. The National Assembly enacted the necessary legislation in 1967.[136] A complementary statute, the 1967 Mines and Minerals Act, applying to both public and private mineral rights, brought the colonial proclamations up to date in anticipation of greater prospecting activity. This act had no adverse effect upon mineral rights in the privately held areas.[137]

Charter Consolidated, which followed the BSAC and is related to the Anglo-American Corporation, acquired the mineral rights in the freehold areas[138]—the Gaborone, Lobatse, and Tuli blocks—while the Tati Company held them in the Tati Concession, where gold mining first began.[139] Once mining became a reality, the government stipulated that private owners of mineral rights would be liable to taxation on their rights, but that this taxation would be reduced in proportion to expenditures on prospecting. Designed to induce those holding minerals rights on private land to undertake serious prospecting or to tax those who did not prospect,[140] this legislation (the 1972 Mineral Rights Tax Act) prompted the Charter Consolidated to give up its mining rights in the three freehold blocks.[141]

The first mining complex involving external private and public capital was a copper-nickel mine at Selebi-Phikwe in the Bamangwato area, which was covered by the 1959 agreement. A massive undertaking that preoccupied Botswana government officials,[142] this mining complex required the financial and technical resources of four significant South African elements, which were often combined with other foreign components. The government negotiated a R 13.5 million loan with the Industrial Development Corporation, a South African parastatal body, thus making an exception to its general policy of avoiding public sector assistance from South Africa.[143]

South African private investment was also involved through the well-known South African transnational firm of Anglo-American Corporation,[144] which held 30 percent of the shares in Botswana RST (BRST). American Metal Climax (AMAX), an American multinational mining corporation, also owned 30 percent of the shares in BRST, which, in turn, held 85 percent interest in BCL, with the government of Botswana owning the remaining 15 percent. Both multinationals cooperated to provide a P 8.9 million loan through the BRST.[145] Also the importation of goods and supplies for the construction of the mine and its accompanying infrastructure (the Shashe project) generated considerable revenue under the terms of the newly revised SACU agreement with South Africa. Finally, the mine intended to sell sulfur, a byproduct of its operations, to a South African fertilizer company.[146]

In planning the creation of linkages[147]—other industries that can sell and purchase goods and services to and from the Shashe project—the government attempted to develop its own electrical power capacity to avoid increasing its reliance upon the South African Electricity Supply Commission,[148] which furnished electrical power until its own coal-fed generators came into operation in 1987.[149] The electrical generators are fueled by coal from the nearby Morupule coal mine, but the Botswana Power Corporation imported South African coal until the boiler design was modified to handle local coal. The coal mine at Morupule is a part of the Anglo-American Corporation,[150] while the funding for the power station came from a loan of Canadian $30 million from the Canadian International Development Agency.[151]

The development of coal mining seems to be the only significant backward economic linkage in the Shashe project,[152] although overall electric power generation still lags behind consumption, with the shortfall being met by imported South African power. The level of these imports had dropped to 6 percent of Botswana's power supplies by 1989–1990.[153]

Technical and environmental difficulties that required extensive financial restructuring in 1978 plagued the BCL mine.[154] Because the copper-nickel matte from the mine is not locally refined, no value was added to the ore, which was shipped to the AMAX's refinery at Port Nickel, Louisiana.[155] The West German firm Metallgesellschaft AG purchased all the copper and two-thirds of the nickel produced at the Louisiana refinery.[156] Although it is Botswana's largest private sector employer with about 4,500 employees,[157] the project has not developed any forward economic linkages.[158] Not only was it unable to produce elemental sulfur,[159] but also the international market for copper and nickel has been quite depressed, making the venture unprofitable.[160] In 1985 the AMAX refinery in Louisiana was closed down,[161] and BCL arranged for the termination of its exclusive supply contract with AMAX at the end of July 1985, a decision that entailed a contract to pay AMAX P 63 million over five years.[162] The matte is now being refined in Zimbabwe and Norway.[163]

Diamond mining, however, has been much more promising, with prospecting dating back to 1955.[164] De Beers, the South African mining house that acquired mining rights in the BP from the BSAC in 1892,[165] undertook the operation. This search lasted until 1967, when a significant strike was made roughly 110 miles west of Francistown at Orapa.[166] The Orapa discovery was the second largest kimberlite diamond pipe ever found outside the Soviet Union.[167] An earlier discovery in 1967 had been made 25 miles southeast of Orapa at Lethlakane.[168] By 1976 the geologists had located yet another diamond pipe roughly 71 miles northwest of Lobatse at Jwaneng.[169]

Here again, the Botswana government turned to a South African multinational enterprise, De Beers, for the expertise and capital needed to mine the diamonds. In 1969 the De Beers Botswana Mining Company, known as Debswana, was created to undertake mining operations at Orapa. The government of Botswana held 15 percent of the shares in Debswana, while De Beers held the remaining 85 percent. De Beers invested P 25 million to bring the Orapa mine into production by 1971.[170] Using a mixture of dividends, royalties, and taxation, the government of Botswana realized roughly 57.5 percent of the profits of the Orapa mine.[171]

Encouraged by the quality of the diamond finds at Lethlakane and the inaccessibility of the diamond mining sites, which enhanced their industrial security, the government later bargained for greater benefits from De Beers. Roughly 65 to 70 percent of the profits of the Debswana now accrues to the government,[172] which currently owns half the shares of Debswana.[173] When the Jwaneng diamond mine became operational in 1982, total diamond production at the three mines (Orapa, Lethlakane, and Jwaneng) increased so rapidly that Botswana even surpassed South Africa in terms of output by 1983.[174]

These two projects relied upon private venture capital and, in the case of the infrastructure for the Shashe complex, overseas public capital, and both have had only limited forward or backward economic linkages. In the case of the diamond mining industry, the stones are marketed through the Central Selling Organization (CSO) in London, a De Beers monopoly serving South Africa, Botswana,[175] and the former Soviet Union (in a discrete fashion).[176] De Beers has established as forward linkages a diamond sorting operation, known as the Botswana Diamond Valuing Company,[177] and a diamond cutting enterprise in Gaborone.[178] Both types of mining, especially the Debswana enterprise, are more capital than labor intensive,[179] and the diamond mining industry has generated far more revenue than any other enterprise,[180] despite a slump in the market in 1981–1982.[181]

Particularly in diamond mining, Botswana depends upon De Beers, which is part of the Anglo-American family. This has proven distasteful to the government, which has preferred to diversify commercial operations,[182] even though it does have a 50 percent share of Debswana and participates in the management of the corporation.

When it sold the stockpile of diamonds acquired from 1982 to 1985 to De Beers, Debswana acquired twenty million shares of the corporation worth $380 million, equivalent to a 2.6 percent interest in this business.[183] It also acquired two seats on the board of directors of De Beers in Johannesburg and on the Diamond Trading Company in London, which sells to both retailers and cutters. Some argued that this arrangement improved the standing of De Beers, showing it had become less of a South African enterprise.[184] A less charitable interpretation was that Botswana aided South Africa's economic aims during a time of increasing international sanctions.[185]

Those distressed about the closer ties between large South African firms and Botswana find equally troubling the arrangement for mining soda ash at Sua Pan in the Makgadikgadi depression 112 miles northwest of Francistown.[186] Such an arrangement dates back at least to 1963 when the Legislative Council of the BP brought it up, probably expecting to attract the RST.[187] In 1984 South African authorities attempted to induce Botswana to sign a nonaggression treaty as a condition for a business deal involving Sua Pan. Botswana rejected such a linkage, wanting no part of any agreement that implied it could not control the political and military activities of South African refugees or that it would legitimate apartheid.[188] Here low politics served as a lever to move into the high politics area. The South African government was involved in what David A. Baldwin has termed economic statecraft,[189] with the Pretoria authorities using similar inducements and threats to secure a bilateral agreement with Botswana similar to the 1984 Nkomati Accord between South Africa and Mozambique.[190]

South Africa was involved because it provides the principal market[191] for the sale of common salt and soda ash (known as sodium carbonate) extracted from the brine at Sua Pan.[192] South Africa imported 100,000 tons of salt and 250,000 tons of soda ash each year,[193] much of it from six US companies operating as a cartel known the American Natural Soda Ash Corporation (ANSAC).[194] This importation pattern suggested that once the US government passed sanctions legislation in 1986, South African importers anticipated that their American supply would be at risk.[195] So South Africa considered building a synthetic soda ash plant.[196] The president of ANSAC attempted to persuade South African firms not to change suppliers by switching to Sua Pan soda ash, and this American marketing offensive was blunted by South African foreign minister Pik Botha, who assured Botswana that SACU would afford the necessary tariff protection for the sale of soda ash to South Africa.[197]

Lest the Sua Pan project take on more of a South African image than necessary, Botswana attempted to secure regional participation of the Zimbabwean Industrial Development Corporation and of Malawi and Zambia. It also sought to attract the interest of the Commonwealth Development Corporation and of the International Finance Corporation.[198] As a result of a P 736 million arrangement signed in Gaborone at the end of 1988, Botswana controls slightly less than half (48 percent) of the equity in the holding company for the project, known as Soda Ash Botswana Limited, while the remaining 52 percent is held by De Beers, the Anglo-American Corporation, and the African Explosives and Chemical Industries (AECI).[199] Anglo-American in turn, has a 38 percent equity in AECI. Given this configuration, Botswana is anxious to have the project regarded as a SADCC one.[200]

Because of the infant industry provision in the 1969 SACU agreement permitting a protective tariff for beginning enterprises,[201] manufacturing would seem to be a particularly attractive sector for South African and overseas investors.[202] Although the local market is small, Botswana has access to the entire customs union area.[203] The difficulty, though, is that currently Botswana lacks managerial talent,[204] the Batswana having allocated their own talent, time, and capital to the cattle industry rather than to the manufacturing sector.[205]

In 1980, 45 manufacturing firms with more than ten employees were owned by non-nationals, and 26 other such firms were owned by both nationals and non-nationals; the comparable figure for wholly local firms in that year was 13.[206] South African investors supplied roughly two-thirds of the capital of the foreign-owned firms in Botswana.[207] By 1984 the number of foreign-owned establishments had more than doubled to 122, while the jointly owned firms jumped to 55, and the number of purely locally owned firms increased to 32.[208]

Helped by the local commercial banking sector, the Zimbabwean and South African business communities, and Bill Mackintyre, a retired American banking executive, the Botswana Development Corporation (BDC) examined the possibilities of opening a capital market and even a stock exchange in Botswana to tap local funds.[209] Foreign firms could sell their shares on this market, and more than a dozen local firms could use the market to raise capital.[210] In 1989 the BDC launched Stockbrokers Botswana Limited to handle bonds and promissory notes, followed later by equity financing and perhaps the sale of treasury bills.[211]

After the renegotiation of the SACU agreement, the Botswana government used the infant industry clause of that agreement to secure protection for a brewery built by a West German firm.[212] This was one of the few cases in which Botswana has taken advantage of that particular clause (the Kgalakgadi Soap Industries in Gaborone and a flour mill are the other examples[213]). This commercial venture with the Brau Finaz, a member of the Oetker Group, involved a majority shareholding by the BDC.[214] The BDC preferred this overseas company to the South African Breweries, a firm that had captured 90 percent of the Botswana beer market by 1973.[215] From its base in Botswana, protected by the eight-year tariff for newly established industries authorized by the 1969 customs agreement, Brau Finaz expected to penetrate the South African market, something it never accomplished.[216] The two brands that Brau Finaz brewed were not exceptionally popular in Botswana, and by 1978 the West German firm had sold out to the South African Breweries, which ran the operation profitably.[217] South African Breweries, in turn, came under the control of the Anglo-American Corporation in 1983.[218] This is not the only time that a private enterprise met with technical difficulties; the Selebi-Phikwe copper-nickel mining operation also suffered setbacks and high levels of debt.[219]

The possibility of increased economic sanctions against South Africa caused some South African industrialists to focus on Botswana as an investment haven.[220] The Zimbabwean government, with a free trade agreement with Botswana known as the open general import license, suggested that South African manufactured goods would travel under the protection of a Botswana label. Such a license provides that a Zimbabwean importer need not have a permit to import goods from Botswana with a minimum of one-fifth (for textiles) to one-fourth (for nontextile items) Botswana content. Zimbabwean officials have coordinated their trade monitoring activities with authorities in Botswana to curb such activity by South African business firms with operations in Botswana. The increased bilateral trade between Botswana and Zimbabwe from 1985 onward reflected the growing use of Botswana as a trade conduit by South African firms anxious to circumvent trade sanctions.[221]

ATTRACTING PUBLIC FOREIGN AID DONORS

During most of the colonial era, the UK was quite parsimonious toward the BP.[222] This scrimping was due not only to the general British policy that colonies should be financially self-sustaining but also to the anticipated transfer of the HCT to South Africa, whose taxpayers would thereafter assume the British financial burdens. The early years were marked by treasury subventions, especially for the railways, and they were subsequently supplemented by income from Pretoria under the terms of the 1910 SACU agreement.[223] By 1929 the

British government went beyond simple administrative grants and began to consider additional expenditures under the various Colonial Development and Welfare Acts.[224]

The South African government was willing to help the BP in 1936, thereby supplementing funds from the British Exchequer. The Hertzog government appropriated public funds to subsidize joint Anglo–South African cooperation on technical projects in the HCT, presumably as part of an incremental approach to the transfer of the HCT to the Union. Daniel F. Malan's Purified National Party in the South African House of Assembly and the Tswana leadership in the Protectorate were opposed to this early exercise in South African functionalism, and the South African appropriation was never spent.[225] This is yet another example of the melding of low and high politics.

Particularly after 1955, as the British began to develop infrastructure in the Protectorate, the level of financial support increased[226] and economic planning became institutionalized.[227] Yet even at independence, President Khama was disappointed at the sparseness of the infrastructure bequeathed to the Batswana by the British.[228]. A year after independence, Botswana was exceptionally dependent upon the British Exchequer, which accounted for roughly 90 percent of its overseas aid funds.[229] A British nongovernmental organization, the Oxford Committee for Famine Relief, furnished funds to deal with the famine resulting from the long drought in the 1960s.[230] By 1972 Botswana was able to dispense with British grants to balance its recurrent budget.[231] The challenges for Botswana's political leadership were to increase foreign aid, to diversify the number of donors, to reduce the influence of any single national donor, and to keep foreign public debt servicing costs low.

South African foreign aid, as distinct from revenues derived from the 1910 and 1969 SACU agreements, was politically unpalatable. Unlike Malawi, Botswana has not sought such public funding.[232] This has not meant, however, that the Gaborone authorities have turned away South African private investors and funds. Quite the contrary. But with the closing of the door to the South African government and with the unwillingness or inability of the Zimbabwean government to provide public funds other than those connected with such specific public utilities as the railways and postal and telegraphic services, Botswana had to look beyond its neighbors for financial transfers and assistance with which to improve its socioeconomic structure.

One of the more obvious external sources of aid has been the United Nations. As early as 1954, BP officials turned to the UN specialized agencies for supplemental technical assistance in the medical field.[233] The UN also furnished food to the Batswana during the devastating drought of the 1960s.[234] Access to the UN was improved with the admission of Botswana to that organization in 1966, and President Khama's choice of the first ambassador to the UN (and to the United States as well), Zachariah K. Matthews,[235] was prudential, considering that four of his former students (from Fort Hare University in the Cape) were already UN ambassadors.[236] In addition, Matthews had contacts in the ecclesiastical community from his service as secretary of the Geneva-based African Section of the Division of Inter-Church Aid, Refugee, and World Service of the World Council of Churches.[237]

Not only was the UN family of intergovernmental organizations a potential and welcome source of technical assistance and funds to fortify the British contribution, but also the family enabled Botswana to secure diplomatic contacts with a wide range of potential donors at a minimal cost. In particular, links with the International Bank for Reconstruction and Development (World Bank) and the International Monetary Fund in Washington, D.C., could provide the economic advice and studies previously provided by the British government. In 1983 a team sent by the International Bank to appraise the quality of the management of Botswana's public sector[238] was very favorably impressed with the ability of Botswana's civil servants to manage foreign technical aid as well as to work harmoniously with foreign donors.[239]

Foreign donors were attracted to Botswana not only because of its fine planning performance and fiscal probity but also because of the quality of its democratic, nonracial order.[240] In addition to furnishing economic assistance and other material benefits to the newly independent Republic of Botswana, the UN, particularly the General Assembly, had the advantage in 1966 of being insulated from Cold War pressures and of being receptive to the needs and aspirations of Third World states. Other intergovernmental bodies, such as the Commonwealth of Nations and the Organization of African Unity, provided useful forums in which to exchange views and to cultivate diplomatic and symbolic support, especially in terms of relations with minority-ruled neighboring states.[241]

Less than a decade after independence, Botswana's principal patron was no longer the former metropole but Sweden,[242] which began its aid shortly before independence.[243] In 1975–1976 Botswana ranked first in the amount of per capita of Swedish International Development Authority (SIDA) aid allocations, with the funds earmarked for educational, road-building, and water supply programs.[244] The Swedes were particularly intent on helping Botswana because of its dependence upon its minority-ruled neighboring states.[245]

An analysis of the patterns of foreign assistance shows that aid donors have a tendency to specialize in different functional areas: Canada, for example, is interested in the minerals and mining area, while the United States is concerned with managerial skills, Sweden deals with water supplies, and Norway concentrates on village health and transportation.[246] Persons from the Dutch, UN, Swedish, Norwegian, West German, Danish, Canadian, and British volunteer services, as well as members of the US Peace Corps function at both the national and local levels in technical and supervisory capacities.[247]

During the 1980s there was a shift in the rank order of the major donors of foreign assistance to Botswana, along with a greater local capacity for undertaking capital projects because of a buoyant economy. Between roughly three-fifths and three-fourths of Botswana's bilateral aid comes from only four donor nations: the UK, Sweden, the Federal Republic of Germany, and the United States. Three international organizations (the European Community, the UN Development Program, and the World Food Program) supply from three-fifths to four-fifths of the multilateral aid. In 1981 the first-ranked foreign donor was the UK ($16.6 million), but by 1986 Sweden was the first-ranked ($16.3 million), with the UK dropping to fourth place (with $9.9 million) in 1986. The West Germans were exceptionally active during this period, ranking first or tied for first for four of the six years, with contributions ranging from $12.5 million to $24.2 million. American aid during this time varied between $11 million and $17 million. The foreign aid data for the 1981–1986 period clearly indicate that bilateral aid usually consists of roughly two-thirds to four-fifths of all Botswana's foreign aid.[248]

Nowadays it is probable that Botswana will have to expect reduced foreign aid. This can be attributed less to Botswana's performance levels and more to rapid change in the regional political and global economic environment,[249] including what G.M. Erich Leistner of the Africa Institute has referred to as "aid fatigue."[250] Neighboring Namibia has become independent as well as a fellow SADCC member, and it has been actively competing for aid donors,[251] especially in North America and Western Europe. The Unified German Republic, which has historic and ethnic links to the German-speaking whites there,[252] has become the top-ranked donor for Namibia.[253] It is likely that the Scandinavian donors will begin to switch their interest and aid to Namibia in the aftermath of its quarter-century war for independence.[254] Notwithstanding such aid (and investment) competition from SADCC states, the new Mandela government in South Africa bodes well for Botswana in terms of reduced military threats and destabilization.[255] In sum, Botswana will doubtless want a proportionate regional share of the South African peace dividend.

CHAPTER NINE

Migrant Labor

THE EVOLUTION OF MIGRANT LABOR

President Khama acknowledged during the founding of the SADCC that political independence without economic support in the southern African region was incomplete independence. He recognized both the reality of interdependence and the need to reduce the asymmetry between South Africa and the majority-ruled states. Such a reduction is a cardinal principle of the SADCC, formed just before Sir Seretse died in 1980.[1] One glaring imbalance in the Botswanan–South African relationship has been in the labor sector, where Botswana has imported skilled labor from South Africa while almost always exporting unskilled labor to South Africa.[2] Along with low levels of manufacturing to generate employment for its citizens, this imbalance limits autonomy for Botswana.

As noted in Chapter Six, Botswana seeks to fill both public and private positions with local personnel, thus importing fewer skilled laborers and simultaneously reducing its dependence. Botswana has turned to outside nations, international organizations, and regional institutions for financial and technical assistance to remedy the shortfall in highly educated persons.

The system of contract laborers migrating temporarily from the BP to South Africa reflects the decline of gold mining in the BP and its displacement by the larger, more powerful mining industry of South Africa. Small-scale gold mining operations in the Tati area of the BP employed more Africans from nearby Southern Rhodesia than from the BP, suggesting that local mining operations were too small to employ sizable numbers of Batswana. Indeed, the Bakwena of southeastern

Botswana initially sought employment in the diamond industry in Kimberley in the Cape in the 1870s.[3]

Although I focus on migrant gold miners, the South African gold mines are certainly not the sole employers who use short-term labor contracts.[4] Batswana have been employed in unskilled labor on South African farms, in other types of mining, and in other neighboring territories and states. The data from the gold mines, however, are usually more systematically kept and are more readily available to researchers.[5] As of 30 June 1986, of the 28,244 Batswana nationals employed in South Africa, 21,686 worked in mining and quarrying, 1,511 in the agricultural sector, 1,107 in domestic services, 1,064 in the manufacturing sector, 591 in the electricity, gas, and water services, 547 in the transport, storage, and communication industries, 520 in wholesale and retail trade, and the remaining 160 in the field of finance and insurance.[6] Moreover, Batswana have also worked in neighboring Zimbabwe[7] and Namibia,[8] although these data are very skimpy and not as carefully kept as those for South Africa. In all likelihood, they lived in areas of Botswana bordering on Zimbabwe and Namibia, crossing the border to work in the homes and farms of the resident whites or perhaps in small-scale mining operations. It is doubtful that they were recruited in as systematic a fashion or in as large numbers as those who went south to the gold mines in the Witwatersrand.[9]

On 20 May 1961 the South African minister of Bantu administration and development appointed G. F. Van L. Froneman, MP, to chair a ten-person interdepartmental committee to report on the number and occupations of foreign Africans in South Africa, the privileges they enjoyed, the problems their presence created, and how such problems could be resolved. Although the committee visited Mafikeng, no British or African officials from the BP gave written or oral evidence to the committee. The Froneman Committee completed its report eleven months later[10] and sent it to Parliament in early 1963.[11] Parliament, however, did not undertake a full-scale debate on the report, and the minister of Bantu administration and development inexplicably declined to make a statement to the House of Assembly even two years after the report had been tabled on 24 January 1963.[12] Earlier, when questioned in Parliament about the Froneman Committee, the deputy minister of this department indicated that it was rare to table the reports of interdepartmental committees.[13]

Following the tabling of that report, the South African government began to constrain and monitor the influx of foreign migrant workers. Although the Natives (Abolition of Passes and Coordination of Documents) Act No. 67 of 1952 required Africans from South Africa and the HCT to have identity documents as of 1958,[14] it was not until the passage of the Bantu Laws Amendment Act No. 76 of 1963 that Pretoria adopted measures controlling the entry of nationals of the HCT.[15] The Froneman Committee found that HCT and other foreign Africans had unfettered access to South Africa, and many chose to remain in South Africa. This, in turn, put severe strains on the South African economy in terms of the provision of social and educational services and tended to diminish economic opportunities for African nationals of South Africa. Hence Pretoria welcomed the idea of regulating the influx of foreign Africans, including those from the HCT.[16] The 1963 legislation, coupled with the creation of a large number of passport control posts on the borders with the HCT, was intended to regulate the BP labor traffic flow.[17]

Because change in climate adversely affected the miners' health, the South African government would not permit the Witwatersrand mines to employ those who lived north of the twenty-second parallel.[18] This meant that while the Native Recruiting Corporation (NRC), which had operated in the BP since 1912, could work in the southern part of the Protectorate,[19] north of that twenty-second parallel was considered out of bounds as a tropical area.[20] By 1934, however, an increase in the price of gold on world markets and improvements in tropical medicine forced the Witwatersrand mines to move the recruiting catchment area further to the north to recruit more miners.[21] The WNLA assumed recruiting responsibilities north of the twenty-second parallel.[22]

Although it developed recruiting depots in the north of the country, the WNLA was more successful in locating potential miners in Namibia, Angola, Malawi, and Zambia than in northern Botswana;[23] yet a substantial upsurge in recruitment occurred in that part of Botswana from 1974 to 1977.[24] Even though the geographically dispersed Basarwa are sometimes involved,[25] the bulk of the Batswana who work in the South African mines reside in the southeastern portion of the country.[26] These two recruiting organizations (NRC and WNLA), which have been significant transnational actors in the labor field during the present century, merged in 1977 to form the Employment Bureau of Africa (TEBA).[27]

The literature about migrant (or circular or oscillating[28]) labor contains four explanations for the steady exodus of younger Batswana men to South Africa's mines. The writers of the dependency school of international and comparative politics, who regarded Botswana as a peripheral labor reserve for the South African core, perceive Botswana's golden age in the nineteenth century as a period in which the country was economically self-sufficient and had a flourishing regional trade. This golden age vanished, averred these exponents of dependency theory, because the colonial authorities created shortages of land. They argued that local taxation to support the minimal administrative structure in the BP was geared to maintain law and order. The colonial system, they argued, benefited the resident white population and the Batswana rulers and elites, who permitted mine agents to recruit within their chiefly domains.. Adherents of the dependency school asserted that the South African mining industry and its local and overseas shareholders were the major beneficiaries of this inexpensive, unorganized, and politically docile labor force.[29]

A second, less complex, explanation for the exodus involved access to ready cash to pay different types of taxes, from hut taxes to school fees.[30] The society's wealthier elements secured the requisite cash for these expenses through the sale of livestock. Cattle holding for the Batswana was a functional equivalent of a Western banking system; cattle were a visible and liquid asset as well as a form of equity. From 1924 until 1941, South African restrictions upon the export of BP beef to the Union adversely affected Batswana cattle owners, whose beasts could not meet the minimum weight standards.[31]

A third explanation was historical. In the past, Batswana went to the mines as a type of regimental labor to raise funds for a tribal project or individuals went as a type of tribally imposed fine for wrongdoing.[32] A fourth explanation concerned achievement and ascriptive criteria. Those Batswana who either had little or no formal education[33] or who were members of ethnic groups that have traditionally ranked low in the Tswana sociopolitical system migrated to the mines.[34]

Batswana migrated to the mines for specific economic goals, which could be achieved by working for a specific number of contract periods varying from nine to fifteen months each.[35] This goal-oriented employment was known as "target work."[36] Given the salience of livestock in Tswana society, one such target was the acquisition of a modest herd, which could insure minimal security needs.[37] In addition, the miner who intended to establish himself as a farmer could use his savings to purchase agricultural implements to complement his livestock, some of which could supply draft power.[38] In this sense, a trip to South Africa could lead to greater agricultural inputs, but it is debatable whether such capital improvements would insure a prosperous farming career or lead to agricultural self-sufficiency in a nation plagued with recurrent drought and small amounts of fertile land.[39]

THE DIRECTION AND AMOUNT OF MONETARY BENEFITS

As early as 1899, the BP derived much of its operating expenses from a hut tax upon the migrant worker.[40] This worker would be taxed in the BP before leaving or in South Africa itself by the appropriate tribal authority;[41] over time, however, the process became routinized in South Africa itself with the creation of what was called the Agency in the Witwatersrand, which in 1933 began to handle taxation for Basuto nationals employed in the area.[42] In 1938 the BP began to use its services.[43] Eventually it catered to, and was financially supported by, all three HCT,[44] functioning as an unofficial consular office on the Rand.[45] Headed by a BP district officer, the section of the Agency that catered to Batswana nationals was located in Randfontein.[46] In 1973 a bilateral South African-Botswana labor treaty officially recognized the Botswana labor representative at Roodepoort, in the Witwatersrand metropolitan area.[47] Prior to the treaty, the UK's Consulate-General in Johannesburg undertook the labor representation function.[48]

Officials in the labor office are neither private citizens nor diplomats of Botswana. Although their office is in Roodepoort, their residence is in Dobsonville, an African township in Johannesburg.[49] This quasi-diplomatic status[50] represented a blend between the economic realities of Botswana and its foreign policy preferences, which the late President Khama established. In his 1969 address to the OAU,[51] he announced that Botswana would not "consider an exchange of diplomatic representatives until South Africa can fully guarantee that Botswana's representatives will in all respects be treated in the same way as diplomats from other countries."[52] Nevertheless, a recent study published under the auspices of the International Labor Organization indicated that the Roodepoort office actually performed consular tasks for Batswana in the Witwatersrand area of South Africa.[53] The functioning of the Roodepoort office is yet another illustration of the merging of low and high politics in different issue areas. Here Botswana reaped economic benefits at a politically acceptable cost.

Since 1910 the principal vehicle for cash transfers to Botswana was the voluntary deferred pay scheme whereby the miner received a portion of his earnings in Botswana at the end of the contract. Advantageous to the mines and to the receiving state, this scheme insured that the miner would return home to collect his deferred pay[54] and would not become a permanent part of the South African economy.[55] In addition, the mines earned interest on the miners' wages that could be held for those with deferred pay schemes. This interest was returned to the sending state to finance sporting and medical facilities.[56]

Batswana miners purchased such South African goods as clothes, bicycles, and radios, which they took back home with them.[57] This was a boon to South African manufacturers and retailers. According to 1976 Botswana Central Statistics Office data, for example, the miners spent a total of P 13.71 million in South Africa, which comprised 42 percent of their earnings during that year. In addition, they brought back not only P 1.70 million in the form of cash but also P 4.50 million in the form of purchases. Their deferred pay amounted to P 11.52 million that year and represented roughly a third of their total annual earnings of P 32.17 million.[58] Roughly 5 percent of the Batswana miners earn wages sufficiently high to be subject to South African income tax.[59]

In the Botswana national accounts, only that portion of the migrant miners' income remitted to Botswana was considered as part of the gross national product (GNP), but not of the gross domestic product (GDP).[60] Under the terms of the 1973 bilateral treaty, these earnings were subject to Botswana taxation and were deducted from the employees' pay by the employers and sent to the proper offices in Botswana. The Roodepoort Labor Office certified that the employees paid the requisite taxes.[61] In his classic study of migrant labor, Isaac Schapera estimated that about 46 percent of the migrants' earnings were returned directly or indirectly to Botswana.[62]

John R. Harris' research indicated that about two-thirds of the miners' earnings returned directly or indirectly to Botswana.[63] The difference in the Harris and Schapera estimates can probably be explained not only by the different data bases but also by the data processing techniques used in the two studies. The miners' wages had a multiplier effect within the Botswanan domestic economy, that is, spending generated further income through purchases and investments and these, in turn, generated employment opportunities. The multiplier effect in Botswana perhaps was smaller than the one and one-half estimated for Lesotho, a nation that depended much more heavily upon the South African mining industry for employing its nationals than does Botswana.[64]

While a small proportion (2.6 percent) of Botswana nationals earned their living as migrant laborers in South Africa and their remittances constituted 3 percent of the Botswanan GNP in 1983,[65] this was still significant in terms of what David Jones termed "the network of income transfers."[66] Such income transfers are extremely important to the rural poor, especially those whose households are headed by women. These women not only could receive remittances and goods from their absent family members but also could earn a modest income from brewing sorghum beer, which they sold to returning migrant mine workers.[67]

THE LIABILITIES OF MIGRANT LABOR IN SOUTHERN AFRICA

Like most states in the region, Botswana has more job seekers than jobs.[68] Thus working in South African mines was lucrative, largely because the pay levels for unskilled work in Botswana were less than those in South Africa.[69] Considering the recurrent mine labor patterns, that is, contract, return home, another contract, and so on,[70] as well as the bachelor nature of the mining compounds where the African miners live,[71] it is hardly surprising that this type of cyclical migration to South Africa created problems. A predominately rural society with a communal land tenure system, Botswana lacked manpower for raising staple crops and for animal husbandry. The work thus devolved upon women and children who remained on the lands.[72] Men also might be absent when crucial agricultural choices, such as when to plow and which crops to plant, needed to be made, thereby undercutting the effectiveness of agricultural extension work involving their families.[73]

In addition to depleting agricultural areas of labor in the fields and pastures, the migrant labor system weakened cohesion among the various ethnic groupings and eroded traditional deference to chiefs,[74] largely because of the cosmopolitan effect of travel to another country and exposure to a wider range of ethnic groups and ideas in the mines.[75] It also subjected them to South African racial practices and policies.[76] Additionally, returning miners could use their wages to invest in cattle, which are a status symbol within Tswana society. Even during the colonial era, the chiefs complained about the irreverent and insouciant attitudes of returning mine workers who believed they were better than those people who had remained in Botswana.[77] Other individuals used labor contracts to evade such onerous obligations of Tswana society as regimental labor[78]—those collective, unpaid tasks which Batswana age-set groups undertook at the chief's request, such as construction or maintenance of tribal property.[79]

Further, international migrant labor often put pressure upon marriage and child rearing because wives and families could not accompany mine workers; rather they lived in the compounds like bachelors.[80] This style reflected the prevailing South African governmental view until the 1980s[81] that Africans had no right to remain in urban, commercial areas except by request and thus they were principally short-term employees who can be rotated into and out of the work site depending upon the economic situation.[82] Recently, the Chamber of Mines has begun to consider better housing arrangements, but this change has been slow and did not include miners from Botswana.[83] Secular and clerical critics of the migrant labor system charged that the system extracted an exorbitant social and moral price. They argued that marital infidelity, family desertion, delayed marriages, illegitimate births, homosexuality, drunkenness, and reduced parental authority were some of the byproducts of this pattern of disjointed residence and work place.[84]

At various times, the synod of the largest branch of the Dutch Reformed Church in South Africa, the *Nederduits Gereformeerde Kerk*, took issue with the migratory labor system and recognized its shortcomings, particularly in terms of African family life.[85] Yet it did not call for the system's termination.[86] The Anglican Dean of Johannesburg (now the Archbishop of Cape Town and a Nobel Prize laureate), Desmond Tutu, criticized this labor system for the social maladies that it engendered,[87] and the South African Council of Churches also was disturbed about the moral costs of migrant labor.[88]

Batswana migrant miners are among the least educated men in the society. Unlike university students, they do not return to Botswana with highly valued skills, and they bring little to the local or national economy in terms of readily transferable skills.[89] The South African gold mining industry, with its powerful white miners' union, has insured that little, if any, technology transfer occurred from the better skilled white miners to the novice African miners, who were customarily relegated to the ranks of the unskilled and semi-skilled employees.[90] White miners sustained this technology gap, which was reinforced by racial attitudes and mining legislation, thereby protecting their privileged status.[91] The Batswana miners might improve their earnings through repeated contracts, but, because of the South African color bar, they stood little chance of becoming highly skilled miners who could look forward to greater opportunities and remuneration in the smaller mines of Botswana.[92]

THE FUTURE OF MIGRANT LABOR IN BOTSWANA

Since Botswana's independence the annual number of legal migrants to the South African mines has fluctuated between 14,000 and 24,000 men.[93] Three SADCC member states, however, did not follow Botswana's policy regarding migrant labor and forbade their citizens to be officially recruited for mine labor in South Africa. Tanzania started this policy in 1959, followed by Zambia in 1966,[94] and then by Malawi in 1974.[95] Mozambique permitted its citizens to work as miners in South Africa, although the numbers have fallen dramatically.[96] By 1981 the flow from Zimbabwe had practically ended.[97]

Such a shift in employment patterns in the South African mines was significant for regional labor-exporting states. Foreign migrant workers were gradually replaced by those from South Africa.[98] From 1964 to 1984, the proportion of non-South African black workers in these mines has dropped from 64.1 percent to 39.4 percent, even though the total of such workers employed jumped from 388,800 to 495,080 during that same period.[99] Real wages also rose for the mine workers,[100] and the mines demonstrated greater interest in what might be called career miners[101] rather than in neophyte miners.[102]

These changes suggested that South African mines might be less able to absorb Batswana work seekers, preferring to employ miners from the homelands.[103] Had the West tightened economic sanctions against South Africa, it was conceivable that the Pretoria regime could have passed on this economic hardship to it neighbors by reducing the number of, or even eliminating, foreign nationals employed in South Africa.[104]

How would such a situation affect the Batswana migrant miner workers? Would they be repatriated? There is the additional consideration of what policies the Mandela government would adopt regarding foreign migratory workers, who have usually been less well organized and vocal than their South African counterparts. A reduction in migrant labor flows would accelerate the urbanization of Botswana, as the newly unemployed drifted from rural areas to urban ones in search of work.[105] This would certainly increase the pressure on Botswana to create even more employment options,[106] something the Gaborone authorities could temporize about as long as the South African mines offered such opportunities to the least skilled Batswana.[107]

There are two principal points about changes in migrant labor patterns. The first is the rate of change: whether the closure of the South African mining labor market would occur slowly or suddenly and unexpectedly.[108] Botswana would need time to make economic adjustments to this loss or reduction of foreign employment for its nationals. Second, Botswana (as well as other southern African labor-exporting states) is anxious to see that its miners in South Africa improve their working conditions.[109] These concerns reflect the reality that there are few, if any, competitive employment opportunities available for these migrant miners in Botswana.[110]

Batswana miners are in a weak bargaining position relative to the South African mining houses, which operate in a buyers' market. In a desperate economic situation,[111] they have few, if any, bargaining counters[112] given their needs, education, and skills. Their employers, however, have had the luxury of being able to pit one regional labor-exporting nation against another should it appear that the exporters would act in concert to bargain for higher pay rates and improved conditions in the work place.[113]

Recruitment to the South African mines has dropped steadily since 1976[114] because of greater use of capital rather than labor intensive mining technology, pressures to hire local Africans, and the costs of transporting miners from their homes to the mines.[115] Mine recruiting areas within Botswana have correspondingly shrunk to the southeastern portion of the nation, which has traditionally been the most significant labor-exporting region.[116] South African mining recruiters moved the economic catchment area to Bophuthatswana, which contributed one-fourth of the labor the mines required.[117] This shift to the South African homelands, according to Vice President Peter Mmusi, reflected official pressure from Pretoria on the mine labor recruiters to give preference to the homelands. Sometimes, he claimed, the authorities in Gaborone were successful in blocking this South African pressure on the mine labor recruiters, although he did not indicate when and how often the government did this.[118] This would suggest that bargaining was a component of the low politics of migrant labor.

In 1977 and 1978, several southern African ministers of labor met in Maseru and Lusaka, respectively, to explore a planned phase-out of migrant mine labor.[119] On 31 January 1980, in Gaborone, eight of the nine SADCC states (all those except Angola) created the Southern African Labor Commission (SALC), which sponsored workshops and held an annual meeting of ministers of labor. By 1987 the ministers had approved "a Model Labour Migration Agreement with South Africa" to help member states with regard to their migrant workers.[120] A SADCC sectoral paper urged that the suppliers adopt a uniform rate for mine recruiting fees for their citizens so that they could secure greater earnings without jeopardizing their access to the South African mine labor market.[121] This short-run strategy would be valuable only to the extent that such additional revenues could be plowed back into the creation of domestic employment opportunities for displaced or repatriated miners.[122]

In Botswana the present trend is for the South African mines to continue the contracts of older, better skilled miners and to reduce the recruitment of young, inexperienced miners. Thus the average

Motswana mine worker was thirty-two years old in 1986; that average age was twenty-five a decade earlier. Now only 1.6 percent of the new mine laborers in South Africa are from Botswana.[123] As the recruitment area shifted to the southeastern parts of the country, the response of those in the northern and western parts of the country was to trek to the urban areas in search of work,[124] causing high urbanization rates, especially in Gaborone.[125]

Clearly, Botswana was vulnerable to South African counter-sanctions involving the repatriation of its migrant mine workers.[126] In 1985 South African President P. W. Botha, apparently acting with the concurrence of the State Security Council,[127] openly spoke about the repatriation of foreign mine workers as a South African counter to Western sanctions.[128] The National Union of Mineworkers and the Chamber of Mines took strong exception to this position.[129] Had the challenge materialized, Botswana's optimal response would have been to create greater rural employment opportunities,[130] which was made even more difficult because of the current high level of population growth, which will double the population in twenty years. Such a population explosion has profound adverse consequences for the environment.[131]

CHAPTER TEN

Conclusion

THE POLITICS OF DISENGAGEMENT

Botswana's weakness can be traced to its landlocked position, its location in southern Africa, its lack of water, and its modest infrastructure. From the standpoint of international politics, what is crucial, however, is Botswana's propinquity to South Africa. Jack D. Parson averred that its long frontier with South Africa provided Botswana with political visibility and that, without that strategic location, Botswana would be just another Third World state.[1]

His argument underscores the significance of being South Africa's neighbor. The juxtaposition of a weak, African majority-ruled state next door to what was a powerful minority-ruled state attracted the attention of many Western donor states anxious to change the political landscape of southern Africa by eliminating or weakening apartheid in South Africa. Weakness is relative, and that of Botswana is ever more apparent when compared to South Africa, one of the most powerful states in the continent. Consequently, when other states did something for, or about, Botswana, it often meant doing something about, or perhaps against, South Africa. Interest in Botswana was typically a byproduct of fascination with or repugnance to apartheid in South Africa.

Botswana's relationship with South Africa (and Zimbabwe, for that matter) can be examined in terms of high and low politics; that is, it contains security and nonsecurity dimensions. In terms of high politics, the animosity between Botswana and South Africa was high. Their racial attitudes and policies differed markedly. The Botswanan position —clearly spelled out by its foreign minister Dr. Chiepe in her 1985 address to the United Nations Security Council—rested upon a perception of South African apartheid as the problem and the eradication of apartheid as the solution.[2] Yet the leaders of minority-ruled South Africa insisted, particularly in the United Nations, that their racially stratified governmental system was a domestic matter and hence non-negotiable, especially with foreign nations. Consequently, South Africa, to a much greater extent than other states, harped upon the sanctity of sovereignty and preferred an international and regional system based upon the fundamental precepts of noninterference in domestic affairs.[3]

South African authorities wanted to participate fully in international affairs, but not at the expense of dismantling the system of apartheid. South Africa has also paid the price of diplomatic isolation for its unyielding stance against international intrusions to alter its domestic order.[4] High politics intruded here because South African dissidents, who included a small number of radical whites in addition to the politically disadvantaged blacks, insisted upon reordering the South African system with the help of foreign states and sympathetic groups. Their help was sought because of the weakness (in all but numbers) of the disaffected elements within South Africa. There was both a push and a pull for some of the younger, more militant South Africans, many of whom escaped apartheid by journeying north to Botswana.

South African refugees (and, to a lesser extent, those from pre-independent Namibia) in Botswana epitomized the gulf separating the two neighboring states. Had the refugees simply headed north, left the region, and taken up an apolitical life in the remainder of Africa or in the West, the Pretoria regime would have been relieved. Instead, refugees tended to become politicized and even joined various liberation groups, such as the ANC and the Pan-Africanist Congress of South Africa, which aimed to supplement political tactics with military activity. Some refugees returned as armed insurgents, intent upon changing the racial and political balance of power by violent means. Armed struggle necessitated operations against South African property as well as civil and military authorities. Also, it challenged contiguous, host states, which would be at risk by providing what Pretoria regarded as aid and comfort to their enemies. In short, depending upon how one wanted to use the terms, destabilization begot destabilization.[5]

Consequently, refugee policy and security policy were the twin components of high politics for Botswana because they were bound up with regime change in South Africa. It would be myopic to restrict such high politics to South Africa, considering the difficulties Botswana experienced in the aftermath of Zimbabwe's independence. Sympathizers of Joshua Nkomo's ZAPU sought refuge in Botswana, and there were occasional skirmishes between the BDF and the Zimbabwean armed forces. Based upon past trends in Africa, similar security problems may arise between Botswana and Namibia. The unity and national reconciliation that SWAPO of Namibia has tried to foster could be sorely tested in post-independence Namibia when and if the Namibians' expectations for the even-handed allocation of perquisites and services, including employment, are frustrated.[6] Political fault lines may run parallel to those of the several ethnic groups within Namibia, and disgruntled members of minority groups could flee the majority-ruled regime in Windhoek, taking their politics with them into Botswana.

Less episodic than high politics, low politics propelled moves to expand the economic distance between Botswana and South Africa and, conversely, to diminish that distance between Botswana and its SADCC partners. On a sector by sector basis, Botswana increasingly relied upon the resources of its British metropole and, after its independence, upon those of the majority-ruled states in the region. Botswana also has sought aid from other states in Africa and from the international community, using such resources to improve its production and distribution of economic, social, and public goods. To replace the South African presence or assistance seemingly meant to displace that presence or assistance. The reality was more complicated. What Botswana sought to regulate was South African public and private influence stemming from its roles as an employer of migrant labor, as a source of private investment capital, as a supplier of finished goods and products, and as a customer for Botswana's produce.

The nature of the South African connection with Botswana lay at the heart of low politics. This relationship was decidedly interdependent,[7] yet the interdependence was asymmetrical, favoring South Africa.[8] South Africa, in turn, served as the pivot of southern Africa,[9] while Botswana could not muster or project enough military and economic power to function as a regional power. If one regarded dependence in relational terms, that is, the ability of "one country . . . [to] inflict grave damage on another without incurring comparable harm sufficient to deter it from doing so,"[10] then one could characterize Botswana's position as one of dependence vis-à-vis South Africa.[11] Dependence thus entailed the possibility of influence exerted upon one or more nations, across a number of issue areas; the differential in national capabilities could span a wide range.[12] Although some scholars have dismissed the phrases *high* and *low politics*, arguing that only high politics are worthy of a political scientist's attention,[13] that myopic view ignores the role of economic statecraft in international relations. I have shown instances where

Botswana's low politics blends into high politics and where the distinction between the two realms of politics fades in practice (although not in analysis).

Botswana's effort to replace and to diminish the South African contribution to its economy was less an exercise in autarky than a denial to white-ruled South Africa of opportunities to harness the human and nonhuman resources the Pretoria regime needed to perpetuate apartheid. In South African political circles it became commonplace to discuss plans for constitutional engineering (usually termed political dispensations), and this appealed to the ruling minority. These new dispensations, however, did not envision a unitary state with black African majority rule.[14]

The Mandela regime has been admitted to the OAU,[15] following its recognition by the various African states, and the new South African government has rejoined the Commonwealth of Nations[16] and become a member of SADC.[17] At that point, with international respectability regained for South Africa and with Namibia now a member of the OAU, the Commonwealth,[18] and SADC,[19] Botswana would have lost its special standing, according to Parson's thesis. At that point, there would be little, if any, incentive to disengage from relations with South Africa. Thereafter, it could become just another Third World state. Presumably, anti-colonial violence would end and interracial conflict in the region would be reduced, particularly if and when internal political accommodations are reached in both Angola and Mozambique.

Along with other OAU members, Botswana refused to recognize South Africa's fragmentation into a metropole and different ethnic peripheral units termed Bantustans or homelands. One of the former homelands, known as Bophuthatswana, was an ethnic archipelago of Tswana-speakers related to their cousins in Botswana. Only one of the seven component parts of Bophuthatswana abutted on Botswana.[20] Officially, the two neighbors had little to do with each other, with Botswana concerned that none of its acts suggested that it diplomatically recognized Bophuthatswana.[21] Particularly in the 1970s, speculation centered on the possibility of an incorporation of at least a portion of the homeland by Botswana, but nothing ever came of it,[22] and on 6 December 1977 South Africa granted the homeland its independence.[23] The officials in Gaborone wanted to negotiate directly with their counterparts in Pretoria, rather than with those in the capital of Bophuthatswana.[24] In Chapter Seven, I indicated the lengths to which Bophuthatswana went to maneuver Botswana into recognizing its statehood in the railway crew and transit rights episode of 1986–1987.

Except for Malawi, no SADCC states exchanged diplomats with

South Africa. Botswana did not do so to show its displeasure with South African apartheid. The Masire government maintained the policy enunciated by President Khama, who insisted upon equality of treatment of the diplomats,[25] even though the South African foreign minister suggested that Botswana's diplomats would be allowed to occupy premises in the white suburbs of Pretoria and Cape Town.[26] Despite the housing exception, Botswana recognized that these courtesies would be extended only to diplomats. That was the rub.[27] As a result, Botswana adopted a policy termed "telephone diplomacy,"[28] which attempted to maintain links with South Africa at the least possible political[29] and economic cost.[30] At the end of 1992, however, both governments established closer links, terming them the "Office of the Botswana Representative" in South Africa and the "Office of the South African Representative," with the latter located in Gaborone. The announcement, which Botswana's minister for external affairs made on 30 December 1992, did not indicate where the Botswanan office would be sited.[31] An external affairs official admitted that Piet Barnard, the South African representative in Botswana, had not been accorded diplomatic status, probably because the South African regime did not grant such status to Zibani Ntakhwana, Barnard's opposite number in South Africa. Hardly embassies, these offices ranked at the bottom of the diplomatic order of precedence.[32] The 1992 arrangement suggested a very cautious response to the erosion of apartheid, but one that went beyond telephone diplomacy and the Roodepoort office of the labor representative. By July 1994 the two nations had established complete diplomatic relations with each other.[33]

For a variety of reasons, South African political elites have long wanted hegemony over English-speaking southern Africa, using economic inducements to achieve that goal. Functionalist thought, anticipating that economic cooperation will subsequently be transmuted into political integration, played a large role in the various schemes designed to link the parts of the old British sphere of influence in Africa.[34] Earlier I indicated that South Africa unsuccessfully used economic blandishments to win over BP's African elites to the idea of incorporation in South Africa in the 1930s. In his 1963 address to the Transvaal National Party congress, Prime Minister Hendrik F. Verwoerd adumbrated the idea of a southern African common market linking the three HCT, South Africa, and the homelands.[35] The Batswana declined his offer.[36] He took up the theme of the common market once again in his speech to the 1964 Cape National Party congress.[37] In 1979 the South Africans refurbished this idea, calling it CONSAS, an organization that would stretch as far north as the

Zambezi River. South Africans expected that CONSAS would extend to the three BLS states, Namibia, Southern Rhodesia, and the two homelands that had achieved independence (Transkei and Bophuthatswana).[38] Once more, Botswana refused to join this South African-dominated group.[39]

Botswana's attempts to distance itself from South Africa could be interpreted in terms of low politics. The driving force of Botswana's economy was to create an infrastructure that would improve its citizens' standard of living and, in the process, deal with the lack of gainful employment within Botswana since the beginning of this century. This shortfall between the number of able-bodied Batswana and the number of jobs available was a major reason for the export of migrant labor to South African farms and mines.

Severe social, moral, and agricultural costs were associated with this pattern of oscillating labor, with some analysts viewing Botswana as little more than a labor catchment area for South Africa.[40] The migrant labor sector, as shown in Chapter Nine, was very salient in 1985, when President Botha hinted that, in the face of increasing Western sanctions, South Africa might consider repatriating foreign migrant workers.[41] His successor, President De Klerk, let the matter drop. Taking a longer perspective, however, protectionist pressure is likely in post-apartheid South Africa. Employers will probably hire South African, rather than foreign, nationals, if only to meet the expectations of the underemployed and unemployed Africans.[42] In addition, the SALC has not proved to be a useful bargaining instrument against the South African Chamber of Mines.[43]

This leads to the related issue of South African private sector investment. Regarding the diamond mining industry, the Anglo-American Corporation of South Africa plays a significant role in Botswana's economy through its Debswana subsidiary. It is noteworthy that no South African officials were invited to Sir Seretse's funeral in 1980, even though many other heads of state and government were.[44] A private South African citizen, Harry Oppenheimer, laid a wreath at Sir Seretse's grave in Serowe.[45] This is indicative of the public political space that Botswana maintains between itself and the Pretoria regime and of the close ties between Botswana and the South African diamond mining firm of De Beers, which the Oppenheimer family controls.

Although it contributes to Botswana's foreign exchange earnings and provided a major source of tax revenue for Gaborone, diamond mining is fundamentally a capital rather than a labor intensive industry, with few forward and backward economic linkages; it neither generates a large number of jobs nor spurs the creation of ancillary industries to supply the mines or to use its products to create additional goods or services. Its complex marketing and decision-making structure ties Botswana to South Africa in such a way that it could have helped shield South Africa against economic sanctions.[46] The Batswana, in turn, are apprehensive about the preeminent role the South African multinational Anglo-American Corporation[47] has assumed in their economy;[48] they are keen to reduce their reliance upon diamond export earnings,[49] which constituted 80 percent of Botswana's exports in 1990.[50]

Disengagement can be challenging, given the texture of Botswana's economy and its links to both the north and the south. The key here, was the nature of the exchange arrangement and Botswana's ability to manipulate its environment to its advantage. Because of its political or economic bargaining position and skills,[51] Botswana achieved exceptional success in renegotiating a new contract with De Beers in the 1970s;[52] observers claimed that the Anglo-American Corporation was willing to sustain considerable losses in the Selebi-Phikwe copper-nickel mine venture to guarantee its access to the valuable diamond pipes.[53]

Botswana needed greater public and private investment to diversify its economy. The threat of foreign economic pressure against South Africa served as an incentive for overseas and private South African investors to increase investments in Botswana,[54] which tried to interest Americans[55] and Britons[56] in local business opportunities, and its local stockbrokerage operations was likely to attract savings that otherwise might have been deployed outside the country.

In the airline transportation sector, the international airport at Gaborone enabled Botswana to bypass the Jan Smuts Airport hub in Johannesburg. Air Botswana and Namib Air (now Air Namibia) have cooperated to provide a regular link to Windhoek.[57] Such a scheduled east-west airline route provides the transportation for a vacation package for Botswana and Namibia. This would tap the lucrative German market, which has a historical affinity for Namibia.[58] This air link was a first step in the creation of a stronger transportation tie that might eventually include the trans-Kalahari railroad.[59] The idea of this tie originated in the colonial era but is now eclipsed by the construction of a highway to Namibia.[60] Another nettlesome matter is the extent to which Western-owned airlines will make use of the Sir Seretse Khama Airport in Gaborone for international flights that critics once regarded as a means of circumventing bans on air travel to South Africa.[61] Economies of scale and underutilization of aircraft are problems that might be resolved by greater economic cooperation within the SADC framework.[62]

The more difficult task, though, will be to strengthen the newly acquired Botswana Railways, which belonged to the National Railways of Zimbabwe. The transfer from Harare to Gaborone cost the latter roughly P 87 million in compensation for the fixed assets, although the takeover generated about 2,000 new jobs for Batswana.[63] With South Africa willing both to engage in what Jan Loubser, former general manager of the South African Railways, dubbed "transport diplomacy,"[64] and to use its railway network to secure political ends,[65] Botswana could reduce its railway dependence upon South Africa by utilizing the ports in Mozambique, but the main drawback for Botswana of Maputo or of Beira is that Cape Town has the only available cold storage transit facilities for Botswana's beef exports.[66]

COPING WITH CLIENTAGE

By joining with other majority-ruled states in southern Africa, Botswana increased its leverage relative to South Africa. That regional leverage stemmed from SADCC, a loose organization of majority-ruled states in the southern third of the African continent whose secretariat was located in Gaborone. SADCC represented a counterweight to the CONSAS—South Africa and its four internationally unrecognized homelands of Transkei, Venda, Bophuthatswana, and Ciskei.

Disengagement was one way to dilute South African power, especially economic power. By loosening its ties to South Africa, Botswana attempted to deny white South African decision-makers the opportunity of using low politics to the Pretoria regime's advantage. This stratagem did not guarantee Botswana protection against the epitome of high politics, SADF raids, with a foreign policy that reflected the dominance of the South African military establishment during the P.W. Botha era.[67] The Pretoria government developed an array of covert economic, military, and psychological techniques to destabilize neighboring states whose policies it perceived as threatening.[68]

Repugnant as these policies may have been to Botswana and its fellow SADCC members, they underscored the fundamental asymmetry of power within the region. Post-apartheid South Africa will still be a dominant player in the southern African region. Whatever else apartheid may have been, it certainly was a distributive system that awarded public and private goods disproportionately to a numerical minority. The end of apartheid in South Africa alters the balance of internal power, which changes the principles upon which goods and services are distributed within that political system. Presumably, this internal readjustment would benefit South African foreign policy to the extent that foreign policy had represented only the wishes of the dominant minority.

The end of apartheid, however, will not necessarily end conflict and initiate cooperation in southern Africa. The mixture of conflict and cooperation between South Africa and Botswana will probably be less conflictual, at least in the high politics arena. Conflicts in the high politics areas will not attract quite the international attention and support they have in the past, if only because of the diminished salience of the Cold War and the erosion of white rule in South Africa.[69] Both these features facilitated international coalition-building, occasional external intrusion, and rhetorical behavior in lieu of countervailing power.

South Africa still will retain the economic pride of place in southern Africa, even though it will devote considerable economic resources to redistributive programs, while Zimbabwe probably will continue to have the second-ranked economy in the region.[70] Botswana may aspire for third-place economic ranking, based upon its past economic performance. At present, and in the future, Botswana will need all the diplomatic help it can muster in bargaining with South Africa. Although the dismantling of apartheid will probably create savings in administrative and security budgets,[71] these peace dividends are likely to be plowed back into meliorative policies that the newly enfranchised African majority will have come to expect.[72]

The peace process in southern Africa will enable newly recognized players, with claims to international recognition and resources, to change the nature of the economic ententes. The group known as the Front Line States ended its existence on 30 July 1994.[73] The Mandela government is less likely to have the resources to aid neighboring states in their recovery from their wars of independence and probably will need much of the savings from reducing the size of the SADF to dismantle the homeland apparatuses and to reintegrate their personnel into the South African economic and political mainstream. Homeland and defense budgets can be reduced, with the savings applied to meeting the elementary needs of the majority population.[74] Consequently, post-apartheid South Africa is likely to be amenable to renegotiating the SACU, this time with Namibia as a member.[75] A corresponding readjustment of the Rand Monetary Area for Lesotho, Namibia, and Swaziland is equally probable.

With the demise of apartheid and the termination of civil wars in Angola and Mozambique, Botswana's neighborhood will have undergone a sea change. But it is still likely that bargaining groups will be formed to deal with both South Africa and with the industrialized north. A reinvigorated southern Africa will contribute new members to the ACP (African, Caribbean, and Pacific) group within the wider context of the Lomé Convention linking the First and Third Worlds.

Peace in southern Africa, welcome though it will be to the Batswana and their neighbors, will not radically change the nature of international stratification in the world, particularly in terms of the north-south divide. Botswana will still remain weak, which is as much a geographical legacy as an imperial one. Like that of other similar small states throughout the world, its weakness will be reflected in a profile of dependence upon South Africa and the industrialized states of the West. Skilled statecraft, however, has enabled Botswana to enjoy a type of limited freedom of maneuver through what John Ravenhill has termed "collective clientelism."[76] Its fate was shared within the company of the other small states in Africa and the Third World. This might not have pleased all the Batswana, but at least it was an improvement upon permanent thralldom to South Africa. What has been called "Finlandization" was an even less appealing alternative for Botswana's burden of weakness.[77]

AUTONOMY IN SOUTHERN AFRICA: A REPRISE

Does Parson's hypothesis about the dwindling significance of Botswana hold true? Will Botswana pass into oblivion and will southern Africa be of little account in world affairs?[78]

From the regional perspective, the admission of a majority-ruled South Africa to SADC will mean that South Africa's domestic political agenda will probably differ from what it was during the apartheid era. SADC will need to take this change into account,[79] which should come as no shock to those careful observers who, for instance, realized that the foreign policy goals of Malan differed considerably from those of his predecessor, Smuts. The difference between those two prime ministers was clearly exhibited in their approach to the international status of Namibia. Nevertheless, the imbalances in the regional system will still favor South Africa, while Zimbabwe attempts to hold to the second-ranked position.[80]

The end of apartheid has signaled different leaders, not different national rank orders. Botswana still will be flanked by powerful states on its eastern and southern borders. Zambia, with a newly elected president, faces severe economic difficulties and will probably be a pliant neighbor.[81] Botswana's other neighbor, Namibia, is busy meeting the basic human needs of the majority, while trying to secure private and public funds to offset the loss of pre-independence South African budget subventions.[82]

Botswana's search for autonomy continues. Its regional environment has been transformed since 1966. The Soviet Union, which played a significant part in arranging the combined departure of the Cubans from Angola and the SADF from Namibia,[83] is no longer a powerful actor in the region. Politically fragmented and weakened, it is now an aid recipient, not a donor, leaving the West in a favorable position with regard to southern Africa. Christopher Coker[84] and Ted Morello[85] have argued that the new scramble will be for finite external funding. Donor states and organizations are likely to take a hard look at regime qualities, particularly in the area of human rights protection,[86] and Botswana was concerned that external funding may dwindle because of its high level of foreign exchange holdings.[87] As a number of observers have suggested, Botswana's economic growth has not entailed much economic development, so that there are glaring inequities in the distribution of wealth within the nation.[88]

The focus on autonomy does not signify an unrealistic interest in autarky,[89] but rather a concern for enlarging the scope of choice[90] or preferences[91] and with creating political space in which to maneuver.[92] Autonomy stands as antipodal to the *dependencia* approach.[93] *Dependencia* offers political or economic leaders little scope for choice,[94] is rather rigid and doctrinaire about how dependency can be reversed,[95] provides economic planners with little explanatory or predictive tools about managing their own economy,[96] and is a self-reinforcing notion.[97]

By combining this concern for autonomy with the better known concepts of high and low politics, I have traced Botswana's relations with its neighboring states over time and over different economic, military, and political matters. This provides a more satisfactory way of studying change and highlights the sectors in which dependence has decreased since the colonial era. The essential question becomes: how much room for maneuver and for choice did Botswana have in a given sector at a given moment and did it expand that room and the range of choices? Which sectors proved easier to manage? Which required outside funding? Which required outside expertise?

Part of the explanation for Botswana's increasing autonomy was political change in the regional system in the form of British and Portuguese decolonization, which made a difference in the nature of the high politics involved. Equally significant was the willingness of Western powers and international organizations to fund Botswana's attempts to reduce dependence upon its powerful neighbors. Some of the funding could be interpreted as a tacit price some states paid to continue trade with, and investment in, South Africa.[98] Botswana, in sum, had a welter of friends internationally and few enemies.

The challenge facing Botswana is no longer one of high politics: the South African military establishment no longer enjoys the power it had in the days of President P. W. Botha; the refugee issue has become less nettlesome following the return of the Dukwe residents to Zimbabwe; and, aside from the Sidudu/Kasikili Island dispute, there are no irredentist irritants between Botswana and its neighbors. The other exception, however, is the construction of a large BDF airfield at Molepolole at a cost of P 1 billion as a replacement for the one in Gaborone. The project has alarmed the foreign minister of Namibia and aroused the concern of the Swedish and Norwegian governments.[99]

The two significant challenges facing Botswana for the rest of the decade will be in the low politics area. The first concerns the reversal of some, if not most, of the environmental damage that has come primarily from expanding the national cattle herd and the rangeland, which is a serious problem of long-term environmental degradation here.[100] The second challenge will be the conduct of trade within two different zones, namely, the Southern African Custom Union zone of Botswana, Lesotho, Swaziland, Namibia, and South Africa and the Preferential Trade Area of Zimbabwe and Zambia.[101] What will be of lasting importance will be the nature of the economic competition between Botswana and Zimbabwe, which has caused ill will in the past and required the leaders of both states to draw down on their reserves of political capital to resolve amicably.[102]

Notes

PREFACE

1. *The Third Wave: Democratization in the Late Twentieth Century* (Norman: University of Oklahoma Press, 1991). This classic work includes extensive references to South Africa.

2. Marina Ottaway provides a lucid analysis of this period of South African political history in her *South Africa: The Struggle for a New Order* (Washington, DC: Brookings Institution, 1993).

3. The term southern Africa, as used in this study, includes the ten states of Angola, Botswana, Lesotho, Malawi, Mozambique, Namibia, South Africa, Swaziland, Zambia, and Zimbabwe.

4. The term Botswana is a geographical one, referring to the nation-state, whose citizens are known collectively as Batswana and whose indigenous language is Setswana.

5. Charles Harvey, *Botswana: Is the Economic Miracle Over?*, Discussion Paper no. 298 (Brighton: University of Sussex, Institute of Development Studies, 1992), 3. John Battersby, a veteran correspondent, wrote that Botswana's economy has been "outperforming every economy in the world." ("Striving for Links after Decades of Hostility," CSM, 21 September 1994, 8).

6. John D. Holm termed Botswana "the only uninterrupted liberal democracy in postcolonial Africa" ("Botswana: One African Success Story," CH 93, no. 583 [May 1994]:198), while Keith Somerville regarded it as "the most politically stable . . . state in southern Africa" ("Botswana at the Crossroads," WT 50, no. 2 [February 1994]:22).

7. Harvey, *Botswana*, 4.

8. Professor I. William Zartman observed that "The most important relations of any country . . . are its relations with its neighbors, since it is here that the greatest need to deal with issues on a day-to-day basis arises." "Decision-Making among African Governments on Inter-African Affairs," JDS 2, no. 2 (January 1966):98.

9. Frederic S. Pearson and J. Martin Rochester (*International Relations: The Global Condition in the Late Twentieth Century*, second ed. [New York: Random House, 1988], 327) define "'High politics'. . . [as] those issues involving the most crucial and the most controversial interests of states (especially military security issues)," while "'low politics' refers to those issues that are relatively narrow, technical and noncontroversial (for example, setting international mail rates, sharing weather forecasting data or cancer research findings, or managing river basins)."

10. See Arnold H. Isaacs, *Dependence Relations between Botswana, Lesotho, Swaziland and the Republic of South Africa: A Literature Study Based on Johan Galtung's Theory of Imperialism*, Research Reports no. 15 (Leiden: African Studies Centre, 1982), and Bruce Couperthwaithe, comp., "The Bechuanaland Protectorate," RRJ 18, no. 1 (1951):27–71.

11. Ronald T. Libby, *The Politics of Economic Power in Southern Africa* (Princeton, NJ: Princeton University Press, 1987), 110, n. 1 and 131, n. 17.

12. The best-known example is Joseph Hanlon, *Beggar Your Neighbours: Apartheid Power in South Africa* (Bloomington: Indiana University Press, 1986), 4.

13. Deon J. Geldenhuys, *The Diplomacy of Isolation: South African Foreign Policy Making* (New York: St. Martin's Press, 1984), 102, 153–154, and 163.

14. Olayiwala Abegunrin, *Economic Dependence and Regional Cooperation in Southern Africa: SADCC and South Africa in Confrontation*, Studies in African Economic and Social Development, vol. 2 (Lewiston, NY: The Edwin Mellen Press, 1990), 225.

15. Alvin Y. So provides a thorough review of the dependency literature in his *Social Change and Development: Modernization, Dependency, and World-System Theories*, Sage Library of Social Research no. 178 (Newbury Park, CA: Sage Publications, 1990), 91–165.

16. See Margaret C. Lee, *SADCC: The Political Economy of Development in Southern Africa* (Nashville, TN: Winston-Derek Publishers, 1989), especially 14–19 and 271–274.

17. *Regional Cooperation in Southern Africa: A Post-Apartheid Perspective*, Seminar Proceedings no. 22, ed. Bertil Odén and Haroub Othman (Uppsala: SIAS, 1989), is an example of this type of creativity.

18. "Southern Africa in Conflict: Problems Enough To Share," in *South Africa in Southern Africa: Domestic Chance and International Conflict*, ed. Edmond J. Keller and Louis A. Picard (Boulder, CO: Lynne Rienner Publishers, 1989), 203, 206, and 213.

19. Alan Riding, *Distant Neighbors: A Portrait of the Mexicans* (New York: Viking Books, 1989, originally published in 1984).

20. Two notable exceptions are Heige Hveem, "If Not Global, Then (Inter-) Regional: The Mini-NIEO Alternative," in Odén and Othman, *Regional Cooperation*, 186 and 191, and Libby, *The Politics of Economic Power*, 110, n. 1 and 131, n. 17.

21. *Finlandization: Towards a General Theory of Adaptive Politics* (Aldershot: Avebury, 1988), 43, n. 39, 45, and 69–70.

22. (New Haven: YUP, 1982), 16–17.

23. I follow the distinction between external and internal dependence developed in Wolfgang Schneider-Barthold's "Determinants and Forms of External and Internal Dependence in Rhodesia and Namibia: Possible Solutions to the Problem of Twofold Dependence," in *Perspectives of Independent Development in Southern Africa: The Cases of Zimbabwe and Namibia*, Occasional Papers of the German Development Institute no. 62, ed. Harmut Brandt et al. ([West] Berlin: German Development Institute, 1980), 1–2. The element of international asymmetry is certainly part of the pattern of relations between a dominant and a subordinate state, as explained in David B. Abernathy, "Dominant-Subordinant Relationships: How Shall We Define Them? How Do We Compare Them?" in *Dominant Powers and Subordinate States: The United States in Latin America and the Soviet Union in Eastern Europe*, ed. Jan F. Triska (Durham, NC: Duke University Press, 1986), 104–107.

24. *Small Is Dangerous: Micro States in a Macro World: Report of a Study Group of the David Davies Memorial Institute of International Studies*, ed. Sheila Harden (New York: St. Martin's Press, 1985), 137. James A. Caporaso provides an excellent cluster of indicators in his "Dependence, Dependency, and Power in the Global System: A Structural and Behavioral Analysis," IntOrg 32, no. 1 (Winter 1978):25–26.

25. See Charles Harvey and Stephen R. Lewis, Jr., *Policy Choice and Development Performance in Botswana* (New York: St. Martin's Press, 1990), 11, 41, 64–65, and 320.

26. James J. Zaffiro, "Evolution of Foreign Policy Decision-Making in Botswana: Domestic, Regional, and International Factors" (Paper delivered at the thirty-third annual meeting of the African Studies Association, Baltimore, 1–4 November 1990), 36.

27. Robert H. Jackson, *Quasi-States: Sovereignty. International Relations, and the Third World*, Cambridge Series in International Relations, no. 12 (Cambridge: CUP, 1990), 194.

CHAPTER ONE

1. See the commentary on, and the text of, the 1969 Lusaka Manifesto in Kenneth W. Grundy, *Confrontation and Accommodation in Southern Africa*, Perspectives on Southern Africa no. 10 (Berkeley: UCP, 1973), 113–117 and 315–323 (Appendix 2), respectively.

2. Willie Henderson, "Seretse Khama and the Institutionalisation of the Botswana State," in *Botswana: Education, Culture, and Politics: Proceedings of a Conference Held in the Centre of African Studies, University of Edinburgh, 15 & 16 December 1988*, Seminar Proceedings no. 29 (Edinburgh: University of Edinburgh, Centre of African Studies, 1990), 235, and Arne Tostensen, *Dependence and Collective Self-Reliance in Southern Africa: The Case of the Southern African Development Coordination Committee (SADCC)*, Research Report no. 62 (Uppsala: SIAS, 1982), 15.

3. Three examples are: international or symbolic legitimation dependency (evident in Botswana's refusal to sanction apartheid by exchanging ambassadors with Pretoria and to recognize Bophuthatswana, a Tswana

homeland), migrant labor dependency, and retail merchandise sales dependency. See Henderson, "Seretse Khama," 221 and 237; Roger Martin, *Southern Africa: The Price of Apartheid: A Political Risk Analysis*, Special Report no. 1130 (London: EIU, 1988), 29–32; and Stephen R. Lewis, Jr., *Economic Realities in Southern Africa (or, One Hundred Million Futures)*, Discussion Paper no. 232 (Brighton: University of Sussex, Institute of Development Studies, 1987), 1 and 34.

4. For the notion of vulnerability and its application to Botswana, consult Carol R. Hansen, "South Africa as a Force for Regional Stability or Instability" (Ph.D. diss., Harvard University, 1985), 99, 101–102, 163–164, and 187, and "Walking a Tight Rope," MWD, 24–30 October 1987, 2 (editorial).

5. "The Zairian Crisis and American Foreign Policy," in *African Crisis Areas and U.S. Foreign Policy*, ed. Gerald J. Bender, James S. Coleman, and Richard L. Sklar (Berkeley: UCP, 1985), 219.

6. Richard F. Weisfelder, who has provided the most rigorous definition of this behavior, indicated that "Destabilization involves preemptive intervention whereby a state or other international actor covertly orchestrates disruption of the economic, political[,] and social systems of target states," adding that it "attains its objectives through indirect and covert means that violate accepted international standards and would otherwise trigger global condemnation and countervailing sanctions." ("Destabilization in Southern Africa: Conflict Management and Conflict Accentuation" [Preliminary draft of a paper delivered at the twenty-fifth annual meeting of the African Studies Association, Washington, DC, 4–7 November 1982], 2—3).

7. John Imrie and Thomas Young, "South Africa and Botswana: [A] Case of Destabilisation?" IAB 14, no. 1 (1990):15–16, and Gerald L'Ange, "Countries in the Cross-Fire," in *Challenge: Southern Africa within the African Revolutionary Context: An Overview*, ed. Al J. Venter (Gibraltar: Ashanti Publishing, Ltd., 1989), 332 and 352.

8. King George VI and his family visited Botswana in 1947 as part of the Royal Tour to South Africa, while Princess Marina (Queen Elizabeth II's aunt) represented the queen at the 1966 independence celebration. Queen Elizabeth II visited Botswana in 1979, and Prince Charles visited Botswana in 1984. Sir R. Peter Fawcus remarked that "The real legacy of Colonial [sic] rule in Botswana, strikingly demonstrated to us during our visit, is the exceptionally warm and friendly relations which exist between the Botswana Government and people and the British." ("Botswana Revisited," BNR 19 [1987], 171).

9. The African Governance Program of the Carter Center of Emory University rated Botswana (along with Gambia, Mauritius, Namibia, and Senegal) as having a democratic political system. Eight African states were classified as authoritarian, two as directed democracies, and twenty-five others were designated as "regimes in transition" (which were grouped according to whether their commitment to a democratic system was ambiguous [eleven], moderate [ten], and strong [four]). "Political Systems" and "Regimes in Transition/Strength of Commitment to Democracy," *Africa Demos* 1, no. 2 (January 1991):7 (both articles).

10. Philip H. Frankel, "The Foreign Policy of Swaziland" (M.A. thesis, University of the Witwatersrand, 1976), 161–162.

11. Very little has been published on the Asian population in Botswana, which is quite small and located in urban areas. See Saroj N. Parratt, "Muslims in Botswana," AS 48, no. 1 (1989):71–82.

12. See Q. Neil Parsons, "Seretse Khama and the Ba[ma]ngwato Succession Crisis, 1948–1953," in *Succession to High Office in Botswana: Three Case Studies*, ed. Jack D. Parson, Monographs in International Studies, Africa series no. 54 (Athens: Ohio University Press, 1990), 73–95, especially 78–84, and 351–364 (Appendix K).

13. Willie Henderson, "Independent Botswana: A Reappraisal of Foreign Policy Options," AA 73, no. 290 (January 1974):40–41, and Seretse Khama, *From the Frontline: Speeches of Sir Seretse Khama*, ed. Gwendolen M. Carter and E. Philip Morgan (London: Rex Collings, 1980), 56–62, especially 56.

14. "Botswana: Economy Sparkles," FM 96, no. 2 (12 April 1985):53.

15. *Macro-Economic Management and Bureaucracy: The Case of Botswana*, Research Report no. 59 (Uppsala: SIAS, 1981), 19.

16. "Economic Cooperation in Sub-Saharan Africa," *Mining Survey* (Johannesburg), 2 (1989):11 and 18.

17. Louis A. Picard, *The Politics of Development in Botswana: A Model for Success?* (Boulder, CO: Lynne Rienner Publishers, 1987), 235; Christopher L. Colclough and Stephen J. McCarthy, *The Political Economy of Botswana: A Study in Growth and Distribution* (New York: OUP, 1980), 76–79, 81–85, 90, and 141–158; and Nimrod Raphaeli, Jacques Roumani, and A. C. MacKeller, *Public Sector Management in Botswana: Lessons in Pragmatism*, World Bank Staff Working Papers no. 709 (Washington, DC: The World Bank, 1984), 37–59.

18. Lynda Schuster, "Surviving without South Africa: Namibia: Realism Key for Economy," CSM, 13 April 1989, 3.

19. "The Small State in International Politics," in *Small States and International Relations*, ed. August Schou and Arne O. Brundtland, Nobel Symposium no. 17 (New York: John Wiley & Sons, Inc., 1971), 32 (italics in the original).

20. "Introduction," in *South Africa in Southern Africa: The Intensifying Vortex of Violence*, ed. Thomas M. Callaghy (New York: Praeger Publishers, 1983), 7.

21. For contrasting interpretations, consult Deon J. Geldenhuys, "South Africa: A Stabilising or Destabilising Influence in Southern Africa?," in *On the Razor's Edge: Prospects for Political Stability in Southern Africa*, ed. Calvin A. Woodward, Communications of the Africa Institute of South Africa no. 46 (Pretoria: AISA, 1986), 59–75; Elling N. Tjønneland, *Pax Pretoriana: The Fall of Apartheid and the Politics of Destabilisation*, Discussion Paper no. 2 (Uppsala: SIAS, 1989), 16–24; and Martin, *Southern Africa*, 5–11, 33–56, and 126–128.

22. This and the preceding paragraph draw upon John A. Vasquez, *The Power of Power Politics: A Critique* (New Brunswick, NJ: Rutgers University Press, 1983), 13–37; Paul R. Viotti and Mark V. Kauppi, *International Relations Theory: Realism, Pluralism, Globalism* (New York: Macmillan Publishing Company, 1987), 7, 10, 33, 60–67, 193, 400, and 592; Robert L. Pfaltzgraff, Jr., "International Relations Theory: Retrospect and Prospect," IA

50, no. 1 (January 1974) 28–31; Arend Lijphart, "The Structure of the Theoretical Revolution in International Relations," ISQ 18, no. 1 (March 1974):43–44; and Robert O. Keohane and Joseph S. Nye, *Power and Interdependence: World Politics in Transition* (Boston: Little, Brown and Company, 1977), 24 and 46.

23. "Public Opinion and Regional Integration," Intorg 24, no. 4 (Autumn 1970):770.

24. Eritrea is an obvious exception to this. For a current assessment, consult Jeffrey Herbst, "The Creation and Maintenance of National Boundaries in Africa," IntOrg 43, no. 4 (Autumn 1989):673–692.

25. Even though Namibia was under South African control at this time, the white residents of the Ghanzi enclave in western Botswana seemed uninterested in joining neighboring Namibia, an idea which Lord Harlech, the British high commissioner in South Africa, was considering in 1944 (PRO, file D.O. 116/8/25, Lord Harlech to Lord Cranbourne [Secretary of State for Dominion Affairs], 5 June 1944 as cited in Harold H. Robertson, "From Protectorate to Republic: The Political History of Botswana, 1926–1966" [Ph.D. diss., Dalhousie University, 1979], 246, n. 16).

26. See James H. Polhemus, "Botswana's Role in the Liberation of Southern Africa," in *The Evolution of Modern Botswana: Politics and Rural Development in Southern Africa*, ed. Louis A. Picard (London: Rex Collings; Lincoln: University of Nebraska Press, 1985), 228–270 and 322–328.

27. Seretse Khama, "Address on Botswana and Southern Africa to the Foreign Policy Society, Copenhagen, 13 November 1970," in Khama, *From the Frontline*, 106; Rolf Bodenmüller, *Botswana, Lesotho, and Swaziland: Their External Relations and Policy and Attitudes towards South Africa* (Pretoria: AISA, 1973), 85-86; and Martin, *Southern Africa*, 36-37.

28. Athaliah Molokomme, "Mine Labour Migration from Botswana to South Africa: Some Practical Legal Issues," in Louis Molamu, Athaliah Molokomme, and Gloria Somolekae, *Perceptions of Batswana Mineworkers towards the South African Gold Mines with Special Reference to Living and Working Conditions, Legal Issues, and Trade Unions*, International Migration for Employment Working Paper no. 36 (Geneva: ILO, 1988), 41 and 51; Martin, *Southern Africa*, 40–42; and Douglas G. Anglin, "Southern Africa under Siege: Options for the Frontline States," JMAS 26, no. 4 (December 1988) 557–558.

29. BNAORH, 60 (22 November 1977), 17 (policy statement of the minister of external affairs). These and other points of conflict and cooperation are discussed in Richard Dale, "Botswana's Relations with Bophuthatswana: The Politics of Ethnicity, Legitimacy, and Propinquity in Southern Africa," JCH 17, no. 2 (December 1992):1–19.

30. Stanley Hoffman emphasized the connotative significance of high politics when he used the equivalent German expression *Grosspolitik* ("Discord in Community: The North Atlantic Area as a Partial International System," IntOrg 17, no. 3 [Summer 1963]:531).

31. See Samuel C. Chime's near-encyclopedic study, *Integration and Politics among African States: Limitations and Horizons of Mid-Term Theorizing* (Uppsala: SIAS, 1977), and Martin Holland's "A Rejoinder: The European Community and Regional Integration in Southern Africa: A

Misplaced Analogy," PSAJPS 10, no. 2 (December 1983):38–50.

32. The South African political scientist Peter Vale has characterized this approach as "the politics of assertive incorporation" ("Regional Policy: The Compulsion To Incorporate," in *South Africa in Crisis*, ed. Jesmond Blumenfeld [London: Croom Helm Ltd., 1987], 181–184).

33. For a comparative analysis of the two organizations, see Deon J. Geldenhuys, *The Constellation of Southern African States and the Southern African Development Co-ordination Council* [sic., i.e., Conference]: *Towards a New Regional Stalemate?* Special Study (Braamfontein: SAIIA, 1981).

34. Viotti and Kauppi, *International Relations Theory*, 7–10 and 192–193; Samuel P. Huntington, "Transnational Organizations in World Politics," WP 25, no. 3 (April 1973):333–368; and Joseph S. Nye, Jr. and Robert O. Keohane, "Transnational Relations and World Politics: A Conclusion," IntOrg 25, no. 3 (Summer 1971):729 (quotation). The subject matter of high and low politics is graphically displayed in Leon N. Lindberg and Stuart A. Scheingold, *Europe's Would-Be Polity: Patterns of Change in the European Community* (Englewood Cliffs, NJ: Prentice-Hall, Inc., 1970), 263 (figure 8.1).

35. Joseph S. Nye, Jr., *Peace in Parts: Integration and Conflict in Regional Organization* (Boston: Little, Brown and Company, 1971), 41, n. 55.

36. The term was apparently coined by Dr. J.G.H. Loubser, former manager of the South African Transport Services (see his *Transport Diplomacy with Special Reference to Southern Africa* [Sandton: Southern African Editorial Services (Pty.) Ltd., 1980]).

37. John Imrie and Donald Wilson, "Botswana in the 1990s: Prospects for Prosperity, Stability and Security," in *Southern Africa at the Crossroads?: Prospects for Stability and Development in the 1990s*, ed. Larry Benjamin and Christopher Gregory (Rivonia: Justified Press, 1992), 46.

38. Concern for Botswana's ability to weather the imposition of economic sanctions against South Africa antedated independence, as shown by R. M. Bostock, "Sanctions and the High Commission Territories," in *Sanctions against South Africa*, ed. Ronald Segal (Baltimore: Penguin Books, 1964), 204–233.

39. Sullivan, "Southern Africa in Conflict," 303 and Richard F. Weisfelder, "SADCC as a Counter-Dependency Strategy: How Much Collective Clout?" in Keller and Picard, *South Africa in Southern Africa*, 173.

40. See Steven J. Brams, "Transaction Flows in the International System," APSR 60, 4 (December 1966):898.

41. United States. Congress. House of Representatives. Committee on Foreign Affairs. Subcommittee on Africa, *Regional Destabilization in Southern Africa: Hearing.* 97th Congress. 2d Session, 8 December 1982. Committee Print (Washington, DC: USGPO, 1983), 166.

42. Lewis, *Economic Realities*, 18; Lee, *SADCC*, 273; Gavin Maasdorp, "The Southern African Development Co-ordination Conference (SADCC)," in *South Africa in Southern Africa: Economic Interaction*, ed. G.M. Erich Leistner and Peter Esterhuysen, Research Communications Series no. 51 (Pretoria: AISA, 1988), 82; Douglas G. Anglin, "Economic Liberation and Regional Cooperation in Southern Africa: SADCC and PTA," IntOrg 37, no. 4 (Autumn 1983):706; and Henry Bienen, "Economic Interests and Security Issues in

Southern Africa," in Robert I. Rotberg et al., *South Africa and Its Neighbors: Regional Security and Self-Interest* (Lexington, Mass.: Lexington Books 1985), 84.

43. See both the list of "measures or events which increase or decrease Botswana's dependence on South Africa" in Bertil Odén, *The Macroeconomic Position of Botswana*, Research Report no. 6 (Uppsala: SIAS, 1981), 44–45, and Harvey and Lewis, *Policy Choice*, 320–321.

44. *Collective Clientelism: The Lomé Conventions and North-South Relations* (New York: Columbia University Press, 1985), 3.

45. *Ideology and Development in Africa*, 308.

46. "Seretse Khama: A Personal Appreciation," AA 89, no. 354 (January 1990):44.

47. This analysis draws upon Viotti and Kauppi, *International Relations Theory*, 9–10 and 399–401; Tony Smith, "The Underdevelopment of Development Literature: The Case of Dependency Theory," WP 31, no. 2 (January 1979):247–288, especially 283–284; Imrie and Thomas, "South Africa and Botswana," 16; and Michael Clough and Jeffrey Herbst, *South Africa's Changing Regional Strategy: Beyond Destabilization*, Critical Issues, 1989, no. 4 (New York: Council on Foreign Relations, 1989), 17.

48. Lee, *SADCC*, 14, 19, and 264.

CHAPTER TWO

1. *Apartheid's Second Front: South Africa's War against Its Neighbours* (Harmondsworth: Penguin Books Ltd., 1986), 46.

2. *Structural Conflict: The Third World against Global Liberalism* (Berkeley: UCP, 1985), 113, 120, 122, 128, 176–178, 181, 226, and 268.

3. Anthony Sillery, *The Bechuanaland Protectorate* (Cape Town: Geoffrey Cumberlege, OUP, 1952), 58 and 78.

4. Ibid., 78–79.

5. Tony Hawkins, "Rhodesia Booms, So Why the Fears?" *The Star*, 9 October 1974, 2d c.l.e., 29.

6. "Republic and Protectorates: We Will Never Link—Premier," RDM, 5 September 1962, m.f.e., 1-2.

7. SAPHAD, 5 (25 January 1963), col. 233.

8. Henry John May, *The South African Constitution*, 3d ed. (Cape Town: Juta & Co., Limited, 1955), 19-21, 124-125, 517, and 626–627.

9. "S. A. To Renounce Claims," *The Star*, 5 February 1969, 2d c.l.e., 13, and SAPSD, 1969, 1 (13 March 1969), cols. 785–786 (2d reading debate).

10. Louis A. Picard, "From Bechuanaland to Botswana: An Overview" in Picard, *The Evolution*, 5.

11. Jeffrey Butler, Robert I. Rotberg, and John Adams, *The Black Homelands of South Africa: The Political and Economic Development of Bophuthatswana and Kwazulu*, Perspectives on Southern Africa no. 21 (Berkeley: UCP, 1977), 159, n. 3.

12. SA, *Summary of the Report of the Commission for the Socio-Economic Development of the Bantu Areas within the Union of South Africa*. U.G.

61/1955 (Pretoria: GP, 1955), 181; SAPHAD, 90 (20 January 1956), col. 192; SAPHAD, 91 (14 May 1956), col. 5309; and SAPHAD, 91 (16 May 1956), col. 5504.

13. "Nationalists and Native Policy," CT, 10 November 1925, 9.

14. Don Knowler, "Botswana Worried over New Homeland," *The Star*, 26 August 1977, s.p.e., 18.

15. BNAORH, 60 (22 November 1977), 17.

16. Wallace Sokolsky, "The Establishment of the British Protectorate in Bechuanaland" (M.A. thesis, Columbia University, 1951), 47–79.

17. SAPHAD, 20 (26 January 1933), col. 130 (Mr. A.S. van Hees).

18. Ronald Hyam, *The Failure of South African Expansion, 1908–1948* (London: Macmillan Press, 1972), 49, 53, and 68.

19. Jack R. Bermingham, "The Settler/Imperial Complex and the Bechuanaland Protectorate" (Ph.D. diss., University of California, Santa Barbara, 1979), 31 and 151–152.

20. Derek Smith, "Africans Claim Tuli and Tati Blocks: Bechuana Seeks U.N. Aid," RDM, 11 June 1964, m.f.e., 13.

21. SA, *Negotiations regarding the Transfer to the Union of South Africa of the Government of Basutoland, the Bechuanaland Protectorate, and Swaziland, 1910–1939* (Pretoria: GP, 1952), 12.

22. Robertson, "From Protectorate to Republic," 181–182.

23. Hyam, *The Failure*, 74–75.

24. Newell M. Stultz, *Afrikaner Politics in South Africa, 1934-1948*, Perspectives on Southern Africa no. 13 (Berkeley: UCP, 1974), 19–21, 30–32, and 47–48.

25. Leonard M. Thompson, *The Unification of South Africa, 1902-1910* (Oxford: Clarendon Press, 1960), 124–127 and 271–79.

26. Geldenhuys, *The Diplomacy of Isolation*, 20–21.

27. UNGA res. 1817 (XVII) of 18 December 1962, operative para. 6.

28. *Documents and Speeches on Commonwealth Affairs, 1931–1952*, 2 vols., ed. Nicholas Mansergh (London: OUP, 1953), vol. 2, 929.

29. "Britain and S.A. Disagree on Meaning of a Word," *The Star*, 6 July 1956, c.l.e., 1.

30. The attitudes of the Batswana until the Second World War are examined in June B. Rampa, "Euro-African Reactions to Incorporation: The Bechuanaland Case (c. 1908–1940)" (B.A. thesis, University College of Botswana, 1978), 20–34.

31. Hyam, *The Failure*, 77.

32. BPNACM, 3d sess. (15 November 1921), 8, 10, and 12–13; 5th sess. (16–17 March 1925), 4–11; 15th sess. (10 July 1933), 34–35; and BPAACM, 25th sess. (29 April 1944), 87–89.

33. "Case for Incorporation of Protectorates," EPH, 22 October 1953, 7.

34. Deon J. Geldenhuys, "South Africa's Regional Policy" in *Changing Realities in Southern Africa: Implications for American Policy*, ed. Michael Clough, Research Series no. 47 (Berkeley: University of California Institute of International Studies, 1982), 134, 150–152, and 156.

35. SA, *Negotiations*, 17 and 45.

36. SAPHAD, 26 (25 March 1936), col. 1916, and 27 (11 June 1936), cols.

5918–5941.

37. Robertson, "From Protectorate to Republic," 206–211.

38. SA, *Negotiations*, 46-50.

39. SRLAD, 13 (26 April 1933), cols. 541–542 (prime minister's speech).

40. Hanlon, *Apartheid's Second Front*, 39.

41. Letter to me from Dr. Thomas P. Ofcansky, US Department of Defense analyst, Washington, DC, dated 28 March 1990.

42. See Mirjana Roth's "'If You Give Us Rights We Will Fight': Black Involvement in the Second World War," SAHJ, 15 (November 1983):85–104.

43. Letter of 21 May 1921 from Sir H. Roland M. Bourne to H. J. Stanley (imperial secretary to the high commissioner), letter of 24 May 1921 from Stanley to Bourne, letter of 19 July 1921 from Bourne to Sir Henry C. M. Lambert (head of the Dominions Department of the Colonial Office), and letter of 4 August 1921 from Bourne to the private secretary of Prime Minister Smuts, TCAD, PM 1/1/411, file folder 150/20.

44. Michael Crowder, *The Flogging of Phinehas McIntosh: A Tale of Colonial Folly and Injustice: Bechuanaland, 1933* (New Haven: YUP, 1988), 52–61, 63–64, 67, 69, 71–72, 81, 85–86, 88–89, 94–95, 98, 102–103, 111–112, 119, 122, and 124.

45. SAPHAD, 42 (4 April 1941), cols. 5882–5883.

46. UKPHCD, 592 (21 July 1958), cols. 11–12 (written answers), and SAPHAD, 105 (3 May 1960), cols. 6592–6593 and 6610 (Mr. J.A.L. Basson and the minister of defense, respectively).

47. "The Evolution of Modern Botswana: Historical Revisions," in Picard, *The Evolution*, 34–36.

48. BPEACM, 12th sess. (3–12 March 1930), 39–40 (comments of the Acting Resident Commissioner Charles F. Rey and Mr. H. C. Weatherilt).

49. See Paul R. Maylam, *Rhodes, the Tswana, and the British: Colonial Collaboration and Conflict in the Bechuanaland Protectorate, 1885-1899*, Contributions in Comparative Colonial Studies no. 4 (Westport, CT: Greenwood Press, 1980), especially 34, 63–64, 66–71, 99, 149–152, 155–156, 162–168, 170–173, 175–179, 189, 191–194, 200, and 218–220.

50. Ibid., 195.

51. Linda Van Buren, "Forging Links to the North Is a Formidable Task," AB 148 (December 1990):35.

52. Martin Chanock, *Britain, Rhodesia, and South Africa, 1900–45: Unconsummated Union* (Totowa, NJ: Frank Cass and Company, 1977), 75–76.

53. Maylam, *Rhodes*, 197-198.

54. Anthony Sillery, *Founding a Protectorate: History of Bechuanaland, 1885–1895*, Studies in African History, Anthropology, and Ethnology, vol. 3 (The Hague: Mouton & Co., 1965), 127.

55. Philip R. Warhurst, "Rhodesia and Her Neighbours, 1900–23" (D.Phil. diss., University of Oxford, 1970), 394.

56. *Proceedings at the Eighteenth Ordinary General Meeting and at an Extraordinary General Meeting of the British South Africa Company, Great Hall, Cannon Street Hotel, 27th February, 1913* (s.l.: n.p., 1913), 10.

57. Letter of 12 March 1913 from Prime Minister Botha to High Commissioner Lord Gladstone reprinted in UKCRO, *Basutoland, the*

Bechuanaland Protectorate, and Swaziland: History of Discussions with the Union of South Africa, 1909–1939, cmd. 8707 (London: HMSO, 1952), 12.

58. Parsons, "The Evolution," 35.

59. Hugh I. Wetherell, "The Rhodesias and Amalgamation: Settler Sub-Imperialism and the Imperial Response, 1914–48" (D.Phil. diss., University of Rhodesia, 1977), 78–81, 88–89, 99–100, 105–106, and 116.

60. Robertson, "From Protectorate to Republic," 179 and 246.

61. Henderson M. Tapela, "The Tati District of Botswana, 1866–1969" (D.Phil. diss., University of Sussex, 1976), 191.

62. Debate of 18 May 1921 on Mr. Moffat's motion on the Tati district, as reported in the RH, 27 May 1921, w.e., 22–23.

63. Warhurst, "Rhodesia and Her Neighbours," 397–401.

64. UKPHCD, 185 (15 June 1925), cols. 11–12 (oral answers); 199 (18 November 1926), cols. 1963–1964 (oral answers); 217 (14 May 1928), col. 642 (oral answers); and 237 (24 March 1930), col. 48 (written answers).

65. SRLAD, 3 (10 June 1925), cols. 1327–1328; 7 (5 June 1928), cols. 595–596; 12 (11 May 1932), col. 1752; 13 (12 April 1933); and 13 (26 April 1933), cols. 531–543.

66. Ibid., 13 (26 April 1933), col. 531.

67. "Walvis Bay Our Future Port: Southern Rhodesia Premier's Declaration," BC, 13 November 1929, 5 and 3 [sic].

68. J.R.T. Wood, *The Welensky Papers: A History of the Federation of Rhodesia and Nyasaland* (Durban: Graham Publishing Company [Pty.] Ltd., 1983), 146–147, 155–158, and 160–161.

69. "Bechuanaland Afrikaners' Petition," CT, 9 September 1963, l.f.e., 3, and UKPHCD, 692 (23 March 1964), col. 27 (written answers).

70. "Whites Claim Territory Not Part of Bechuanaland," RDM, 15 February 1964, 2d ed., 9.

71. Derek Smith, "Tati Whites Rebel at Bechuana Self[-]rule," RDM, 7 April 1964, 2d ed., 3.

72. Derek Smith, "Africans Claim Tuli and Tati Blocks: Bechuana Seeks U.N. Aid," RDM, 11 June 1964, m.f.e., 13.

73. "Bechuanaland: Republicanism Revived," *News/Check* (Johannesburg) 2, no. 12 (20 December 1963):7.

74. Prime Minister Huggins defined the northern part of the BP as everything " . . . lying north of a line running from the Limpopo [River] along the northern boundary of the Bakgatla Reserve and the southern boundary of the Bamangwato Reserve westward to the north-west corner of the Bakwena Reserve and thence along the former common boundary of the Northern and Southern Protectorates to the eastern border of South-West Africa." Minute of Prime Minister Huggins, 26 March 1935, as published in UKCRO, *Basutoland, The Bechuanaland Protectorate*, 129.

75. SRLAD, 6 (27 May 1927), col. 821 (Captain Bertin).

76. ibid., 13 (26 April 1933), col. 538 (Mr. Fletcher).

77. "A Prior and Better Claim: Colony and the Transfer of Bechuanaland," BC, 15 April 1938, 7.

78. BPEACM, 44th sess. (9 March 1949), 35–42; 45th sess. (13 October 1949), 82–86; 46th sess. (6–10 March 1950); 51st sess. (6 November 1952),

41-59.

79. BPAACM, 31st sess. (21 June 1950), 75–76.

80. "Bechuanaland Opposition to Incorporation in Union [Is] Almost 100 Per Cent.," *The Star*, 3 November 1949, c.l.e., 9, and "Bechuanaland Eager To Join [Central] African Federation," *The Star*, 1 June 1950, s.p.e., 17.

81. "Time To Give Our View" (editorial), BC, 27 October 1949, 6, and "Rhodesia Not Butting In" (editorial), BC, 31 October 1949, 6.

82. "Rhodesian Mission to Britain," *The Star*, 8 November 1949, c.l.e., 1.

83. M. N. Smith, "We Have A Good Claim to Northern Bechuanaland," *The Chronicle* (Bulawayo), 26 April 1956, 8, and "But Union Does Not Think So," *The Chronicle*, 26 April 1956, 8.

84. "Rhodesian Claims to Bechuanaland Kept Alive," *The Star*, 5 June 1956, c.l.e., 2.

85. "Protectorates Issue Seen as Rallying Point for H.N.P.," *The Star*, 22 December 1949, c.l.e., 3.

86. "'Allegations a Little Unfair'," *The Friend* (Bloemfontein), 23 December 1949, 1.

87. W. A. Gonlonton, "Rhodesia and Bechuanaland [—I]: Malan's Claim Utterly Baseless," NR 18, no. 976 (6 April 1951):10–11 and "Rhodesia and Bechuanaland—II: Rhodesia's Claims to Prior Consideration," NR 18, no. 977 (13 April 1951):10–12.

88. A. I. Asiwaju, "Partitioned Culture Areas: A Checklist," in *Partitioned Africans: Ethnic Relations across Africa's International Boundaries, 1884–1984*, ed. A. I. Asiwaju (New York: St. Martin's Press, 1985), 256, and Parsons, "The Evolution," 27–28.

89. James J. Zaffiro, *From Police Network to Station of the Nation: A Political History of Broadcasting in Botswana, 1927–1991* (Gaborone: BS, 1991), 40, 66, and 87.

90. Louis A. Picard, "Role Changes among Field Administrators in Botswana: Administrative Attitudes and Social Change" (Ph.D. diss., University of Wisconsin, Madison, 1977), 548–551.

91. Diana S. Wylie, *A Little God: The Twilight of Patriarchy in a Southern African Chiefdom* (Hanover, NH: Wesleyan University Press, University Press of New England, 1990), 162–172.

92. Ian Brownlie, with the assistance of Ian R. Burns, *African Boundaries: A Legal and Diplomatic Encyclopedia* (Berkeley: UCP, 1979), 1090.

93. C. C. Worrall and E. B[rian]. Egner, *Bechuanaland Protectorate— Southern Rhodesia Boundary Commission: Joint Report* (s.l.: n.p., 1959), 1–11 and annexure B, 1–6.

94. BNAORH, 70 (27 February 1981), 59.

95. Lynn Berat *Walvis Bay: Decolonization and International Law* (New Haven: YUP, 1990), especially 68–89 and 155–175, and John Battersby, "Cold War Legacy: Namibian Sovereignty Complete as S. Africa Withdraws from Port," CSM, 1 March 1994, 7.

96. Consult Michael Crowder's archivally based analysis, "Tshekedi Khama, Smuts, and South West Africa," JMAS 25, no. 1 (March 1987):25–42.

97. Tshekedi Khama, *The Case for Bechuanaland* (s.l: n.p., [1946]), unpaginated introduction and chaps. 1 and 5–9.

98. Mary Benson, *Tshekedi Khama* (London: Faber and Faber, 1960), 153 and 156.

99. UKPHCD, 427 (14 October 1946, written answers), col. 17.

100. Ibid., 430 (25 November 1946, written answers), cols. 201-202.

101. Ibid., (21 November 1946, oral answers), cols. 1012–1013.

102. Khama, *The Case*, chaps. 5–9.

103. M.E.A. Laschinger, "The Khamas and Their British Campaigns" (Paper [no. RHC/BCP/63/2] delivered at the postgraduate seminar on the recent history of the Commonwealth and British colonial policy since Chamberlain, ICSUL, 7 May 1964), 1–9.

104. UNGA doc. A/4926 (UNGAOR, 16th sess., suppl. no. 12A), 5, 7–8, and 28–31.

105. Judith P. Gregory, "The Conflict over the International Status of South West Africa, 1946–1961" (M.A. thesis, University of Virginia, 1962), 110 and 112, n. 4.

106. William U. Crowell, "The Evolution of South African Control over South West Africa (Namibia)" (Ph.D. diss., St. John's University, 1975), 292–294.

107. SA, *Report of the Commission of Enquiry into South West Africa Affairs, 1962–1963*, R.P. no. 12/1964 (Pretoria: GP, 1964), 49.

108. BPEACM, 12th sess. (3–12 March 1930), 12.

109. LNPMCM, 3d sess. (20 July–10 August 1923), 102; 4th sess. (24 June–8 July 1924), 57; 6th sess. (26 June–10 July 1925), 58–59, 61, and 177; 7th sess. (19–30 October 1925), 16–17 and 216–217; 11th sess. (20 June–6 July 1927), 96; 18th sess. (18 June–1 July 1930), 132 and 204; and LNOJ 7, no. 3 (March 1926), 375–377.

110. SRLAD, 32, pt. 2 (20 June 1951), col. 2903.

111. F. A. Low, "Rhodesia May Ask for the Caprivi Strip," *The Star*, 22 December 1953, c.l.e., 19.

112. Peter Gibbs, *The History of the British South Africa Police, vol. 2: The Right of the Line, 1903–1939* (Salisbury: Kingstons Limited, 1974), 102–109.

113. SAPSD, 1951, 4 (18 June 1951), cols. 6491–6493.

114. Chanock, *Britain, Rhodesia, and South Africa*, 118.

115. SAPSD, 1951, 4 (18 June 1951), col. 6497. This idea had surfaced in Northern Rhodesia at least as early as 1932, according to Wetherell's "The Rhodesias," 178.

116. In 1945 there was a suggestion in the Dominions Office to consider detaching the Strip from South West Africa and adding it to the BP (PRO, file D. O. 35/1119, commentary of Mr. J. P. Parker of the Dominions Office on a report filed by Evelyn Baring, the British High Commissioner in South Africa, 5 December 1945 as cited in André Du Pisani *SWA/Namibia: The Politics of Continuity and Change* [Johannesburg: Jonathan Ball Publishers, 1985), 112 and 126, n. 19).

117. Thomas Tlou, "A Political History of Northwestern Botswana to 1906" (Ph.D. diss., University of Wisconsin, Madison, 1972), 283–285.

118. Sillery, *The Bechuanaland Protectorate*, 190 and 192-193, and Asiwaju, "Partitioned Culture Areas," 256.

119. BPLCORH, 9 (22 November 1963), 123–128.

120. "Envoy Exchange—On Conditions: Bechuanas 'Won't Be Stooges'," RDM, 9 September 1965, m.f.e., 2.

121. "Bechuanaland Okays S.W.A. Boundary Work," MMPG, 8 January 1965, 2.

122. "Problems for Land Owners," MMPG, 30 July 1965, 5.

123. BNAORH, 21 (17 March 1967), 99–100.

124. Ibid., 70 (27 February 1981), 59 (Mr. Gaseitsiwe), and 74 (18 August 1982), 187–188 (Mr. Monwela), 189–190 (Mr. Magang), 190 (attorney-general), and 193–194 (minister of external affairs). Brownlie (African Boundaries, 1078) suggested that demarcation of the southern boundary of the Strip was needed.

125. Theo-Ben Gurirab, "The Kasikili Island Situation: Statement Made in the National Assembly, Namibia, May 26, 1992," SAPEM 6, no. 2 (November 1992), 24.

126. Ibid., 25, and Tiyanjana Maluwa, "Disputed Sovereignty over Sidudu (or Kasikili) Island (Botswana-Namibia)," SAPEM 6, no. 2 (November 1992):20–21.

127. "Is Causing Tension," CRBNLS, no. 1—1993 (1 March 1993), 14.

128. "A Territorial Dispute with Namibia Has Been Averted," CRNBLS, no. 3—1992 (14 August 1992):25.

129. Gurirab, "The Kasikili Island Situation," 26.

130. "Botswana's National Development and Geopolitical Situation: A Politico-Geographical Study of an Ideological Frontier" (M.A. thesis, McMaster University, 1969), 122–173.

131. "Zambia Lays Out Red Carpet for Seretse," The Star, 27 April 1965, c.l.e., 23.

132. "Kaunda's Visit to Botswana [Is] 'Symbolic'," The Star, 21 May 1968, c.l.e., 5.

133. Khama, From the Frontline, 131–134.

134. Asiwaju, "Partitioned Culture Areas," 256.

135. "Barotseland: The Secessionist Challenge to Zambia," JMAS, 6, no. 3 (October, 1968), 355 and 358.

136. Louis in. Ebert III (a US Department of State officer), "Some International Legal Aspects of the Botswana-Zambia Boundary Question" (M.S. thesis, George Washington University, 1971), 23–24.

137. Q. Neil Parsons, "A New Link between Two Nations: Economics of the Zambia-Botswana Highway," Enterprise (Lusaka), 1974, no. 3, 56.

138. My interview with Mr. Kenneth J. Mommsen, representative of the Mine Labor Organization, Kasane, Botswana, 27 July 1976 (hereafter cited as Mommsen interview).

139. Bertram A. Young, Bechuanaland (London: HMSO, 1966), 97.

140. "Africa: Captain Nelson's Freedom Ferry," Time 83, no. 15 (10 April 1964):38, and "Freedom Ferry: Zambesi Crossing Last Hurdle for Refugees," The Star, 23 September 1964, c.l.e., 28–29.

141. "Freedom Ferry: Zambesi Crossing," 28–29.

142. BNAORH, 44, pt. 1 (14 March 1973), 64–65.

143. My interview with Mr. Ambrose B. Masalila, District Commissioner,

Kasane, Botswana, 26 July 1976.

144. "South Africa Questions Botswana's Claim to Narrow Border Strip," ST, 29 March 1970, 1 as cited in Ebert, "Some International Legal Aspects," 24 and 90, n. 5.

145. SAPHAD, 30 (3 September 1970), col. 3279 (the foreign minister).

146. "How Can a Pinpoint Support a Bridge?" *The Star*, 4 April 1970, s.p.e., 5, and Arnold Benjamin, "Middle of Nowhere," *The Star*, 18 April 1970, c.l.s.e., 11.

147. "Diplomatic Crisis over Botswana Road Issue," *The Star*, 21 April 1970, 2d c.l.e., 32.

148. "Botswana-Zambia Road To Rely on Ferry," RH, 3 April 1970, 7, and "No Bridge Plan for Zambezi—Botswana," RH, 14 April 1970, 5.

149. "R 180m Zambezi Bridge," RDM, 15 November 1983, m.f.e., 4.

150. "South Korean Firm Will Build Orapa-Serowe Road," QERNBLS, 1986, no. 1 (12 March 1986):37.

151. Barbara Cole, *The Elite: The Story of the Rhodesian Special Air Service* (Amanzimtoti, Natal: Three Knights Publishing, 1984), 296–304.

152. Dan Van Der Vat, "Road Plan Alarms S[.] Africa," *The Times* (London), 29 May 1970, f.e., 10.

153. "We Didn't Try To Kill Nkomo—Gen[.] Walls," *The Star*, 21 April 1979, i.a.w.e., 5.

154. Ron Reid Daly, as told to Peter Stiff, *Selous Scouts: Top Secret War* (Alberton, Transvaal: Galago Publishing [Pty.] Ltd., 1982), 655–671.

155. Bob Hitchcock, "'Botswana Roads Not for Army'," RDM, 31 January 1973, m.f.e., 3.

156. "South Africa's Outward Policy May Be Jeopardised: Botswana–Zambia Road Dispute Mars Relations," ST, 31 May 1970, 10.

157. BPLAORH, 15 (dated only December 1965), i.

158. "Challenge to S.A. on Botswana Border," RDM, 13 April 1970, m.f.e., 1, as cited in Ebert, "Some International Legal Aspects," 26 and 90, n. 11.

159. Russell W. Howe, "US Road Is Helping Botswana," *The Baltimore Sun*, 10 September 1970, A–4, as cited in Ebert, "Some International Legal Aspects," 36 and 91, n. 25.

160. BNAORH, 70 (27 February 1981), 59.

161. Serfontein, "South Africa's Outward Policy," 10, and letter from Yeta III, Paramount Chief of Barotseland, to G.G.P. Lyons, resident magistrate, Mongu, dated 8 September 1919, NASA, file KDE 2/10/2.

162. Memorandum on "the Rhodesian Problem" from the BSAC to the Colonial Office, 3 March 1921, PRO, C.O. file 417/670/10375, as cited in Wetherell, "The Rhodesias," 70–71, n. 2.

163. The speeches of Messrs. Knight and Norris in the *Debates* of the Northern Rhodesian Legislative Council, 4th session, 17 and 21 December 1932, cols. 142 and 301, respectively, as cited in Wetherell, "The Rhodesias," 178, nn. 2–3, respectively.

164. Richard Dale, "Botswana," in *Southern Africa in Perspective: Essays in Regional Politics*, ed. Christian P. Potholm and Richard Dale (New York: The Free Press, 1972), 111 and 354, nn. 7–8.

CHAPTER THREE

1. *Refugees in International Politics* (New York: Columbia University Press, 1987), 71.

2. Kirsten Alnaes, "Oral Tradition and Identity: The Herero in Botswana," in *The Societies of Southern Africa in the 19th and 20th Centuries*, 11, Collected Seminar Papers no. 27 (London: ICSUL, 1981), 16–17.

3. Peter H. Katjavivi, "The Herero Community in Botswana and Its Role in the Campaign against South Africa's Attempt To Incorporate Namibia" (Paper delivered at the seminar of the Yale University Southern African Research Program, 7 December 1988), 10–15.

4. Horst Drechsler, *"Let Us Die Fighting": The Struggle of the Herero and Nama against German Imperialism*, translated by Bernd Zollner (London: Zed Press, 1980), 202–203 and 238–239.

5. Wylie, *A Little God*, 168–170.

6. Tom Lodge, *Black Politics in South Africa since 1945* (New York: Longman Inc., 1983), 273–278.

7. James H. Polhemus, "The Refugee Factor in Botswana," IM 4, no. 1 (March 1985):31–32.

8. Christian P. Potholm, "Wanderers on the Face of Africa: Refugees in Kenya, Tanzania, Zambia, and Botswana," RT 261 (January 1976):86–90.

9. Polhemus, "The Refugee Factor," 34–35 and 40–43.

10. *Linkage Politics: Essays on the Convergence of National and International Systems*, ed. James N. Rosenau (New York: The Free Press, 1969).

11. "Candidates' Views on Foreign Policy," CSM, 17 October 1988, 14.

12. T. F. Betts, *Refugees: Bechuanaland Protectorate* (Mafeking: n.p., 1961), 7. BNA, file SM. 97.

13. G. H. Cunningham, "Confidential Memorandum" (s.l.: n.p., circa June 1965), [1]. Africa Bureau Papers, MSS Afr. s. 1681, box 218, file 6, RHL.

14. R. Nengwekhulu, "Some Findings on the Origins of Political Parties in Botswana," PBJAS 1, no. 2 (June 1979):56–74.

15. Parsons, "The Evolution," 37–38.

16. Robertson, "From Protectorate to Republic," 170.

17. Letsoko N. Moerane, "The Role of the Legco [Legislative Council] in the Formation of Political Parties in [the] Bechuanaland Protectorate" (B.A. thesis, University College of Botswana, 1982), 16–20.

18. BPJACM, 7th sess. (15 April 1958), 85 (Dr. S. M. Molema).

19. BPLCORH, 9 (18 November 1963), 2–3 (R. Peter Fawcus, Her Majesty's commissioner for the BP).

20. "Deported Men Set Free," *The Times*, 8 November 1962, l.l.e., 10, and "Thank You, Sir John," *Contact* (Cape Town) 5, no. 23 (15 November 1962):2.

21. Edwin S. Munger, *Bechuanaland: Pan-African Outpost or Bantu Homeland?* (London: OUP, 1965), 20.

22. "Freedom Ferry: Zambesi Crossing," 28–29.

23. "Refugees on the Way to Tanganyika," *The Star*, 26 July 1963, 1st s.p.e., 3.

24. "Refugee Flight," *The Star*, 28 November 1963, c.l.e., 3.

25. "Botswana: Home to 500 'Freedom' Refugees," *The Star*, 12 July 1968, 2d c.l.e., 24.

26. SAPHAD, 87 (23 March 1955), cols. 3122–3127 (minister of the interior), 3130–3131 (minister of the interior), and 3164 (minister of the interior and Mr. Mitchell).

27. Ibid., 6 (29 April 1963), cols. 4913–4915 (minister of foreign affairs).

28. Ibid., 9 (24 January 1964), col. 254.

29. "Schoeman Acts on 'Refugee Flights'," *The Star*, 13 September 1963, 1st s.p.e., 1.

30. Jack Halpern, *South Africa's Hostages: Basutoland, Bechuanaland, and Swaziland* (Baltimore: Penguin Books, 1965), 35–37.

31. Eric Robins, *White Queen in Africa* (London: Robert Hale Ltd., 1967), 135.

32. Lauritz Strydom, *Rivonia Unmasked!* (Johannesburg: Voortrekkerspers, 1965), 50–52.

33. Wilf Nussey, "Career of a White in Black African Politics Is Over, *The Star*, 8 December 1981, l.f.e., 29.

34. "Schoeman Acts," 1.

35. "Curbing Refugees: Check-Point Airfields Listed," *The Star*, 17 September 1963, c.l.e., 3.

36. SAPHAD, 6 (26 April 1963), col. 4817.

37. Ibid., 9 (10 February 1964), cols. 1051–1053 (minister of transport).

38. UKPHCD, 685 (25 November 1963), cols. 4–5 (oral answers).

39. SAPHAD, 15 (7 June 1965), cols. 7296–7297 (minister of justice).

40. Earlier (SAPHAD, 12 [10 June 1964], col. 7638), the minister of justice stated that Algeria, Congo, Ghana, and Tanganyika had served as host nations for what he termed "sabotage camps."

41. Ibid., 15 (11 June 1965), cols. 7916–7918.

42. Ibid., 17 (21 September 1966), cols. 2549–2550, 2557, and 2558.

43. BPLAORH, 15 (8 December 1965), 56–57 (Prime Minister Khama).

44. BPLCORH, 12 (17 November 1964), 13–14 (chief secretary).

45. SAPHAD, 21 (22 May 1967), col. 6480 (minister of justice).

46. UKHCD, 624 (26 May 1960), cols. 653–658 (oral answers).

47. SAPSD, 1962, 2 (20 March 1962), cols. 2297–2298 (minister of justice).

48. BNAORH, 19 (6 October 1966), 12 (presidential address).

49. BPLCORH, 9 (19 November 1963), 46 (the chief secretary), and 11 (25 August 1964), 40–41 (the chief secretary).

50. Cato Aall, *Refugee Situation in Bechuanaland, June, 1965* (Gaberones, Francistown, Lusaka: International Refugee Council of Zambia, June–July, 1965), 4.

51. Polhemus, "The Refugee," 37.

52. My background interview, on a not-for-attribution basis, with a well-informed expert on these matters, Gaborone, 29 March 1985.

53. BNAORH, 21 (14 March 1967), 43–44 (minister of state).

54. "U.N. Refugee Officials in Botswana," *The Star*, 28 March 1967, c.l.e., 5.

55. BNAORH, 22, pt. 1 (23 August 1967), 76–79.

56. Jenny Zetterqvist, *Refugees in Botswana in the Light of International Law*, Research Report no. 87 (Uppsala: SIAS, 1990), 28, 75, and 78.

57. BNAORH, 22, pt. 1 (23 August 1967), 77 (minister of state).

58. "Botswana To Make Refugees Citizens," *The Star*, 27 September 1967, c.l.e., 9.

59. BNAORH, 22, pt. 1 (23 August 1967), 78 (Mr. Matante) and 76 (minister of state).

60. "Extradition Talks Near Finality," *The Star*, 19 February 1968, c.l.e., 6.

61. BNAORH, 25 (7 August 1968), 37–38, 47, 49–52 (minister of state).

62. BGG, 7, no. 18 (2 May 1969), D.155–D.162.

63. Ibid., 7, no. 5 (7 February 1969), E.75–E.139.

64. Zetterqvist, *Refugees*, 28–29, 43–44, and 75.

65. Roger Southall, "Botswana as a Host Country for Refugees," JCCP 22, no. 2 (July 1984) 164.

66. *"Now in the Future Is It Peace or War?": A Report on Refugees from South Africa and on the Issues Involved* (London: Amnesty International, 1963), 7.

67. "Centre Is for Refuge, Not Sabotage," *The Star*, 30 May 1964, s.p.e., 3.

68. "Sequel to Wrecking of Hostel: Fear Stalks Refugees in Francistown" *The Star*, 1 August 1964, c.l.s.e., 11.

69. Jane W. Jacqz, *Refugee Students from Southern Africa: Report of a Workshop on the Training and Utilization of Refugee Students from Southern Africa Sponsored by the African-American Institute and Syracuse University at Lublin House, New York City, April 18–19, 1967* (New York: African-American Institute, 1967), 33.

70. "Refugee Camp Burnt Down," *The Star*, 31 October 1966, c.l.e., 3.

71. "Joint Committee on the High Commission Territories: Secretary's Report, February 1967," [1]. Africa Bureau Papers, MSS Afr. s. 1681, box 218, file 7, RHL.

72. Southall, "Botswana" 163.

73. Margaret Legum, "Problems of Asylum for Southern African Refugees," in *Refugee Problems in Africa*, ed. Sven Hamrell (Uppsala: SIAS, 1967), 54, n. 1.

74. Z[achariah]. K. Matthews, "The Role of Voluntary Organisations in the Refugee Situation in Africa," in Hamrell, *Refugee Problems*, 104.

75. Polhemus, "The Refugee," 40.

76. Southall, "Botswana," 163.

77. "Refugees in Botswana: A Policy of Resettlement," *Kutlwano* (Gaborone) 9, no. 7 (July 1970):[15]–[18].

78. David Potten, "Etsha: A Successful Resettlement Scheme," BNR, 8 (1976) 115.

79. Zetterqvist, *Refugees in Botswana*, 22 and 35.

80. Southall, "Botswana," 164.

81. UN doc. 5/12307, 28 March 1977, 5–6, 13–16, and 33–36.

82. The Lutheran World Federation, Department of World Service, *Botswana Refugee Program: Annual Report, 1978* (s.l.: n.p, n.d.), 6-16.

83. UN doc. 5/17453, 11 September 1985, 6–7.

84. Zetterqvist, *Refugees in Botswana*, 35 and 38.

85. Medard Rwelamira, *Refugees in a Chess Game: Reflections on Botswana, Lesotho, and Swaziland Refugee Policies*, Research Report no. 88 (Uppsala: SIAS, 1990), 38.

86. *LWS/WS Botswana: 1985 Annual Report* (s.l.: n.p., n.d.), 3.

87. "Refugee Community Dwindles," MWD, 26 January–1 February 1990, 2.

88. UN doc. 5/17453, 20–21.

89. BNAORH, 22, pt. 2 (28 August 1967), 167–194 (minister of state's motion on the Luke Report on Localization and Training).

90. Ibid., 70 (20 March 1981), 359–371 and (27 March 1981), 434–441 (debates on Mr. Oteng's motion on localization in the private sector).

91. Ibid., (26 March 1981), 422 (minister of home affairs, introducing the second reading of the bill).

92. Zetterqvist, *Refugees in Botswana*, 63–65.

93. Southall, "Botswana," 174, and Richard F. Weisfelder, "Human Rights under Majority Rule in Southern Africa: The Mote in Thy Brother's Eye," in *Human Rights and Development in Africa*, ed. Claude E. Welch, Jr., and Ronald I. Meltzer (Albany: State University of New York Press, 1984), 97–98.

94. UNSCOR, 32d yr., *Resolutions and Decisions*, 2 (res. 403 [1977] of 14 January 1977, para. eight of the preamble).

95. "Khama Gets U.N. Refugee Award," MMBG, 28 April 1978, 1.

96. Hanlon, *Beggar*, 220 and 222–225.

97. John A. Marcum, "The Exile Condition and Revolutionary Effectiveness: Southern African Liberation Movements," in Potholm and Dale, *Southern Africa in Perspective*, 262–275 and 380–388, and Cato Aall, "Refugee Problems in Southern Africa," in Hamrell, Refugee Problems, 33.

98. "Lobatsi Inquiry into Explosion in Vehicle," *The Star*, 19 September 1963, c.l.e., 5.

99. Gordon Winter, *Inside BOSS: South Africa's Secret Police* (London: Allen Lane, Penguin Books Ltd., 1981), 75–76.

100. "Sabotage Suspected in Gutted Plane," *The Star*, 29 August 1963, 1st s.p.e., 1.

101. BPPARC, 1963, 8–9.

102. BPLCORH, 9 (18 November 1963), 10 (first reading), (19 November 1963), 40–43 (second reading), (20 November 1963), 65 (committee), and (21 November), 85 (third reading).

103. BPSL, 1963, 357–358.

104. Halpern, *South Africa's Hostages*, 459–460.

105. "Extradition between South Africa and Its Nearest Neighbours Presents Immense Complexities: Why There Is No Treaty Yet," *The Star*, 7 September 1965, c.l.e., 20.

106. "Bechuanaland Blast: No Arrests Yet," *The Star*, 27 July 1964, c.l.e., 1.

107. BPPARC, 1964, 8.

108. Munger (*Bechuanaland*, 104) entertained the idea of freelance violence in Francistown in 1963 but noted that there was no concrete evidence

to sustain or refute the allegation.

109. Sue Leeman, "ANC 'Still Operates from Botswana'," *The Star*, 22 November 1986, i.a.w.e., 1. Stephen Ellis and Tsepo Sechaba (pseud.) have demonstrated that the ANC and its military wing Umkhonto we Sizwe did have members or agents in Botswana and that they were monitored by the Gaborone authorities and/or South African intelligence operatives (*Comrades against Apartheid: The ANC & the South African Communist Party in Exile* [London: James Currey, 1992], 50, 53, 77, 84, 101, 116–117, 119, 152, 154, 170–171, and 195).

110. Polhemus, "Botswana's Role," 265, and "4 South Africans Jailed," BDN, 12 August 1986, 1.

111. "South African Pressure for a Non-Aggression Pact Is Being Resisted," QERNBLS, no. 2—1984 (15 June 1984):24.

112. "Despite Recent Expulsions of ANC Members," CRNBLS, no. 2—1986 (16 June 1986):28.

113. Barnett F. Baron, "Southern African Student Exiles: The Function of Politics" (Ph.D. diss., Yale University, 1969), 174.

114. Polhemus, "The Refugee," 41–42.

115. Zwelakhe Sisulu, "Guer[r]illas Won't Stop: Botswana 'Unable To Check ANC and PAC'," SP, 28 January 1979, 1.

116. "Refugees To Strictly Live [sic] at Dukwe Camp," BDN, 23 February 1983, 1.

117. Winter, *Inside BOSS*, 31–32.

118. Polhemus, "The Refugee," 35.

119. BNAORH, 86, pt. 2 (15 April 1986), 954–958 (minister of presidential affairs and public administration).

120. BGG 15, no. 103 (23 May 1986):A.23–A.33 (text of the 1986 act).

121. Bojosi Otlhogile, "National Security Act: Dusk for Democracy?" MWD, 10 May 1986, 4, and Sandy Grant and E. Brian Egner, "The Private Press and Democracy," in *Democracy in Botswana: The Proceedings of a Symposium Held in Gaborone, 1–5 August 1988*, ed. John D. Holm and Patrick P. Molutsi (Athens: Ohio University Press, 1989), 247 and 261, n. 2.

122. Oagile K. Dingake, "Opposition Spokesmen Slam [the National] Security Act," MWD, 10 May 1986, 3.

123. "The Proposed National Security Act: A New So Wide To Catch Us All?," MWD 5 April 1986, 4.

124. "Bitter over Tiro Death," *The Star*, 5 February 1974, 2d c.l.e., 1.

125. "Bombed Refugee Lived Here for More Than [a] Year," BDN, 17 May 1985, 1.

126. Munger, *Bechuanaland*, 108–111.

127. Daly, *Selous Scouts*, 369 and 375–385.

128. "Halfway House for Political Refugees," *The Star*, 16 October 1975, s.p.e., 28.

129. "And Batswana of Namibian Origin Are To Return Home," CRNBLS, no. 3—1992 (14 August 1992):25.

130. "Botswana: Worried about Soweto Refugees," AC 18, no. 6 (5 August 1977), 1.

131. Southall, "Botswana," 156.

132. Mxolisi Mgxashe, "Refugee Death Toll Increases in 19 Y[ea]rs," BG, 21 June 1985, 4 and 7.

133. Annick Billard, "The Protection of Refugees: Priority Number One," *Refugees* (Geneva), 32 (August 1986):17–18.

134. Q. Neil Parsons, "The Idea of Democracy and the Emergence of an Educated Elite in Botswana, 1931–1960," in *Botswana: Education, Culture, and Politics*, 191, and Charles W. Gossett, "The Civil Service in Botswana: Personnel Policies in Comparative Perspective" (Ph.D. diss., Stanford University, 1986), 128 and 399.

135. Shelly Pitterman, "A Comparative Survey of Two Decades of International Assistance to Refugees in Africa," AT 31, no. 1 (First Quarter 1984):35.

136. "Zimbabwe Refugees Are To Be Repatriated," CRNBLS no. 2—1989 (14 June 1989):26, and "Refugee Community Dwindles," 2.

137. Keto Segwai, "Nkomo Visit Augurs Return Home," MWD, 21–27 May 1988, 4, and Rampholo Molefhe, "Zim[babwe] Refugee Campaign Producing Results Despite Some Apprehensions," MWD, 28 May–3 June 1988, 8.

138. Cheryl Benard, "Politics and the Refugee Experience," PSQ 101, no. 4 (1986):621.

CHAPTER FOUR

1. Quill (i.e., H.C.L.) Hermans, "Towards Budgetary Independence: A Review of Botswana's Financial History, 1900 to 1973," BNR 6 (1974), 102.

2. Chanock, *Britain, Rhodesia, and South Africa*, 208.

3. Lewis H. Gann, "The Development of Southern Rhodesia's Military System, 1890–1953," in National Archives of Rhodesia, *Occasional Papers*, n.s. no. 1 (Salisbury: GP, 1965), 60–82.

4. "Police Flown from Rhodesia to Serowe," *The Star*, 2 June 1952, c.l.e., 1.

5. BPEACM, 51st sess. (3 November 1952), 10.

6. Chester A. Crocker (later US Assistant Secretary of State for African Affairs), "The Military Transfer of Power in Africa: A Comparative Study of Change in the British and French Systems of Order" (Ph.D. diss., The Johns Hopkins University, 1972), 302.

7. BPPARC, 1965, 7.

8. Ibid., 1962, 7.

9. Ibid., 1964, 5–6.

10. Ibid., 1965, 7 and 24.

11. Anthony Clayton, *The Thin Blue Line: Studies in Law Enforcement in Late Colonial Africa*, Oxford Development Records Project Report [no.] 1 (Oxford: [University of Oxford] RHL, circa 1985), 195.

12. According to Jonathan Bloch and Patrick Fitzgerald (*British Intelligence and Covert Action: Africa, Middle East, and Europe since 1945* [Dingle, Ireland: Brandon Book Publishers, Ltd., and London: Junction Books Ltd., 1983], 181), the station not only broadcast programs into Southern

Rhodesia but also was used in electronic eavesdropping on the rebellious territory, probably as a means of tracking Southern Rhodesia's sanctions-busting efforts.

13. "Bush Radio Sabotage Feared: British Troops Were 'Forced' on Seretse," *The Star*, 27 December 1965, c.l.e., 1.

14. BPLAORH, 15 (13 December 1965), 116.

15. "Mrs. White's Visit Leads to New Speculation," RDM, 24 December 1965, m.f.e., 3.

16. "Bush Radio Sabotage Feared," 1.

17. "Freedom Radio Threat to Khama's Life-Line," *The Star*, 18 December 1965, c.e., 1.

18. "B.B.C. Station Is 'Military Base' Now," *The Star*, 10 May 1966, 2d s.p.e., 19.

19. Ralph Cohen, "Threat of Sabotage over Anti-U.D.I. Radio," RDM, 8 December 1965, 2d ed., 1.

20. BPLAORH, 17 (16 March 1966), 19–25.

21. Ibid., 16 (24–25 January 1966), 6, 8–9, 13–14, 17, 19, 23, 24, and 36.

22. "No Army Wanted," *The Star*, 24 August 1966, c.l.e., 14.

23. BP, *Memorandum on Bechuanaland's Financial Needs, 1966–71* (Gaberones: Ministry of Finance), publication date and page(s) not given, as cited in Gilfred L. Gunderson, "Nation-Building and the Administrative State: The Case of Botswana" (Ph.D. diss., University of California, Berkeley, 1970), 399, 421, n. 138, and 465.

24. UK, *Agreement between the Government of the United Kingdom . . . and the Government of Botswana regarding the Status of the Armed Forces of the United Kingdom in Botswana. Gaberones, 30 September 1966.* Cmnd 3190. Treaty Series no. 5 (1967) (London: HMSO, 1967), 2–[3].

25. George E. Moose, "French Military Policy in Africa," in *Arms and the African: Military Influences on Africa's International Relations*, ed. William J. Foltz and Henry S. Bienen (New Haven: YUP, 1985), 61–62.

26. Botswana, *Transitional Plan for Social and Economic Development* (Gaberones: GP, 1966), 101.

27. BPARC, 1967, 24.

28. UK, *Exchange of Letters between the Government of the United Kingdom of Great Britain and Northern Ireland and the Government of Botswana for the Provision of Personnel of the United Kingdom Armed Forces To Assist in the Training of the Police Forces of Botswana, Gaberones, 9 October 1968.* Cmd. no. 3937, Treaty Series No. 37 (1969) (London: HMSO, 1969), 3–[6].

29. BPARC, 1967, 1, and BPARC, 1968, 1.

30. UKPHLD, 307 (5 February 1970), cols. 746–747.

31. Mr. Matante's motion on prostitution in BNAORH, 27, pt. 1 (21 March 1969), 138–162, especially 140.

32. BPARC, 1967, 6.

33. Ibid.; BPARC, 1968, 6; and BPARC, 1969, 6.

34. The Prevention of Violence Abroad Law No. 32 of 1963 in BPSL, 47 (1963), 357–358.

35. BNAORH, 19 (6 October 1966), 12.

36. "Botswana Captures 13 More Terrorists," *The Star*, 6 September 1967, c.l.e., 1.

37. "Guer[r]illas Back from Prison: Trained Terrorists Will Fight Again," *The Star*, 3 February 1969, 2d c.l.e., 9.

38. "Botswana Warns Guer[r]illas," *The Star*, 27 October 1966, c.l.e., 1.

39. David Martin and Phyllis Johnson, *The Struggle for Zimbabwe: The Chimurenga War* (London and New York: Monthly Review Press, 1981), 3, 10, 69–70, 77, 83–84, 86–87, 112, 174, 190, 203, 205, 223, 278, and 322.

40. Paul L. Moorcroft, *African Nemesis: War and Revolution in Southern Africa, 1945-2010* (London: Brassey's [UK], 1990), 126–127, and "Police in Rhodesia: Seretse: Ask S.A. To Quit," *The Star*, 10 January 1969, 2d c.l.e., 1.

41. UN doc. 5/7781/Add. 2/Annex, 9 March 1967 (UNSCOR, 22d yr., suppl. for January–March 1967, 156).

42. Vincent B. Khapoya, "A Comparative Study of African Policies toward Liberation Movements in Southern and Colonized Africa" (Ph.D. diss., University of Denver, 1974), 77–78 and 86.

43. Botswana, *National Development Plan, 1968-73* (Gaberones: GP, 1968), 70 and 86–87, with my computations based on tables VII (p. 86) and IX (p. 87).

44. Botswana, *National Development Plan, 1970-75* (Gaborone: GP, 1970), 129.

45. Ibid.

46. Ibid., 131.

47. Khama, *From the Frontline*, 82 and 103.

48. BNAORH, 23 (9 January 1968), 27–29; 34 (30 October 1970), 94–95; 35 (16 December 1970), 68–69; and Samuel Moribame, "MPs' Accusations over Dube Kidnap," BDN, 22 November 1974, 1.

49. "The Capture of Persons in Foreign Territory for Offenses Committed Extraterritorially," SAYIL, 3 (1977), 183–184.

50. "Dingake Can Now Be Quoted in SA," MWD, 9–15 February 1990, 3.

51. UKPHLD, 312 (10 November 1970), cols. 594–596.

52. UN doc. 5/12262, 22 December 1976 (UNSCOR, 31st Yr., suppl. for October–December 1976, 56–57).

53. UNSCOR, 32d Yr., 1983d mtg. (12 January 1977), 3–11; 1984th mtg. (13 January 1977), 1–17; and 1985th mtg. (14 January 1977), 1–23.

54. "Invite Us, Rhodesia Asks UN," *The Star*, 15 January 1977, i.a.w.e., 3, and "Let Us Explain—Rhodesia," *The Star*, 22 January 1977, i.a.w.e., 5.

55. UNSCOR, 32d yr., *Resolutions and Decisions*, 1–2 (res. 403 [1977] of 14 January 1977).

56. UN doc. 5/12307, 28 March 1977 (UNSCOR, 32d yr., suppl. for January–March 1977, 21–47), and UN doc. 5/12326, 9 May 1977 (UNSCOR, 32d yr., suppl. for April–June 1977, 36).

57. For a discussion of the 1977 legislation, consult Richard Dale, "The Creation and Use of the Botswana Defence Force," RT 290 (April 1984):216–235, especially 220–222.

58. "Chief with the Common Touch," *The Star*, 21 November 1977, s.p.e., 22.

59. Masoabi Motseta, "Botswana General without an Army," RDM, 19 April 1977, m.f.e., 9.

60. Data furnished to me by Lt. Col. Pheto, BDF, Seretse Khama Barracks, Mogoditshane, 16 June 1987 (hereafter cited as Pheto data).

61. BNAORH 69, 397–408 (2 December 1980), especially 397, 399–400, 402-403, and 405, and Moeng Pheto, "Foreign Enlistment," *Sethamo: Newsletter of the BDF* (Gaborone), 1–2 (1981):14.

62. Richard Lee, "The Gods Must Be, Crazy, but the State Has a Plan: Government Policies towards the San in Namibia and Botswana," in *Namibia 1884–1984: Readings on Namibia's History and Society*, ed. Brian Wood (London: Namibia Support Committee in cooperation with the United Nations Institute for Namibia, Lusaka, 1988), 539–546.

63. "Others to Botswana: Bushmen To Be Resettled in the RSA," WA, 16 February 1990, 1–2, and Page Snyman, "Will BaSarwa Mercenaries Be Brought to Book?," MWD, 14–20 September 1990, 16 (letter to the editor).

64. Allen Pizzey, "The Unwanted Army," *The Star*, 13 April 1978, s.p.e., 20; "Anger over Trigger-Happy Botswana Soldiers," *The Star*, 2 May 1990, i.a.w.e., 11; and "Gloss Fades on Botswana," *The Aida Parker Newsletter* (Aukland Park), no. 136 (May 1990):5.

65. Letter to me from Lt. Col. Werner M. Zepp, Security Assistance Officer, US Embassy, Gaborone, dated 19 June 1987 (hereafter cited as 1987 Zepp letter).

66. "Tuli Deaths: Soldier Acquitted," RDM, 14 November 1978, m.f.e., 1.

67. "Gaborone Admits Two Shot," *The Star*, 31 October 1983, w.n.s.p.e., 1.

68. "BDF Soldiers Given 33 Y[ea]rs for Murder," BDN, 5 October 1984, 1.

69. "Soldiers Given Presidential Mercy," BDN, 29 November 1984, 1.

70. "Roadblock Killing: Police Arrest Soldier," *The Gazette* (Gaborone), 13 May 1987, 1.

71. "Archibold [sic, i.e., Archibald] Awarded over P 200[,]000," MWD, 8–14 September 1989, 3.

72. "Killings," MWD, 27 April–3 May 1990, 2 (editorial).

73. Pizzey, "The Unwanted Army," 20.

74. M. S. Merafhe, "The Role of the Army in a Society," *Sethamo*, 1-2 (1981):[4]-5.

75. "BDF: Reaching Out to Civilians," MWD, 27 October–2 November 1989, 2. Samuel Decalo, a political scientist at the University of Natal at Durban, argued that such an ascriptive appointment has made civilian control effective in Botswana. This stratagem has also been employed in Swaziland, Gabon, and Zambia ("Towards Understanding the Sources of Civilian Rule in Africa, 1960–1990," JCAS 10, no. 1 [1991]:70, 72–73, and 80).

76. "Kgosi Seretse Khama Installation," *Kutlwano* 18, no. 6 (June 1979):6.

77. "Ian Khama for Sandhurst," *The Star*, 24 April 1972, 1st c.l.e., 14.

78. Letter to me from Mr. J. W. Hunt, signed by Mr. M.G.H. White, Central Library, Royal Military Academy, Sandhurst, dated 27 July 1983.

79. Data furnished to me by Lt. Col. Zepp, 6 July 1987 (hereafter cited as Zepp data).

80. Letter to me from Captain Dane L. Rota, Department of Social Sciences, US Military Academy, West Point, N.Y., dated 21 September 1988.

81. Paul Ellman, "SAS To Train Botswana Army," *Guardian* (London), 13 February 1986, 1 and 32.

82. Gerald L'Ange, "US Troops 'Mass' on Borders," *The Star*, 22 January 1992, i.a.w.e., 11.

83. 1987 Zepp letter.

84. Personnel, equipment, and armaments data are given in MB, 1985–1986 (London: IISS, 1985), 92. Because more recent data (MB, 1990–1991 [London: Brassey's, 1990], 126) are not especially detailed, I relied on the earlier set, as checked and revised by Lt. Col. Zepp (1987 Zepp letter and data), and supplemented by Lt. Col. Moeng Pheto (Pheto data and my interview with Lt. Col. Pheto, Seretse Khama Barracks, Mogoditshane, 16 June 1987).

85. Zepp data.

86. "Botswana Starts Air Force," *The Star*, 27 October 1977, s.p.e., 9.

87. Ken Vernon, "Jet Fighters Beef up Strike Capability of Air Force: Botswana Arms against Future Border Violations," *The Star*, 12 May 1988, l.e., 9.

88. MB, 1990–1991, 126 and Zepp data.

89. MB, 1982–1983 (London: IISS, 1982), 73, and 1987 Zepp letter.

90. Lloyd L. Mathews, "Botswana," in *World Armies*, 2d ed., ed. John Keegan (Detroit: Gale Research Company, 1983), 64.

91. USDS, *United States Treaties and Other International Agreements*, 32, pt. 1 (1979–1980) (Washington, DC: USGPO, 1983), 957–959.

92. 1987 Zepp letter.

93. Zepp data.

94. Patrick Lawrence, "Sympathy But No Aid for ANC," RDM, 15 December 1981, m.f.e., 11.

95. J.D.F. Jones, "Botswana President Attacks Pretoria," FT, 18 December 1981, 3 and Zepp data.

96. Letter to me from Lt. Col. Zepp, dated 9 October 1986.

97. *Foreign Military Sales, Foreign Military Construction Sales, and Military Assistance Facts as of September 30, 1987* (s.l.: Defense Security Assistance Agency, Comptroller, Data Management Division, n.d.), 28–29, 78–79, and 86–87.

98. Gerald L'Ange, "US Supplies Sophisticated Weapons to Botswana," *The Star*, 15 February 1989, i.a.w.e., 11.

99. James J. Zaffiro, "The U.S. and Botswana in the 1990s: Eroding Continuity in a Changing Region," JCAS 10, no. 1 (1991) 25–26.

100. "African Ground Forces," in *African Armies: Evolution and Capabilities*, ed. Bruce E. Arlinghaus and Pauline H. Baker (Boulder, CO: Westview Press, 1986), 115.

101. The analysis in this paragraph draws upon ibid., 113–140, and Zepp data.

102. Dennis Gordon, "Rhodesians Hit Botswana Base," RDM, 17 May 1977, m.f.e., 1, and Dennis Gordon, "Rhodesian Attack 'Planned in Advance'," RDM, 18 May 1977, m.f.e., 6.

103. BNAORH, 61 (28 February 1978), 84 (statement of the vice-

president); "15 Die after Hot Pursuit," *The Star*, 4 March 1978, i.a.w.e., 2; and "Situation on Border 'Tense'," *The Star*, 4 March 1978, i.a.w.e., 2.

104. "Rhodesians Abduct 14, Blow [Up] Ferry," BDN, 18 April 1979, 1.

105. "Botswana, Rhodesia in Air Battle," *The Star*, 11 August 1979, i.a.w.e., 3.

106. "Botswana Arrests 60 Guer[r]illas," *The Star*, 22 January 1979, s.p.e., 3.

107. Brendan Nicholson, "Flight of Zipra Refugees Raises Unwelcome Echoes," *The Star*, 9 November 1982, l.f.e., 21.

108. "Botswana: A Refuge for Rebels," *The Star*, 28 October 1982, l.f.e., 17.

109. Robin Drew, "Zimbabwe in Fury at Nkomo's Escape," *The Star*, 10 March 1983, w.n.c.l.e., 1.

110. Norman Chandler, "Zimbabwean Troops Deep in Botswana," RDM, 8 October 1983, m.f.e., 1; BNAORH, 78 (9 November 1983), 9 (minister of public service and information); Norman Chandler, "A New Border War Brewing," RDM, 11 November 1983, m.f.e., 10; and Norman Chandler, "Botswana Steps Up Security along Border," RDM, 19 December 1983, m.f.e., 5.

111. *African Nemesis*, 303–304 and 323.

112. *Apartheid's Second Front*, 56–58 and 72–73.

113. "'Peace' from the Barrel of a Gun: Nonaggression Pacts and State Terror in Southern Africa," in *Terrible beyond Endurance?: The Foreign Policy of State Terrorism*, ed. Michael Stohl and George A. Lopez, Contributions in Political Science no. 180 (Westport, CT: Greenwood Press, 1988), 292–293.

114. Hanlon, *Beggar*, 180.

115. Willem Steenkamp, *Borderstrike! South Africa into Angola* (Durban: Butterworths Publishers, 1983), 1–263.

116. Helmoed-Römer Heitman, *South African War Machine* (Novato, CA: Presidio Press, 1985), 138, 157, and 165.

117. "Botswana Warns Pretoria and Swapo," *Sowetan* (Johannesburg), 27 May 1981, 6.

118. "SA-Botswana in Contact on 'Incidents'," RDM, 20 March 1981, m.f.e., 3.

119. "Shot Marines 'Were Inside Botswana'," RDM, 27 October 1984, m.f.e., 2.

120. Wilf Nussey, "Masire Fears SA [Is] Gearing for Attack," *The Star*, 2 December 1981, l.f.e., 29.

121. Dave Spiro, "Botswana: We Shot Down Piper," *The Citizen* (Johannesburg), 18 December 1982, 3.

122. "Botswana Claims SA Troops 'Poaching'," *The Star*, 15 April 1980, s.p.e., 1.

123. "SA Claims Botswana Territory," BDN, 21 December 1984, 1.

124. For an inventory of, and statistics on, South African cross-border attacks on Botswana from 1985 to 1989 compiled by the BDF and the BPF, consult Phyllis Johnson and David Martin, *Apartheid Terrorism: The Destabilization Report* (London: The Commonwealth Secretariat in association

with James Currey Ltd., London, and Indiana University Press, Bloomington, 1989), 103–110.

125. The narrative of the 1985 SADF raid in this and subsequent paragraphs is a composite account, based upon the following contemporary sources: "Eleven Killed in SA Raid on Gaborone," BDN, 14 June 1985, 1; "Botswana Fears Some People 'Kidnapped'," *The Citizen*, 15 June 1985, 2; Gerald L'Ange, "Raiders Used Road Spikes To Stop BDF," *The Star*, 15 June 1985, l.f.e., 1; Stephan Terblanche, "ANC Was Ready To Strike Today . . . So Army Struck First: The Guns of Gaborone," ST, 16 June 1985, 1–2; FBISDRMEA 5, no. 116 (17 June 1985):U7–U8; "Botswana Denies Getting Warning of SA Raid," *The Citizen*, 19 June 1985, 8; Gwen Ansell, "SADF Raids Gaborone," BG, 19 June 1985, 1–2; "ANC Terror Hide-Outs Destroyed," "Botswana 'Activated' by ANC," and "The Latest," *Paratus* (Pretoria) 36, no. 7 (July 1985):18–19, 19–21, and 21, respectively; "SA Killer Squad Consisted of More Than 50 Armed Men," BDN, 1 July 1985, 2; ARBPS 22, no. 6 (15 July 1985):7668; and "South African Attack on Botswana," *Briefing Paper on Southern Africa* (London: IDAFSA) 18 (September 1985):[3]-[4].

126. There was speculation that the 1985 raid was launched from Zeerust in the Transvaal, but this has not been confirmed (Howard Barrell, "Botswana: The Raid That Backfired," NA 215 [August 1985]:28). This was plausible, considering that there was a SADF base in Zeerust (Gavin Cawthra, *Brute Force: The Apartheid War Machine* [London: IDAFSA, 1986], 224 [map titled "South Africa: Military Deployment"]). According to one account (Ansell, "SADF Raids Gaborone," 1), the attack force was rumored to have a reserve of armored vehicles and tanks should additional force be needed. If so, then Zeerust would have been the logical place for positioning an armored column close to the Tlokweng border post outside Gaborone.

127. The 1978 Defense Amendment Act allowed the minister of defense to have access to a six-mile zone along South Africa's borders, while farms along the border must be effectively occupied (Loraine Gordon et al. [comp.], SRRSA, 1978 [Johannesburg: SAIRR, 1979], 61, and "South Africa Imposes Rules on Border Farmers," NYT, 7 May 1983, f.e., 5). Such regulations could permit the establishment of small, clandestine, forward SADF bases or assembly points for cross-border raids.

128. Jowitt Mbongwe, "BDF Reviews Operational Strategy," BDN, 19 June 1985, 1.

129. In addition, Simon Hirschfeldt, the commissioner of the BPF, indicated that the police force was not given advanced warning of the raid by the SADF (FBISDRMEA 5, no. 117 [18 June 1985]:U1).

130. See William J. Foltz, "The Militarization of Africa," in Foltz and Bienen, *Arms and the African*, 172.

131. "Pretoria Is Invited To Identify any ANC Bases," QERNBLS, no. 3—1983 (12 September 1983):22.

132. "We Warned Them—Pik," *The Citizen*, 15 June 1985, 2.

133. UNSC doc. S/PV 2598, 21 June 1985, 4–19.

134. UNSC doc. S/PV 2599, 21 June 1985, 31–36.

135. Ibid., 78.

136. UNSC doc. S/RES/568, 21 June 1985 (res. 568 [1985]), operative

paras. 1, 5, and 8.

137. UNSC doc. S/17453, 11 September 1985, 10–13.

138. Marshall Tladi, "SA Has Not Responded to Our Demand," BDN, 1 November 1985, 1.

139. "House Hit in SADF Raid Is Rebuilt as a Memorial," *The Star*, 21 July 1986, i.a.w.e., 4.

140. The narrative of the 1986 SADF attack is a composite account, based upon the following contemporary sources: SAD, 23 May 1986, 440 and 442; FBISDRMEA 5, no. 96 (19 May 1986):U5, U7–U8, and U11–U13; FBISDRMEA 5, no. 97 (20 May 1986):U1–U10; FBISDRMEA 5, no. 98 (21 May 1986):U1–U6 and U8–U10; FBISDRMEA 5, no. 99 (22 May 1986):U1–U5; FBISDRMEA 5, no. 100 (23 May 1986):U1; FBISDRMEA 5, no.101 (27 May 1986):U3; ARBPS 23, no. 5 (15 June 1986):8073–8079; "Eminent Persons Are in Gaborone," BDN, 25 February 1986, 1; and Edward Kwakwa, "South Africa's May 1986 Military Incursions into Neighboring African States," YJIL 12, no. 2 (Summer 1987):421–443.

141. UNSC doc. provisional S/PV 2684, 22 May 1986, 21–28/30 (South African delegate); UNSC doc. provisional S/PV 2686, 23 May 1986, 51–61 (Botswanan delegate) and 127–128/130 (voting); and Zoriana Pysariwsky, "Veto Angers Africans," *The Times*, 26 May 1986, 5.

142. Steven K. Metz, "Pretoria's 'Total Strategy' and Low-Intensity Warfare in Southern Africa," CS 6, no. 4 (1987):437–469, especially 446–458.

143. Bernhard Weimer and Olaf Claus, "A Changing Southern Africa: What Role for Botswana?," in *Botswana: The Political Economy of Democratic Development*, ed. Stephen J. Stedman (Boulder, CO: Lynne Rienner Publishers, 1993), 193.

144. The (English) text of the proposed treaty is published in Olaf Claus, *Botswana: Südafrikanisches Homeland oder unabhänginger Frontstaat? Zur Handlungsfreiheit eines "kleinen" Staates gegenüber seinem "mächtigen" Nachbarn*, Arbeiten aus dem Institut für Afrika-Kunde, Heft 82 (Hamburg: Institut für Afrika-Kunde im Verband der Stiftung Deutsches Übersee-Institut, 1992), 221–226.

145. "Terrorists Entering via Botswana, Says Vlok," *The Star*, 28 September 1988, i.a.w.e., 5.

146. "Botswana Orders ANC Rep[resentative] Out," MWD, 8 March 1986, 1.

147. "Botswana Pledge on Armed Raids," *The Citizen*, 3 March 1987, 13.

148. "ANC Men Jailed in Botswana," *The Star*, 19 July 1989, i.a.w.e., 8.

149. BNAORH, 86, pt. 2 (16 April 1986), 963–964 (Mr. Dabutha), 966 (Mr. Dabutha), 972 (Mr. Tlhomelang), 985 (minister of presidential affairs and public administration), and 997 (Mr. Tlhomelang).

150. "National Security Act, No. 11 of 1986," BGG 15, no. 103 (23 May 1986):A.23–A.33 (Supplement A), especially sections three (prejudicial acts) and ten (presumption).

151. Dingake, "Opposition Spokesmen Slam Security Act," 3, and Otlhogile, "National Security Act," 4.

152. Grant and Egner, "The Private Press and Democracy," 247, 250–252, 254, and 261–262.

153. "And the Trial Starts of Captured South African Commandos," CRNBLS, no. 4—1988 (18 November 1988):25–26, and "And the Two Captured Commandos Are Sentenced," CRNBLS, no. 1—1989 (27 February 1989):28–29.

154. James J. Zaffiro, "Botswana's Foreign Policy and the Exit of the Superpowers from Southern Africa," AI 22, no. 2 (1992):99.

155. Weimer and Claus, "A Changing Southern Africa," 198–200.

156. "Cash for Police Shoots Up," *The Star*, 27 March 1991, i.a.w.e., 13.

157. Laurie Nathan, *Marching to a Different Drum: A Description and Assessment of the Namibian Police and Defence Force*, Southern African Perspectives: A Working Paper Series, no. 4 (Bellville: University of the Western Cape, Centre for Southern African Studies, 1990), 5–19, especially 12–13.

158. "A Troop Contingent Has Been Sent to Somalia," CRBNLS, no. 1—1993 (1 March 1993):14.

159. "Botswana Forces Arrive in Tete for UN Mission," FBISDRSSA 93-074 (20 April 1993):24.

160. See the suggestions in Simon J. Baynham, "Regional Security in the Third World with Specific Reference to Southern Africa," SRSA 16, no. 1 (March 1994):105–107.

CHAPTER FIVE

1. Anthony J. Dachs, *The Road to the North: The Origin and Force of a Slogan*, Local series pamphlet no. 23 (Salisbury: The Central Africa Historical Association, 1969), 2–3.

2. Q. Neil Parsons, "Education and Development in Pre-Colonial and Colonial Botswana to 1965," in *Education for Development in Botswana*, ed. Michael Crowder (Gaborone: Macmillan Botswana Publishing Co. [Pty.] Ltd., 1984), 39.

3. Marshall R. Singer, *Weak States in a World of Powers: The Dynamics of International Relations* (New York: The Free Press, 1972), 149–172 and 396–399.

4. Edmond A. Watters III, "Botswana: The Roots of Educational Development and the Evolution of Formal and Informal Education" (Ed.D. diss., Lehigh University, 1973), 88.

5. Parsons, "Education and Development," 40.

6. Watters, "Botswana," 195.

7. H.C.L. Hermans, "Botswana's Options for Independent Existence," in *Land-Locked Countries of Africa*, ed. Zdenek Cervenka (Uppsala: SIAS, 1973), 203, and letter to the writer from H.C.L. Hermans, permanent secretary of the ministry of finance and development planning, Gaborone, dated 28 November 1974.

8. Ernest P. Lekhela, "The Origin, Development, and Role of Missionary Teacher-Training Institutions for the Africans of the North-Western Cape (An Historical-Critical Study of the Period 1850–1954)" (D.Ed. diss., University of South Africa, 1970), 505.

9. Benson, *Tshekedi Khama*, 41 and 87–88.

10.   Edgar H. Brookes, *A South African Pilgrimage* (Johannesburg: Ravan Press, 1977), 25, 49, and 63.

11.   BPEDAR, 1951, 21.

12.   Letter to me from H.C.L. Hermans, chief, world bank regional mission, Bangkok, dated 23 February 1987 (hereafter cited as 1987 Hermans letter).

13.   W. L. Maree, *Uit Duisternis Geroep: Die Sendingswerk van die Nederduitse Gereformeerde Kerk onder die Bakgatlavolk van Wes-Transvaal en Betjoeanaland* (Johannesburg: Voortrekkerspers Beperk, 1966), 257.

14.   Benson, *Tshekedi Khama*, 277.

15.   High Commissioner for Basutoland, the Bechuanaland Protectorate, and Swaziland, *Lands of Opportunity: Basutoland, Bechuanaland, [and] Swaziland* (Pretoria: author, 1958), 6.

16.   UK. Commission on Financial and Economic Position of the Bechuanaland Protectorate, *Financial and Economic Position of the Bechuanaland Protectorate: Report of the Commission Appointed by the Secretary of State for Dominion Affairs*, Cmd. 4368 (London: HMSO, 1933) (hereafter cited as Pim Report), 83–84 and 86.

17.   Watters, "Botswana," 116–117, 156–157, and 188.

18.   SRLAD, 58 (16 October 1964), cols. 1925–1926.

19.   Parsons, "Education and Development," 39.

20.   BPEDAR, 1948, 17.

21.   *Report on [the] Education of Europeans in the Bechuanaland Protectorate* (Pretoria: National Bureau of Educational and Social Research for the Union of South Africa, 1939), 5 (italics in the original).

22.   Ibid.

23.   Watters, "Botswana," 57–58, 105, 107–108, 113, 139, 141–143, 190–191, and 201–202.

24.   Michael O. M. Seboni, "The Development of Education in the Bechuanaland Protectorate (1824-1944): An Historical Survey" (M.Ed. thesis, University of South Africa, 1947), 15 and 19.

25.   Letter to me from the late Connie Minchin, Mafikeng, former member of the BP Department of Education from 1946 to 1952, dated 12 November 1986 (hereafter cited as Minchin letter), and Parsons, "Education and Development," 39.

26.   "Phasing Out Afrikaans," *The Star*, 8 February 1967, c.l.e., 8.

27.   BPLAORH 14 (13 July 1965), 132–133; BNAORH 41, pt. 1 (30 August 1972), 32; 52 (13 March 1975), 207 (speech of Mr. G. S. Mosinyi) and 220 (14 March 1975); 54 (25 November 1975), 7–8; and 57 (10 December 1976), 146.

28.   My interview with the Rev. Hugh Brown, headmaster, Broadhurst Primary School, Gaborone, 11 June 1987.

29.   BPEACM, 42d sess. (5 April 1948), 4.

30.   Parsons, "Education and Development," 39.

31.   "Bantu Education Ends Community: Gaunt Reminder of Mission Days," *The Star*, 27 January 1969, 2d c.l.e., 12.

32.   Lentlhabile Maano, "Moeding College Celebrates 20 Y[ea]rs,"

Kutlwano 20, no. 5 (May 1982) 8–10, and Alec C. Campbell, *The Guide to Botswana*, 2d ed. (Johannesburg and Gaborone: Winchester Press, 1979), 373.

33.   Ernst G. Malherbe, *Never a Dull Moment* (Cape Town: Howard Timmins [Pty.] Ltd. S.A., 1981), 167–168.

34.   Seboni, "The Development of Education," 24.

35.   W. L. Maree, "A Century of Grace for [the] D. R. Church in Botswana," DRC *Africa News* (Pretoria) 2, no. 5 (May 1977):1–5, and Minchin letter.

36.   BPNACM, 16th sess. (11-13 February 1935), 10–11 and 49–54; 18th sess. (4 March 1937), 7; and 21st sess. (27-28 March 1940), 14–22, 25–26, 35, 37–38, and 40; and BPAACM, 26th sess. (30 April–7 May 1945), 9, 111, and 126.

37.   "UB Graduation Ceremony," *Kutlwano* 23, no. 11 (November 1985):4.

38.   Kathleen M. Mulligan, "Alfred E. Jennings: The Political Activities of the London Missionary Society in Bechuanaland, 1900–1935" (Ph.D. diss., St. John's University, 1974), 383, 387, and 468.

39.   B. K. Murray, "Black Admissions to the University of the Witwatersrand, 1922–1939," SAHJ 14 (November 1984):35–53.

40.   Richard Dale, "The 'Functional Web of Interdependence' between Pre-Independent Botswana and South Africa: A Preliminary Study," BNR 6 (1974), 124–125.

41.   Robertson, "From Protectorate to Republic," 283–284.

42.   "Botswana's Man Meets Old Friends at U.N.," *The Star*, 28 October 1966, s.p.e., 8.

43.   UKCOBPR, 1961–1962 (London: HMSO, 1964), 52.

44.   Richard P. Stevens, "Southern Africa's Multiracial University," AR 9, no. 3 (March 1964):17–18, and Dale, "The 'Functional Web'," 125.

45.   Parsons, "The Evolution," 35.

46.   "Legal Developments since Independence," MWD, 18 October 1986, 11.

47.   SAPHAD, 21 (16 June 1933), col. 1068, and Charles F. Rey, *Monarch of All I Survey: Bechuanaland Diaries, 1929-37*, ed. Q. Neil Parsons and Michael Crowder (Gaborone: BS; New York: Lilian Barber Press, Inc.; and London: James Currey Ltd., 1988), 240, n. 12 and 263, n. 11.

48.   Charmaine Muir, "Magang Calls for Localisation of [the] Legal Profession," BDN, 15 September 1983, 4.

49.   My interview with Spencer P. Minchin, of the Mafikeng legal firm of Minchin and Kelly, Gaborone, 7 July 1976. A list of the names and addresses of the members of the bar of Botswana was published in the BGG 10, no. 37 (28 July 1972):440–441 (Government Notice no. 226 of 1972).

50.   "SA Judges for Botswana," *The Star*, 6 February 1981, s.p.e., 3.

51.   Akinola Aguda, "Legal Development in Botswana from 1885 to 1966," BNR 5 (1973), 56–57.

52.   "Resignation Denial by Bench Head," *The Star*, 16 February 1970, 2d c.l.e., 7, and Kevin Stocks, "Dendy-Young: He Walks the Wilgespruit Tightrope," *The Star*, 8 June 1973, 2d c.l.e., 27.

53.   Letter to me from T. W. Baxter, Director of the National Archives of Rhodesia, Salisbury, dated 10 January 1968.

54.   BNAORH, 23 (8 January 1968), 15 (address by President Khama).

55.   Colclough and McCarthy, *The Political Economy*, 249.

56.   BPLAORH, 14 (14 July 1965), 207–210 (motion), and BNAORH, 24 (3 April 1968), 548–559 (motion).

57.   Parsons, "The Evolution," 35.

58.   BED, *Report of the Education Department for the Years 1965 and 1966* (Gaberones: GP, n.d.), 25–29.

59.   BDIPER, LPSSSO, 1970 (s.l.: GP, 1970), [2]–[12].

60.   Christopher Colclough, "Some Lessons from Botswana's Experience with Manpower Planning," BNR 8 (1976), 132–133.

61.   John W. Hanson, *Secondary Level Teachers: Supply and Demand in Botswana*, Country Study no. 1 (East Lansing: Michigan State University, Institute for International Studies in Education and the African Studies Center, 1968), 19.

62.   Watters, " Botswana," 242–243.

63.   Hanson, *Secondary Level Teachers*, 19.

64.   Letter to me from Professor E. Philip Morgan, School of Public and Environmental Studies, Indiana University, Bloomington, Indiana, dated 19 October 1986 (hereafter cited as 1986 Morgan letter).

65.   Letter to me from Kevin Lowther, deputy chief, east and southern Africa division, US Peace Corps, Washington, DC, dated 26 September 1968.

66.   BNAOR, 21 (15 March 1967), 50–51.

67.   Bessie Head, *Serowe: Village of the Rain Wind* (London: Heinemann Educational Books Ltd., 1981), 135–138.

68.   "Dorothy Yates, Bushveld Teacher," *The Star*, 3 August 1972, 1st c.l.e., B8.

69.   1987 Hermans letter.

70.   Vicki Rosenthal, "Maru a Pula: 'School That Split a Nation . . . '," RDM, 14 November 1973, m.f.e., 15.

71.   1986 Morgan letter.

72.   Letter to me from Brenda P. Joy, secretary to the headmaster, Maru-a-Pula School, Gaborone, dated 16 April 1985.

73.   [Maru-a-Pula School], "Full Time Teaching Staff—May, 1987," 1, and my interview with Mr. David Matthews, headmaster of Maru-a-Pula School, Gaborone, 22 June 1987 (hereafter cited as Matthews interview).

74.   Gossett, "The Civil Service," 358.

75.   Sam Kauffmann, "Young Professionals Stifled in Botswana," CSM, 22 April 1991, 12–13, and Matthews interview.

76.   D. J. Jerling, "Thanks, SAVS, for Building That School," *The Star*, 30 July 1968, 2d c.l.e., 20 (letter to the editor).

77.   Letter to me from the Rev. James H. Robinson, executive director, Operation Crossroads Africa, Inc., New York, dated 23 February 1968.

78.   Watters, "Botswana," 240–241.

79.   Cynthia M. Magagulu, "The Multi-National University in Africa: An Analysis of the Development and Demise of the University of Botswana, Lesotho, and Swaziland" (Ph.D. diss., University of Maryland, 1978), 119–120.

80.   E. Jefferson Murphy, *Creative Philanthropy: Carnegie Corporation and Africa, 1953-1973* (New York: Columbia University Teachers College

Press, 1976), 180–185.

81.   Pius XII College, *Statistical Abstracts of Student Enrolment for the Academic Year 1963* (Roma: Pius XIII College, Office of the Registrar, 1963), 1–4, [8], and [28], and Magagulu, "The Multi-National University," 235b.

82.   Colclough and McCarthy, *The Political Economy*, 250–251.

83.   Kebareng Solomon, "How [the] University of Botswana Came About," BDN, 10 November 1986, 3.

84.   Kgomotso Mogapi, "Education and Cultural Identity," in Crowder, Education for Development, 187–190.

85.   Michael Crowder, "Introduction," in *Essays on the History of Botswana: A Bibliography of History Research Essays Presented in Part[ial] Fulfilment of the B.A. Degree of the University of Botswana*, comp. Kevin Shillington (Gaborone: UB Department of History, 1984), iii–iv.

86.   Kebareng Solomon, "Varsity Library Exhibits Inter-African Co-operation," BDN, 6 October 1986, 1.

87.   "American Scholarships Available," MMPG, 23 April 1965, 2, and "Scholarships Offered in USA," MMPG, 23 July 1965, 13.

88.   UNESCO Expanded Programme of Technical Assistance, *Bechuanaland Educational Planning Mission, July-September 1964*. UN doc. EPTA/EDPLAN/BECH (Paris: UNESCO, 1964), iii–xi.

89.   Khama, *From the Frontline*, 25.

90.   BDIPER, LPSSSO, 1974/75 (s.l.: GP, n.d.), [1], [4]–[7], [16]–23, and 25–27.

91.   Ibid., [16]–17, 23, and 25–27.

92.   1987 Hermans letter.

93.   1986 Morgan letter.

94.   James H. Polhemus, "Botswana Votes: Parties and Elections in an African Democracy," JMAS 21, no. 3 (September 1983):401–402.

95.   "Botswana's Museum: Help from S.A. and Rhodesia," *The Star*, 3 October 1967, c.l.e., 10.

96.   NMB, 1968 Annual Report (Gaborone: GP, n.d.), 4.

97.   Doreen Nteta, "The Museum Service in Botswana," BNR 5 (1973), 215.

98.   NMAG, *Annual Report 1970-1973* (Gaborone: GP, n.d.), 4.

99.   Doreen Nteta, "Museum Training," ZV 9, no. 4 (1982):24–25.

100.   Quett K. J. Masire, "Presidential Address Delivered at the Annual General Meeting of the Botswana Society Held on 22 March 1972," BNR 4 (1972), unpaginated, and 1986 Morgan letter.

101.   UKPHCD, 348 (6 June 1939), col. 191.

102.   Sara Pienaar, *South Africa and International Relations between the Two World Wars: The League of Nations Dimension* (Johannesburg: Witwatersrand University Press, 1987), 157–165.

103.   An invaluable checklist of services performed by these two neighbors appears in Couperthwaite, "Bechuanaland," 66–69.

104.   See Peter Vale, "Prospects for Transplanting European Models of Regional Integration to Southern Africa," PSAJPS 9, no. 2 (December 1982):32–41, especially 34 and 39.

105.   SAPSD, 1931 (6 May 1931), cols. 466–467 (minister of lands).

106. Ibid., 1935 (22 March 1935), cols. 167–168 (minister of lands).

107. Letter to me from the director, National Parks Board of Trustees, Pretoria, dated 19 April 1968 (hereafter cited as 1968 National Parks letter).

108. Letter to me from Dr. G. De Graaff, assistant director (scientific liaison and publications), National Parks Board of Trustees, Pretoria, dated 6 January 1976.

109. 1968 National Parks letter.

110. James Clarke, "A Way of Spreading Out the Tourists," *The Star*, i.a.w.e., 7 November 1990, 9.

111. K. L. Tinley, *An Ecological Reconnaissance of the Moremi Wildlife Reserve, Northern Okovango [sic] Swamps, Botswana* (Johannesburg: Okovango [sic] Wildlife Society, 1966), introduction (unpaginated).

112. Okavango Wildlife Society, *The Moremi Wildlife Reserve* (Bramley, Johannesburg: author, n.d.), [4], and "Okavango Society To Show Films," *The Star*, 22 June 1973, 2d c.l.e., 20.

113. G. M. Erich Leistner, "Co-operation for Development in Southern Africa," in *Accelerated Development in Southern Africa*, ed. John Barratt, Simond Brand, David S. Collier, and Kurt Glaser (London: The Macmillan Press Ltd., 1974), 574–575.

114. James Clarke, "South Africa Sits on Its Scientific Treasure Chest: So Much Wildlife Research Is Yet To Be Done," *The Star*, 19 August 1972, l.s.e., 10.

115. F. Zumpt, "A Trip to a Game Paradise: 1. An Introduction to Why and How," AWL 13, no. 3 (September 1959):1.

116. "Big Conference on Wildlife for Pretoria," *The Star*, 8 March 1973, 2d c.l.e., 12.

117. For an excellent synopsis of research on the Okavango, consult D. H. Potten and W. S. Pintz, "Exploitating [sic] the Okavango: Past Proposals, Present Investigations, and Future Prospects," in *Proceedings of the Symposium on the Okavango Delta and Its Future Utilisation, National Museum, Gaborone, Botswana, August 30th to September 2nd, 1976* (Gaborone: BS, n.d.), 315–336.

118. Ibid., 315–316.

119. SA. Department of Irrigation, *Report of the Kalahari Reconnaissance of 1925* (Pretoria: GPO, 1925), 9.

120. L. A. Mackenzie, *Report on the Kalahari Expedition, 1945 (Being a Further Investigation into the Water Resources of the Kalahari and Their Relationship to the Climate of South Africa)*. U.G. no. 28—1946 (Pretoria: GP, 1946).

121. "International Water Link for S.A. Mooted," *The Star*, 17 April 1969, 2d c.l.e., 30.

122. Letter to me from Professor D. C. Midgley, Department of Civil Engineering, University of the Witwatersrand, dated 18 July 1968.

123. "Water Search: Now for the Zambezi," FM 95, no. 6 (8 February 1985):77.

124. For evidence of environmental concerns about aqueducts see "Water Project Worries Maun Residents," MWD, 30 November–6 December 1990, 1; "Gov[ernmen]t Back-Tracks on Okavango," 1–24 January 1991, 5; and

"Greenpeace Trio 'Not Persuaded'," MWD, 1–7 February 1991, 1 and 3–4.

125. Pim Report, 14–16, 27–28, 88, 118–119, 121–122, 126–132, 135, and 153–155.

126. D. M. Joubert, "The Contribution of SARCCUS to Development and Co-operation in Southern Africa," SAJAA 3, no. 1 (1973):1–6.

127. SAPHAD, 3 (20 February 1925), cols. 133–134.

128. Letter to me from the secretary, embassy of South Africa, Washington, DC, dated 27 December 1967 (hereafter cited as 1967 SA embassy letter).

129. "South Africa Helps Emerging Black States," Bantu (Pretoria) 14, no. 4 (April 1967):2.

130. Leistner, "Co-operation for Development," 568.

131. Stephen J. Ettinger, "South Africa's Weight Restrictions on Cattle Exports from Bechuanaland, 1924–41," BNR 4 (1972), 21–29.

132. SAPHAD, 22 (13 February 1968), cols. 411–412.

133. "Starting Point of New Era," MMPG, 25 February 1949, 1, and 1967 SA embassy letter.

134. "Concern over Okavango Tsetse," MMPG, 15 January 1965, 11, and BNAORH, 23 (11 January 1968), 9 (speech of President Khama).

135. B. C. Jansen, "The Onderstepoort Veterinary Research Institute in Relation to Animal Diseases in Southern Africa," SAJAA 2 (1972):47–54.

136. SAPHAD, 44 (29 May 1973), col. 7777 (speech of the minister of agriculture).

137. 1967 SA embassy letter.

138. G. M. Erich Leistner, "Economic Interdependence in Southern Africa," AIB 26, no. 4 (1986), supplement 4, 13.

139. J. H. Moolman, "Technical and Scientific Co-operation," in International Relations in Southern Africa: Papers Presented at a Symposium Held in Pretoria on 7 June 1973, ed. Denis Venter (Braamfontein: SAIIA, 1974), 32.

140. H. C. Biggs, Report on the Marketing of Agricultural Produce and Some Aspects of the Marketing of Livestock in Bechuanaland (London: MOD, 1966), 5, 49, and 54.

141. Derek J. Hudson, "Botswana's Membership of the Southern African Customs Union," in Papers on the Economy of Botswana, ed. Charles Harvey (London: Heinemann Educational Books, Ltd., 1981), 136.

142. Letter to me from Dr. G. M. Erich Leistner, Director of the Africa Institute, Pretoria, dated 14 February 1990.

143. "Medical Team for Rodent Research," MMPG, 9 July 1965, 6.

144. "Bechuanaland Protectorate," MMPG, 24 May 1946, 1.

145. David R. Massey, "Labor Migration and Rural Development in Botswana" (Ph.D. diss., Boston University, 1981), 129.

146. Pim Report, 76.

147. Andrew C. S. Mushingeh, "A History of Disease and Medicine in Botswana, 1820–1945" (Ph.D. diss., University of Cambridge, 1984), 321–322.

148. Ibid., 326 and 356, n. 77.

149. Ibid., 364, n. 149.

150. Ibid., 330–331.

151. "Seretse's Cousin in Kidney Operation," *The Star*, 14 February 1973, 2d c.l.e., 3, and "Young Desert Doctor 'Saved Herself'," *The Star*, 15 July 1976, s.p.e., 3.

152. "'Outwards' Policy Is for Safety: Vorster," *The Star*, 12 September 1968, 2d c.l.e., 1 and 3.

153. L.M. Irwig and W.G. Maxwell, "Report on a Medical Programme Undertaken in Northern Ngamiland, Botswana, by the Students' Medical Council of the University of the Witwatersrand Medical School in December, 1968" (Johannesburg: n.p., 1969).

154. Serara S. Kupe, "A History of the Evolution of Nursing Education in Botswana, 1922–1980" (Ed.D. diss., Columbia University Teachers College, 1987), 133–134.

155. Gossett, "The Civil Service," 372, n. 69.

156. Kupe, "A History," 159–160.

157. Ibid., 197.

158. Ibid., 169 and 287–290, and "Charlotte Searle: Nurses' President," *The Star*, 29 October 1973, 2d c.l.e., B5.

159. SAPSD, 1938 (21 September 1938), cols. 310–312.

160. *Report to the Government of Bechuanaland on the Bushman Survey* (Gaberones: Bechuanaland Government, 1965), 7–8 and 11.

161. Letter to me from Professor Phillip V. Tobias, Department of Anatomy, University of the Witwatersrand Medical School, dated 24 July 1968, as well as numerous scholarly reports and publications which Professor Tobias sent to me.

162. BGG 5, no. 47 (20 October 1967):B.231–B.233.

163. BNAORH, 22, pt. 1 (24 and 25 August 1967), 106–108 and 146–148 (introductory and concluding remarks, respectively, of the minister of home affairs during the 2d reading debate).

164. Isebill V. Gruhn, "Functionalism in Africa: Scientific and Technical Integration" (Ph.D. diss., University of California, Berkeley, 1967), 39, 46, and 55–56.

165. Ibid., 61–63.

166. Ibid., 86–88.

167. In 1976, seventy-two separate BNA files listed under the heading of the CCTA in the BNA catalog (in the 5503 through 5517 and the 5627 series) were closed to researchers.

168. BNAORH, 28 (12 May 1969), 2–3.

169. Maswgo A. Mpotokwane, "Tourism and Environmental Issues in Botswana," in *Tourism in Botswana: Proceedings of a Symposium Held in Gaborone, Botswana, 15–19 October 1990*, ed. Linda Pfotenhauer (Gaborone: BS, 1991), 149.

170. "Down in the Dumps? Then Take to the Dunes!," *The Star*, 26 June 1972, 1st c.l.e., 21.

171. Mark and Delia Owens, *Cry of the Kalahari* (Boston: Houghton Mifflin Company, 1984), 170 and 331.

172. BPIBBR, 1964 (London: HMSO, 1965), 61.

173. Ibid., 1965 (London: HMSO, 1966), 71.

174. Wolfgang Von Richter and Thomas M. Butynski, "Hunting in

Botswana," BNR 5 (1973), 191–208, and J. L. Dawson, "The Birds of Kutse Game Reserve," BNR 7 (1975), 141–150.

175. *Biographies of Trainees, Botswana I: Peace Corps Training Project at Syracuse University, August 31–December 12, 1966* (s.l.: n.p., n.d.), 1-24.

176. Letters to me from Kevin Lowther, operations officer for Botswana, US Peace Corps, Washington, D. C., dated 14 February 1968 and 22 March 1968.

177. BDIPER, LPSSSO, 1973/74 (s.l.: GP, n.d.), 18.

178. Rodger Yeager, "Democratic Pluralism and Ecological Crisis in Botswana," JDA 23, no. 3 (April 1989):401, n. 28.

179. David S. Cownie, "Regional Cooperation for Development: A Review and Critique of the Southern African Development Coordination Conference," CBAA 18, no. 1 (1985–1986):35.

180. Owens, *Cry*, 331.

181. W. Sheppe, "A Note on Research into Mammals of the Chobe River Flood-Plain," BNR 4 (1972), 281.

182. BDWNP, *Report of the Department of Wildlife and National Parks for the Period March 1965 to December 1968* (Gaborone: GP, n.d.), 1-3 and 11–12.

183. C.M.H. Jennings, J.P.F. Sellschop, B. Th. Verhagen, and M. T. Jones, "Environmental Isotopes as an Aid to [the] Investigation of Ground Water Problems in Botswana," BNR 5 (1973), 179 and 182.

184. H. J. Cooke, "The Problem of Drought in Botswana," in *Proceedings of the Symposium on Drought in Botswana, National Museum, Gaborone, Botswana, June 5th to 8th, 1978*, ed. Madalon T. Hinchley (Gaborone: BS in collaboration with Clark University Press, 1979), 10–11.

185. Cownie, "Regional Cooperation," 35.

186. *Southern Africa: Toward Economic Liberation: Papers Presented at the Arusha and Lusaka Meetings of the Southern Africa Development Co-ordination Conference*, ed. Amon J. Nsekela (London: Rex Collings, 1981), 160–166.

187. "Chinese Offer Crops for a Friendly Vote," *The Star*, 18 February 1969, 2d c.l.e., 35.

188. Harvey and Lewis, *Policy Choice*, 103.

189. Cownie, "Regional Cooperation," 35.

190. Deon Du Plessis, "Botswana Wins a Biological War," *The Star*, 31 October 1979, s.p.e., 8.

191. E. Philip Morgan, "Botswana: Development, Democracy, and Vulnerability," in *Southern Africa: The Continuing Crisis*, ed. Gwendolen M. Carter and Patrick O'Meara, 2d ed. (Bloomington: Indiana University Press, 1982), 242.

192. "Give What You Can: And So They Did," *The Star*, 8 June 1976, s.p.e., 20.

193. T. C. Luke, *Report on Localisation and Training* (Mafeking: Bechuanaland Press, 1966) (hereafter cited as the Luke Report), 80, 82, 139, and 143.

194. UKMOD, *The Development of the Bechuanaland Economy: Report of the Ministry of Overseas Development Economic Survey Mission* (November

1965) (Gaberones: GP, n.d.) (hereafter cited as the Porter Report), 31.

195. Isebill V. Gruhn, "Towards Scientific and Technological Independence?," JMAS 22, no. 1 (March 1984):11–14.

196. Derek J. Hudson, "The Taxation of Income from Cattle Farming," in Harvey, *Papers*, 68.

197. "Botswana Resumes Beef Exports to the EEC," AB, 35 (July 1981):4, and "Vaccines: Botswana," ARBFETS 15, no. 5 (30 June 1978):4725.

198. Letter to me from Mr. Phalaagae S. Tau, second secretary, embassy of Botswana, Washington, DC, dated 24 October 1991.

199. BNAOR, 31, pt. 2 (25-26 March 1970), 418–419 and 424–456, respectively (Mr. Matante's motion).

200. "Khama III," RDM, 30 June 1980, m.f.e., 2.

201. G. M. Erich Leistner, "Migration of High-Level African Manpower to South Africa," AI 23, no. 4 (1993):220.

202. LPSSSO, 1970, [9]–[11].

203. R. H. Johnson, "The Journal of the Medical and Dental Association of Botswana," BNR 4 (1972), 286–287.

204. Cownie, "Regional Cooperation," 35.

205. 1986 Morgan letter.

CHAPTER SIX

1. R. Frederic Morton, "Introduction: Seeing Botswana as a Whole," in *The Birth of Botswana: A History of the Bechuanaland Protectorate from 1910 to 1966*, ed. R. Frederic Morton and Jeff Ramsay (Gaborone: Longman Botswana, 1987), 3.

2. Picard, *The Politics of Development*, 72.

3. Letter to the writer from Dr. Q. Neil Parsons, Botswana Society, Gaborone, dated 4 January 1988 (hereafter cited as Parsons letter).

4. Philip E. Chartrand, "Churchill and Rhodesia in 1921: A Study of British Colonial Decision-Making" (Ph.D. diss., Syracuse University, 1974), 163–164.

5. Hyam, *The Failure*, 3.

6. Charles Jeffries, *The Colonial Office* (London: George Allen & Unwin, Ltd., 1956), 26.

7. Hyam, *The Failure*, 3.

8. J.A. Cross, *Whitehall and the Commonwealth: British Departmental Organisation for Commonwealth Relations, 1900–1966* (London: Routledge and Kegan Paul, 1967), 52.

9. Joe Garner, *The Commonwealth Office, 1925–68* (London: Heinemann Educational Books, Ltd., 1978), 130 and 413.

10. William M. Hailey (Lord Hailey), *The Republic of South Africa and the High Commission Territories* (London: OUP, 1963), 1–2.

11. Anthony Sillery, *Botswana: A Short Political History*, Studies in African History no. 8 (London: Methuen & Co., Ltd., 1974), 158.

12. Garner, *The Commonwealth Office*, 413.

13. "Bechuanaland," *The Times*, 16 June 1896, 15.

14.   Gossett, "The Civil Service," 184–186.

15.   "Bechuanaland—IV: Defects of Protectorate Government," *The Star*, 4 February 1938, s.p.e., 27.

16.   Rey, *Monarch of All I Survey*, 91–92 (entry for 7–8 December 1931).

17.   Anthony Sillery, "The British Protectorates in Africa—II," *The Fortnightly* (London) 71 (n.s.), no. 1021 (n.s.) (January 1952):26–29.

18.   Hugh Ashton, "The High Commission Territories," in *Handbook on Race Relations in South Africa*, ed. Ellen Hellmann (Cape Town: Geoffrey Cumberlege, OUP, 1949), 708.

19.   Graham T. Allison, *Essence of Decision: Explaining the Cuban Missile Crisis* (Boston: Little, Brown and Company, 1971), 176 and 316, n. 71.

20.   Letter to me from H.C.L. Hermans, permanent secretary, ministry of finance and development planning, Gaborone, dated 10 April 1973 (hereafter cited as 1973 Hermans letter).

21.   Mulligan, "Alfred E. Jennings," 462–463, n. 2.

22.   Robertson, "From Protectorate to Republic," 145.

23.   BPAACM, 38th sess. (22 May 1958), 67–68.

24.   UKPHCD, 484 (22 February 1951), cols. 1423–1424 (oral answers); 544 (21 July 1955), cols. 559–560 (oral answers); and 585 (3 April 1958), col. 175 (written answers).

25.   Ibid., 621 (12 April 1960), cols. 120–121 (written answers); 649 (14 November 1961), col. 198 (oral answers); and 674 (26 March 1963), cols. 141–142 (written answers).

26.   Ibid., 589 (12 June 1958), col. 384 (oral answers).

27.   Ibid., 623 (12 May 1960), cols. 77–78 (written answers).

28.   Ibid., 555 (5 July 1956), col. 1509 (oral answers).

29.   UKPHLD, 172 (27 June 1951), cols. 406–407 (debate on the banishment of Seretse and Tshekedi Khama).

30.   William H. Clark, "Banishment of Tshekedi," *The Times*, 12 June 1951, l.l.a.e., 7 (letter to the editor).

31.   UKPHCD, 621 (12 April 1960), cols. 120–121 (written answers).

32.   Ibid., 484 (22 February 1951), cols. 1423–1424.

33.   "Role Changes," 151–156 and 217, n. 88. Sir R. Peter Fawcus, a retired queen's commissioner for the BP, did not think that the HCT suffered as a result of the link with the CRO. He thought that the critical matter was the competence and concern of those officials in London who bore the responsibility for the management of the HCT (letter to me from Sir R. Peter Fawcus, Killin, Scotland, dated 9 December 1986 [hereafter cited as Fawcus letter]).

34.   Parsons letter.

35.   1973 Hermans letter.

36.   Parsons, "Seretse Khama and the Ba[ma]ngwato Succession Crisis, 1948-1953," 75–84.

37.   Sillery, *The Bechuanaland Protectorate*, 174 and 210–211.

38.   John L. Comoroff, "Competition for Office and Political Processes among the Barolong Boo Ratshidi of the South Africa-Botswana Borderland" (Ph.D. diss., University of London, 1973), 6–7 and 34.

39.   BPEACM, 2d sess. (31 October–5 November 1921), 7–8 and 29–30.

40.   Ibid., 4th sess. (3–6 March 1924), 16; 9th sess. (17–26 September 1928), 39 and 46–47; 10th sess. (11–19 February 1929), 12; 11th sess. (19–27 August 1929), 7, 9, and 29; 12th sess. (3–12 March 1930), 34; 18th sess. (3–6 December 1934), 53; 19th sess. (28–29 March 1935), 24–25; 31st sess. (9–13 March 1942), 74; 35th sess. (20–24 March 1944), 82–83; 38th sess. (25–30 March 1946), 44–47; and 53d sess. (17–19 August 1953), 41–44.

41.   Neither Kenneth R. D. Manungo's study ("The Role of the 'Native' Advisory Council in the Administration of [the] Bechuanaland Protectorate [1919–1960]" [B.A. thesis, University College of Botswana, 1977]) nor Robertson's careful investigation ("From Protectorate to Republic") contains any references to this council's discussing the possible relocation of the Imperial Reserve.

42.   At its initial meeting, the resident commissioner indicated that the council's concerns should not extend beyond the BP (BPNACM, 1st sess. [2 November 1920], 7 and annexure B). Perhaps this included the siting of the Imperial Reserve, but it certainly did not include matters of "low politics," as the minutes of subsequent sessions clearly indicated.

43.   Robertson, "From Protectorate to Republic," 400.

44.   Pim Report, 50 and 147–149.

45.   Charles F. Rey, "Notes by [the] Resident Commissioner, Bechuanaland Protectorate[,] on High Commission Territories Memorandum," March 1936, 48–49, in BNA file S458/2.

46.   "High Commission Territories Committee: Notes for Consideration," n.d., 34–35, enclosure in letter from Sir William H. Clark, British high commissioner, Cape Town, to Charles F. Rey, resident commissioner of the BP, dated 20 February 1936 in BNA file S458/1 and Robertson, "From Protectorate to Republic," 213–214.

47.   PRO file DO 35/1172/Y708/18, as cited in Deon J. Geldenhuys, "The Effects of South Africa's Racial Policy on Anglo-South African Relations, 1945–1961" (Ph.D. diss., University of Cambridge, 1977), 124–125 and 125, nn. 389–391, and Fawcus letter.

48.   Gossett, "The Civil Service," 344, and 1973 Hermans letter.

49.   BNDP, 1968–73 (Gaberones: GP, 1968), 67, and 1973 Hermans letter.

50.   Fawcus letter.

51.   Sillery, "The British Protectorates," 30.

52.   Richard D. Kauzlarich, "Development in Botswana: The Possibility of Regional Integration" (M.A. thesis, Indiana University, 1967), 5–6.

53.   Fawcus letter.

54.   Arthur J. A. Douglas (BP administration secretary) Papers, Files A and B, RHL, as cited in Robertson, "From Protectorate to Republic," 452, nn. 20–21.

55.   Campbell, *The Guide*, 612.

56.   BPLCORH, 2 (26 September 1961), 6 (speech of the government secretary).

57.   Fawcus letter.

58.   BPLCORH, 2 (26–27 September 1961), 6–51 (debate on the motion on the site for administrative and legislative headquarters).

59.   Richard Dale, "The Tale of Two Towns (Mafeking and Gaberones), and the Political Modernization of Botswana," SAIPAJPA 4, 2 (March 1969):133–134 and 139–140.

60.   Modisaotsile M. Hulela, "The Role of the European Advisory Council in the Administration of [the] Bechuanaland Protectorate (1920–1960)" (B.A. thesis, University College of Botswana, 1978), 41.

61.   Alan C. G. Best, "Central Trading in Botswana, 1890–1968," EG 46, no. 4 (October 1970):608–609.

62.   BNAOR, 27, pt. 1 (18 March 1969), 33 (minister of finance).

63.   Ann M. Burton, "Treasury Control and Colonial Policy in the Late Nineteenth Century," PA 44 (Summer, 1966):169–192.

64.   Halpern, South Africa's Hostages, 110–111 and 126.

65.   Ibid., 109, 125, and 264.

66.   Letter to me from Miss J.A.V. Rose, Government Archivist, Gaborone, dated 23 April 1976. I am most grateful for the cooperation and assistance of Miss Rose and Mr. E. B. Gwabini, the Senior Archives Assistant who consulted the personnel records.

67.   The category of dual nationality applied to the BP but was only used once (UKPHCD, 575 [29 October 1957], cols. 41–42 [written answers]) in answering questions in the House of Commons. Mr. Gwabini did not employ the category of dual citizen.

68.   Parsons letter.

69.   Ibid.

70.   BPAACM, 27th sess. (1 May 1946), 88.

71.   1973 Hermans letter.

72.   Fawcus letter. This is corroborated by Q. Neil Parsons, "Colonel Rey and the Colonial Rulers of Botswana: Mercenary and Missionary Traditions in Administration, 1884–1955," in People and Empires in African History: Essays in Memory of Michael Crowder, ed. J. F. Ade Ajayi and J. D. Y. Peel (New York: Longman, 1992), 208–209.

73.   Gunderson, "Nation-Building," 227–228.

74.   George Katsande, "The Evolution of the Bechuanaland Protectorate African Civil Service in a Colonial Context, c. 1895–1965" (B.A. thesis, University College of Botswana, 1982), 9–16.

75.   "Discrimination against South Africans Denied," The Star, 8 March 1966, c.l.e., 9.

76.   "Many S. Africans To Leave Bechuanaland," RDM, 3 March 1966, 2d ed., 6.

77.   Parsons letter.

78.   Picard, The Politics of Development, 77–78 and 92, n. 13.

79.   This position is, however, more restrictive than the one used locally just before independence. See BP, The Development of the Public Service, Legislative Council Paper no. 20 of 1964/65 (s.l.: Bechuanaland Press, n.d.), 62.

80.   Carl G. Widstrand and Zdenek Cervenka, Scandinavian Development Agreements with African Countries [Uppsala: SIAS, 1971], 43, 55, and 62.

81.   Hans-Erik Soonlike, "The Union of South Africa and the Question of the Incorporation of the Protectorates, 1933–1939" (BA [Hons.] thesis,

University of Cape Town, 1969), 27.

82. Ibid., 28–29.

83. UKCRO, *Report of a Mission to the Bechuanaland Protectorate To Investigate the Possibilities of Economic Development in the Western Kalahari, 1952* (London: HMSO, 1954).

84. *Basutoland, Bechuanaland Protectorate & Swaziland: Report of an Economic Survey Mission* (London: HMSO, 1960) (hereafter cited as the Morse Report).

85. USDS, Office of Media Services. *Bureau of Public Affairs, Background Notes: Bechuanaland*, Publication no. 8046 (Washington, DC: The Bureau, 1966), 4.

86. "Bechuanaland's New Diplomatic Status," *The Star*, 19 October 1964, c.l.e., 15.

87. Parsons letter.

88. BNAORH, 21 (16 March 1967), 80.

89. Here I employ Professor Picard's definition of localization (Picard, *The Politics of Development*, 278): "The replacement of colonial administrators with citizens of the newly independent country. Unlike the term 'Africanization,' localization does not imply racial exclusiveness."

90. BP, *The Development of the Public Service*, 26–27 and 63–66.

91. BPLCORH, 9 (19 November 1963), 32–33 (the chief secretary, moving the 2d reading of the 1963 Overseas Service Bill).

92. Gunderson, "Nation-Building," 235–238.

93. Patrick P. Molutsi, "International Influences on Botswana's Democracy," in Stedman, *Botswana*, 57, and Picard, *The Politics of Development*, 215.

94. Letter to me from E. Philip Morgan, Assistant to the Director, Africa-Asia Program, Syracuse University, dated 11 March 1968, and Picard, "Role Changes," 508, n. 10.

95. Fawcus letter. One of the Americans served as assistant to the resident commissioner ("Africa-Asia Public Service Fellows, 1964–1965," 15 May 1964, 1, in Anthony Sillery Papers, MSS Afr. s. 1611, file 2, RHL).

96. "Peace Corps Wave Flies In," *The Star*, 24 December 1966, i.a.w.e., 7.

97. Parsons letter.

98. Parsons letter, and BNAORH, 41, pt. 1 (28 August 1972), 4–5.

99. Johannes C. N. Mentz, "Localization and Training in the Botswana Public Service, 1966–1976" (D.Litt. et Phil., diss., University of South Africa, 1981), 247, 259, and 357.

100. Picard, *The Politics*, 209 and 211.

101. Ibid., 209

102. Ibid., 217.

103. Johannes C. N. Mentz and Louis A. Picard, "Human Resource Development in Botswana: A Shrinking Political Issue: [A] Preliminary Survey of Issues" (Paper delivered at the conference on the political economy of Botswana, Johns Hopkins University School of Advanced International Studies, Washington, DC, 12–13 April 1991), 2.

104. Ibid., 11, and James H. Cobbe, "Possible Negative Side Effects of

Aid to South Africa's Neighbours," AA 89, no. 354 (January 1990):89.

105.   Leistner, "Migration of High-Level African Manpower," 219–220 and 222–223, and Hussein Solomon, "Migration in Southern Africa: A Comparative Perspective," AI 24, no. 1 (1994):62, 64, and 67–69.

106.   Mentz, "Localization," 322, 339–340, and 342.

107.   Ibid., 322.

108.   Peter D. Bell, "The Ford Foundation as a Transnational Actor," IntOrg 25, no. 3 (Summer 1971):465–478.

109.   Mentz, "Localization," 373.

110.   Stephen R. Lewis, Jr., "Policymaking and Economic Performance: Botswana in Comparative Perspective," in Stedman, *Botswana*, 23.

111.   Cobbe, "Possible Negative Side Effects," 88–90.

112.   "International Influences," 57.

113.   "Human Resource Development," 3 and 13–14.

CHAPTER SEVEN

1.   *Transport Diplomacy*, 3.

2.   Martin, *Southern Africa*, 3 and 73.

3.   Botswana. Information Branch, *Republic of Botswana Fact Sheet* (Gaberones: author, 1966), 5.

4.   UKCOBPR, 1965, 136–137.

5.   Botswana. Information Branch, *Republic of Botswana Fact Sheet*, 5.

6.   Penelope Hartland-Thunberg, *Botswana: An African Growth Economy* (Boulder, CO: Westview Press, 1978), 33.

7.   Barbara Ntombingwenya, "The Development of Transport Infrastructure in the Bechuanaland Protectorate, 1885–1966," BNR 16 (1984), 76.

8.   Botswana. Information Branch, *Republic of Botswana Fact Sheet*, 5.

9.   "Funding Obtained for Orapa-Serowe Road," QERNBLS, no. 1—1985 (11 March 1985):32.

10.   Jeanne Hoes, "The Bid To Open Up the Hinterland," AB 75 (November 1984):34–35.

11.   Stephen J. McCarthy, "Infrastructural Development: Domestic and International Issues," in *Botswana's Economy since Independence*, ed. M. A. Oommen, F. K. Inganji, and L. D. Ngcongco (New Delhi: Tata-McGraw Hill Publishing Company, Ltd., 1983), 183–185.

12.   Douglas G. Anglin and Timothy M. Shaw, *Zambia's Foreign Policy: Studies in Diplomacy and Dependence* (Boulder, CO: Westview Press, 1979), 8–9, 17, and 23.

13.   Hoes, "The Bid," 34–35.

14.   Guy Arnold and Ruth Weiss, *Strategic Highways of Africa* (New York: St. Martin's Press, 1977), 40–41.

15.   Julian Burgess, *Interdependence in Southern Africa: Trade and Transport Links in South, Central, and East Africa*, EIU Special Report no. 32 (London: EIU, 1976), 90.

16.   "Work To Start on a New Road to Namibia," CRNBLS, no. 2—1989 (27 February 1989):36.

17. Dale Lautenbach, "Namibia Seeking More Gateways to [the] Outside World," *The Star*, 1 May 1991, i.a.w.e., 14.

18. "Trans-Kgalagadi Road," MWD, 7 September 1985, 3.

19. Hartland-Thunberg, *Botswana*, 32.

20. "April 5: D-Day for Expatriate Drivers," BDN, 11 March 1986, 1.

21. "Transport Dilemma," BG, 12 July 1985, 1.

22. Hanlon, *Beggar*, 70–71.

23. Gavin G. Maasdorp, *Transport Policies and Economic Development in Southern Africa: A Comparative Study in Eight Countries* (Durban: University of Natal, Economic Research Unit, 1984), 170.

24. "Government Reviews Regulations Affecting Cargo Haulers," MWD, 23 August 1986, 1.

25. Gavin G. Maasdorp, *Current Political and Economic Factors in Transportation in Southern Africa*, Occasional Paper (Braamfontein: SAIIA, 1988), 7.

26. *Botswana '86: An Official Handbook*, ed. Tom Obondo-Okoyo (Gaborone: Department of Information, Publications Division, 1986), 164.

27. Hartland-Thunberg, *Botswana*, 29.

28. Robert I. Rotberg, "South Africa's Regional Hegemony," in *Regional Conflict and U.S. Policy: Angola and Mozambique*, ed. Richard J. Bloomfield (Algonac, Mich.: Reference Publications, Inc., 1988), 81.

29. Campbell, *The Guide*, 230.

30. Colclough and McCarthy, *The Political Economy*, 158.

31. Douglas G. Anglin, "The Politics of Transit Routes in Land-Locked Southern Africa," in Cervenka, *Land-Locked Countries*, 118, n. 6.

32. Hartland-Thunberg, *Botswana*, 30.

33. Burgess, *Interdependence*, 27.

34. Frank Austin, *The Rhodesia Railways: A Short History* (Bulawayo: Rhodesia Railways Public Relations Branch, 1968), 15–16.

35. Hartland-Thunberg, *Botswana*, 30.

36. Ibid.

37. BNAORH, 22, pt. 2 (30 August 1967), 240–242, and Colclough and McCarthy, *The Political Economy*, 161.

38. BNAORH, 69 (18 November 1980), 16–17.

39. Obondo-Okoyo, *Botswana '86*, 165.

40. Southern Rhodesia, *Report of the Beit Bridge Rail Link Commission, 1967*, C.S.R. 10—1967 (Salisbury: GP, 1967), 7.

41. UN doc. 5/7781/Add. 2, annex, 9 March 1967 (UNSCOR, 22d yr., suppl. for January–March 1967, 159).

42. Ibid., 159–160.

43. SRPD, 66 (3 February 1967), col. 1128.

44. SRPHAD, 88 (10 September 1974), cols. 585–586.

45. ACRASD, 1974–1975 (London: Rex Collings, 1975), B365.

46. Stewart Dalby, "Despite Sanctions and Sentiment Botswana Railway Runs a Rhodesian Lifeline," FT, 26 May 1976, 29.

47. "Botswana Railways Taking Shape," *Africa* (London) 84 (August 1978), 116.

48. Dalby, "Despite Sanctions and Sentiment," 29.

49. "Botswana Railways Taking Shape," 116.

50. Kebareng Solomon, "Blackbeard Receives 10 Loco-Engines," BDN, 6 October 1986, 2.

51. Lentlhabile Maano, "Railway Gets P 14 Million Swedish Grant," BDN, 14 February 1986, 1.

52. Molefe Mmamapilo, "P 6m Rail Repair [Workshop] Well Underway," BDN, 10 March 1986, 3.

53. "Railway Supplementary Contract Is Signed," BDN, 1 September 1986, 3.

54. Solomon, "Blackbeard Receives 10 Loco-Engines," 2.

55. "Opposition: Locating HQ in Francistown? Botswana Railways Coming on Stream," MWD, 11 October 1986, 1 and 3.

56. "Botswana: The Transport Weapon," AC 28, no. 4 (18 February 1987):7.

57. "Government Seeks Way Out of Mangope Impasse: Botswana Wants Train Handover at Ramatlabama," MWD, 10 January 1987, 1.

58. "New Handover Arrangements with SATS Keeps Railway Traffic Moving," CRNBLS, no. 2—1987 (13 May 1987):42.

59. Zenaide Vendeiro, "New Rail Link Cuts Bop[huthatswana] Visa Demands," The Star, 16 February 1987, s.p.e., 3.

60. "Railway Takeover Arrangements Are Completed," CRNBLS, no. 2—1989 (14 June 1989):35.

61. J.G.H. Loubser, "Transportation Co-operation," in Leistner and Esterhuysen, South Africa in Southern Africa, 135.

62. "South African Initiatives in Intraregional Railway Transport," in Leistner and Esterhuysen, South Africa in Southern Africa, 143.

63. Cole, The Elite, 296–304.

64. "Surviving a Cold Shoulder from the North," South (London) 4 (January–February 1981):54.

65. "South African Initiatives," 143.

66. BNAORH, 62 (25 July 1978), 151 (speech of the assistant minister of finance and development planning during the second reading debate on the Gaborone and Francistown Oil Storage Deports Loan [Authorization] Bill).

67. "Mmusi Gets 5-m Dollars from Arabs," MMBG, 21 February 1975, 5.

68. "Botswana Stores Oil," The Star, 23 March 1982, l.f.e., 6.

69. BNAORH, 48 (6 December 1973), 228–229 (statement of the minister of state on the oil boycott).

70. Hanlon, Beggar, 74–75.

71. "EEC Agree To Finance Oil Survey," BDN, 13 August 1986, 1.

72. "Botswana Steps Up Oil Exploration," AB 99 (November 1986):46.

73. Hans-Jürgen Bocker, "Air Transport Potential and Problems of Developing Countries with Special Reference to Botswana" (D.Comm. diss., University of South Africa, 1978), 341–342, 356, 367, and 386–387.

74. Munger, Bechuanaland, 70.

75. Campbell, The Guide, 509.

76. UKCROBPR, 1947 (London: HMSO, 1949), 39.

77. Ibid., 1948 (London: HMSO, n.d.), 33.

78. UKCOBPR, 1961–1962, 75–76.

79. The Porter Report, 62–63.

80. Bocker, "Air Transport Potential," 273–274, and Robert L. Curry, *Small Is Profitable for Air Botswana*, Studies in Development Management no. 4 ([Gaborone]: Institute of Development Management, 1978), 4–6.

81. "And Air Botswana Is To Become a Fully Fledged Parastatal," CRNBLS, no. 4—1987 (23 November 1987):30.

82. Curry, *Small Is Profitable*, 3 and 8–9.

83. "Finance for Building Kasane Airport Has Been Secured," CRNBLS, no. 2—1988 (8 June 1988):38.

84. "And Air Botswana," 30.

85. "Air Botswana Adds a Jet to Its Fleet," CRNBLS, no. 3—1989 (3 September 1989):31.

86. Bocker, "Air Transport Potential," 274.

87. "But a Modest Expansion Programme for the Airline Is Being Implemented," QERNBLS, no. 1—1986 (12 March 1986):36.

88. Bocker, "Air Transport Potential," 282.

89. Hugh Quigley, "Botswana Carrier Brings Maintenance Home," AB 100 (December 1986):57.

90. "Air Botswana Recruits Local Pilots," MWD, 21 June 1986, 5.

91. Botswana, *Transitional Plan*, 78–79.

92. BNAORH, 69 (4 December 1980), 472 (statement of the minister of finance and development planning).

93. Ibid., 61 (23 March 1978), 425.

94. Ibid., (22 March 1978), 421, and (23 March 1978), 425–430.

95. Ibid., 426.

96. Ibid., (22 March 1978), 422 (Mr. Kwelagobe).

97. Ibid., (23 March 1978), 425 (Messrs. Kwelagobe and Mpho).

98. "Seretse Khama Airport Operational," BDN, 11 December 1984, 1.

99. D. H. Patrick, *Botswana: An Economic Survey and Businessman's Guide* (s.l.: Barclays Bank of Botswana Limited, 1985), 40.

100. "Air Botswana Has Increased Its Passenger Traffic," CRNBLS, no. 2—1991 (10 June 1991):39.

101. "BA Is the New Operator to Gaborone," CRNBLS, no. 1—1988 (29 February 1988):35–36.

102. "UTA Puts on a Weekly Flight to Paris," CRNBLS, no. 1—1990 (13 March 1990):33.

103. "Air Botswana Flies to Windhoek," MWD, 25 February to 4 March 1989, 1.

104. "Gov[ernmen]t Plans To Take Control of Airspace," BDN, 11 April 1988, 1 and 3.

105. "Plessey Radar To Establish a New Flight Information Region," CRNBLS, no. 2—1990 (11 June 1990):39. The transfer from South African to Botswanan control took place in October 1991 ("Botswana Now Controls Its Own Air Space," CRNBLS, no. 1—1992 [28 February 1992]:27).

106. Nussey, "Masire Fears SA [Is] Gearing for Attack," 29. This happened again in 1992 and evoked another protest ("South African Invasion of Botswana's Air Space Is Condemned," CRBNLS, no. 1—1993 [1 March 1993]:14).

107.   Johnson and Martin, *Apartheid Terrorism*, 110–111.

108.   Douglas G. Anglin, "The Frontline States and Sanctions against South Africa," in *Sanctioning Apartheid*, ed. Robert E. Edgar (Trenton, NJ: Africa World Press, 1990), 268–271.

109.   Jack D. Parson, "The Potential for South African Sanctions Busting in Southern Africa: The Case of Botswana," in Edgar, *Sanctioning Apartheid*, 305–306.

110.   Anglin, "The Frontline States and Sanctions," 269 and 287, n. 45.

111.   Hans-Jürgen Bocker, *A Study of the Air Traffic Potential of the Republic of Botswana: A Survey Conducted on Behalf of Esquire Airways Botswana* (Pretoria: University of South Africa, Bureau of Market Research, circa 1972), 49–50, 55, 60, and 62.

112.   My interview with David W. Joy, manager for Botswana of British Caledonian Airways, Gaborone, 4 June 1987.

113.   Peter Maphangela, "Air Botswana Builds Maintenance Hanger," BDN, 16 January 1986, 2.

114.   Hartland-Thunberg, *Botswana*, 35.

115.   Bocker, *A Study*, 62.

116.   "Air Botswana Plans New Jet Services," CRNBLS, no. 1—1992 (28 February 1992):33, and Tutu Tsiang, "An Overview of Tourism in Botswana," in Pfotenhauer, *Tourism in Botswana*, 29.

117.   "Aviation Infrastructure Is To Be Developed," CRNBLS, no. 2—1989 (14 June 1989):35.

118.   Harold M. Prowse, "Wildlife Administration and the Safari Industry in Botswana" (Ph.D. diss., University of Michigan, 1974), 43 and 352, n. 25.

119.   Ibid., 10, 24, 40, 81, 105, and 109.

120.   Ibid., 80.

121.   The Porter Report, 35–37.

122.   Ibid., 34–35.

123.   Prowse, "Wildlife," 226.

124.   Ibid., 260, 262, and 264.

125.   Mommsen interview.

126.   Prowse, "Wildlife," 120–132.

127.   Bocker, *A Study*, 1–4.

128.   Prowse, "Wildlife," 107–108, 110–111, 137–139, 175, and 245–246.

129.   Ibid., 200–202, 257, 260, 262, and 288–291.

130.   Bocker, *A Study*, 9, 44–45, and 62.

131.   Letter to me from Mrs. E. B. Mathe, Controller of Tourism, Gaborone, dated 11 November 1975 (hereafter cited as Mathe letter).

132.   BCSO, *Tourist Statistics, 1975* (Gaborone: GP, 1976), i.

133.   Mathe letter.

134.   G. M. Erich Leistner, "Constellation of Southern African States (Economic Aspects)," in *Alternative Structures for Southern Africa Interaction: A Collection of Addresses Presented at a Seminar Given by the Institute of Foreign and Comparative Law, University of South Africa* (Pretoria: AISA, 1982), 31.

135.   Letter to me from Chawa Bogosi, Director of the Tourism Development Unit, Gaborone, dated 7 July 1987 (hereafter cited as Bogosi

letter).

136. My computations based on BCSO, *Tourist Statistics, 1989* (Gaborone: CSO, 1990), 13.

137. Lewis, *Economic Realities*, 40, n. 24.

138. Isaac N. Mazonde, "Bordermanship: A Factor of Economic Differentiation among the Afrikaner and English Settlers in the Tuli Bloc, Eastern Botswana," BNR 22 (1990), 79–89.

139. Hanlon, *Beggar*, 62 and 285.

140. "Let's Protect Our Game," BDN, 19 September 1986, 1 (editorial).

141. Dorian Wild, "Third Link in Temptation Chain," *The Star*, 21 July 1971, 1st c.l.e., 25.

142. Jonathan Crush and Paul Wellings, "The Southern African Pleasure Periphery, 1966–83," JMAS 21, no. 4 (December 1983):677 and 683–687, and letter to me from Edwin S. Munger, Munger Africana Library, California Institute of Technology, Pasadena, CA, dated 15 December 1986 (hereafter cited as Munger letter).

143. BNAORH, 27, pt. 1 (21 March 1969), 138–161 (Mr. Matante's motion); 36 pt. 1 (16 March 1971), 177–179, and (17 March 1971) 207–209 (Mr. Matante's motion); and 36, pt. 2 (18 March 1971), 217–227 (Mr. Matante's motion).

144. Ibid., 36, pt. 3 (25 March 1971), 374–375 (speech of the minister of commerce, industry, and water affairs, introducing the second reading of the Casino Bill).

145. Paul Devitt, "A Note on Tourism in Botswana," in *Tourism in Africa and the Management of Related Resources: Proceedings of a Seminar Held in the Centre of African Studies, University of Edinburgh, 3rd and 4th May 1974* (Edinburgh: University of Edinburgh Centre of African Studies, circa 1974), 95.

146. My interview with Chawa Bogosi, director of the Tourism Development Unit, Gaborone, 2 June 1987 (hereafter cited as Bogosi interview).

147. Crush and Wellings, "The Southern African Pleasure Periphery," 689.

148. *The Contribution of the Tourist Industry to the Economy of the Republic of Botswana* ([Gaborone]: Kalahari Conservation Society, 1985), 36 and 51.

149. BCSO, *Tourist Statistics*, 1989, 27.

150. Fowkes, *The Contribution*, 45.

151. Bogosi letter.

152. Bogosi interview and Masego A. Mpotokwane, "Tourism and Environmental Issues in Botswana," in Pfotenhauer, *Tourism in Botswana*, 154.

153. M. J. Roberts, B. R. Ingram, and John D. and Sandra Fowkes, *A Profile of the Independent Tourist Visiting Botswana in 1985* ([Gaborone]: Kalahari Conservation Society, circa 1985), 4–5 and 32.

154. Ken Vernon, "Enormous New Fees 'May Kill Botswana Safari Industry'," *The Star*, 18 January 1989, i.a.w.e., 12–13.

155. Ibid.

156. Carolyn P. Widd, "Game Parks Should Not Be Preserve of the Very Rich," *The Star*, 25 January 1989, i.a.w.e., 9 (letter to the editor).

157.   Magdeline Rantu, "Botswana Participates for the First Time in AIET," BDN, 13 January 1986, 1.

158.   "EEC To Provide Technical Aid to Tourism Dev[elopment]. Unit," BDN, 17 January 1986, 1.

159.   Bogosi interview.

160.   Ibid.

161.   Ibid.

162.   Roger Murray, "Hopes of Tapping Package Tour Market," AB 63 (November 1983):54.

163.   Jansen Kaekwe, "Tourism Rekindled in Chobe," BDN, 2 June 1980, 2.

164.   Linda Van Buren, "New Tourism Policy Seeks a Degree of Regulation," AB 148 (December 1990):46.

165.   As Quill Hermans, assisted by Simon Stone, has pointed out ("Opportunities and Problems of Tourism in the Economy of Botswana," in Pfotenhauer, Tourism in Botswana, 225–240, especially 226–227), the data set for Botswana is not as accurate, or as carefully measured, as it should be.

166.   Jenny Cargill, "Freeloading in Paradise," AB 73 (September 1984): 65.

167.   Paul Ranto, "Botswana Gets Big Size [sic] of Africa's Tourists['] Cake," Kutlwano 15, no. 4 (April 1976):6.

168.   "Southern Sun Gloom over Hotel Bookings," The Star, 25 June 1977, i.a.w.e., 17.

169.   Therese Anders, "Fifty-Percent Drop in SA Visitors to Botswana, The Star, 1 June 1990, i.a.w.e., 1.

170.   Barbara B. Brown, "South Africa's Foreign Policy towards Its Black Neighbors" (Ph.D. diss., Boston University, 1979), 141, n. 54.

171.   Linda Van Buren, "Forging Links to the North Is a Formidable Task," AB 148 (December 1990):37.

172.   Richard Mordi, "Public Attitudes toward Wildlife in Botswana" (Ph.D. diss., Yale University, 1987), 24.

173.   Carolyn F. Eagle, "[The] Kalahari Conservation Society," Kutlwano 21, no. 7 (June 1983):16–17.

174.   John D. Holm, "How Effective Are Interest Groups in Representing Their Members?", in Holm and Molutsi, Democracy in Botswana, 149–153.

175.   D. C. Parry and B. M. Campbell, "Wildlife Management Areas of Botswana," BNR 22 (1990), 73–74 and 76.

176.   John S. Morrison, "Developmental Optimism and State Failure in Africa: How To Understand Botswana's Relative Success?" (Ph.D. diss., University of Wisconsin, Madison, 1987), 530.

177.   Ranto, "Botswana Gets Big Size," 10.

178.   Couperthwaite, "Bechuanaland," 38.

179.   The Morse Report, 78–79.

180.   Bernard Mayson, "Internal Communications in Botswana," AW, January 1968, 7.

181.   BP, Staff List, April 1st, 1945, 23.

182.   Mayson, "Internal Communications," 7.

183.   "Protectorate Postal Links To Change," The Star, 27 March 1963,

2d s.p.e., 3.

184.   SAPHAD, 6 (23 April 1963), col. 4535.

185.   Ibid., 45 (23 March 1973), cols. 518–520.

186.   Letter to me from the Postmaster General of South Africa, Pretoria, dated 18 April 1968.

187.   Zaffiro, *From Police Network to Station*, 2–3.

188.   UKCROBPR, 1949 (London: HMSO, n.d.), 33.

189.   James J. Zaffiro, "Twin Births: African Nationalism and Government Information Management in the Bechuanaland Protectorate, 1957–1966," IJAHS 22, no. 1 (1989):57.

190.   "Radio Back in Bechuanaland," *The Star*, 1 February 1964, c.l.s.e., 11.

191.   "ZND: Africa's Newest Radio Station," *The Star*, 29 April 1964, c.l.e., 11.

192.   Patrick, *Botswana*, 42.

193.   Zaffiro, "Twin Births," 69.

194.   SAPHAD, 17 (9 August 1966), col. 406.

195.   "Regering Bewus van Radio-Gevaar," *Dagbreek en Sondagnuus* (Johannesburg), 20 May 1962, 1, as cited and translated in "Nats. Fear Non-Apartheid Radio Broadcasts," *Contact* (Cape Town), 31 May 1962, 6.

196.   "Lobatsi on the Air in August," *The Star*, 26 July 1962, c.l.e., 1.

197.   "Protectorates on Air Soon," ST, 11 August 1963, 4.

198.   UKHCD, 732 (26 July 1966), col. 215 (written answers), and UKPHLD, 307 (5 February 1970), col. 747.

199.   "Botswana Is on the Line . . . ," *The Star*, 12 November 1973, 2d c.l.e., 33.

200.   "Earth Station Now Working!," BDN, 30 January 1980, 1.

201.   Ibid., and "Linking the World by Satellite," BDN, 7 February 1980, 3.

202.   "Southern Africa," ARBEFTS 19, no. 5 (30 June 1982):6463.

203.   "Zimbabwe," ARBEFTS 19, no. 2 (31 March 1982):6353.

204.   "Telecommunications Facilities Are Further Upgraded," CRNBLS, no. 1—1988 (29 February 1988):36.

205.   J. Derek Jones, "'Mahoko a Becwana': The Second seTswana [sic] Newspaper," BNR 4 (1972):112–120.

206.   Q. Neil Parsons, "The Tswana Press: An Outline of Its History since 1856," *Kutlwano* 7, no. 8 (August 1968):6–7.

207.   "About Us," *Kutlwano* [1], no. 1 (January 1962):1.

208.   Parsons, "The Tswana Press," 7.

209.   Young, *Bechuanaland*, 118.

210.   James J. Zaffiro, "The Press and Political Opposition in an African Democracy: The Case of Botswana," JCCP 27, no. 1 (March 1989):62.

211.   Munger letter.

212.   Halpern, *South Africa's Hostages*, 289–291.

213.   Letter to me from Joe Podbrey, editor, *Mafeking Mail*, Mafikeng, dated 25 September 1972.

214.   Letter to me from Pule Shabangu, distribution manager, Text Publications, Mafikeng, dated 8 October 1990.

215.   Letter to me from Wilf Nussey, editor, Argus Africa News Service, Johannesburg, dated 15 August 1974.

216.   Data furnished to me by Rev. J. Derek Jones, former mayor of Gaborone and general manager of the Botswana Book Center, Gaborone, 17 June 1987 (hereafter cited as Jones data).

217.   Letter to me from A.J.W.L. Richards, manager, *The Chronicle* and *The Sunday News*, Bulawayo, dated 10 November 1975.

218.   Jones data.

219.   Letter to me from the secretary (signature unclear), Suidwes-Drukkery Bpk., Windhoek, dated 11 January 1968.

220.   Letter to me from K. L. Lakemeier, Advertising Manager, *Windhoek Advertiser* and *Allgemeine Zeitung*, Windhoek, dated 11 October 1974.

221.   Jones data.

222.   Grant and Egner, "The Private Press," 254.

223.   "Letlhakane Daily News Distribution Centre" BDN, 28 July 1986, 2.

224.   "Government Ministers Hint at Press Curbs," CRNBLS, no. 2—1987 (13 May 1987):28.

225.   "Two New Newspapers in Botswana," *The Star*, 2 November 1982, l.f.e., 4.

226.   Zaffiro, "The Press and Political Opposition," 65.

227.   "'20 Years of Progress' amidst the Growing Crisis in Southern Africa," ACRASD, 1986–1987, B642.

228.   Grant and Egner, "The Private Press," 247–250, 258, and 260.

229.   My interview with Tom Obondo-Okoyo, deputy director (production), Department of Information and Broadcasting, Gaborone, 9 June 1987 (hereafter cited as Obondo-Okoyo interview), and James J. Zaffiro, "Mass Media, Politics and Society in Botswana: The 1990s and Beyond," AT 40, no. 1 (First Quarter 1993):16–17.

230.   "A 'Yes' to Continental Network," BDN, 4 July 1986, 1 (editorial).

231.   George A. Ngwa, "The Pan-African News Agency: A Regional Response to Global News Flow Problems" (Ph.D. diss., Southern Illinois University at Carbondale, 1989), 76–78.

232.   Obondo-Okoyo interview.

233.   Q. Neil Parsons, "Some Thoughts on Publishing in Botswana," BLAJ 4, no. 2 (August 1982):19.

234.   Sue C. Brothers, "The Development of Botswana's National Library Service," BNR 23 (1991):72–74.

235.   Stephen R. Lewis, Jr., *The Economics of Apartheid* (New York: Council on Foreign Relations Press, 1990), 85 and 94.

236.   Grant and Egner, "The Private Press," 250.

237.   My interview with Riecks Morake, deputy director (programs), Department of Information and Broadcasting, Gaborone, 2 June 1987, and Zaffiro, *From Police Network To Station*, 73.

238.   Grant and Egner, "The Private Press," 259–261.

239.   Jones data and Abagail Nwako, "Publishing in Botswana: Its History, Problems and Prospects" (M.L.S. thesis, Loughborough University of Technology, 1982), 3 and 75–82.

CHAPTER EIGHT

1. Tjønneland, *Pax Pretoriana*, 16 and 21, and Imrie and Young, "South Africa and Botswana", 4–21.

2. Richard J. Payne, *The Nonsuperpowers and South Africa: Implications for U.S. Policy* (Bloomington: Indiana University Press, 1990), 216.

3. For the text, see BP, *Orders in Council and High Commissioner's Proclamations and Notices Issued during the Period from the 9th May 1891 to the 30th June 1914*, ed. M. Williams (Mafeking: Mafeking Mail Printers, 1915), 367–369 (with the 1911 and 1913 protocols found on pp. 373–374 and 378–379, respectively).

4. "Southern African Customs Union," SBR, July 1970, 7.

5. Hendrik J.P.L. Kruger, "Customs Unions in South Africa" (M.Com. thesis, University of South Africa, 1956), 188–189.

6. James H. Cobbe, "The South African Trade Control System and Neighbouring States," SAJE 42, no. 4 (December 1974):439.

7. Ettinger, "South Africa's Weight Restrictions," 21–23.

8. Michael Hubbard, *Agricultural Exports and Economic Growth: A Study of the Botswana Beef Industry* (London: KPI Limited, 1986), 83.

9. "Southern African Customs Union," 7.

10. Ettinger, "South Africa's Weight Restrictions," 26–28.

11. "Southern African Customs Union," 7–8.

12. Hudson, "Botswana's Membership," 132.

13. "The Economics of the Customs Union between Botswana, Lesotho, Swaziland, and South Africa" (Ph.D. diss., University of Michigan, 1974), 64.

14. Ibid., 92, and "Southern African Customs Agreement," 8.

15. Hudson, "Botswana's Membership," 132.

16. E. J. Van der Merwe, "The Customs Agreement between Botswana, Lesotho, Swaziland, and the Republic of South Africa," SAJAA 2 (1972):69.

17. Hermans, "Towards Budgetary Independence," 99.

18. Gavin G. Maasdorp, "The Southern African Customs Union: An Assessment," JCAS 2, no. 1 (October 1982):87–88.

19. Colclough and McCarthy, *The Political Economy*, 78.

20. Peter M. Landell-Mills, "The 1969 Southern African Customs Union Agreement," JMAS 9, no. 2 (August 1971):272.

21. Hermans, "Towards Budgetary Independence," 99.

22. "Botswana Seeks New S.A. Customs Pact," *The Star*, 30 September 1966, c.l.e., 21.

23. Botswana, *Transitional Plan*, 10.

24. Biff Turner, "A Fresh Start for the Southern African Customs Union," AA 70, no. 280 (July 1971):271–273.

25. Ettinger, "The Economics," 59.

26. "Vorster Goes Ahead with Policy: Moves To Widen Contacts," *The Star*, 25 April 1969, 2d c.l.e., 19, and Turner, "A Fresh Start," 272–273.

27. Peter Robson, "Economic Integration in Southern Africa," JMAS 5, no. 4 (December 1967):477–478.

28. A.M.R. Ramolefe and A.J.G.M. Sanders, "The Structural Pattern of

African Regionalism: The South[ern] African Customs and Monetary Union,"
CILJSA 6, no. 1 (March 1973):83 and 87.

29. SAPHAD, 28 (23 February 1970), col. 1772 (speech of the minister
of economic affairs when moving parliamentary approval of the 1969 customs
union agreement).

30. For the text, see BGG 7, no. 64 (12 December 1969):E.337–E.348.

31. Ramolefe and Sanders, "The Structural Pattern," 97–98.

32. Van der Merwe, "The Customs Union Agreement," 71–72.

33. Ibid., 67.

34. Hudson, "Botswana's Membership," 136–137. Maasdorp ("The
Southern African Customs Union," 96, n. 38) has commented on the absence
of any literature explaining how the figure of 1.42 was selected.

35. Van der Merwe, "The Customs Union Agreement," 73–74.

36. Hudson, "Botswana's Membership," 135 and 140.

37. Van der Merwe, "The Customs Union Agreement," 74.

38. Hudson, "Botswana's Membership," 135.

39. Ibid., 141–144.

40. Maasdorp, "The Southern African Customs Union," 97 and 103.

41. Jasper Mortimer, "Meanwhile . . . BLS States Grapple with [the]
Customs Union," AB 64 (December 1983):23. In August 1993 an attempt was
made to reexamine SACU by the appointment of a technical committee (Gavin
Maasdorp, "The Future Structure of Trade Integration and Development
Cooperation in Southern Africa," AI 24, no. 1 [1994]:8).

42. Porter Report, 11.

43. Leistner, "The External Sector," 124.

44. Christopher Colclough, "Dependent Development in Southern Africa,
1960–80: National Strategy Options in a Regional Context," in Oommen,
Botswana's Economy, 11.

45. Earl L. McFarland, Jr., "Benefits to the RSA of Her Exports to the
BLS Countries," in Oommen, Botswana's Economy, 268.

46. Colclough and McCarthy, The Political Economy, 71.

47. Jumanne H. Wagao, "Trade Relations among SADCC Countries," in
SADCC: Prospects for Disengagement and Development in Southern Africa, ed.
Samir Amin, Derrick Chitala, and Ibbo Mandaza (London and Atlantic
Highlands, NJ: Zed Books, Ltd.; Tokyo: The United Nations University, 1987),
154 (table 7.6).

48. E. O. Ochieng, "Botswana's Foreign Trade Structure: Dependence
Versus Diversification," in Proceedings of the Seminar on Botswana's External
Trade in Light of the Lomé Convention Held at the National Museum & Art
Gallery, Gaborone, 30-31 October 1978), ed. Joachim Jeske (Gaborone:
University College of Botswana, National Institute of Development and
Cultural Research, 1978), 48.

49. "Foreign Trade," CPBLS, 1988–89, 34.

50. Derek J. Hudson, "[A] Brief Chronology of Customs Agreements in
Southern Africa," BNR 11 (1979):91–92.

51. Ibid., 92–93.

52. Ibid., 93.

53. Ettinger, "The Economics," 141.

54. Hubbard, *Agricultural Exports*, 95–96, 114, 125, 127, 130, and 132.

55. SRLAD, 18 (8 June 1938), col. 1851 (speech of the minister of finance and commerce, when moving parliamentary approval of the customs agreement between the BP and Southern Rhodesia).

56. UNSC doc. S/7781/Add. 2/Annex, 9 March 1967 (UNSCOR, 22d Yr., suppl. for January–March 1967, 156).

57. UNSC doc. S/8786, Annex II, 28 August 1968 (UNSCOR, 23rd Yr., suppl. for July–September 1968, 177–181).

58. BGG 8, no. 3 (9 January 1970):D.2 (Statutory Instrument no. 2 of 1970).

59. Ettinger, "The Economics," 141.

60. Henry S. Bienen, "Economic Interests and Security Issues in Southern Africa," in Rotberg, *South Africa and Its Neighbors*, 84.

61. Colleen L. Morna, "Botswana: Temporary Truce on the Trade Front," *South* 89 (March 1988):50.

62. Hudson, "[A] Brief Chronology," 93.

63. Johannes Pilane, "Botswana, Zimbabwe Sign Trade Agreement," BDN, 13 September 1988, 1.

64. Ivan Farai, "New Trade Pact Saves Botswana Market," AB 117 (May 1988):25.

65. Ibid.

66. Anglin, "Economic Liberation," 690–691.

67. Morna, "Botswana: Temporary Truce," 50.

68. Morrison, "Developmental Optimism," 516.

69. "Foreign Trade," *Country Profile: Namibia, 1989–90* (London: EIU, 1989), 41–42.

70. Roger Murray, *Namibia Through the 1990s: Turning Rich Resources into Growth*, Special Report no. M211 (London: EIU, 1992), 102.

71. SRPHAD 1 (11 June 1924), cols. 98–111 (debate on Mr. Thompson's motion proposing a railway link between Southern Rhodesia and Walvis Bay), and J.L.S. Jeffares, *Report on Rhodesia-Walvis Bay Reconnaissance Survey*. CSR 13—1932 (Salisbury: GP, 1932).

72. Letter to me from G. M. Erich Leistner, director of the Africa Institute of South Africa, Pretoria, dated 12 February 1990.

73. Ngila R. L. Mwase, "Reflections on the Proposed Botswana-Namibia Trans-Kalahari Railway," EAER, n.s. 3, no. 1 (December 1987):73.

74. "The New Road to Namibia Begins To Take Shape," CRNBLS, no. 2—1990 (11 June 1990):38.

75. "Trade Patterns," in Nsekela, *Southern Africa*, 235.

76. Wagao, "Trade Relations among SADCC Countries," 152.

77. "South Korean Firm Will Build Orapa-Serowe Road," QERNBLS, no. 1—1986 (12 March 1986):37.

78. "More Finance Sought for Kazungula Road," QERNBLS, no. 2—1982 (2 June 1982):25. Murray (*Namibia Through the 1990s*, 109) is more optimistic about funding.

79. UKCROBPR, 1949, 13.

80. Ibid., 1950 (London: HMSO, 1951), 13.

81. Ibid., 1953, (London: HMSO, 1955), 20.

82. Basil C. Muzorewa, "The Development of the Money Economy and an Analysis of the Monetary and Financial System in the Republic of Botswana" (M.Phil. thesis, University of Leeds, 1976), 77.

83. Derek J. Hudson, "The Establishment of Botswana's Central Bank and the Introduction of the New Currency, BNR 10 (1978):134–135.

84. Botswana, *Transitional Plan*, 5.

85. Hans-Erik Dahl, *Botswana's First Independence Decade, 1966–1976: A Survey*, Economic Papers no. 6 (Bergen: University of Bergen, Institute of Economics, 1978), 23.

86. Hudson, "The Establishment," 120, 123, and 135.

87. BPLCORH, 3 (25 and 27 October 1961, speech of the development secretary in the second reading of the Post Office Savings Bank and Savings Certificate Bill), 28 and 78. The South African connection can be explained because the British forbade a colonial dependency from investing those funds acquired in its own territory in that same territory (Muzorewa, "The Development," 76).

88. "B.P. Will Operate Its Own Savings Bank," MMPG, 9 March 1962, 6.

89. "Savings Bank in B.P. from January 1st," MMPG, 7 December 1962, 1, and "P.O. Savings Bank Board Members," MMPG, 6 August 1965, 2.

90. Muzorewa, "The Development," 75.

91. Hudson, "The Establishment," 126 and 135.

92. "Limits on Bank Lending Have Been Lifted," QERNBLS, no. 3—1983 (12 September 1983):23, and "Commercial Banking Corporation Has Intensified," CRNBLS, no. 3—1991 (8 August 1991):33.

93. Rangarirai Shoko, "Zimbabwe Banks Branch into Botswana," AB 141 (May 1990):141, and "First National Has Taken Over BCCI's Local Subsidiary," CRNBLS, no. 4—1991 (3 December 1991):33.

94. Muzorewa, "The Development," 173–175.

95. UKCOBPR, 1933, 26.

96. Economic Department of the South African Reserve Bank, "The South African Reserve Bank: Its History, Functions, and Growth," SBR, February 1973:3.

97. Basil C. Muzorewa, "Botswana's Share of Revenue from the Use of Rand Currency: A Note," BNR 6 (1974):225–227.

98. UKPHCD, 629 (8 November 1960), col. 39 (written answers).

99. "End of a Five-Coin Country," *The Star*, 10 November 1965, c.l.e., 6.

100. Muzorewa, "The Development," 177 and 183–186.

101. The name Pula (meaning rain in Setswana) was chosen after asking the public of Botswana to suggest appropriate names. The Pula is divided into one hundred Thebe (meaning shield in Setswana) ("Botswana: New National Currency: A Milestone Is Achieved," SCR, September 1976:8–9).

102. "Botswana's Monetary Independence: Real or Imagined?" IDSB 11, no. 4 (1980):40.

103. Ettinger, "Economics," 252–253 and 258.

104. Charles Harvey, "Successful Adjustment in Botswana," IDSB 16, no. 3 (July 1985):47.

105.   Botswana, *Transitional Plan*, 5 and 10.

106.   Ibid., 10.

107.   E.Y. Ablo and Derek J. Hudson, "Monetary Policy of Botswana," in Oommen, *Botswana's Economy*, 93.

108.   Botswana, *Transitional Plan*, 10.

109.   "Stockbrokers Botswana Commences Trading," CRNBLS, no. 3—1989 (3 September 1989):28. By 1991 there were no more than ten stock markets operating in the entire continent ("Stock Markets Lag," *The Star*, 19-25 November 1992, i.w.e., 19).

110.   Linda Van Buren, "Botswana Share Market Has Spectacular First Year," AB 148 (December 1990):28.

111.   "Cash and Customs Dealings with S.A.: Black States Seek a Bigger Say," *The Star*, 1 September 1969, 2d c.l.e., 1 and 3.

112.   Botswana, *A Monetary System for Botswana*, Government Paper no. 1 of 1975 (Gaborone: GP, 1975), 2.

113.   Francis d'A. Collings et al., "The Rand and the Monetary Systems of Botswana, Lesotho, and Swaziland," JMAS 16, no. 1 (March 1978):101-102.

114.   H.C.L. Hermans, "Botswana Establishes Its Own Currency and Reserves," AD 10, no. 9 (September 1976):895.

115.   Hudson, "The Establishment," 120.

116.   E. O. Ochieng, "The Implications of Pegging the Botswana Pula to the U.S. Dollar," PBJAS 2, no. 1 (February 1980):49.

117.   Hudson, "The Establishment," 120.

118.   Charles Harvey, *The Use of Monetary Policy in Botswana in Good Times and Bad*, Discussion Paper no. 204 (Brighton: University of Sussex, Institute of Development Studies, 1985), 9, and Ochieng, "The Implications," 52.

119.   "Foreign Trade," CPBLS, 1988–89, 34.

120.   "Last Year's Visible Trade Deficit Was Far Lower," CRNBLS, no. 2—1985 (12 June 1985):46.

121.   "The Pula Has Been Revalued by 3 Per Cent," CRNBLS, no. 3—1985 (30 August 1985):35, and Harvey, *The Use of Monetary Policy*, 9.

122.   "But the Pula Strengthens against Major Currencies," CRNBLS, no. 3—1986 (28 August 1986):33.

123.   "Diamond Sales Have Continued To Rise in Value," CRNBLS, no. 4—1984 (7 December 1984):30.

124.   Harvey and Lewis, *Policy Choice*, 206, and Charles Harvey, *Botswana*, 28.

125.   Ibid., 12.

126.   "Exchange Controls Have Been Relaxed," CRNBLS, no. 3—1985 (30 August 1985):36-37.

127.   Philippus Smit, *Botswana: Resources and Development*, Communications of the Africa Institute no. 13 (Pretoria: AISA, 1970), 202.

128.   Ibid., 203, and Campbell, *The Guide*, 523.

129.   "Gold Output Is To Expand," CRNBLS, no. 2—1987 (13 May 1987):39.

130.   "The Map Nora Gold Mine Is Redesigned," no. 2—1990 (11 June 1990):37.

131. "The Map Nora Gold Mine Is To Open in 1989," CRNBLS, no. 1—1988 (29 February 1988):33.

132. "The Story of the Tati Concession: A Link with Lobengula, King of the Matabele," SA 62, no. 3207 (8 July 1950):27.

133. Michael Crowder, "Tshekedi Khama and Mining in Botswana, 1929–1959" (Paper delivered at the African studies seminar, University of the Witwatersrand, 3 June 1985), 2–4.

134. Ibid., 5–14 and 16.

135. F. Taylor Ostrander, "Botswana Nickel-Copper: A Case Study in Private Investment's Contribution to Economic Development," in Barratt, *Accelerated Development*, 536–537.

136. BNAORH, 22, pt. 1 (25 August 1967), 151 (minister of local government and lands, introducing the second reading of the Mineral Rights in Tribal Territories Bill).

137. Ibid., 22, pt. 2 (28 August 1967), 195 (minister of commerce, industry, and water affairs, introducing the second reading of the Mines and Minerals Bill).

138. James H. Cobbe, *Governments and Mining Companies in Developing Countries* (Boulder, CO: Westview Press, 1979), 190 and 221, n. 31.

139. J. Nganunu, "Botswana's Minerals and Mining Policy," in Oommen, *Botswana's Economy*, 225.

140. BNAORH, 41, pt. 2 (12 September 1972), 233–234 and 236–237 (minister of finance and development planning, introducing the second reading of the Mineral Rights Tax Bill).

141. Cobbe, *Governments and Mining Companies*, 221, n. 31.

142. Harvey and Lewis, *Policy Choice*, 52.

143. Cobbe, *Governments and Mining*, 196–197.

144. David H. Lewis, "The Theory and Practice of Direct Foreign Investment in Less Developed Countries: A Study of Copper-Nickel Mining in Botswana" (M.A. thesis, University of Cape Town, 1974), 48 and 160.

145. M. C. Tibone, "The Shashe Nickel-Copper Project," in Oommen, *Botswana's Economy*, 240 and 242.

146. Cobbe, *Governments and Mining*, 197 and 213.

147. David H. Lewis, "Direct Foreign Investment and Linkages in a Less Developed Country," BNR 7 (1975):82–86.

148. Hanlon, *Beggar*, 231.

149. T. J. Denis Fair, "The Regional Interchange of Power Supplies," in Leistner and Esterhuysen, *South Africa in Southern Africa*, 171.

150. Lewis, "Direct Foreign Investment," 83–84.

151. Cobbe, *Governments and Mining*, 198.

152. Lewis, "Direct Foreign Investment," 83.

153. "Electricity," CPBLS, 1991–1992, 26.

154. Stephen R. Lewis, Jr., "The Impact of the Shashe Project on Botswana's Economy," in Harvey, *Papers*, 107–108, and Baledzi Gaolathe, "Mining Development: Environment, Social Costs, Retained Value, and Shadow Wage Rates," in Harvey, *Papers*, 88–91.

155. Lewis, "Direct Foreign Investment," 85.

156. Cobbe, *Governments and Mining*, 196.

157.   Hanlon, *Beggar*, 226.

158.   Lewis, "Direct Foreign Investment," 85–86.

159.   Lewis, "The Impact," 105 and 107.

160.   Hanlon, *Beggar*, 226, and Lewis, "The Impact," 109.

161.   "While Negotiations on a Further Debt Rescheduling Continue," CRNBLS, no. 4—1987 (23 November 1987):26.

162.   "Although an Accounting Change Reduced the Net Loss for the Year," CRNBLS, no. 2—1987 (13 May 1987):38.

163.   "Copper-Nickel," CPBLS, 1988–89, 25.

164.   L. G. Nchindo, "Diamonds in Botswana," in Oommen, *Botswana's Economy*, 233.

165.   Pim Report, 21.

166.   Nchindo, "Diamonds," 233, and Cobbe, *Governments and Mining*, 203.

167.   The first largest such pipe outside the Soviet Union is in Tanzania (Cobbe, *Governments and Mining*, 203).

168.   Ibid., and Campbell, *The Guide*, 529.

169.   Cobbe, *Governments and Mining*, 205, and Campbell, *The Guide*, 341.

170.   Nchindo, "Diamonds," 233.

171.   Cobbe, *Governments and Mining*, 204.

172.   Ibid., 204–209.

173.   Robert L. Curry, Jr., "Botswana's Macroeconomic Management of Its Mineral-Based Growth: It Used Mining Revenues for Development and Services But Must Now Broaden the Beneficiaries," AJES 46, no. 4 (October 1987):481.

174.   Patrick, *Botswana*, 17.

175.   Cobbe, *Governments and Mining*, 205–206.

176.   Kurt M. Campbell, *Soviet Policy towards South Africa* (New York: St. Martin's Press, 1986), 101–104.

177.   Cobbe, *Governments and Mining*, 205–206.

178.   Patrick, *Botswana*, 18.

179.   Robson Silitshena, "Mining and Development Strategy in Botswana," in *Natural Resources and National Welfare: The Case of Copper*, ed. Ann Seidman (New York: Praeger Publishers, 1975), 399.

180.   Nchindo, "Diamonds," 237–238.

181.   Stephen R. Lewis, Jr., "Botswana: Diamonds, Drought, Development, and Democracy," *CSIS Africa Notes*, no. 47 (11 September 1985):3.

182.   Hanlon, *Beggar*, 226–227, and Colclough and McCarthy, *The Political Economy*, 156–158.

183.   "De Beers Has Bought Debswana's Entire Stockpile," CRNBLS, no. 3—1987 (14 August 1987):32.

184.   "And the Company Will Have Its First Black Directors," CRNBLS, no. 3—1987 (14 August 1987):33.

185.   Parson, "The Potential," 307–308, and Colleen L. Morna, "Ashes and Diamonds," AR 34, no. 1 (January–February 1989):22.

186.   Tony Tembo, "Does Sua Pan Snub SADCC?," AB 126 (February 1989):40.

187. BPLCRH, 8 (19 April 1963), 189 (remarks of the acting development secretary).

188. Hanlon, *Beggar*, 221.

189. *Economic Statecraft* (Princeton, NJ: Princeton University Press, 1985), 13–14, 30, 32, and 35.

190. "Intense Pressure on Botswana and Lesotho," FPRSA, no. 55 (November–December 1984):12.

191. "A Decision over the Soda Ash Project May Be Imminent," QERNBLS, no. 4—1984 (7 December 1984):32.

192. Maggie Jonas, "Low World Prices Dictate Mining Future," AB 97 (September 1986):60.

193. Geoffrey King, "Sua Pan's Future Hangs in Balance," AB 112 (December 1987):18.

194. "Soda Ash: Sanctions Beget Protectionism," *The Economist* (London), 305, no. 7521 (24 October 1987):95–96.

195. R. Frederic Morton, "South African Capital in Southern Africa: Botswana's Sua Pan Project" (Paper delivered at the third symposium on post-apartheid South Africa, Pittsburgh, 17–19 March 1988), 3.

196. "A Decision," 32.

197. "Soda Ash," 95–96, and King, "Sua Pan's Future," 18.

198. Methaetsile Leepile, "Zim[babwe] To Invest in Sua," MWD, 23–31 March 1989, 1–2.

199. "Who's Who in Soda Ash," MWD, 26 November–2 December 1988, 1–2.

200. Leepile, "Zim[babwe] To Invest," 1–2.

201. Colclough and McCarthy, *The Political Economy*, 164.

202. Alan W. Whiteside, *Investment Opportunities in Southern Africa: The Business Climate in the SADCC States*, Occasional Paper (Braamfontein: SAIIA, 1987), 1–5 and 8–9.

203. Colclough and McCarthy, *The Political Economy*, 4 and 164.

204. Nelson P. Mayo, "Constraints on Industrialisation in Botswana," in Oommen, *Botswana's Economy*, 221–222.

205. Hubbard, *Agricultural Exports*, 7, 43–44, 168, 171, and 173.

206. Patrick, *Botswana*, 33.

207. Hanlon, *Beggar*, 228 (Hanlon, however, gives no date for these official Botswana financial data [ibid., 337, n. 33]).

208. Patrick, *Botswana*, 33.

209. Lerato Molodi and Methaetsile Leepile, "BDC Plans Stock Market," MWD, 19–25 November 1988, 1–2.

210. Gwen Ansell, "Stockbrokers Boost Capital Market," AB 125 (January 1989):36.

211. "Stockbrokers Botswana Commences Trading," 28, and Molodi and Leepile, "BDC Plans," 1.

212. Hanlon, *Beggar*, 231.

213. Stephen R. Lewis, Jr., and Jennifer Sharpley, *Botswana's Industrialisation*, Discussion Paper no. 45 (Brighton: University of Sussex, Institute of Development Studies, 1988), 42, and Hanlon, *Beggar*, 231.

214. Charles Harvey, "Foreign Investment in Manufacturing: The Case of

Botswana's Brewery," in Harvey, *Papers*, 212–213.

215.   Ibid.

216.   Ibid., 215–217.

217.   Ibid., 216–218.

218.   Hanlon, *Beggar*, 68.

219.   Harvey, "Foreign Investment," 219.

220.   Anglin, "The Frontline States and Sanctions against South Africa," 278.

221.   "SA Companies Probe Frontline Markets," CT, 3 February 1987, 10.

222.   Picard, *The Politics of Development*, 96–97.

223.   Hermans, "Towards Budgetary Independence," 91–92.

224.   Keith F. Jones, "Britain's Contribution to Botswana's Public Debt, 1956–1976," BNR 9 (1977):113.

225.   Rey, *Monarch*, 191 (entry for 22 November 1935), 202 (entry for 1–2 April 1936), 259, n. 14, and 260, n. 7.

226.   Hermans, "Towards Budgetary Independence," 93–95.

227.   Andrew Murray and Q. Neil Parsons, "The Modern Economic History of Botswana," in *Studies in the Economic History of Southern Africa*, vol. 1: *The Front-Line States*, ed. Zbigniew A. Konczacki, Jane L. Parpart, and Timothy M. Shaw (London: Frank Cass & Co., Ltd., 1990), 171–177.

228.   Khama, *From the Frontline*, 98–100.

229.   UKPHCD, 753 (9 November 1967), col. 1229 (oral answers).

230.   Picard, *The Politics of Development*, 235.

231.   Hermans, "Towards Budgetary Independence," 89.

232.   Suresh C. Saxena, *Foreign Policy of African States: Politics of Dependence and Confrontation* (New Delhi: Deep and Deep Publications, 1982), 81–83 and 87.

233.   UKPHCD, 531 (21 October 1954), cols. 1353–1354 (oral answers).

234.   "7,350 Tons of Food for Bechuanas," *The Star*, 30 July 1965, s.p.e., 7.

235.   See "Z. K. Matthews Remembered," *Kutlwano* 10, no. 9 (September 1971):6–8.

236.   "Botswana's Man Meets Old Friends at U.N.," *The Star*, 28 October 1966, s.p.e., 8.

237.   "New Post for Dr. Matthews," *The Star*, 10 September 1966, w.a.e., 4.

238.   Raphaeli, *Public Sector Management*, preface.

239.   Ibid., 7, 9–10, 13–14, 36, 39, 42, and 54–55.

240.   Michael Stevens, "Aid Management in Botswana: From One to Many Donors," in Harvey, *Papers*, 167–168.

241.   Colclough and McCarthy, *The Political Economy*, 48.

242.   Ibid., 96–97 and 102.

243.   "Swedish Aid Fund Announced: R 460,000 for Bechuanaland, Basutoland," *The Star*, 29 March 1966, c.l.e., 4.

244.   Roger Leys, "Scandinavian Development Assistance to BLS: Liberation Support or Neo-Colonialism?" (Paper delivered at the conference on conflict and change in southern Africa: Scandinavian and Canadian perspectives and policy options, Ottawa, 19–22 February 1978), 4. Botswana

also ranked first in terms of Norwegian per capita aid (*Botswana: Country Study and Norwegian Review*, ed. Per Granberg and J. R. Parkison [Bergen: Chr. Michelsen Institute, 1988], 161, as cited in Molutsi, "International Influences," 55 and 61, n. 4).

245.   Bertil Odén, *The Macroeconomic Position of Botswana*, Research Report no. 60 (Uppsala: SIAS, 1981), 5.

246.   Raphaeli, *Public Sector Management*, 40–42 and 46.

247.   Molutsi, "International Influences," 57, and Picard, *The Politics*, 215. In 1989 there were more U.S. Peace Corps volunteers in Botswana (roughly 200) than in any other African host nation ("The New US Embassy Opens," CRNBLS, no. 4—1989 (22 December 1989]:26).

248.   Computed from "Gross Official Development Assistance," CPBLS, 1988–89, 40.

249.   Douglas G. Anglin, "Southern African Responses to Eastern European Developments," JMAS 28, no. 3 (September 1990):436–439 and 453.

250.   "The Role of Foreign Aid in Africa," AI 20, no. 4 (1990):210.

251.   David Simon, *Independent Namibia: One Year On*, Conflict Studies no. 239 (London: Research Institute for the Study of Conflict and Terrorism, 1991), 15–16 and 24.

252.   Vivienne Jabri, *Mediating Conflict: Decision-Making and Western Intervention in Namibia* (Manchester: Manchester University Press, 1990), 65 and 69.

253.   Murray, *Namibia Through the 1990s*, 103.

254.   Ibid., 103–104.

255.   Clough and Herbst, *South Africa's Changing Regional Strategy*, 8–9, 24, 28, and 30.

CHAPTER NINE

1.   "In Memoriam: Opening Statement of the Southern African Development Coordination Summit, Lusaka, 1 April 1980, by the Chairman, His Excellency Sir Seretse Khama, President of Botswana," SADEX 2, no. 3 (May–June 1980):18–19.

2.   In this chapter, I will not consider two groups of individuals who travel in different directions. The first are skilled South African expatriates employed in Botswana (and other SADCC states) and the second are skilled Batswana who leave Botswana to work in South Africa. There are not very full data about either group. On the South Africans, consult Lewis, *Economic Realities*, 15. On the Batswana, see Gossett, "The Civil Service," 204–205; "Botswana Concerned about Loss of Workers," *The Star*, 3 October 1985, s.p.e., 9; and Dale, "Botswana's Relations," 16.

3.   Isaac Schapera, *Migrant Labour and Tribal Life: A Study of Conditions in the Bechuanaland Protectorate* (London: Geoffrey Cumberlege, OUP, 1947), 25, 27, and 145.

4.   Carol Kerven, *Botswana Mine Labour Migration to South Africa*, National Migration Study Issue Paper no. 3. Revised [ed.] ([Gaborone]: Central Statistics Office, Ministry of Finance and Development Planning, and Rural

Sociology Unit, Ministry of Agriculture, 1980), 15 and 20–26, and John Taylor, "The Reorganization of Mine Labor Recruitment in Southern Africa: Evidence from Botswana," IMR 24, no. 2 (Summer 1990):254.

5. Jeremy A. Peat, "Employment Creation: Problems and Policies," in Oommen, *Botswana's Economy*, 192.

6. SA. Central Statistical Service, *South African Labour Statistics, 1987* (Pretoria: n.p., n.d.), table 6.2.2., as cited in G. M. Erich Leistner, "Labour Migration" in Leistner and Esterhuysen, *South Africa in Southern Africa*, 125.

7. Schapera, *Migrant Labour*, 25, 27, 47, 68–69, and 72.

8. John Taylor, "Mine Labour Recruitment in the Bechuanaland Protectorate," BNR 10 (1978):101–102.

9. My interview with Bias Mookodi, manager of the Employment Bureau of Africa, Gaborone, 3 July 1987 (hereafter cited as Mookodi interview).

10. SA. Committee re Foreign Bantu, *Report*. R.N. 11/254 (Pretoria: n.p., 1962), 1–3 and 5–5(a) (hereafter cited as Froneman report).

11. Ken Owen, *Foreign Africans: Summary of the Report of the Froneman Committee*. R.R. 111/64 (Johannesburg: SAIRR, 1964), 2.

12. Ibid., and SAPHAD, 14 (9 April 1965), col. 4340.

13. SAPHAD, 3 (13 April 1962), col. 3887.

14. Froneman Report, 76–78, and SRRSA, 1963 (Johannesburg: SAIRR, 1964), 143–144.

15. SRRSA, 1963, 145–146.

16. Froneman Report, 96–111, 180–181, and 203.

17. Wilhelmus J. Breytenbach, *Migratory Labour Arrangements in Southern Africa*, rev. ed., Communications of the Africa Institute no. 33 (Pretoria: AISA, 1979), 17.

18. Taylor, "Mine Labour Recruitment," 101.

19. Ibid., 100–101 and 104, and John Taylor, "Some Consequences of Recent Reductions in Mine Labour Recruitment in Botswana," *Geography* (Sheffield), 71, pt. 1 (January 1986):37.

20. Taylor, "Mine Labour Recruitment," 102.

21. Ibid., 101–103.

22. Ibid., 103, 105–106, and 111.

23. Ibid., 106.

24. Pauline Cuzen, *The History of TEBA in Botswana* (s.l.: n.p., 1985), 82.

25. Wylie, *A Little God*, 89, and Janet G. Hermans, "The Basarwa of Botswana: A Case Study in Development" (M.A. thesis, The American University, 1980), 102.

26. Kerven, *Botswana Mine Labour*, 1.

27. Taylor, "Some Consequences," 37.

28. The terms in parentheses appear in Walter Elkin "Labor Migration from Botswana, Lesotho, and Swaziland," EDCC 28, no. 3 (April 1980):585.

29. For a clear, and well-documented, exposition of this school of analysis, consult Donald K. Kowet, *Land, Labour Migration and Politics in Southern Africa: Botswana, Lesotho, and Swaziland* (Uppsala: SIAS, 1978); Massey, "Labor Migration"; and Jack D. Parson, "The 'Labor Reserve' in Historical Perspective: Toward a Political Economy of the Bechuanaland

Protectorate," in Picard, *The Evolution*, 40–57.

30. Kerven, *Botswana Mine Labour*, 7–8.

31. David R. Massey, *The Development of a Labor Reserve: The Impact of Colonial Rule on Botswana*, Working Papers no. 34 (Boston: Boston University African Studies Center, 1980), 17 and 19.

32. Isaac Schapera, *Tribal Innovators: Tswana Chiefs and Social Change, 1795–1940*, London School of Economics Monographs on Social Anthropology no. 43 (London: Athlone Press; New York: Humanities Press, 1970), 117–118.

33. Kerven, *Botswana Mine Labour*, 54–55.

34. Ibid., 72–74.

35. Francis Wilson, "International Migration in Southern Africa," IMR 10, no. 4 (Winter 1976):459.

36. Elkin, "Labor Migration," 590 (quotation).

37. Kerven, *Botswana Mine Labour*, viii and 74–76.

38. Ibid., viii, x, and 74.

39. Ibid., 82–83.

40. Picard, *The Politics of Development*, 111.

41. Pim Report, 39–40 and 42.

42. Young, *Bechuanaland*, 103.

43. Schapera, *Migrant Labour*, 27.

44. Young, *Bechuanaland*, 103–104.

45. Schapera, *Migrant Labour*, 78.

46. Ibid., 207, and Picard, "Role Changes," 263–264 and 295, n. 33.

47. SA, *Agreement between the Government of the Republic of South Africa and the Government of the Republic of Botswana Relating to the Establishment of an Office for a Botswana Government Labour Representative in South Africa, Botswana Citizens in the Republic of South Africa, and the Movement of Such Persons across the International Border*. Treaty Series no. 3/1973 (Pretoria: GP, n.d.), 3, 5, 7, 9, 11, and 13.

48. "African Heads New Aid Office," *The Star*, 6 July 1971, 1st c.l.e., 6.

49. Mookodi interview.

50. "'Necklace Threat' Sends Officials Home," *The Star*, 19 September 1986, s.p.e., 11.

51. Khama, *From the Frontline*, 33.

52. Ibid., 47.

53. Molokomme, "Mine Labour Migration," 41, 43–44, and 51.

54. Schapera, *Migrant Labour*, 106–108 and 205.

55. The Froneman Committee had expressed its concern about foreign Africans remaining in South Africa rather than returning to their countries of origin (Froneman report, 30–31).

56. Enclosures entitled "Annual disbursement from deferred pay interest fund from 1960 to 1965" in letter to Dr. G. M. Erich Leistner, Africa Institute, Pretoria, from John Lang, acting public relations adviser, Transvaal and Orange Free State Chamber of Mines, Johannesburg, dated 4 November 1965 in AISA file 3650 (Diverse).

57. Kerven, *Botswana Mine Labour*, 64–65.

58. Ray Weeden and Odd Ystgaard, "Railways, Immigrants, Mining, and Cattle: Problems of Measurement in Botswana's National Income Accounts,"

in Harvey, *Papers*, 249 (I computed the percentage from appendix 14.D, pt. 1, which inadvertently omitted the millions).

59. Mookodi interview.

60. Weeden and Ystgaard, "Railways," 238.

61. Articles 4(a)(i), 4(a) (ii), and 4(a) (iv) of the 1973 treaty cited in n. 47 above.

62. *Migrant Labour*, 210.

63. *Labor Migration from Botswana to South African Mines: Economic Effects*, Working Papers no. 80 (Boston: Boston University African Studies Center, 1983), 17.

64. James H. Cobbe, "Consequences for Lesotho of Changing South African Labour Demand," AA 85, no. 338 (January 1986):37–38.

65. Alan W. Whiteside, *Past Trends and Future Prospects for Labour Migration to South Africa*, Occasional paper (Braamfontein: SAIIA, 1985), 5.

66. "Arable Agriculture in Botswana: A Case for Subsidies," in Harvey, *Papers*, 38 (for quotation).

67. Steven J. Haggblade, "The Shebeen Queen or Sorghum Beer in Botswana: The Impact of Factory Brews on a Cottage Industry" (Ph.D. diss., Michigan State University, 1984), 30–32, 79–81, 130, and 148–149.

68. Lewis, "Botswana," 2.

69. Harris, *Labor Migration*, 15.

70. Harris (ibid., 7) noted that miners in his sample had a mean number of 5.9 mine labor contracts, spread out over an average of 51 months on such work in South Africa.

71. Jonathan Crush and Wilmot James, "Depopulating the Compounds: Migrant Labour and Mine Housing in South Africa," WD 19, no. 4 (April 1991):302 and 304.

72. Schapera, *Migrant Labour*, 164–166 and 196.

73. Elkan, "Labor Migration," 592.

74. Schapera, *Migrant Labour*, 168–170.

75. Schapera, *Tribal Innovators*, 236.

76. Ibid., 231.

77. Schapera, *Migrant Labour*, 169, and BPNACM, 17th sess. (21 May 1936), 56–59.

78. Schapera, *Migrant Labour*, 169, 172, and 196–197.

79. Schapera, *Tribal Innovators*, 73–74.

80. Clyde Winters, "The Importance of Mine Workers in Southern Africa," JAS 4, no. 4 (Winter 1977–1978):452, 457–458, and 460–462.

81. Letter to me from Dr. G. M. Erich Leistner, director, Africa Institute of South Africa, Pretoria, dated 12 February 1990.

82. Winters, "The Importance," 458, and Merle Lipton, "Men of Two Worlds: Migrant Labour in South Africa," *Optima* (Marshalltown) 29, nos. 2–3 (28 November 1980):75–76, 88, and 93.

83. Crush and James, "Depopulating the Compounds," 302, 304–306, 310, and 312.

84. Schapera, *Migrant Labour*, 196; Barbara B. Brown, "The Impact of Male Labour Migration on Women in Botswana," AA 82, no. 328 (July 1983) 371; and Francis Wilson, *Migrant Labour in South Africa: Report to the South*

African Council of Churches (Johannesburg: The South African Council of Churches and Spro-Cas, 1972), 178–182.

85. "Migrant Labour Sets Problems," *The Star*, 30 October 1965, w.a.e., 8; "Migrant Labour 'Cancer': D.R.C.," *The Star*, 12 September 1968, 2d c.l.e., 1; "Church and Migratory Labour," *The Star*, 29 December 1969, 2d c.l.e., 9; "Synod Deplores Migrant Labour System Evils," *The Star*, 20 October 1970, 2d c.l.e., 9; and "That Concomitant," *The Star*, 21 October 1970, 2d c.l.e., 24 (editorial).

86. Peter Randall, *Migratory Labour in South Africa: A Talk Given to a Christian Institute Study Group, Johannesburg, March, 1967*, Topical Talks no. 1 (Johannesburg: SAIRR, 1967), 7–8.

87. "Migratory Labour 'an Evil System'," *The Star*, 19 January 1976, c.l.h.e., 19.

88. John W. de Grunchy, *The Church Struggle in South Africa*, second ed. (Grand Rapids, Mich.: William B. Eerdmans Publishing Co., 1986), 116.

89. Mookodi interview.

90. Harold H. G. Henry, "The Basutoland Economy: A Case Study of Backwardness in a Traditional Economy" (Ph.D. diss., Cornell University, 1964), 106.

91. G. V. Doxey, *The Industrial Colour Bar in South Africa* (Cape Town: OUP, 1961), 116–126 and 158–162.

92. Louis Molamu, "Botswana Labour Migration: The Case of Returnee Migrant Workers," in *Botswana: Education, Culture, and Politics*, 253–254.

93. Libby, *The Politics of Economic Power*, 38–39.

94. R. Mansell Prothero, "Foreign Migrant Labour for South Africa," IMR 8, no. 3 (Fall 1974):388.

95. Libby, *The Politics of Economic Power*, 198. Nevertheless, according to Breytenbach (*Migratory Labour*, 30), in 1978 the flow of Malawians to the South African mines resumed.

96. Libby, *The Politics of Economic Power*, 206, n. 22.

97. Hanlon, *Beggar*, 76 and 186.

98. Ibid., 76–77.

99. Libby, *The Politics*, 38–39 and 41.

100. Hanlon, *Beggar*, 76–77.

101. Taylor, "Some Consequences," 38.

102. Jack D. Parson, "Toward a Political Economy of Post-Colonial Societies: State and Society in Contemporary Botswana" (Paper delivered at the twenty-fifth annual meeting of the African Studies Association, Washington, DC, 4–7 November 1982), 22.

103. Libby, *The Politics*, 40–41.

104. Gary Thatcher, "Southern African Nations Would Feel Kick from Sanctions," CSM, 28 July 1986, 3 and 5.

105. Morrison, "Developmental Optimism," 481–482.

106. Molamu, "Botswana Labour Migration," 252–255.

107. Hansen, "South Africa," 204–205.

108. Gwen Ansell, "Migrant Labour: End of an Era?" *Kutlwano* 24, no. 8 (August 1986):14.

109. Molamu, "Botswana Labour Migration," 246.

110.   Cuzen, *The History*, 91.

111.   Mookodi interview.

112.   Henry ("The Basutoland Economy," 129–130) suggested a system of dual monopolies: one for the labor-exporting states and one for the labor importers.

113.   G. M. Erich Leistner, "Foreign Bantu Workers in South Africa: Their Present Position in the Economy," SAJE 35, no. 1 (March 1967):42.

114.   Taylor, "Some Consequences," 38.

115.   R. Majelantle and X. Mhozya, *Prospects for Absorbing Mineworkers into the Botswana Economy*, International Migration for Employment Working Paper no. 40 (Geneva: ILO, 1988), 1 and 11.

116.   Molamu, "Botswana Labour Migration," 250.

117.   Ansell, "Migrant Labour," 14.

118.   Ibid.

119.   "Countering the Migrant Flow," NA 158 (November 1980):31.

120.   "Southern Africa Labour Commission," in *Yearbook of International Organizations, 1991/92*, 28th ed., ed. Union of International Associations, vol. 1 (Munich: K. G. Saur Verlag KG, 1991), 1275–1276.

121.   "Employment and Skills," in Nsekela, *Southern Africa*, 204–205.

122.   Alan Whiteside (*Labour Migration in Southern Africa*, Southern African Issues [Braamfontein: SAIIA, 1988], 41) argued that the SALC's desire to withdraw laborers from South Africa was primarily a protest against the apartheid system. He pointedly asked what the SALC's policy on withdrawal would be once majority rule were established in South Africa.

123.   Ansell, "Migrant Labour," 14.

124.   Taylor, "Some Consequences," 41 and 43.

125.   Morrison, "Developmental Optimism," 481–482.

126.   Reginald H. Green, *Economic Sanctions against South Africa. No. 3. South Africa: The Impact of Sanctions on Southern African Economies* ([London]: Africa Bureau, 1981 reprint), 12.

127.   "Pretoria's Threatened Retaliation through Repatriation," MWD, 23 November 1985, 2 (editorial).

128.   "As South Africa Threatens Migrants with Expulsion," QERNBLS, no. 3—1985 (30 August 1985):38–39.

129.   "Pretoria's Threatened Retaliation," 2.

130.   Green, *Economic Sanctions*, 19.

131.   Mordi, "Public Attitudes," 6 and 28.

CHAPTER TEN

1.   *Botswana: Liberal Democracy and the Labor Reserve in Southern Africa* (Boulder, CO: Westview Press, 1984), 112.

2.   UNSC doc. provisional S/PV 2598, 21 June 1985, 4–19, especially 18.

3.   Pienaar, *South Africa and International Relations*, 18–21, 99, and 179, and Gerhard Erasmus, "White South Africans and the United Nations," IAB 9, no. 3 (1985):26–40, especially 29–31.

4.   For a comprehensive account of this isolation, which places South

Africa within a much larger comparative framework, see Deon J. Geldenhuys, *Isolated States: A Comparative Analysis*, Cambridge Studies in International Relations no. 15 (Cambridge: CUP, 1990).

5. For a range of perspectives on this controversial topic, consult Geldenhuys, "South Africa: A Stabilising or Destabilising Influence," 59–75; Metz, "Pretoria's 'Total Strategy,'" 437–469; and Kwakwa, "South Africa's May 1986 Military Incursions," 421–443.

6. See Murray, *Namibia through the 1990s*, 22–24.

7. Charles Harvey and Stephen R. Lewis, Jr., "Southern African Interdependence: Its Effects on SADCC and on Botswana" (Brighton: University of Sussex, Institute of Development Studies, unpublished typescript, 1987), 1.

8. Kent H. Butts and Paul R. Thomas, *The Geopolitics of Southern Africa: South Africa as a Regional Superpower* (Boulder, CO: Westview Press, 1986), 160.

9. Herbert W. Nickel, "Forging a Western Consensus on South Africa," in *Europe, America[,] and South Africa*, ed. Gregory F. Treverton. Europe/America [series no.] 7 (New York: Council on Foreign Relations, 1988), 100.

10. Charles W. Stahl and W. R. Böhning, "Reducing Dependence on Migration in Southern Africa," in *Black Migration to South Africa: A Selection of Policy-Oriented Research*, ed. W. R. Böhning (Geneva: ILO, 1981), 148–149.

11. John Barratt, *South Africa and Its Neighbours: Co-operation or Conflict?*, Occasional Paper (Braamfontein: SAIIA, 1988), 2.

12. See the commentary on the domain, range, scope, target, and weight of influence (or power) in Harold D. Lasswell and Abraham Kaplan, *Power and Society: A Framework for Political Inquiry*, Yale Law School Studies, vol. 2 (New Haven: YUP, 1950), 73; Karl W. Deutsch, *The Analysis of International Relations*, 2d ed. (Englewood Cliffs, NJ: Prentice-Hall, Inc., 1978), 32–44; Robert A. Dahl, *Modern Political Analysis*, 2d ed. (Englewood Cliffs, NJ: Prentice-Hall, Inc., 1970), 18; and Baldwin, *Economic Statecraft*, 16–17.

13. Baldwin, *Economic Statecraft*, 61.

14. Consult Joseph Lelyveld, *Move Your Shadow: South Africa, Black and White* (New York: Elisabeth Sifton Books, Penguin Books, 1985), 52–74, 138–140, and 348–354.

15. "S. Africa Joins OAU," CSM, 14 June 1994, 6.

16. Garner Thompson, "Historic Service at Westminster Abbey as SA Rejoins Commonwealth: 'Prodigal Son' Now Back in Fold," *The Star*, 21–27 July 1994, i.w.e., 5.

17. Alide Dasnois, "World Must 'Tap Peace Dividend' and Invest in the Region: SADC Embraces SA," *The Star*, 25–31 August 1994, i.w.e., 1.

18. Simon, *Independent Namibia*, 21.

19. "Change to SADC," ARBPSCS 29, no. 6 (1–31 August 1992):10672.

20. C. Bauer and D. P. Wessels, "Bophuthatswana: Its Creation and Quest for International Recognition," JCH 17, no. 1 (June 1992):19–25 and 30–33.

21. Dale, "Botswana's Relations," 12.

22. "Mangope Opts for Botswana Union," *The Star*, 10 September 1973, 2d c.l.e., 7; "Union with Botswana: May Be Considered—Chief Mangope," MMBG, 14 September 1973, 1; "No Federation with Homelands, Says Khama," MMBG, 30 August 1974, 1; and Dale, "Botswana's Relations," 9–13.

23. Bauer and Wessels, "Bophuthatswana," 21–25.

24. Dale, "Botswana's Relations," 8 and 17–18.

25. "Khama Would Gladly Exchange Diplomats," *The Star*, 9 July 1966, i.a.w.e., 5, and "Botswana Restates Conditions for Envoy," *The Star*, 17 August 1967, c.l.e., 13.

26. "Diplomatic Suburbs: Botswana's Proviso," *The Star*, 5 September 1967, c.l.e., 9.

27. Khama, *From the Frontline*, 106.

28. Johan F. Kirsten, "Botswana se Internasionale Politieke Verhoudinge" (D.Phil. diss., Potchefstroom University, 1984), 129.

29. James J. Zaffiro, "State Formation and Pre-Independence Foreign Policy-Making in the Bechuanaland Protectorate" (Paper delivered at the thirty-fourth annual meeting of the African Studies Association, St. Louis, 22–26 November 1991), 14.

30. "Black Envoys in Pretoria Foreseen," *The Star*, 21 December 1966, s.p.e., 3.

31. "Botswana, S. Africa Agree To Establish Reciprocal Missions," BDN, 31 December 1992, 1.

32. Gerald L'Ange, "The Unspoken Art of the Diplomatic Community," *The Star*, 17–23 September 1992, i.w.e., 7.

33. James J. Zaffiro, "Redesigning External Policy for the Next Quarter-Century: The New World Order from a Botswana Perspective" (Draft version of a paper delivered at the thirty-seventh annual meeting of the African Studies Association, Toronto, 3–6 November 1994), 6.

34. Deon J. Geldenhuys, "South Africa's Regional Policy," in *Regional Co-operation: The Record and Outlook*, Special Study (Braamfontein: SAIIA, 1984), 105–109.

35. "Reports Have Been 'Distorted': Premier Denies Any Take-Over Offer," *The Star*, 6 September 1963, c.l.e., 7, and *Dr. H. F. Verwoerd on I. Crisis in World Conscience[;] II. The Road to Freedom for: Basutoland[,] Bechuanaland[,] [and] Swaziland*, Fact Paper 107 (Pretoria: SA, Department of Information, 1963), 15.

36. "Bechuana Reaction: All Condemn Verwoerd," *The Star*, 22 November 1963, c.l.e., 1.

37. "Verwoerd Offers Major Trade Links: He Suggests 'Common Market' with Friendly Countries in Africa," *The Star*, 27 August 1964, c.l.e., 1 and 3.

38. Geldenhuys, *The Constellation*, 2–4.

39. Theo Malan, "The South African Black States' and Neighbouring Black Africa's Response to South Africa's Proposed Constellation of Southern African States," in *The Constellation of States*, ed. Wilhelmus J. Breytenbach (Johannesburg: South Africa Foundation), 60.

40. Tidimane Ntsabane, "Development of Underdevelopment: A Comparative Study of the Transkei and Botswana" (M.S. thesis, University of Wisconsin, Madison, 1983), 61–93.

41. Stephen R. Lewis, Jr., "Southern African Interdependence," *CSIS Africa Notes*, no. 56 (27 March 1986):3.

42. Alan W. Whiteside, "Labour Flows, Refugees, AIDS and the Environment," in *Towards a Post-Apartheid Future: Political and Economic Relations in Southern Africa*, ed. Gavin G. Maasdorp and Alan W. Whiteside (New York: St. Martin's Press, 1992), 162–163.

43. Ibid., 161.

44. "SA Not at Funeral," *The Star*, 24 July 1980, s.p.e., 7.

45. "Botswana," ACRASD, 1980–1981, B659.

46. Moorsom, *The Scope*, 33.

47. Hanlon, *Beggar*, 227.

48. Colclough and McCarthy, *The Political Economy*, 156–158, and Keith Jefferis, "Botswana and Diamond-Dependent Development: Are Botswana's Fortunes Too Closely Tied with DeBeers'?," SAPEM 4, no. 12 (September 1991):19–22.

49. "Botswana Diversifies," *The Star*, 10 August 1988, i.a.w.e., 19.

50. Guy C. Z. Mhone, "Botswana: Debunking the Myth of Africa's Economic Cinderella," SAPEM 6, no. 12 (September 1993):43.

51. Harvey and Lewis, *Policy Choice*, 8.

52. Nchindo, "Diamonds in Botswana," 233–234.

53. David Pallister, Sarah Stewart, and Ian Lepper, *South Africa Inc.: The Oppenheimer Empire*, revised and updated ed. (New Haven: YUP, 1988), 246–248.

54. Charles M. Becker, "The Impact of Sanctions on South Africa and Its Periphery," ASR 31, no. 2 (September 1988):84–85.

55. "Seventeen US Business Executives Pay Botswana a Visit," BG, 31 March 1989, 11.

56. "London Chamber Organises Botswana Visit," BG, 14 April 1989, 13.

57. Linchwe Kgaswe, "Inaugural Flight Successful," BG, 7 April 1989, 12.

58. "ITB Berlin Generates More Tourists for Botswana," BG, 14 April 1989, 14.

59. Richard F. Weisfelder, "Prospects for the Future: An Evaluation of Political Trends and Research Priorities in Botswana," in Picard, *The Evolution*, 281.

60. Linda Van Buren, "Trans-Kalahari Highway Is under Construction," AB 169 (September 1992):30–31.

61. Anglin, "The Frontline States," 269–270.

62. "Air Botswana's Financial Difficulties Continue," CRBNLS, no. 1—1993 (1 March 1993):20.

63. "A Compensation Deal Is Concluded with NRZ," CRNBLS, no. 3—1988 (2 September 1988):31.

64. Loubser, *Transport Diplomacy*, 5.

65. Joseph Hanlon, *SADCC: Progress, Projects & Prospects: The Trade and Investment Future of The Southern African Development Coordination Conference*, Special Report no. 182 (London: EIU, 1984), 34.

66. "China Continues Railway Upgrading," CRNBLS, no. 3—1987 (14 August 1987):35.

67. Philip H. Frankel, *Pretoria's Praetorians: Civil-Military Relations in*

South Africa (New York: CUP, 1984), 105 and 149.

68. Kenneth W. Grundy, *The Militarization of South African Politics* (Bloomington: Indiana University Press, 1986), 94–102.

69. See Christopher Coker, "'Experiencing' Southern Africa in the Twenty-First Century," IA 67, no. 2 (April 1991):281–282.

70. Payne, *The Nonsuperpowers*, 206.

71. Millard W. Arnold, "Southern Africa in the Year 2000: An Optimistic Scenario," *CSIS Africa Notes*, no. 122 (28 March 1991):4.

72. Coker, "'Experiencing' Southern Africa," 287.

73. "Group Welcomes S. Africa into Regional Fold," CSM, 1 August 1994, 2.

74. Weimer and Claus, "A Changing Southern Africa," 186. In 1990 the De Klerk government began to reduce the defense budget (David E. Albright, "South Africa in Southern Africa," in *Regional Hegemons: Threat Perception and Strategic Response*, ed. David J. Myers [Boulder, CO: Westview Press, 1991], 138).

75. Bernhard Weimer, "The Southern African Development Co-ordination Conference (SADCC): Past and Future," AI 21, no. 2 (1991):84–85.

76. The concept is elaborated in Ravenhill, *Collective Clientelism*, 22–23.

77. Consult Steven L. Spiegel, *Dominance and Diversity: The International Hierarchy* (Boston: Little, Brown and Company, 1972), 203, and Richard A. Bitzinger, "'Finlandization:' A Dirty Word?," CSM, 28 August 1989, 18.

78. See G. M. Erich Leistner's rebuttal to Christopher Coker's argument that South and southern Africa will decline in importance (Coker, "'Experiencing' Southern Africa," 283), in G. M. Erich Leistner, "Post-Apartheid South Africa and Africa," AI 20, no. 3 (1990):138.

79. Richard F. Weisfelder, "SADCC after Apartheid," TF 8, no. 3 (Fall 1991):7.

80. Ibid., 14.

81. John Battersby, "New Zambia Leader Faces Economy in Ruin," CSM, 18 November 1991, 8.

82. Udo Froese, "Forgetting Namibia," SAFR 16, no. 11 (November 1990):8.

83. Peter Vanneman, "Soviet Foreign Policy for Angola/Namibia in the 1980s: A Strategy of Coercive Diplomacy," in *Disengagement from Southwest Africa: The Prospects for Peace in Angola and Namibia*, ed. Owen E. Kahn (New Brunswick, NJ: Transaction Publishers, 1991), 69–92.

84. "'Experiencing' Southern Africa," 288–291.

85. "Africans Decry Potential Loss of Aid," CSM, 23 April 1990, 6.

86. See Weisfelder, "SADCC after Apartheid," 8, and Simon Baynham, "The New World Order: Regional and International Implications for Southern Africa," AI 22, no. 2 (1992):86–87.

87. Douglas Tsiako, "Rumours of Aid-Threat Dismissed," MWD, 12–18 January 1990, 2. This point has attracted attention, with Mr. Crosswaite, the economic adviser to the European Community mission in Gaborone, hinting that some of these savings should be used to reduce the hardships of rural dwellers (Tsiako, "Rumours," 2), while Charles Harvey and Stephen R. Lewis,

Jr. (*Policy Choices*, 12) suggested that they be spent for "sustainable development."

88. These criticisms are expressed in Mhone, "Botswana: Debunking the Myth, 40–41; Mohamed H. Abucar and Patrick P. Molutsi, "Environmental Policy in Botswana: A Critique," AT 40, no. 1 (First Quarter 1993):68–73; Kenneth Good, "Interpreting the Exceptionality of Botswana," JMAS 30, no. 1 (March 1992):76–80; and Robert L. Curry, Jr., "Poverty and Mass Unemployment in Mineral-Rich Botswana," AJES 46, no. 1 (January 1987): 71–75.

89. Philip J. Steenkamp, "'Cinderella of the Empire?': Development Policy in Bechuanaland in the 1930s," JSAS 17, no. 2 (June 1991):306.

90. Robert A. Packenham equates autonomy with choice (in his chapter on "The Dependency Perspective and Analytic Dependency" in *North/South Relations: Studies of Dependency Reversal*, ed. Charles F. Moran, George A. Modelski, and Caleb M. Clark [New York: Praeger Publishers, 1983], 41).

91. Joel S. Migdal indicates that, at least in the domestic arena, autonomy "means that state officials can act upon their own preferences" (in his *Strong Societies and Weak States: State-Society Relations and State Capabilities in the Third World* [Princeton, NJ: Princeton University Press, 1988], 6, n. 5).

92. Payne, *The Nonsuperpowers*, 209.

93. Packenham ("The Dependency Perspective," 41) implies that there is an inverse relationship between autonomy and dependency, so that enhancing the former diminishes the latter.

94. Baldwin, *Economic Statecraft*, 55, n. 14.

95. Packenham, "The Dependency Perspective," 32.

96. James C. W. Ahiakpor, "The Success and Failure of Dependency Theory: The Experience of Ghana," IntOrg 39, no. 3 (Summer 1985):550–551.

97. Stephen D. Krasner, *Structural Conflict: The Third World against Global Liberalism* (Berkeley: UCP, 1985), 43.

98. This appeared to be a common element in the southern African policies of the British, West German, and Japanese governments (see Payne, *The Nonsuperpowers*, 51–52, 83, 87, and 102).

99. "And a Large Airbase is Being Built at Molepolole," CRNBLS, no. 1—1992 (28 February 1992):27; Fernando Goncalvez, "Mystery Surrounds Construction of a Massive Airbase in Botswana," SAPEM 6, no. 12 (September 1993):12; "Military Base Sparks Tension," ARBPSCS 31, no. 2 (1–28 February 1994):11320; and "Gaborone: Aid and Military Expenditure," SAPEM 6, no. 1 (October 1992):6.

100. Weimer and Claus, "A Changing Southern Africa," 187 and 196–198, and Yeager, "Democratic Pluralism," 390–399.

101. See the extended discussion in Weimer, "The Southern African Development Co-ordination Conference," 81–82 and 84–86, and in Peter N. Takirambudde, "Rethinking Regional Integration Structures and Strategies in Eastern and Southern Africa," AI 23, no. 3 (1993):149–158.

102. See "Business Seeks an End to Botswana-Zimbabwe Disputes" and "And Has Called for Import Surcharges To Be Lifted," CRNBLS, no. 1—1993 (1 March 1993):21 and 22, respectively.

Selected Bibliography

REFERENCE SOURCES

Imrie, John. "Botswana Politics and Related Developments from 1978." *Southern African Update: A Bibliographical Survey* (Braamfontein) 3, no. 2 (October 1988):29–36.

Morton, Fred, Murray, Andrew, and Ramsay, Jeff. *Historical Dictionary of Botswana*. Metuchen, NJ: Scarecrow Press, new ed., 1989.

Wiseman, John A. *Botswana*. World Biographical Series no. 150. Oxford, Santa Barbara, CA: Clio Press, 1992.

BOOKS

Amin, Santir, Chitala, Derrick, and Mandaza, Ibbo, eds. *SADCC: Prospects for Disengagement and Development in Southern Africa*. London: Zed Books, 1987.

Asiwaju, A.I., ed. *Partitioned Africans: Ethnic Relations across Africa's International Boundaries, 1884–1984*. New York: St. Martin's Press, 1985.

Bodenmüller, Rolf. *Botswana, Lesotho, and Swaziland: Their External Relations and Policy and Attitudes towards South Africa*. Pretoria: Africa Institute of South Africa, 1973.

Brandt, Harmut, et al. *Perspectives of Independent Development in Southern Africa: The Cases of Zimbabwe and Namibia*. Occasional Papers of the German Development Institute no. 62. Berlin: German Development Institute, 1980.

Breytenbach, Wilhelmus J. *Migratory Labour Arrangements in Southern Africa*. Communications of the Africa Institute no. 33. Pretoria: Africa Institute of South Africa, rev. ed., 1979.

Carter, Gwendolen M., and O'Meara, Patrick, eds. *Southern Africa: The Continuing Crisis*. Bloomington: Indiana University Press, 1982.

Cervenka, Zdenek, ed. *Land-locked Countries of Africa*. Uppsala: Scandinavian Institute of African Studies, 1973.

Chanock, Martin. *Britain, Rhodesia, and South Africa*. Totowa, NJ: Frank Cass, 1977.

Clough, Michael, ed. *Changing Realities in Southern Africa: Implications for American Policy*. Research Series no. 47. Berkeley: University of California, Institute of International Studies, 1982.

Clough, Michael, and Herbst, Jeffrey. *South Africa's Changing Regional Strategy: Beyond Destabilization*. Critical Issues, 1989, no. 4. New York: Council on Foreign Relations, 1989.

Cobbe, James H. *Governments and Mining Companies in Developing Countries*. Boulder, CO: Westview Press, 1979.

Colclough, Christopher L., and McCarthy, Stephen J. *The Political Economy of Botswana: A Study in Growth and Distribution*. New York: Oxford University Press, 1980.

Crowder, Michael, ed. *Education for Development in Botswana*. Gaborone: Macmillan Botswana Publishing Company, 1984.

Edgar, Robert E., ed. *Sanctioning Apartheid*. Trenton, NJ: Africa World Press, 1990.

Frankel, Philip H. *Pretoria's Praetorians: Civil-Military Relations in South Africa*. New York: Cambridge University Press, 1984.

Geldenhuys, Deon J. *The Diplomacy of Isolation: South African Foreign Policy Making*. New York: St. Martin's Press, 1984.

Grundy, Kenneth W. *Confrontation and Accommodation in Southern Africa*. Perspectives on Southern Africa no. 10. Berkeley: University of California Press, 1973.

―――. *The Militarization of South African Politics*. Bloomington: Indiana University Press, 1986.

Halpern, Jack. *South Africa's Hostages: Basutoland, Bechuanaland and Swaziland*. Baltimore: Penguin Books, 1965.

Hamrell, Sven, ed. *Refugee Problems in Africa*. Uppsala: Scandinavian Institute of African Studies, 1967.

Hanlon, Joseph. *Beggar Your Neighbours: Apartheid Power in South Africa*. Bloomington: Indiana University Press, 1986.

Harvey, Charles, ed. *Papers on the Economy of Botswana*. London: Heinemann Educational Books, 1981.

―――. *The Use of Monetary Policy in Botswana in Good Times and Bad*. Discussion Paper no. 204. Brighton: University of Sussex, Institute of Development Studies, 1985.

Harvey, Charles, and Lewis, Stephen R., Jr. *Policy Choice and Development Performance in Botswana*. New York: St. Martin's Press, 1990.

Holm, John D., and Molutsi, Patrick P., eds. *Democracy in Botswana: The Proceedings of a Symposium Held in Gaborone, 1–5 August 1988*. Athens: Ohio University Press, 1989.

Hubbard, Michael. *Agricultural Exports and Economic Growth: A Study of the Botswana Beef Industry*. London: KPI Limited, 1986.

Isaacs, Arnold H. *Dependence Relations between Botswana, Lesotho, Swaziland and the Republic of South Africa: A Literature Study Based on Johan*

Galtung's Theory of Imperialism. Research Reports no. 15. Leiden: African Studies Centre, 1982.

Jackson, Robert H. *Quasi-States: Sovereignty. International Relations, and the Third World*, Cambridge Series in International Relations no. 12. Cambridge: Cambridge University Press, 1990.

Johnson, Phyllis, and Martin, David. *Apartheid Terrorism: The Destabilization Report*. London: The Commonwealth Secretariat in association with James Currey, London; Bloomington: Indiana University Press, 1989.

Keller, Edmond J., and Picard, Louis A., eds. *South Africa in Southern Africa: Domestic Change and International Conflict*. Boulder, CO: Lynne Rienner Publishers, 1989.

Keohane, Robert O., and Nye, Joseph S. *Power and Interdependence: World Politics in Transition*. Boston: Little, Brown and Company, 1977.

Khama, Seretse. *From the Frontline: Speeches of Sir Seretse Khama*. Edited by Gwendolen M. Carter and E. Philip Morgan. London: Rex Collings, 1980.

Konczacki, Zbigniew, Parpart, Jane L., and Shaw, Timothy M. *Studies in the Economic History of Southern Africa*. vol. I: *The Front-Line States*. London: Frank Cass, 1990.

Kowet, Donald K. *Land, Labour Migration, and Politics in Southern Africa: Botswana, Lesotho, and Swaziland*. Uppsala: Scandinavian Institute of African Studies, 1978.

Lee, Margaret C. *SADCC: The Political Economy of Development in Southern Africa*. Nashville, TN: Winston-Derek Publishers, 1989.

Leistner, G. M. Erich, and Esterhuysen, Pieter, eds. *South Africa in Southern Africa: Economic Interaction*. Research Communications Series no. 51. Pretoria: Africa Institute of South Africa, 1988.

Lewis, Stephen R., Jr. *Economic Realities in Southern Africa, or, One Hundred Million Futures*. Discussion Paper no. 232. Brighton: University of Sussex, Institute of Development Studies, 1987.

Lewis, Stephen R., Jr., and Sharpley, Jennifer. *Botswana's Industrialisation*. Discussion Paper no. 45. Brighton: University of Sussex, Institute of Development Studies, 1988.

Libby, Ronald T. *The Politics of Economic Power in Southern Africa*. Princeton: Princeton University Press, 1987.

Lodge, Tom. *Black Politics in South Africa since 1945*. New York: Longman, 1983.

Maasdorp, Gavin G. *Current Political and Economic Factors in Transportation in Southern Africa*. Occasional Paper. Braamfontein: South African Institute of International Affairs, 1988.

———. *Economic Co-operation in Southern Africa: Prospects for Regional Integration*. Conflict Studies no. 253. London: Research Institute for the Study of Conflict and Terrorism, July–August, 1992.

———. *Transport Policies and Economic Development in Southern Africa: A Comparative Study in Eight Countries*. Durban: University of Natal, Economic Research Unit, 1984.

Majelantle, R., and Mhozya, X. *Prospects for Absorbing Mineworkers into the Botswana Economy*. International Migration for Employment Working Paper no. 40. Geneva: International Labor Organization, 1988.

Martin, David, and Johnson, Phyllis. *The Struggle for Zimbabwe: The Chimurenga War*. London: Monthly Review Press, 1981.

Martin, Roger. *Southern Africa: The Price of Apartheid: A Political Risk Analysis*. Special Report no. 1130. London: Economist Intelligence Unit, 1988.

Maylam, Paul R. *Rhodes, The Tswana, and the British: Colonial Collaboration and Conflict in the Bechuanaland Protectorate, 1885–1899*. Contributions in Comparative Colonial Studies no. 4. Westport, CT: Greenwood Press, 1980.

Migdal, Joel S. *Strong Societies and Weak States: State-Society Relations and State Capabilities in the Third World*. Princeton: Princeton University Press, 1988.

Moorcroft, Paul L. *African Nemesis: War and Revolution in Southern Africa, 1945–2010*. London: Brassey's, 1990.

Moran, Charles F., Modelski, George A., and Clark, Caleb M., eds. *North/South Relations: Studies of Dependency Reversal*. New York: Praeger, 1983.

Morton, R. Frederic, and Ramsay, Jeff. *The Birth of Botswana: A History of the Bechuanaland Protectorate from 1910 to 1966*. Gaborone: Longman Botswana, 1987.

Munger, Edwin S. *Bechuanaland: Pan-African Outpost or Bantu Homeland?* London: Oxford University Press, 1965.

Odén, Bertil. *The Macroeconomic Position of Botswana*. Research Report no. 6. Uppsala: Scandinavian Institute of African Studies, 1981.

Odén, Bertil, and Othman, Haroub. *Regional Cooperation in Southern Africa: A Post-Apartheid Perspective*. Seminar Proceedings no. 22. Uppsala: Scandinavian Institute of African Studies, 1989.

Oommen, M. A., Inganji, F. K., and Ngcongco, L. D., eds. *Botswana's Economy since Independence*. New Delhi: Tata-McGraw Hill, 1983.

Pallister, David, Stewart, Sarah, and Lepper, Ian. *South Africa Inc.: The Oppenheimer Empire*. New Haven: Yale University Press, rev. and updated ed., 1988.

Parson, Jack D., ed. *Succession to High Office in Botswana: Three Case Studies*. Monographs in International Studies, Africa Series no. 54. Athens: Ohio University Press, 1990.

Payne, Richard J. *The Nonsuperpowers and South Africa: Implications for U.S. Policy*. Bloomington: Indiana University Press, 1990.

Pfotenhauer, Linda, ed. *Tourism in Botswana: Proceedings of a Symposium Held in Gaborone, Botswana, 15–19 October 1990*. Gaborone: Botswana Society, 1991.

Picard, Louis A., ed. *The Evolution of Modern Botswana: Politics and Rural Development in Southern Africa*. Lincoln: University of Nebraska Press, 1985.

———. *The Politics of Development in Botswana: A Model for Success?* Boulder, CO: Lynne Rienner Publishers, 1987.

Potholm, Christian P., and Dale, Richard, eds. *Southern Africa in Perspective: Essays in Regional Politics*. New York: Free Press, 1972.

Rey, Charles F. *Monarch of All I Survey: Bechuanaland Diaries. 1929-37.* ed. Q. Neil Parsons and Michael Crowder. Gaborone: BS; New York: Lilian Barber Press, Inc., and London: James Currey Ltd., 1988.

Robins, Eric. *White Queen in Africa.* London: Robert Hale, 1967.

Rotberg, Robert I., and others. *South Africa and Its Neighbors: Regional Security and Self-Interest.* Lexington, MA: Lexington Books, 1985.

Rwelamira, Medard. *Refugees in a Chess Game: Reflections on Botswana, Lesotho, and Swaziland Refugee Policies.* Research Report no. 88. Uppsala: Scandinavian Institute of African Studies, 1990.

Saxena, Suresh C. *Foreign Policy of African States: Politics of Dependence and Confrontation.* New Delhi: Deep and Deep Publications, 1982.

Schapera, Isaac. *Migrant Labour and Tribal Life: A Study of Conditions in the Bechuanaland Protectorate.* London: Geoffrey Cumberlege, Oxford University Press, 1947.

Schou, August, and Brundtland, Arne. *Small States and International Relations.* Nobel Symposium no. 17. New York: John Wiley, 1971.

Shaw, Timothy M., and Heard, Kenneth A., eds. *Cooperation and Conflict in Southern Africa: Papers on a Regional Subsystem.* Washington, DC: University Press of America, 1976.

Sillery, Anthony. *The Bechuanaland Protectorate.* Cape Town: Geoffrey Cumberlege, Oxford University Press, 1952.

———. *Botswana: A Short Political History.* Studies in African History no. 8. London: Methuen & Co., 1974.

———. *Founding a Protectorate: History of Bechuanaland, 1885–1895.* Studies in African History, Anthropology, and Ethnology, vol. 3. The Hague: Mouton, 1965.

Singer, Marshall R. *Weak States in a World of Powers: The Dynamics of International Relations.* New York: Free Press, 1972.

Smit, Philippus. *Botswana: Resources and Development.* Communications of the Africa Institute no. 13. Pretoria: Africa Institute of South Africa, 1970.

Stedman, Stephen J., ed. *Botswana: The Political Economy of Democratic Development.* Boulder, CO: Lynne Rienner Publishers, 1993.

Tjønneland, Elling N. *Pax Pretoriana: The Fall of Apartheid and the Politics of Destabilisation.* Discussion Paper no. 2. Uppsala: Scandinavian Institute of African Studies, 1989.

Tostensen, Arne. *Dependence and Collective Self-Reliance in Southern Africa: The Case of the Southern African Development Coordination Committee (SADCC).* Research Report no. 62. Uppsala: Scandinavian Institute of African Studies, 1982.

Venter, Al J., ed. *Challenge: Southern Africa within the African Revolutionary Context: An Overview.* Gibraltar: Ashanti Publishing, 1989.

Whiteside, Alan W. *Investment Opportunities in Southern Africa: The Business Climate in the SADCC States.* Occasional Paper. Braamfontein: South African Institute of International Affairs, 1987.

———. *Past Trends and Future Prospects for Labour Migration to South Africa.* Occasional Paper. Braamfontein: South African Institute of International Affairs, 1985.

Widstrand, Carl G., and Cervenka, Zdenek. *Scandinavian Development*

Agreements with African Countries. Uppsala: Scandinavian Institute of African Studies, 1971.

Woodward, Calvin A., ed. *On the Razor's Edge: Prospects for Political Stability in Southern Africa*. Communications of the Africa Institute of South Africa no. 46. Pretoria: Africa Institute of South Africa, 1986.

Wylie, Diana S. *A Little God: The Twilight of Patriarchy in a Southern African Chiefdom*. Hanover, NH: Wesleyan University Press, University Press of New England, 1990.

Young, Bertram A. *Bechuanaland*. London: HMSO, 1966.

Zetterqvist, Jenny. *Refugees in Botswana in the Light of International Law*. Research Report no. 87. Uppsala: Scandinavian Institute of African Studies, 1990.

JOURNAL ARTICLES

Anglin, Douglas G. "Economic Liberation and Regional Cooperation in Southern Africa: SADCC and PTA." *International Organization* 37, no. 4 (Autumn 1983):681–711.

———. "Southern Africa under Siege: Options for the Frontline States." *Journal of Modern African Studies* 26, no. 4 (December 1988):549–565.

———. "Southern African Responses to Eastern European Developments." *Journal of Modern African Studies* 28, no. 3 (September 1990):431–455.

Becker, Charles M. "The Impact of Sanctions on South Africa and Its Periphery." *African Studies Review* 31, no. 2 (September 1988):61–88.

Collings, Francis d'A., and others. "The Rand and the Monetary Systems of Botswana, Lesotho, and Swaziland." *Journal of Modern African Studies* 16, no. 1 (March 1978):97–121.

Couperthwaithe, Bruce, comp. "The Bechuanaland Protectorate." *Race Relations Journal* 18, no. 1 (1951):27–71.

Crowder, Michael. "Tshekedi Khama, Smuts, and South West Africa." *Journal of Modern African Studies* 25, no. 1 (March 1987):25–42.

Crush, Jonathan, and Wellings, Paul. "The Southern African Pleasure Periphery, 1966–83." *Journal of Modern African Studies* 21, no. 4 (December 1983):673–698.

Dale, Richard. "Botswana's Relations with Bophuthatswana: The Politics of Ethnicity, Legitimacy, and Propinquity in Southern Africa." *Journal for Contemporary History* 17, no. 2 (December 1992):1–19.

———. "The Creation and Use of the Botswana Defence Force." *Round Table* 290 (April 1984):216–235.

———. "Not Always So Placid a Place: Botswana under Attack." *African Affairs* 86, no. 342 (January 1987):73–91.

———. "The Politics of National Security in Botswana, 1900–1990." *Journal of Contemporary African Studies* 12, no. 1 (1993):40–56.

Ettinger, Stephen J. "The Bechuanaland Protectorate's Participation in Pre-1910 Customs Unions." *Botswana Notes and Records* 7 (1975):49–59.

Good, Kenneth. "Interpreting the Exceptionality of Botswana." *The Journal of Modern African Studies* 30, no. 1 (March 1992):69–95.

Henderson, Willie. "Independent Botswana: A Reappraisal of Foreign Policy Options." *African Affairs* 73, no. 290 (January 1974):37–49.

Herbst, Jeffrey. "The Creation and Maintenance of National Boundaries in Africa." *International Organization* 43, no. 4 (Autumn 1989):673–692.

Holm, John D. "Botswana: One African Success Story." *Current History* 93, no. 583 (May 1994):198–202.

Hudson, Derek J. "The Establishment of Botswana's Central Bank and the Introduction of the New Currency." *Botswana Notes and Records* 10 (1978):119–135.

Jackson, Robert H., and Rosberg, Carl G. "Why Africa's Weak States Persist: The Empirical and Juridical in Statehood." *World Politics* 35, no. 1 (October 1982):1–24.

Jones, Keith F. "Britain's Contribution to Botswana's Public Debt, 1956–1976." *Botswana Notes and Records* 9 (1977):109–117.

Leistner, G. M. Erich. "Post–Apartheid South Africa and Africa." *Africa Insight* 20, no. 3 (1990):138–140.

Maasdorp, Gavin G. "The Southern African Customs Union: An Assessment." *Journal of Contemporary African Studies* 2, no. 1 (October 1982):81–112.

McGowan, Patrick J., and Smith, Dale L. "Economic Dependency in Black Africa: An Analysis of Competing Theories." *International Organization* 32, no. 1 (Winter 1978):179–235.

Niemann, Michael. "Diamonds Are a State's Best Friend: Botswana's Foreign Policy in Southern Africa." *Africa Today* 40, no. 1 (First Quarter 1993):27–47.

Parsons, Q. Neil. "Botswana: An End to Exceptionality?" *Round Table* 325 (January 1993):73–82.

Polhemus, James H. "The Refugee Factor in Botswana." *Immigrants and Minorities* 4, no. 1 (March 1985):28–45.

Somerville, Keith. "Botswana at the Crossroads." *The World Today* 50, no. 2 (February 1994):22–24.

Southall, Roger. "Botswana as a Host Country for Refugees." *Journal of Commonwealth and Comparative Politics* 22, no. 2 (Jul 1984):151–179.

Steenkamp, Philip J. "'Cinderella of the Empire?': Development Policy in Bechuanaland in the 1930s." *Journal of Southern African Studies* 17, no. 2 (June 1991):292–308.

Taylor, John. "The Reorganization of Mine Labor Recruitment in Southern Africa: Evidence from Botswana." *International Migration Review* 24, no. 2 (Summer 1990):250–272.

———. "Some Consequences of Recent Reductions in Mine Labour Recruitment in Botswana." *Geography* 71, pt. 1 (January 1986):34–46.

Weimer, Bernhard. "The Southern African Development Co–ordination Conference (SADCC): Past and Future." *African Insight* 21, no. 2 (1991):78–89.

Zaffiro, James J. "Mass Media, Politics, and Society in Botswana: The 1990s and Beyond." *Africa Today* 40, no. 1 (First Quarter 1993):7–25.

———. "The Press and Political Opposition in an African Democracy: The Case of Botswana." *Journal of Commonwealth and Comparative Politics* 27, no. 1 (March 1989):51–73.

————. "Twin Births: African Nationalism and Government Information Management in the Bechuanaland Protectorate, 1957–1966." *International Journal of African Historical Studies* 22, no. 1(1989):51–77.

————. "The U. S. and Botswana in the 1990s: Eroding Continuity in a Changing Region." *Journal of Contemporary African Studies* 10, no. 1 (1991):18–44.

Zartman, I. William. "Decision–Making among African Governments on Inter-African Affairs." *Journal of Development Studies* 2, no. 2 (January 1966):98–119.

DISSERTATIONS AND THESES

Brown, Barbara B. "South Africa's Foreign Policy towards Its Black Neighbors." Ph.D. dissertation, Boston University, 1979.

Comoroff, John L. "Competition for Office and Political Processes among the Barolong Boo Ratshidi of the South Africa–Botswana Borderland." Ph.D. dissertation, University of London, 1973.

Ebert, Louis V. "Some International Legal Aspects of the Botswana–Zambia Boundary Question." M.S. thesis, George Washington University, 1971.

Ettinger, Stephen J. "The Economics of the Customs Union between Botswana, Lesotho, Swaziland, and South Africa." Ph.D. dissertation, University of Michigan, 1974.

Frankel, Philip H. "The Foreign Policy of Swaziland." M.A. thesis, University of the Witwatersrand, 1976.

Gossett, Charles W. "The Civil Service in Botswana: Personnel Policies in Comparative Perspective." Ph.D. dissertation, Stanford University, 1986.

Grotpeter, John J. "Political Leadership and Political Development in the High Commission Territories." Ph.D. dissertation, Washington University, 1965.

Gruhn, Isebill V. "Functionalism in Africa: Scientific and Technical Integration." Ph.D. dissertation, University of California, Berkeley, 1967.

Hansen, Carol R. "South Africa as a Force for Regional Stability or Instability." Ph.D. dissertation, Harvard University, 1985.

Kupe, Serara S. "A History of the Evolution of Nursing Education in Botswana, 1922–1980." Ed.D. dissertation, Columbia University Teachers College, 1987.

Lewis, David H. "The Theory and Practice of Direct Foreign Investment in Less Developed Countries: A Study of Copper–Nickel Mining in Botswana." M.A. thesis, University of Cape Town, 1974.

Magagulu, Cynthia M. "The Multi-National University in Africa: An Analysis of the Development and Demise of the University of Botswana, Lesotho, and Swaziland." Ph.D. dissertation, University of Maryland, 1978.

Massey, David R. "Labor Migration and Rural Development in Botswana." Ph.D. dissertation, Boston University, 1981.

Mordi, Richard. "Public Attitudes toward Wildlife in Botswana." Ph.D. dissertation, Yale University, 1987.

Morrison, John S. "Developmental Optimism and State Failure in Africa: How To Understand Botswana's Relative Success?" Ph.D. dissertation, University of Wisconsin, Madison, 1987.

Mushingeh, Andrew C. S. "A History of Disease and Medicine in Botswana, 1820–1945." Ph.D. dissertation, University of Cambridge, 1984.

Muzorewa, Basil C. "The Development of the Money Economy and an Analysis of the Monetary and Financial System in the Republic of Botswana." M.Phil. thesis, University of Leeds, 1976.

Ntsabane, Tidimane. "Development of Underdevelopment: A Comparative Study of the Transkei and Botswana." M.S. thesis, University of Wisconsin, Madison, 1983.

Prowse, Harold M. "Wildlife Administration and the Safari Industry in Botswana." Ph.D. dissertation, University of Michigan, 1974.

Robertson, Harold. "From Protectorate to Republic: The Political History of Botswana, 1926–1966." Ph.D. dissertation, Dalhousie University, 1979.

Stahl, Charles W. "A Spatial Theory of Monopsonistic Exploitation and Its Implications for a Development Strategy of the Labor Exporting Countries of Southern Africa." Ph.D. dissertation, University of California, Santa Barbara, 1974.

Tapela, Henderson M. "The Tati District of Botswana, 1866–1969." D.Phil. dissertation, University of Sussex, 1976.

Warhurst, Philip R. "Rhodesia and Her Neighbours, 1900–23." D.Phil. dissertation, University of Oxford, 1970.

Wetherell, Hugh I. "The Rhodesias and Amalgamation: Settler Sub-Imperialism and the Imperial Response, 1914–48." D.Phil. dissertation, University of Rhodesia, 1977.

Index

About the Author

RICHARD DALE, Associate Professor of Political Science, Southern Illinois University at Carbondale, has been engaged in research about Southern Africa for over 30 years. He has visited Botswana and done research there and in four neighboring states on five different occasions and has written at length on the region.

Recent Titles in
Contributions in Political Science

ISBN 0-313-29571-9

90000>

EAN

9 780313 295713

HARDCOVER BAR CODE

DATE DUE

Mak DUE   JUL 2 4 2003

MCK RTC   DEC 0 5 2003